# A HIGHER LIGHT

## Hasidic and Kabbalistic Insights into the Jewish Holidays

At the time of a festival,
the Blessed God illuminates Israel
with a bright light higher
than their knowledge.

Mordechai Joseph Leiner of Izbica (1801-1854),
*Mei HaShiloach* (The Waters of the Shiloach, Isaiah 8:6)
(Bnei Brak, 1995), v.2, p.56.

i

For Danya & Meital,
Shaya & Gavi

# A HIGHER LIGHT
## Hasidic and Kabbalistic Insights into the Jewish Holidays

Published by Kulmus Publishing through lulu.com

**KULMUS**
PUBLISHING

Paperback ISBN 978-1-988947-06-8
Copyright © Larry Tabick 5780/2020
First Edition

Cover © Marc Michaels 5781/2020
Typeset in Goudita SF Light, Garamond and SBL Hebrew.

# TABLE OF CONTENTS

# INTRODUCTION

An old joke says that Jewish holidays may be summed up in three short sentences:

1. They were mean to us.
2. We won.
3. Let's eat!

Like all jokes, this one contains an element of truth. It is almost an accurate thumbnail description of Pesach *seder*, or maybe Chanukah or Purim (with the additional pleasure of serious drinking in the case of the latter), but it hardly covers most of our other annual occasions. Tisha b'Av, for example, might be summarized as:

1. They were mean to us.
2. We lost.
3. Let's not eat!

And Yom Kippur as:

1. We were mean to each other.
2. We all lost.
3. Let's not eat!

Shavuot, on the other hand, doesn't seem to lend itself to this pattern, nor does Sukkot.

Obviously, our festivals are much more nuanced and richly textured that the joke suggests, for each comes with its own background story, principles and practices that have developed over millennia. Nevertheless, what the joke points out is the tendency for us modern Jews to see our ancient fasts and festivals in purely historical, ethnic and ethical ways. Of course, these factors are all present in our traditional understanding of these occasions, but we also have an on-going tradition of seeing them in a spiritual context, as teaching personal lessons in our relationship to the divine. Much of this material can be found in the writings of our great mystics, especially the kabbalists and Hasidic teachers. This book is a modest attempt to bring some of these sources to wider notice. As such it represents a continuation of the project begun with my earlier work, *The Aura of Torah* (JPSA 2014).

Unfortunately, there are no texts offering commentary on the Pesach Haggadah here. I hope in due course to offer a separate compilation of that material.

Some of the texts that follow include references to the sources of quotations, either embedded within them or as notes. With the exception of Biblical references (which can easily be looked up), I have relegated these to the accompanying notes, in order to facilitate ease of reading. Once again, I have avoided third person masculine singular pronouns so that no one should feel excluded. And for ease of reading, I have removed expressions like "peace be upon him" or "of blessed memory," and the like, though these honorifics are liberally spread throughout the literature from which these texts are drawn. They do not add to the substance of the teachings found therein and may easily distract readers. Each numbered section is meant to stand alone; hence the inevitable repetitions of sources or contextual material. In fact, I imagine readers dipping into the book from time to time, rather than reading continuously.

Most books on the Jewish holidays nowadays usually begin their progress through the year at Rosh Hashanah. After all, we do translate that phrase as the New Year. I have chosen not to do that, but to start with Pesach instead. Rosh Hashanah falls on the first days of the seventh, rather than the first, month, and literally means the Head of the Year. I prefer to think of it as the summit of the year, the high ground, as it were, from which we can assess the past, consider our present, and begin to survey the future. Pesach, on the other hand, falls in the first month of the year, known in the Bible as *Aviv* and later as *Nisan*, as is made clear by Exodus chapter 12: "It shall be the first of the months of the year for you" (verse 2). And this is reinforced in the two full lists that the Torah gives us of our most ancient festivals (Leviticus 23 & Numbers 28-29), beginning with Shabbat, but then proceeding through the year starting from Pesach. (Obviously, Purim, Chanukah, Tisha B'Av and Simchat Torah are not included, as they all developed later in after the completion of the Torah or in post-Biblical times.) If nothing else, commencing with Pesach may serve to offer readers a different perspective on the cycle of the year, for we begin with the new life of spring, ascend through summer to the autumn when life slows down, and then make our way back to spring once more. (Apologies to those readers who live in the southern hemisphere where our *chagim* do not match up with this cycle!)

> All the days of the year represent the fulfilment of the holy days, and each person of Israel must sanctify themselves totally on the holy days so that it is within their power to draw down upon themselves the holiness of the festivals throughout the year, and to feel on each of the days of the year the holiness of Rosh Hashanah, Yom Kippur, Sukkot, Pesach, and Shavuot, and even the rabbinically authorized festivals, Chanukah and Purim.
>
> Shalom Rokeach of Belz (d. 1855), *MaHaRaSH miBelza* (Our teacher, the rabbi, Shalom of Belz) (Israel Klepholtz, ed.) (Bnei Brak, 1987), pt. 2, p. 104.

When you, dear reader, delve into this book, may it serve to enhance the holiness of the festivals for you, and in turn, spread spirituality throughout your year.

A word of caution: The texts presented here are not necessarily representative of their sources. They served as jumping off points for my sermons and study sessions, and have been collected here because they inspired me. Hasidism in particular may be somewhat distorted by my choices, since the central factor in reaching a true understanding of that movement in its own terms has been omitted (or re-interpreted), namely, the doctrine of the *tzaddik* as the point of contact between heaven and earth, spiritual and material realms. With that exception, virtually all the teachings of Hasidism have antecedents and parallels elsewhere in Judaism, but rarely are they expressed with such clarity and beauty.

Readers who are new to Kabbalah may be helped by any one of the numerous popular introductory books available nowadays, but I would recommend Joseph Dan, *Kabbalah: A Very Short Introduction* (Oxford University Press, 2006) as a good place to start.

There are innumerable people who have supported me and who therefore have had an impact on this book. Far too many to mention, in fact. But pride of place must be given to my former congregants at *Shir Hayim*/Hampstead Reform Jewish Community (now known as *Mekor Hayim*) in London, England. Many of the texts presented here first formed the basis of my sermons and study sessions in that community, and *Shir Hayim* members were gracious and patient enough to put up with my obsession with Jewish mysticism in all its forms for close to thirty years. It may be wrong to single out any individual, but I have to acknowledge Ms Lois George once again, for encouraging me to collect these texts for publication in the first place.

Thanks are due to the late Prof. Ada Rapaport-Albert of blessed memory who started me on my first very tentative steps in the academic study of Hasidism.

I was privileged to lecture on Kabbalah and Hasidism at the Leo Baeck College in Finchley, London, and some of these texts found their way into my class, but I am most grateful for the confidence that the college authorities have shown in me over my years of teaching there, and for the questioning of my students.

I must give thanks to the people behind the marvelous website www.hebrewbooks.org. Free of charge, they provide access to thousands of traditional Jewish texts, including hundreds from the library of Jewish mysticism. I could never have produced this modest work without them. More recently, I have discovered www.sefaria.com and have added it to the list of resources that I explore to good effect.

The brief biographies of teachers were gleaned primarily from the *Encyclopedia Judaica* (2nd ed.) and the *Yivo Encyclopedia* (https://yivoencyclopedia.org), plus Yitzchak Alfasi's *Encyclopedia*

*LaHasidut: Ishim* (Jerusalem: Mossad HaRav Kook, 1986), and Hebrew Wikipedia (https://he.wikipedia.org).

Gratitude is particularly due to Marc Michaels, of Kulmus Publishing, for his gentle guidance. Without him this book might never have seen the light of day.

Once again, I must acknowledge the love and support of my children, Mikki, Roni and Jeremy, and their spouses, Shoshi and Ariella, and most of all, that of my beloved wife and life companion, Rabbi Dr. Jackie Tabick. Without their warmth, respect and unfailing encouragement, this book would never have been written.

Obviously, any faults that may be found in the book are to be laid at my door.

And beyond all, my thanks to the One Who spoke and the world came into being, the One to Whom all thanks are due.

L.T.
September 2020

כתר
KETER
Crown

בינה
BINAH
Understanding

חכמה
HOCHMAH
Wisdom

גבורה
GEVURAH
Strength

חסד
HESED
Lovingkindness

תפארת
TIFERET
Beauty

הוד
HOD
Majesty

נצח
NETZACH
Victory

יסוד
YESOD
Foundation

מלכות
MALCHUT
Sovereignty

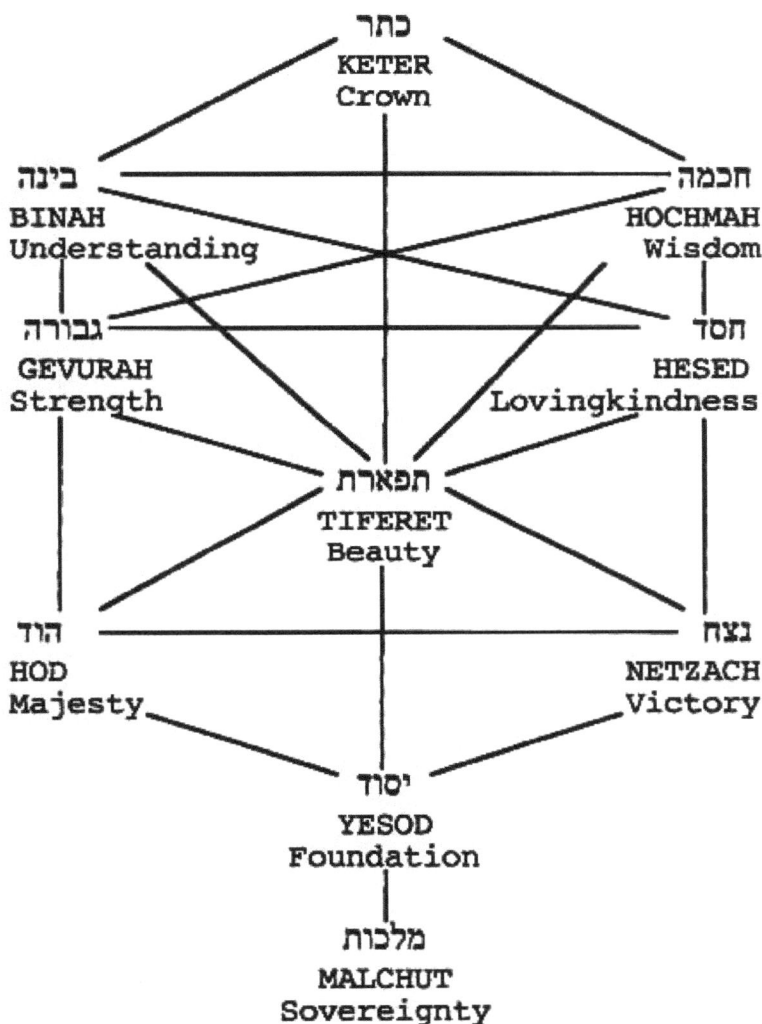

The Ten *Sefirot* as a Tree conveying divine energies
from the Infinite One above to the created universe
below, and vice versa.

# SHABBAT

"A woman blesses the lights from [a book of] Minhagim (Customs).
Library of the Jewish Community, Berlin." Notice that this is an oil lamp
suspended from the ceiling, a type once common in Jewish households.
The Education Center of the National Library of Israel - The National
Library of Israel Collections.

1

# [1] The Name of Shabbat

CONTEXT: Zevi Elimelech of Dinov was a disciple of the Seer of Lublin and Menachem Mendel of Rymanov. The following comes from his major work which weaves Kabbalah and Hasidism together in discussions about the festivals. Here he comments on a curious statement in the Zohar.

TEXT:

It says in the Zohar: "What is Shabbat? It is the name of the Holy Blessed One, the name that is complete on all sides." It seems to me that one may interpret [as follows]: There are twenty-seven letters in the Torah, and each letter contains life-force [deriving] from the revered Tetragrammaton. In that case, within the twenty-seven letters is the power of twenty-seven Tetragrammata, which in *gematria* (numerology) [equals] *SHaBBaT*. Hence, we may interpret: "What is Shabbat? It is the name of the Holy Blessed One, the name that is complete on all sides" – meaning, on all sides are the twenty-seven letters with which the Holy Blessed One created all the worlds with the power of the blessed divine name which is distributed in them, and [God] created the worlds in six days. Shabbat is like the image of the world's soul and form. Therefore, Shabbat is the name of the Holy Blessed One Who gives life to all of them. And since Shabbat is the name of the Holy Blessed One, it is forbidden to mention it in a place where it is forbidden to speak words of Torah. I know some people who are very precise in their actions not to mention the name of Shabbat when it is not necessary. This is correct, since the sages of the Zohar say that it is the name of the Holy Blessed One. The enlightened person will understand [this] matter.

> Zevi Elimelech of Dinov (1785-1841), *Benei Yissachar* (The Sons of Yissachar, I Chronicles 12:33) (Jerusalem, 1983), v.1, p.2a.

NOTES:
**It says in the Zohar...** II, 88b.
**"What is Shabbat? It is the name of the Holy Blessed One..."** In its original Zoharic context, the meaning is that the three meals of Shabbat represent all Ten *Sefirot* and thus a complete divine name. See Daniel C. Matt (trans.), *The Zohar: Pritzker Edition* (Stanford CA: Stanford University Press, 2004-6), v. IV, p.502 n.492.
**There are twenty-seven letters in the Torah...** That is, the normal twenty-two letters plus the five final forms.
**Each letter contains life-force [deriving] from the revered Tetragrammaton...** According to a Kabbalistic view, all the other letters of Hebrew alphabet derive the powers which God employed in the process of Creation from the Four-Letter Divine Name known as the

Tetragrammaton. See Joseph Gikatilla (1248-1325), *Ginat Egoz* (The Nut Garden, Song of Songs 6:11).

**In that case, within the twenty-seven letters is the power of twenty-seven Tetragrammata...** Since each letter is powered by the Four-Letter Name, each contains that name within itself. Hence, we can multiply 27 by 29, giving a total of 702. This is also the total we get when we add up the numerical value of the word *SHaBBaT* (= 300 + 2 + 400).

**Shabbat is like the image of the world's soul and form...** Because it contains the Ten *Sefirot* and combinations of the Tetragrammaton and the letters of the Hebrew alphabet.

COMMENT: In addition to its obvious personal, social and spiritual benefits, Zevi Elimelech of Dinov suggests that it also embodies the divine name in a special way. The Ten Commandments tell us not to take the name of God in vain. Names of God are not to be bandied about, and especially, not to be uttered in unclean places, like toilets. Therefore, according to the Dinover, some people try to refrain from using the word Shabbat when it is not necessary. Perhaps this is extreme, but it points us to a greater reverence for the Seventh Day.


# [2] Zen Shabbat?

CONTEXT: R. Hanoch Henich of Alexander was a disciple of Ya'akov Yitzchak, the Holy Jew, and later of Simchah Bunam of Pshische and of the Kotzker, before becoming a *tzaddik* in his own right. He wrote very little himself, leaving us dependent on his followers to note down his teachings. He was a great believer in doing the *mitzvot* internally as well as externally. Here he recounts what Shabbat felt like in his student days.

TEXT:
[R. Hanoch Henich] related: When we were young [and studying] with the Holy Jew, when Shabbat came we would ask ourselves: What is Shabbat? The *shtreiml* on my head makes Shabbat; the cabbage that we eat is Shabbat, until [these things] made known to us what Shabbat was. And this knowledge remained with us until Shabbat went out. This is the meaning of "it is a holy day" – from when it comes in until when it goes out.
Hanoch Henich of Alexander (Aleksandrow) (1798-1870), *Chashavah L'tovah* ([God] Intended It for Good, Genesis 50:20) (Piotrkov, 1929), p.46.

NOTE:
**The *shtreiml*...** A fur-trimmed hat frequently worn by male Hasidim on Shabbat and festivals.

COMMENT: This enigmatic statement by the Alexanderer *rebbe* has a kind of Zen quality to it, in my view. Shabbat is as Shabbat does, as it were. Shabbat is such an immersive experience that everything, that is part of it – even minor elements like the special clothing, the special food – points to the whole. It is what it is. Nothing else matters. That is what makes Shabbat holy. And its holiness has been internalized.

# SHABBAT AND THE SIX WORKING DAYS

## [3] Elevating the Week I

CONTEXT: This teaching comes from an anthology of sayings attributed to the founder of the modern Hasidic movement.

TEXT:
> On the eve of Shabbat, at *Minchah* and *Kabbalat Shabbat*, all one's words and [fulfilled] commandments for the week are raised up, for then there is an ascent of the worlds.
>> Yisra'el ben Eliezer, Ba'al Shem Tov (1700-1760), *Keter Shem Tov* (The Crown of a Good Name, Pirkei Avot 4:13) (Brooklyn: Kehot Publication Society, 1972), pt. 1, §299, p.77.

NOTES:
**Minchah and Kabbalat Shabbat...** *Minchah* is the afternoon service. On Friday afternoons, it may be followed immediately by *Kabbalat Shabbat*, Receiving/Accepting the Shabbat, prior to praying the Evening Service proper. In the Ashkenazi tradition, *Kabbalat Shabbat* usually consists of Psalms 95-99, 29, the song *Lecha Dodi*, and Psalms 92 and 93.
**An ascent of the worlds...** A term derived from the Lurianic kabbalah, indicating that the multiple levels are existence are all raised and brought into closer proximity to God.

COMMENT: The Ba'al Shem Tov takes the view that not only are we uplifted by the Shabbat, but all the *mitzvot* and Torah study we managed to engage in during the week are also uplifted. This suggests that from the perspective of the day of rest we may able look back over the week and, instead of taking them for granted, recognize the spirituality of the religious acts we undertook during the six working days.

# [4] Elevating the Week II

CONTEXT: Hayyim Haike of Amdur was a controversial student of the Maggid of Mezritch. He scandalized many Hasidim by encouraging his followers to engage in great shouts and even somersaults during prayer, as a mark of their attachment to God.

TEXT:

Whatever one receives of Torah and *mitzvot* throughout the week ascends on Shabbat and causes the flow of the extra soul upon oneself.

Hayyim Haike of Amdur (d. 1787), *Hayyim Va'Hesed* (Life and Lovingkindness, Job 10:12) (Warsaw, 1890), p.21.

NOTE:

**The extra soul...** The Talmud (*Betzah* 16a & *Ta'anit* 27b) says that a Jew acquires an extra soul at the onset of the Shabbat.

COMMENT: For some of us, Shabbat seems to come out of the blue each week (assuming we are keeping it at all, of course). It feels unconnected with the other six days of which it should be the culmination. Clearly, the fault lies in ourselves. If we engaged in Torah and *mitzvot* for at least a few minutes daily from Sunday to Friday, Shabbat itself would take on extra meaning. Rather than an afterthought tagged on to the end of the week, it would feel like an integral part of who we are. And we become worthy to attain that extra soul of which our rabbis speak.

# [5] All Week Long

CONTEXT: The following teaching comes from a book that purports to be the spiritual will of the Ba'al Shem Tov (1700-1760), founder of the modern Hasidic movement. As has long been recognized, this work is not by the Besht, but mostly contains teachings by the man considered to be his successor, Dov Ber, the Maggid of Mezritch (died 1772). The book itself focuses on issues of prayer and *devekut*, attachment to God, itself a key concept of Hasidic thought.

TEXT:

A person should not say, On Shabbat I will pray with concentration (*kavannah*), but not on weekdays. On the contrary, one should not be like servants who serve the king with devotion (*devekut*) when the king is standing before them, but are not quick in their service when the king is not before them. This is not a trustworthy servant. One should realize in faith that it would be bad for oneself if there were no king, and that one should cancel all the watches until one comes before the king, even though one may be unable to speak to him, and it is not appropriate to come before him. Nevertheless, one should do his will, for that would be very great compassion towards him.

> *Tzva'at HaRIBaSH* (The Testament of Rabbi Yisra'el Ba'al Shem) (Brooklyn: Kehot Publishing Society, 1975), §85, p.14a-b.

COMMENT: Of course, Shabbat is meant to be different from the six working days, a weekly opportunity to give ourselves time for spiritual pursuits. On the other hand, this text comes to remind us that confining our religious or spiritual work to Shabbat is little less than a betrayal of all that religion and spirituality are meant to be, of all that our relationship with the divine is meant to be. God cannot be confined to one day per week.

## [6] Three Holinesses

CONTEXT: *Chemdat Yamim* has been of enormous influence within both Sefardi and Ashkenazi ultra-orthodox communities since its appearance in the late seventeenth century, despite its origins in the movement surrounding failed messiah Shabbetai Zevi. Its author remains unidentified.

TEXT:

Look here, within the holiness of the Sabbath three [corollary] holinesses may be mentioned, and they are: [1] holiness of thought, as is written in the *Mechilta* [on] ceasing from the thought of work; also, [2] holiness of speech, which we have mentioned in relation to the Sabbath, as it is written: "[If you refrain from trampling the Sabbath...] and speaking [vain] words" (Isaiah 58:13); and also [3] the holiness of action, as can be cited in any interpretation of the forbidding of work in the holy writings.

The holy person can draw upon these three holinesses each day, whether completely, mostly, or briefly, and each individual is only obligated according to their capacity. Look here, among the requirements for the holiness of thought by which one may be sanctified during the six working days is to think holy thoughts, particularly when engaged in Torah study or prayer. Let all your deeds be for the sake of heaven and unite the "lovers" above. And when engaged in Torah and *mitzvot*, think "I am not here with us today in this world, but in the world of souls (*neshamot*) before the *Shechinah*," and in this way, you will purify your thoughts.

The essence of the thing is to become one who desires solitary meditation, for through this, you demonstrate in the soul that you have no connection with the people of this world at all, as will be true when you have departed [in death], and thus, you will see that you are a sojourner in this world, who wants only to attach their thought to the Rock Who made you, to Whom you will cleave to personally, if you are worthy...

Anon. (17th century), *Chemdat Yamim* (Most Precious of Days) (Jerusalem, 2004), v. 1, p. 30.

NOTES:

**In the *Mechilta*...** This is an ancient halachic *midrash* on the book of Exodus attributed to Rabbi Ishmael. The reference is to *Mechilta* 20:9:1 (*Bachodesh* 7).

**The "lovers" above...** I.e, the *sefirot* of *Tiferet* and *Malchut*.

**I am not here with us today...** Compare Deuteronomy 29:14: "those who are with us today."

COMMENT: If, as frequently stated, Shabbat is a foretaste of the world-to-come, then the *Chemdat Yamim* has taken this sentiment to its logical conclusion. For its author, Shabbat is an opportunity not merely to rest and study Torah, but to separate ourselves from the mundane world and imagine ourselves transported to that perfect world where we can dwell in the unalloyed presence of God. Our observance of the three holinesses he outlines (separation from work, from the thought of work, and from vain words) is our key to achieving this state.

## [7] Spreading Shabbat Over the Week

CONTEXT: The author of this very popular late seventeenth century work was secretly a follower of failed messiah Shabbetai Zevi, but the most zealous opponent could not argue with his elegantly written masterwork of ethics and Kabbalah. Who can disagree with a call to deeper spirituality?

TEXT:

Three are best: thought, speech and action. Every person of Israel should sanctify themselves during the six working days by sanctifying and respecting the *neshamah*, *ruach* and *nefesh*, drawing upon themselves the lights of the great and holy Shabbat. Even poor workers upon whom the yoke of work sits heavily and who have no free time, whom all agree suffer from spiritual deprivation and difficult labor for sustenance and support in this mighty exile – even they, at the moment of prayer, when they willingly set aside their work, should take care to sanctify their thoughts and speech and the rest of their senses at that moment and occasion, in order that in that hour or half-hour, they might sanctify themselves with the holiness of the Shabbat, not ceasing during their prayer for even one word, in such a way that no day is deprived of the Shabbat's holiness. For by sanctifying themselves during the six working days they become able to greet the light of the holiness of the great Shabbat more easily. It is impossible to acquire that holiness of Shabbat without sanctifying themselves throughout the week, for the holiness of the Shabbat is a very supernal holiness, the light of emanation (*atzilut*), and it is impossible for a human being to attain it when they are clothed in the six weekdays over which the thirty-nine categories of work rule.

This may be compared to a garment upon which spots of oil or something similar have fallen. If it is not washed and bleached appropriately, it will be unable to accept any dye. Similarly, it may be compared to a person who lives in a place of darkness and "the shadow of death"; if he were to go out into the light suddenly and be exposed to the full light of the sun, his eyes would be darkened, and he would be unable to appreciate the sweetness of the light. The same applies to someone who comes to receive the light of the Shabbat, but whose soul is dirty, stained with transgressions, over whom the light of the *neshamah* does not rule...

> Anon. (17th century), *Chemdat Yamim* (Most Precious of Days) (Jerusalem, 2004), v. 1, p. 35.

NOTES:

**Three are best...** In the original text, *K'mutav t'lata.* This is actually a pun on a phrase in Talmud, *Ketubbot* 22a, which reads *b'mutav t'lata,* "when three [judges] are sitting."

**Neshamah, ruach and nefesh...** In medieval Jewish thought, these are three souls or soul-levels. Broadly speaking, the *neshamah* represents the intellect or the mind, the *ruach* is the emotional drive and the *nefesh* is that which distinguishes an animate being from the inanimate.

**The light of emanation (*atzilut*)...** *Atzilut* here may refer to the entire sefirotic realm or to the highest of the four worlds, and therefore the furthest removed from the level we normally inhabit.

**The thirty-nine categories of work...** This refers to the types of work prohibited on Shabbat, but obviously permitted during the rest of week. The list may be found in Mishnah, *Shabbat* 7:2.

COMMENT: How are we to think about the interplay between Shabbat and the six working days of the week? The *Chemdat Yamim* suggests that in terms of practice, they should not be opposites. The one being all rest and the other all work. On the contrary, we should see that the spirit of Shabbat infuses our week, particularly when we stop to pray the daily prayers, so that each prayer becomes a mini-Shabbat in itself. And then, those prayers will reinforce and enhance our Shabbat experience, and deepen our spiritual awareness 24/7.

# BE HAPPY

## [8] God's Blessing on the Shabbat

CONTEXT: The following comes from a book attributed to R. Yehudah HeHasid (the Pious), one of the two great leaders of the medieval German pietist movement known to us as the Hasidei Ashkenaz.

TEXT:

> This is the reply that our rabbi Meshullam gave to the heretics who do not light lamps in their homes on Shabbat because the verse says: "Do not kindle a fire in your homes on the Shabbat day" (Exodus 35:3). He answered them: It is written "Then God blessed the seventh day" (Genesis 2:3), but we do not know with what God blessed it, except from what we see of the curses that Job uttered when he cursed his day [of birth] with darkness, as it says: "That night, let thick darkness take it! ... Let it look for light and find none!" (Job 3:8-9). From this generalization [we learn] that the blessing with which the Holy Blessed One blessed the Shabbat was light, meaning, peace in the home. Whatever Job said as a curse, the opposite may be said of Shabbat as a blessing. In Job, it is written: "Let no joy come upon it" (Job 3:7). From this [we learn] that we have to rejoice on Shabbat with songs and praises.
>
> Yehudah ben Shmuel HeHasid of Regensburg (d.1217), *Sefer Hasidim* (The Book of the Pious) (Reuben Margoliot, ed.) (Jerusalem: Mossad HaRav Kook, 1957), § 1147, p. 571. [This piece occurs in almost identical form at §271, pp. 229-230.]

NOTES:

**Our rabbi Meshullam...** This is Meshullam ben Kalonymus (10th-11th century) who was a member of the Kalonymus clan, which included Yehudah HeHasid himself. He was a legal scholar and liturgical poet. The decision referred to here is recorded in *Sefer Mitzvot Gadol* (*SeMaG*, positive commandments 47 & 199) by Moshe of Coucy (13th century France).

**The heretics...** A reference to the Karaites, a Jewish sect that flourished from the 9th to the 12th century. Thereafter, it declined but groups continue to this day. They adhere to a strict interpretation of Exodus 35:3 (quoted above). The normative rabbinic view is that this allows for kindling before Shabbat and letting the fire continue burning during Shabbat itself. Hence, the lighting of candles just before the start of the holy day. (See *Mechilta* on Exodus 35:3.) Sitting in darkness or in the cold on Friday evening would diminish the pleasure of Shabbat.

**Peace in the home…** The connection between peace and light in the home on Shabbat is made in Talmud, *Shabbat* 23b.

COMMENT: R. Meshullam's analysis proceeds from the negative to the positive. Shabbat is opposite of everything that Job wanted his day of birth to be. In other words, Shabbat should be about light and joy: physical and spiritual light, joy in being alive in God's world expressed in song.


## [9] Putting Quarrels to Rest

CONTEXT: The following comes from a book that is still popular in ultra-Orthodox and Hasidic groups, despite being the work of an anonymous supporter of failed messiah Shabbetai Zevi.

TEXT:
You should be happy and rejoice in joy for the bride who is coming amongst us. "And the dove came to him towards evening" (Genesis 8:11), so it is appropriate to make her happy with anything that comes to hand. If you have a quarrel with a friend or any member of your household, you should forgive any sin and not mention any transgression on the Shabbat day, except in love and affection, peace and friendship. Neither should you profane the holiness of Shabbat with any profane thing, for by doing this you damage its holiness and significance. The holiness of Shabbat alludes to a great thing where there is only rest and quiet, and "wickedness will dissipate like smoke."
Anon. (17th century), *Chemdat Yamim* (Most Precious of Days) (Jerusalem, 2004), v. 1, pp. 168-169.

NOTES:
**For the bride who is coming amongst us…** The *Shechinah* or the *Sefirah* of *Malchut*, but also identified with Shabbat. Her bridegroom is the *Sefirah* of *Tiferet*, and those who observe Shabbat are her entourage, accompanying her on her visit to her husband. This imagery lies behind the Friday evening hymn, *L'cha Dodi*.
**"And the dove came to him…"** In Genesis, this refers to the dove that Noah sent out of the Ark to see if the waters had receded. In kabbalistic imagery, the dove represents the *Shechinah*.

**"Wickedness will dissipate like smoke"** ... A phrase depicting a redeemed world, found in the *Amidah* for both Rosh Hashanah and Yom Kippur.

COMMENT: According to the Talmud (*Berachot* 57b), Shabbat is a one-sixtieth, a foretaste, of the world-to-come, a world redeemed from conflict and strife. Therefore, even on this side of the messianic age, our Shabbat experience should be as free of conflict and strife as possible. All the quarrels that inevitably arise between even people in loving relationships need to be set aside, and every effort made to remove sources of further altercations.

## ITS SPIRITUAL MEANING

## [10] Returning to the Root

CONTEXT: Meshullam Feibush of Zbarazh was a student of both Dov Baer, the Maggid of Mezritch and Yechiel Michal, the Maggid of Zlotchov. This text (somewhat abbreviated) comes from his magnum opus, a work describing the Hasidic way of life couched as letters to a friend.

TEXT:

    Shabbat means "being returned" (*hashavah*), for [then] creatures return to their root... [It is] like a small child who goes after childish things and forgets the parent. But after seeing the parent, [the child] throws away everything and attaches itself and runs to the parent because [the child] is "a piece" of [the parent]. The same applies, as it were, when the blessed God makes divine glory shine upon creatures, their faces tend towards [God] with a great longing... Hence, the matter of Shabbat: it is a [case of] being returned to the root, that is to say, the root gives light to the branches, and the branches desire it and take pleasure in it, and long for it. And this is unification with the Blessed God.

    Meshullam Feibush HaLevi Heller of Zbarazh (d. 1785), *Yosher Divrei Emet* (Upright Words of Truth, Ecclesiastes 12:10) (Bnei Brak, 2004), pp.149-150.

NOTES:

**Shabbat means "being returned" (*hashavah*)...** An imaginative derivation, as if it were from the root *SHUV*, to return. Grammatically, though, the noun actually comes from a root (*SH-V-T*) meaning to rest or to cease.

11

**Creatures return to their root...** in the divine realm.

COMMENT: For Meshullam Feibush of Zbarazh, Shabbat is an opportunity for us to reconnect with the spiritual source of our souls, as if we were small children running to hug our parent. For him, Shabbat should be about desire, about love of God. We set aside our normal activities (childish things?) just to be re-united with our Parent for one day out of seven.

## [11] A Day for Souls

CONTEXT: Here the Ba'al Shem Tov offers his view on the meaning of the extra soul that, the Talmud (*Betzah* 16a & *Ta'anit* 27b) says each Jew acquires on Shabbat.

TEXT:
The essential [purpose] of Shabbat is to attach oneself to the blessed God through prayer and Torah. And thus, we read in the Zohar: "This day is a day for souls and not a day for establishing the body." That is to say, the root of souls casts light over the souls that are in bodies and they desire it. This is called the addition of the extra soul, and all this is felt by [those who] are pure of heart.
Yisra'el ben Eliezer, Ba'al Shem Tov (1700-1760), *Keter Shem Tov* (The Crown of a Good Name, Pirkei Avot 4:13) (Brooklyn: Kehot Publication Society, 1972), pt.2, §402, p.118.

NOTES:
**In the Zohar...** II, 205b.
**The root of souls...** Souls are said to have their roots in the world of the *Sefirot*.

COMMENT: All week long our minds are primarily focused on our bodies, our income and outgoings, our appointments and obligations. Now, as Shabbat enters, we can give thought to our souls, our spiritual needs. If our souls do indeed come from the divine realms, then this is our weekly opportunity to reconnect with their source above. But, says the Besht, in order to do this, we have to be pure of heart; we have to set aside all those things that troubled us all week.

# [12] Shabbat as Exodus

CONTEXT: We hear from the Alexanderer *rebbe*, Hanoch Henich, a disciple of the school of Pshische and of Menachem Mendel of Kotzk. This teaching was recorded rather imperfectly by one of his followers.

TEXT:

Moreover, I heard from him on *parashat Bo*: On Shabbat we say "a reminder of the exodus from Egypt" for the essence of Shabbat should be above nature, that is, the annihilation of the qualities before the Eternal, as it is written: "To you, O Eternal, belong the greatness..." [I Chronicles 29:11]. And this too is an "exodus from Egypt," for it is written of all [of the Ten] Plagues "that you may know...," for it brings knowledge to Israel.

This is what I understood of his words, but I do not remember everything. Perhaps a bit has been changed, but this is what I understood.

Hanoch Henich of Alexander (Aleksandrow) (1798-1870), *Chashavah L'tovah* ([God] Intended It for Good, Genesis 50:20) (Piotrkov, 1929), p.5.

NOTES:

**Parashat Bo...** The weekly Torah reading that comprises Exodus 10:1-13:16. It includes the last three plagues of locusts, darkness and the death of the first-born.

**On Shabbat we say...** In the *kiddush* for *Erev Shabbat*.

**The essence of Shabbat should be above nature...** Shabbat should allow us to transcend our natural limitations.

**"To you, O Eternal, belong the greatness..."** Since all attributes and qualities truly belong only to God, we come to realize that what we think of as our own spiritual achievements are as nothing before the divine.

**"That you may know..."** See Exodus 6:7, 10:2.

COMMENT: In the *kiddush* for Friday night we say that Shabbat is both "a memorial of the act of Creation" and "a reminder of the Exodus from Egypt." And these phrases reflect the two explanations given for Shabbat in the two versions of the Ten Commandments, where one (Exodus 20:8-11) refers to Creation and the other (Deuteronomy 5:12-15) the Exodus. For the Alexanderer *rebbe*, this points to Shabbat as an opportunity to transcend our limited physical nature (Creation) and achieve a higher state of consciousness through a kind of spiritual Exodus. And this would bring us to a knowledge that is beyond the capacity of words to express.

# [13] Exodus vs. Creation

CONTEXT: This comes from an anonymous medieval work, one of several, attributed to a legendary Mishnaic teacher who probably lived in the late second century C.E. The book presents as an extensive dialogue between a student of Kabbalah and his mentor.

TEXT:
     ... I said to my teacher: Which is more important [in Judaism]: The Exodus from Egypt or the Creation of the world?

     He replied: The Creation of the world. He continued: We learn this from the use of "remembrance" in relation to the Exodus from Egypt. Thus, it is written, "Remember the Shabbat day" (Exodus 20:8), and it is written, "Remember this day when you came out of Egypt" (Exodus 13:3). Just as there were miracles and wonders performed [at the Exodus], so too were great and wondrous things performed [before] the [first] Shabbat.

     If so, I countered, should we not make a Haggadah to relate the story of Creation? And every Shabbat we should re-tell it.

     He said: My son, don't you say *Vay'chulu* ("Heaven and earth were finished") in your [Friday evening] *kiddush*? *Vay'chulu* contains all of Creation.

     Anon. (14th century), *Sefer HaQanah* (The Book of [Nechunyah ben] HaQanah) (Jerusalem, 1998), p. 153.

NOTES:

***Vay'chulu* ("Heaven and earth were finished")** ... Genesis 2:1-3. This brief biblical passage forms a kind of introduction to the Friday evening *kiddush* proper, namely the blessing over wine, over the day, and over bread. As such, it acts as a parallel to the Pesach Haggadah.

COMMENT: Why would the anonymous teacher rate Creation above the Exodus in importance? Surely, the Exodus is a specifically Jewish event, and thus, central to Jewish identity? Clearly, that is true. But Judaism also has a universal message. Our God is not simply our God, not just the God of the Jews. Our God is concerned for all humanity, because (as we affirm at the inauguration of every Sabbath) our God is the creator of all.

# "AND WAS REFRESHED"

## [14] Preparations for Shabbat

CONTEXT: This comment on the closing word of two biblical verses (Exodus 31:16-17) that form part of the service for Erev Shabbat and the *kiddush* for Shabbat morning, is by Pinchas of Koretz, a younger contemporary of the Ba'al Shem Tov. It contains one of only a handful of references in Hasidic literature to the Besht's only son Zevi.

TEXT:
I heard in his name: "'[God] rested and was refreshed (*vayinafash*)' [Exodus 31:16-17]. When it is Shabbat, Woe (*vai*) my soul is lost! The question is raised: Surely, one should recite this verse at the close of Shabbat, not on the eve of Shabbat." And we also sing it with such a pleasant melody! He explained that when someone is totally ill, they do not feel any pain [in particular limbs] because they have no single limb that is well that that limb should feel pain. But someone who is well [in general] and has a pain in a particular limb, all their limbs feel the pain of that particular limb, and the like. [During] all the ordinary weekdays, a person is ill in all their soul's limbs and do not feel anything, for the reason given above. But when Shabbat comes, and they begin to experience a bit of healing, they feel a great pain, [namely,] the weight of the pain of their soul. Hence, when it is Shabbat [and] they feel the holiness of Shabbat: "Woe, my soul is lost!" for they know and feel their pain and illness.

The great rabbi, our teacher, the rabbi, R. Zevi, the son of R. Israel Ba'al Shem told him that a person should make preparations to be ready to receive the holiness of the Shabbat, as it is written: "They prepared what they had brought" [Exodus 16:5]. And he replied that if a thing is given from above, and one doesn't know how and why it was given, how can a person prepare themselves for it? But, one must guard oneself from anything bad. Hence, "in the days of Rabbi Judah, all their learning was confined to *Nezikin* [Damages]" − [meaning,] one should guard oneself against anything that might cause damage to the soul.

Pinchas of Koretz (1726-1791), *Midrash Pinchas* (Pinchas' Interpretation) (Lemberg, 1874), §108,109, p.14a-b. (Jerusalem, 1971; §§54,55, pp.31-32.)

NOTES:
**The question is raised...** In Talmud *Betzah* 16a & Zohar, II, 204b. In rabbinic literature, *vai* is often interpreted as a cry of anguish, comparable to the Yiddish *oy vey*.

**At the close of Shabbat...** Reflecting the spiritual distress caused by the departure of the holy day.

**"In the days of Rabbi Judah..."** This statement is found in Talmud, *Berachot* 20a. *Nezikin* refers nowadays to the fourth of the six orders of the Mishnah and Talmud, but it may be that in *Berachot* the reference is to the first three tractates of that order (*Bava Kamma, Bava Metzia* and *Bava Batra*, meaning First, Middle, and Last Doors) which originally formed one tractate itself called *Nezikin*.

COMMENT: Does Shabbat bring pain? Perhaps, when its arrival makes us remember how much of our lives are spent worrying about trivialities. In presenting this interpretation, R. Pinchas agrees with the Seer of Lublin (in the passage that follows). But R. Zevi, the son of the Besht, raises the question: Does preparing for Shabbat help to alleviate that spiritual distress that Shabbat itself brings? His answer is no: we can only make efforts to remove causes of distress. The real healing that the holy day brings is unpredictable, a gift from above.

# [15] Oh, My Soul

CONTEXT: Exodus 31:16-17, known from its opening word as *V'sham'ru*, is recited between the *Shema* and its blessings and the *Amidah* in the *Erev Shabbat* service. (It is also sung as the opening section of the *kiddush* for Shabbat morning.) It concludes with the words *shavat vayinafash* ("He [i.e., God] rested and was refreshed"). This phrase raises all kinds of theological questions, but the Talmud, as we shall see, connects *vayinafash* to *nefesh* ("soul"). Our commentator here, the Seer of Lublin, was a disciple of Elimelech of Lyzhansk, was a key figure in the growth and development of Hasidism in Poland, and he quotes the founder of Hasidism as the authority for his interpretation.

TEXT:

I heard that the Rav, the holy man of God, Rabbi Yisra'el, the Ba'al Shem Tov, was very precise about why we say shavat vayinafash [Exodus 31:17] at the start of the sabbath. In accordance with the interpretation [namely,] "Oh (*vai*), my soul is lost!" it would have been sufficient to say it at the moment the sabbath is going out. But it is known that he resolved [the difficulty by saying that we recite it on the eve of the sabbath] in order to add to the love and joy [we experience] from the holy sabbath, when we remember that afterwards the great extra soul [that comes with] the sabbath will cease, as one prolongs a parable or a joke.

Ya'akov Yitzchak HaLevi Horowitz, the Seer of Lublin (1745-1815), *Zikkaron Zot* (A Memorial of This) (Ashdod, 2004), p.157.

NOTES:

**"Oh (*vai*), my soul is lost!"** ... This interpretation is found in the Talmud *Betzah* 16a & Zohar, II, 204b. Rabbinic literature frequently interprets the syllable *vai* as a cry of anguish (woe!). So, the question arises: what anguish is the *nefesh*, the soul, undergoing as a result of the arrival of Shabbat? Hence, the suggestion that perhaps the verses from which this comes should be recited as Shabbat departs instead.

**The great extra soul...** According to the Talmud (*Betzah* 16a & *Ta'anit* 27b), each Jew is granted an extra soul for the duration of the Shabbat.

COMMENT: This text seems to raise the question as to whether any pain or trouble is to be associated with Shabbat. Surely, it is meant to be a day of rest and spiritual joy, not a day of trouble. I would suggest that the pain and trouble is involved in the preparation for Shabbat, rather than in the observance of the day itself. But perhaps the Shabbat itself can bring pain, a spiritual pain when one regrets how we seem to spend so much of the rest of the week on apparently trivial matters and neglect the needs of our soul.

# [16] Shabbat as Form

CONTEXT: Ya'akov Yosef of Polonnoye was the primary disciple of the Ba'al Shem Tov and author of the first Hasidic books to be published. Much of his work consists in innovative applications of the ancient philosophical distinction between matter and form. All things are made up of matter, which is, in itself, formless and uniform. What distinguishes, say, me and my table, is the form. But for Ya'akov Yosef, matter refers to the external aspects of things, their physicality, and form refers to the internal, i.e., the spiritual.

TEXT:

Everything in the universe has external and internal aspects... Thus, the year has internal and external aspects, which are the six working days and Shabbat. Shabbat is called the soul (*nefesh*) and spirit (*neshamah*), as it is said, "[God] rested and was refreshed (*vayinafash*)" (Exodus 31:17). The six working days are the matter.

Thus, humanity contains matter and form, and the purpose [of life] is to make form from matter; hence, "the land shall keep a Shabbat to the Eternal." Understand!

Ya'akov Yosef of Polonnoye (died c.1782), *Toldot Ya'akov Yosef* (The Generations of Jacob Joseph, Genesis 37:2) (Jerusalem, 1973), v. 1, pp. 408-409.

NOTES:

**The six working days and Shabbat...** They are presented in reverse order, with the six working days corresponding to the external or material aspect, and Shabbat to the internal or spiritual aspect.

**"The land shall keep a Shabbat..."** Land represents physical matter, and Shabbat (i.e., the sabbatical year), represents the spiritual.

COMMENT: If Shabbat is just a day to avoid work and be lazy, then we've missed the point of it. It should be our weekly opportunity for spiritual regeneration. All week long our focus has been primarily on our material wellbeing, "our matter", if you will. Now, on Shabbat, we should be devoting time in shul and at home for the revitalization of our "form," our spiritual wellbeing.

# PHYSICAL ASPECTS: HOME, FOOD, CLOTHING

## [17] The *Shechinah* at Home

CONTEXT: *Yalqut Re'uveni* is a seventeenth century anthology of midrashic and kabbalistic texts arranged mainly according to the weekly Torah readings. Occasionally, as here, the selections are summaries rather than exact renderings of the original. Reuven Hoeschke Katz, the compiler, lived in Prague.

TEXT:
"The Israelite people shall keep Shabbat, observing Shabbat throughout their generations (*l'DoRotam*) as a covenant for all time."

Exodus 31:16

In relation to Shabbat, *l'DoRoTam* is written without [vowel letters for "o"]. Thus, it indicates *DiRah* (dwelling). This is to teach us that when Shabbat comes in, the *Shechinah*, the Presence of God, enters. So, look, if the house is arranged with the table [laid] and the bed [made], and candles [lit], the *Shechinah* says: "This is my dwelling." But if not, she says: "This is not the home of a Jew." Similarly, in relation to the *mezuzah l'DoRotam* is written without [the vowel letters for "o"].

Reuven Hoeschke (17th century) (ed.), *Yalqut Re'uveni* (Reuben's Collection) (Warsaw, 1883), v. 1, p. 156. Based on Zohar III, 330a.

NOTES:
***DiRah* (dwelling)...** Reading, *l'DiRoTaM*, "throughout their dwellings", instead of *l'DoRoTam*, "throughout their generations").

**The *mezuzah*...** The small compartment containing two Scriptural passages (Deuteronomy 6:4-9 and 11:13-21) that is fixed to the doorposts of Jewish homes.

***L'DoRotam* is written...** Actually, this word does not occur in relation to the *mezuzah*, but to the *tallit* (prayer shawl), in Numbers 15:38.

COMMENT: What does it mean when this text says that the Shechinah will consider your home her own if it is prepared for the Shabbat? Surely, it means that a home that is ready for the day of rest is a home that is prepared for spirituality. That which seemed abstract is made real.

## [18] Spiritual Enjoyment Through Food

CONTEXT: Ya'akov Yosef of Polonnoye was a close disciple of the Ba'al Shem Tov and our primary source for the latter's teachings. Here, however, he channels the teachings of another preacher of the time whose wisdom might otherwise have been lost to us, Mendel of Bar.

TEXT:

It seems [to me] that I heard this in the name of the preacher (*maggid*), our teacher Mendel [of Bar] ... He explained ... [the talmudic teaching]: "If Israel were to observe two *Shabbatot* according the law, they would be redeemed immediately." Why two *Shabbatot*, and not one? And he explained: A perfect person must observe Shabbat in two aspects. One: through those things that touch upon the body and, two: [through those that touch upon] the soul.

Then he explained with a parable: A king's only son was held captive under harsh conditions. A long time passed and hope of his redemption and return to his father drained away. After much time and [many] years, a letter reached him from his father the king, [saying] that he should not despair and not forget the customs of kingship among the "prairie wolves." For his [the king's] hand is outstretched to restore him to his father through many excuses in war and in peace... Immediately, the king's son became very happy, although this had to be kept secret. It was impossible for him to be happy openly. So, what did he do? He went with the people of his town to an establishment [where they could drink] wine or some other intoxicant, and they experienced a physical happiness with wine while he was happy because of his father's letter. The command to enjoy Shabbat is exactly like this vision. For the body, which is the form, [enjoys itself] with food and drink in order that the righteous might be free to rejoice with the second [type], the happiness of the soul in communion (*devekut*) with the Blessed God all day, so that [their] consciousness never turns from the holiness and awe of the Shabbat...

Ya'akov Yosef of Polonnoye (died c.1782), *Toledot Ya'akov Yosef* (The Generations of Jacob Joseph, Genesis 37:2) (Jerusalem, 1973), v.1, p.231.

NOTES:

**"If Israel were to …"** Talmud, *Shabbat* 118b, but not an exact quotation.

**Among the "prairie wolves" …** I.e., those holding him captive.

**A perfect person…** That is, someone striving to be perfect.

**Must observe Shabbat in two aspects…** The argument pivots. Two consecutive *Shabbatot* have morphed into two aspects of Shabbat observance.

**This had to be kept secret…** To not alert the prince's captors.

COMMENT: If Shabbat is meant to be a spiritual experience, why in our tradition is there an emphasis on the physical pleasures of eating? The Talmud, in *Shabbat* 117b, enjoins the eating of three meals on Shabbat, something few Jews could afford to do the rest of the week. And, by tradition, the foods chosen should ideally include special dishes reserved for the holy day (see Talmud, *Beitzah* 16a). Where is the spiritual value in all this lovely eating? Mendel of Bar takes a rather elitist view. For him, only the "perfect" person (that is, what Hasidism later called the *tzaddik* or *rebbe*) could attain to the spiritual dimension hidden within the physical pleasure of eating. The rest of us, who are rooted in the material world, must content ourselves with the corporeal pleasures. But surely, if we are aware of this teaching, and apply our minds, we too can use the physical to give us space and incentive to attain to the spiritual.

## [19] The Third Meal

CONTEXT: Hanoch Henich of Alexander was a disciple of Simchah Bunam of Pshische and *rebbe* in his own right. The Talmud, in *Shabbat* 117b, enjoins the eating of three meals of Shabbat, as opposed to the two meals on weekdays in poorer cultures. In many Hasidic circles, the third meal, eaten on Shabbat afternoon and into the evening, has a special significance. Accompanied by singing and, in the *rebbe*'s presence, a *d'var torah* (literally, word of Torah, a sermon), it is often given the name *M'laveh Malkah* (accompanying the Queen), symbolizing the departure of the Shabbat Queen/Bride, whom we had welcomed with *L'cha Dodi* on Friday evening.

TEXT:

The [third] Shabbat meal must be prepared [in advance], and not approached in haste. On the contrary, one must calm oneself before the

One Who arranged the meal and Who commanded [us] about the Shabbat meal. And this is the meaning of [the phrase]: "Prepare the meal [of the supernal faith; prepare the meal of the King/Sovereign]." It must be prepared.

> Hanoch Henich of Alexander (Aleksandrow) (1798-1870), *Chashavah L'tovah* ([God] Intended It for Good, Genesis 50:20) (Piotrkov, 1929), p.45.

NOTE:
**"Prepare the meal [of the supernal faith] …"** A quotation from Zohar II, 88b, which was recycled to introduce a *zemirah* (table song) for the third meal attributed to R. Isaac Luria, found in many prayer books.

COMMENT: When the Alexanderer *rebbe* suggests that the third Shabbat meal should be prepared in advance, he doesn't simply mean that it should not just be leftovers thrown together at the last minute. He is referring to spiritual preparation as well. ("One must calm oneself before the One…"). I feel sure that he would not have wanted to restrict this striving for spiritual readiness to the third meal. Each of the three meals of Shabbat offers the potential for a spiritual as well as a gastronomic and social experience.

## [20] Wearing Our Shabbat Best

CONTEXT: The Talmud (in tractate *Shabbat* 113a-114a) recommends that one wear special clothing on Shabbat, or at least clean clothing. Kabbalistic tradition, apparently stemming from the Ari, Isaac Luria, encouraged the wearing of white garments, and some Hasidic communities continue to observe this today. Mordechai of Lachowicze was a Lithuanian Hasidic *rebbe*, a disciple of Shelomo of Karlin. I have been unable to identify his uncle with any certainty.

TEXT:
After this [the main meal of Friday], he would put on his white garments and robe while it was still Friday afternoon. He would not wait until the morning [to do so]. I heard that my uncle, the holy man of Neshchiz related that, as his sainted father departed [this life,] a messenger of the Merciful One came to him [and said] that he would be honored by greeting the Shabbat in the messiah's palace. He went after the messenger and when he arrived at the entrance to the palace, he saw there an honorable old man standing and shining, but not going inside. He asked him [i.e., the messenger]: My holy elder, why is he not going inside? And he replied: He would not be allowed inside until the morning, because it

was his constant practice not to put on his white garment in honor of the holy Shabbat until the morning.

> Mordechai of Lachowicze (Lyakhovichi; 1742-1810) in *Ilana deChayei* (The Tree of Life) (Yitzchak Mordechai Podvah, ed.) (Jerusalem, 1986), pt.2 (Or HaNer), p.11.

NOTES:

**The holy man of Neshchiz...** Possibly Mordechai of Neschiz.

**His sainted father departed...** Is this R. Mordechai's father, or his uncle's?

COMMENT: This obviously absurd story raises a question about the importance of wearing special clothing on Shabbat. For me, it is very much a means of making Shabbat different from the working days that precede it. So, I save my best clothing for the seventh day, eschewing the jeans I wear when I am not working and the sports jackets I wear when I am for a suit with a white shirt and tie. And I do this whether I am expecting to go to synagogue or not, whether I am at home or away. The suit is not for others to see, necessarily. It is for the honor of the holy day alone, and serves to remind me of its sanctity.

# PESACH

THE EGYPTIANS URGE MOSES TO DEPART

And he [Pharaoh] called for Moses and Aaron by night, and said, Rise up, and get
you forth from among my people, both ye and the children of Israel; and go, serve
the Lord, as ye have said ... (Exodus 12, 31)

The Egyptians urge Moses to depart. By Gustave Doré.

# [21] "A Mouth Speaks"

CONTEXT: As is well known, Pesach actually means pass over or spring over and was applied metaphorically to God (or the angel of death) skipping or passing over the homes of the Israelites who had the blood of the Pesach lamb on their doorposts and lintel (see Exodus 12:13,27). Hence, the English rendering "Passover." The following passage "analyzes" the word more imaginatively. Levi Yitzchak of Berditchev was one of the most prominent Hasidic rabbis of his generation and became the subject of many delightful stories.

TEXT:

On the subject of Pesach: It has been found in the words of our rabbis that [*PeSaCH*] may be linguistically related to *PeH SaCH* ("a mouth speaks"). .... A ruler of flesh and blood tells his servants to do such-and-such. While they are still speaking with him, they may be able to seek to overturn the command, but when he has spoken with them and they have left his presence, it is no longer possible to overturn his words. The Holy Blessed One's character is not like that of flesh and blood. Even though the letters [of the Hebrew alphabet] have been emanated, created, formed and made, and their development has reached into this lowly world to accomplish such-and-such, [nevertheless] there are righteous people who can overturn [God's] decisions.

Or alternatively, if God's children repent, then automatically, [the letters] are turned into another configuration, dealing with God's people in a good way, [each] letter resembles the Ruler who speaks with the people while they are still present, because "the whole world is full of God's glory" [Isaiah 6:3] and "there is no place empty of God." And as God's power was then, so it is now. Hence *peh sach* – meaning, "the mouth is speaking," i.e., even though [God] has created all the worlds, God speaks with those who serve God and they are still in God's presence.

Levi Yitzchak of Berditchev (1740-1809), *Qedushat Levi* (The Holiness of Levi) (Munkacs, 1829), p. 61c.

NOTES:

**In the words of our rabbis...** This de-construction of the word Pesach does not appear in rabbinic literature but may have originated in the Kabbalah. (See Hayyim Vital (1542-1620), *Liqqutei Tanakh veTa'amei HaMitzvot* (Gleanings on the Bible and the Meanings of the Commandments) (Jerusalem: Yeshivat Kol Yehudah, 1970), pp.138-139; and *Sha'ar HaKavvanot* (The Gate of Intentions) (Jerusalem: Yeshivat Kol Yehudah, 1985), v. 2, p. 155.

**Emanated, created, formed and made...** The reference here is to the four realms or levels of existence of kabbalistic thought. From highest to lowest, they are *Atzilut* (Emanation), *Beri'ah* (Creation), *Yetzirah* (Formation) and *Asiyah* (Making). The notion that God created the universe with the letters of the Hebrew alphabet goes back at least as far as the *Sefer Yetzirah* (Book of Formation), a work of unknown origin probably written between the third and sixth centuries.

**"There is no place empty of God" ...** A phrase from Elijah's prayer in *Tikkunei HaZohar* §7.

COMMENT: What does Pesach actually mean? Passover, because God/the Angel of Death passed over the houses of the Israelites in Egypt? Skipping, jumping, walking with a limp? The suggestion here is that *Peh Sach* indicates that Pesach was/is a moment of interaction with and revelation of the divine, since in Kabbalistic symbolism, the mouth indicates the *Sefirah* of *Malchut*, which manifests divine activity in the world.

For Levi Yitzchak of Berditchev, *Peh Sach* means, God still speaks to certain people, to those conscious of being in God's presence, i.e., the *tzaddikim*, the righteous, by which he meant the Hasidic *rebbes*.

To me, *Peh Sach* means, the future is not written in stone. God still speaks, and what we think is going to be, may not be. We have the power to change things (for better or for worse). But Levi Isaac is not wrong: those who are conscious of being in God's presence may be precisely those who can change things for the better! For they will see the bigger picture. (Think of Mahatma Gandhi and Martin Luther King, Jr.) And maybe "the righteous" can be us!

## [22] Pesach as Lovingkindness

CONTEXT: Menachem Nachum of Chernobyl was a student of the Maggid of Mezritch, and father of Mordechai of Chernobyl who succeeded him in leading his Hasidic community.

TEXT:

Pesach is "the right arm," that is, on Pesach the forces of love (*hasadim*) are revealed in the world. Pesach is the life force of the entire year, that is, through those forces of love that are brought to bear during Pesach through the medium of the *Seder* and the rest of the things that we do at Pesach. Therefore, our sages taught in their Mishnah [that the world is judged] on Pesach in relation to produce, i.e., food. So, the entire world is sustained through God's great lovingkindness...

Menachem Nachum of Chernobyl (1730-1797), *Me'or Eynayim* (The Light of the Eyes) (n.p., 1952), p. 85.

NOTES:
**Pesach is "the right arm"** ... meaning that it represents the *Sefirah* of *Hesed*, Lovingkindness.
**In their Mishnah...** *Rosh Hashanah* 1:2.

COMMENT: Pesach operates at many levels. The most obvious, the ones we usually think of, are probably the historical and the social, because it tells of the origins of the Jewish people and helps to maintain our Jewish identity and social cohesion. But Pesach also says many important things about God. Perhaps the foremost of these, at least in the mind of Menachem Nachum of Chernobyl, is that Pesach demonstrates divine *Hesed*, not only through the rescue of a slave people, but also through grain harvest being brought in Israel at this time of the year, a grain harvest that, until modern times, had to see people through the summer and into the autumn and winter. Surely, the harvest too is a sign of God's *Hesed*.

# [23] Absorbed in Business

CONTEXT: Yitzchak Meir of Gur (or, Ger) was a disciple of a number of rabbis, including Menachem Mendel of Kotzk, before setting up his own dynasty which persists to this day. The passage below comes from an extensive collection of short sayings by various Hasidic rabbis of the Pshische and Kotzk schools.

TEXT:
On Pesach he said that [the Israelites] had faith to go out into the unsown wilderness without asking how they would be fed. It was a time when each one could establish faith in their heart, [for] in any event, "whoever is granted life, is granted sustenance." Their heads and hearts were not in pursuit of their living, as in these generations.

He used to cry out: What is it with these generations? They are enslaved to the yoke of making a living throughout their days and their lives! Doesn't everyone know that it is the Blessed God Who sustains and nourishes all creatures, and that "whoever is granted life, is granted sustenance"? Of course, it is necessary to engage in business, but don't let your head and your heart be absorbed in it.

Yitzchak Meir of Gur (1789-1866) in Yo'etz Qayyam Qadish Rokotz (ed.), *Siach Sarfei Qodesh* (The Conversation of the Holy Serafim) (Lodz, 1931), pt. 1, p. 16, §60 & §54.

NOTE:
**"Whoever is granted life, is granted sustenance."** A proverb in Aramaic whose origins I have been unable to trace.

COMMENT: Making a living, or trying to make ends meet, is something most adults are engaged in. It is important, even vital since we all have to live. The Gerer *rebbe* calls out to us never to forget the spiritual dimension of life, however hard we may struggle to gain our livelihood, because ultimately, our success or failure in our economic life is in God's hands. The Pesach story itself contains that message.

# [24] Drawing God into Time

CONTEXT: Avraham Yehoshua Heschel of Apt was a disciple of both the Maggid of Mezritch and the Maggid of Zlotchov, as well as a formidable teacher in his own right. Here he comments on a Torah verse that serves as a text for the *kiddush* to be recited on the mornings of the three Pilgrim Festivals: Pesach, Shavuot and Sukkot. This forms part of his discussion of Pesach.

TEXT:
"These are the appointed times (*mo'adei*) of the Eternal, holy gatherings, which you shall proclaim at their appointed times."
Leviticus 23:4

Look here, we recite [the words] "who sanctifies Israel and the festive seasons," yet in truth, time does not apply to God Who is above nature and specific times. But, out of love for Israel, the people whom God had chosen, and for whose sake God had to create all the worlds, and even to initiate time. At the three pilgrimage festivals, God is drawn into time, and there is a revelation of divine light upon the community of Israel.

And how do we, as it were, draw God into time? By attaching ourselves to the beginning of thought, which entered into God's simple will to create time (*ha-Z'MaN*), as it is written: "Israel is holy to the Eternal, the beginning of [God's] produce" (Jeremiah 2:3). We draw down and invite (*maZMiNiM*) the Holy One to dwell in our land, to be, as it were, drawn down into the midst of the worlds. It is at an "appointed time" (*mo'ed*) that we invite the Holy One, and in this way, we invite the God into the midst of time by attaching ourselves to the exalted [attribute] that is above time...

Avraham Yehoshua Heschel of Apt (d.1825), *Ohev Yisra'el* (Lover of Israel) (Zhitomir, 1863), pp. 180-181.

NOTES:

**We recite [the words] "who sanctifies Israel and the festive seasons."** At the end of the third blessing of the *Amidah*, the evening *kiddush* and at the end of the last blessing after the *haftarah* for the three Pilgrim festivals.

**Beginning of thought...** The *Sefirah* of *Hochmah* (Wisdom), also known as *Reishit*, Beginning. Israel too is designated as *Reishit*, Beginning; see below.

**We draw down and invite (*maZMiNiM*)...** The play on words here itself suggests the drawing of God into time.

COMMENT: It seems to me that all of Jewish practice is really about drawing the infinite God into finite time and space, and the only method for achieving this is with the mind. It is as if the "normal" world that we inhabit, filled with objects and emotions, is godless, and that our primary means of touching the infinite, which we of the Jewish faith call "God," is by thoughtful recitation of blessings and prayers, and bringing the divine to mind as we go about our lives.

## *MATZAH*

## [25] Healing on the Inside

CONTEXT: Is there some deeper significance to the eating of *matzah* during Pesach? The rabbi of Ropshitz thought so, and employed concepts derived from Lurianic Kabbalah to explain. His main teacher in Hasidism was Elimelech of Lyzhansk, a disciple of Dov Baer, the Maggid of Mezritch.

TEXT:

The *matzot* that we eat during Pesach are a charm that we may be strengthened in faith. During Sukkot there is the aspect of "surrounding forces (*mekifin*)," just as one puts a bandage and ointment for healing on the outside, while on Pesach one eats *matzah* as an example of healing on the inside.

Naftali Zevi Horowitz of Ropshitz (1760-1827), *Zera Qodesh* (Seed of Holiness, Isaiah 6:12) (Jerusalem, 1971), v. 2, p. 34a.

NOTE:

**"Surrounding forces (*mekifin*)" ...** In this context, the *mekifin* are those spiritual forces that ensure what we might call the structural integrity of objects and creatures in the world.

COMMENT: Some people experience digestive problems at Passover, and I remember one of my teachers saying that Maimonides, speaking as a physician, recommended that we not eat too much *matzah* during the festival. Yet, R. Naftali Zevi of Ropshitz says that *matzah* brings healing from inside. Perhaps he means spiritual healing, for I believe that consuming unleavened bread throughout this week can reinforce our Jewish identity and thus, our connection with our Jewish past and our Jewish future, and beyond that, with the God, whom we believe, ensures our survival and encourages our commitment until the messianic age finally dawns.

# RAIN AND PRODUCE

## [26] When We Stop Mentioning Rain

CONTEXT: It is traditional to mention rain in the second paragraph of the *Amidah*, as one of God's Powers (*Gevurot* – the name given to the second blessing), from Shmini Atzeret until the first day of Pesach. Sephardi practice is to mention dew throughout the spring and summer months instead, while Ashkenazi congregations simply leave omit the phrase. Zevi Elimelech of Dinov was a disciple of a number of rabbis, including the Seer of Lublin. His seminal text, *Benei Yissachar*, is a study of kabbalistic and Hasidic teachings on the Jewish festivals.

TEXT:
We stop mentioning rain during the Festival of Pesach..., because rain represents sustenance..., and the eating of *matzah*, the bread of affliction, is a charm for sustenance. The eating of this *matzah* draws [in its wake] sustenance for the entire year; thus, "at Pesach we are judged regarding produce" ... Therefore, [the phrase] "*matzah*, the bread of affliction" (*MaTZaH, LeCHeM 'oNI*) has the numerical value of [the word for] rain (*GeSHeM*).

Zevi Elimelech of Dinov (1785-1841), *Benei Yissachar* (The Sons of Yissachar, I Chronicles 12:33) (Jerusalem, 1983), v. 1, p. 113b.

NOTES:
**We stop mentioning rain ...** As laid down in the Talmud, *Ta'anit* 4b,
**Rain represents sustenance...** *Ta'anit* 2b.
**The bread of affliction...** *Matzah* is referred to in this way in Deuteronomy 16:3.

29

**"At Pesach we are judged regarding produce"** ... Talmud, *Rosh Hashanah* 16a; Mishnah, *Rosh Hashanah* 1:2.

***MaTZaH, LeCHeM 'oNI ...*** gives us a total of 343, as follows: *M* (40) + *TZ* (90) + *H* (5) + *L* (30) + *CH* (8) + *M* (40) + ' (70) + *N* (50) + *I* (10) = 343.

***GeSHeM...*** also gives us 343: *G* (3) + *SH* (300) + *M* (40). The point seems to be that we can stop praying for rain at Pesach – rain being a key factor in food production – because the *matzah* itself is a prayer for food.

COMMENT: Unlike some other food-symbols of Pesach (bitter herbs, for instance), *matzah* is ambivalent in meaning. One the one hand, it represents the suffering that the Israelites had to endure in Egyptian slavery; hence its description as "the bread of affliction" (Deuteronomy 16:3). On the other hand, it represents freedom because they had to bake it hurriedly in preparation for their departure (see Exodus 12:39). Here it is given new meaning. Pesach represents the start of summer in the Land of Israel and throughout the Near East, and summer means no rain. Hence, the question mark over how much food the land will produce, and that raises the possibility of lean times. So, why do we not pray for good harvests? Because *matzah* itself is that prayer.

## [27] God's Faith in Israel

CONTEXT: Yisra'el of Sadagora was a descendant of the Maggid of Mezritch and an important link in a Hasidic dynasty that continues to this day. Here he employs the same Mishnaic teaching we met in the previous passage, but with radically different results. The sermons in the book from which this is drawn are dated. This one was given on the second day of Pesach 5644 (= 11 April 1884).

TEXT:
"On Pesach we are judged with regard to produce." It is written: "Holy is Israel to the Eternal, the first of God's produce" (Jeremiah 2:3). Pesach [represents] faith, for the Holy Blessed One had faith in Israel and brought them out of Egypt. And God [continued to] have faith in them, that after they had counted off forty-nine days they would accept the Torah. "God's produce" [should be understood] in line with the Scriptural verse "God's produce upon the head of Joseph" (Deuteronomy 33:16). Hence, "on Pesach we are judged with regard to produce" means [we are judged] with regard to what will be produced later on...

Yisra'el Friedman of Sadagora (1853-1907), *Or Yisra'el* (Israel's Light) (1997), p. 112.

NOTES:

**On Pesach we are judged...** The text gives the reference as [Talmud,] *Rosh Hashanah* 16a; this is equivalent to Mishnah, *Rosh Hashanah* 1:2.

**"Holy is Israel to the Eternal, the first of God's produce" (Jeremiah 2:3)** ... For purposes of this *d'rashah*, this verse establishes the relationship between God and Israel as one in which Israel is of special significance to God, as it were, and also as the referent of the word "produce."

**"God's produce upon the head of Joseph"** ... Perhaps the reference here is to the *tzaddik*, the Hasidic *rebbe*, as the channel for God's bounty to his people. Joseph is the archetypal *tzaddik*. In any event, the original text indicates that the conclusion of this exposition is lost.

COMMENT: "Everybody knows" that a primary message of the Days of Awe, Rosh Hashanah and Yom Kippur, is that we are judged for the things that we have done, or failed to do, in the year that has just ended. The *rebbe* of Sadagora seems to be suggesting that on Pesach we are judged for the things that we have yet to do, our intentions, plans and hopes, but that God has faith in our choices. May we be worthy of God's faith in us.


# THE SONG OF SONGS


## [28] The Impenetrability of the Song of Songs

CONTEXT: The Song of Songs (*Shir HaShirim*) is one of the five *megillot*, the five little scrolls in the Bible that are read on different occasions throughout the year. This delightful book of love poetry is read on the intermediate Shabbat of Pesach, or on the eighth day, if there is no intermediate Shabbat. Pinchas of Koretz was a younger contemporary but probably not a disciple of the Ba'al Shem Tov, the founder of the modern Hasidic movement.

TEXT:

We cannot understand anything in the Song of Songs, because "All the Scriptures are holy but the Song of Songs is the Holy of Holies." This is because all the Scriptures are intermediate between the upper worlds and the lower, but the Song of Songs is intermediate between the upper worlds and the Infinite Blessed One, and so we cannot understand it.

Later he put it differently: All the prophets tried to raise this lowly world to the upper world, but the Song of Songs raises the upper worlds to the Infinite Blessed One.

Pinchas of Koretz (1726-1791), *Imre Pinchas* (Pinchas' Sayings) (Tel Aviv: Arnberg, 1974), §191, p. 52.

NOTES:
**"All the Scriptures are holy…"** A quote from Rabbi Akiva in Mishnah, *Yadaim* 3:5. Akiva was a great proponent of the Song of Songs as a mystical text.
**The Scriptures are intermediate between the upper worlds and the lower…** That is, between the world of the *Sefirot* and this created world.
**The upper worlds and the Infinite Blessed One…** The world of the *Sefirot* is emanated from within the unknowable *Ayn Sof*, the Infinite.
**All the prophets tried to raise this lowly world to the upper world…** The prophets are the supposed authors of the second group of Biblical books, the *Nevi'im*. The chief of them, Moses, is the reputed author of the Torah, the first group. The Song of Songs is part of the third, the *Ketuvim*, or Writings.

COMMENT: In kabbalistic thought, the *Sefirot* may be contemplated and analyzed; the Infinite God beyond them may not. All the scriptures of the Hebrew Bible can, potentially, provide us with insights into the realm of the *Sefirot*, but they cannot take us beyond them. According to the Koretzer, only the Song of Songs can do that.

Whether as love poetry or profound mystical text, the Song of Songs remains inexplicable unless we have experienced love or mystical enlightenment for ourselves. The purpose of all the Scriptures is to raise spiritual awareness and promote ethical behavior. It would seem that the Song of Songs can take us into deeper realms.

## [29] Thoughts Riding the Words of Prayer

CONTEXT: Here a verse from the first chapter of the Song of Songs provides a hook upon which to hang a parable about prayer and the thoughts that may prevent full concentration. Although this passage is credited to the Ba'al Shem Tov, the founder of Hasidism, it has long been suspected that the book in which it is located does not actually record his teachings at all, but rather those of the Maggid of Mezritch, his successor.

TEXT:
['To a mare in Pharaoh's chariots have I likened you, my darling (*Ra'yati*).'
Song of Songs 1:9]
If a person is praying, and another thought comes to them, then the "shell" is riding upon the word, for thought rides upon words. Hence it says, "To a mare in Pharaoh's chariots" – "Horses" symbolize "words,"

so when "Pharaoh," i.e. an extraneous thought rides upon them, then "you seem evil to me." It would be better to remain silent. However, words that come from the heart, enter the heart, meaning "the supernal heart," through the breath, as is well known.

> Yisra'el ben Eliezer, Ba'al Shem Tov (1700-1760), *Tzva'at HaRIBaSH* (The Testament of Rabbi Israel Ba'al Shem) (Brooklyn: Kehot Publishing Society, 1975), §71, pp. 21-22.

NOTES:

**My darling (*Ra'yati*)...** In the context, this noun is clearly from the same root that gives us *Re'aH* (friend, companion or neighbor), but the interpretation here treats it as if it came from a similar root that yields *Ra'* (bad, evil). It renders the word as: "you seem evil to me."

**The "shell"** ... In the Lurianic kabbalistic scheme, shells (*kelippot*) represent the force of evil holding divine sparks in captivity. In our context, the extraneous thought is constraining the divine spark within the prayer.

**Words that come from the heart, enter the heart...** an old proverb, recorded as early as the twelfth century by Moses ibn Ezra (c. 1055–after 1135). See Leo Rosten's *Treasury of Jewish Quotations* (London: Bantam, 1977), p. 245.

**"The supernal heart"** ... may refer to the *Sefirah* of *Binah*, Understanding, or to *Malchut*, Sovereignty. In either case, the point is that prayerful words spoken without extraneous thoughts will be received in the realm of the *Sefirot*.

COMMENT: Mostly, we Jews pray from prayer books, reciting the words that others have composed years, perhaps millennia ago. And combined with increasing familiarity, it becomes apparent that our minds may wonder away from the words we are saying. Other thoughts may intrude. What is the status of these extraneous thoughts? The author of this passage suggests that we may think of them as originating in the realms of evil, yet they are somehow "riding" on the words of the prayers themselves. It might seem better not to pray, to remain silent; instead, we are encouraged to persevere, because prayer that is spoken with concentration is the purest form of prayer to which we can aspire.

# [30] Blossoming Souls

CONTEXT: Another verse from Song of Songs, this time interpreted by Elazar of Worms, a central figure in the *Hasidei Ashkenaz*, the Pietists of medieval Germany. He is called the Pharmacist after the name of his primary work, a code of Jewish law of that title.

TEXT:
["I am a rose of Sharon, a lily of the valleys."

Song of Songs 2:1]
"A rose of Sharon, a lily": These are the souls. And it is written "it shall blossom like a rose" (Isaiah 35:2), and "it shall blossom like a lily" (Hosea 14:6) ...

Elazar ben Yehudah of Worms (c.1160-1237), *Perush HaRokeach al HaMegillot* (The Pharmacist's Commentary on the [Five] Scrolls) (Bnei Brak, 1986), v.1, p.112.

COMMENT: What is the soul? In today's scientific thought, perhaps an unanswerable question, and yet, we also seem to know intuitively what we mean by this term. It seems to be tied up with our sense of self, of being alive, of individuality. It represents a certain ineffable quality that makes us who we are. The passage above suggests that our soul is not fixed once and for all. It may be nourished and allowed to grow, like a rose or a lily, or stifled and left to wither. What nourishes the soul? I would suggest: hope and creativity, and the constant pushing back of the boundaries of knowledge, spirituality and righteousness, all tempered by humility.

# [31] The Wall Between Us

CONTEXT: The Song of Songs here depicts the young virile and handsome male lover trying to gain a glimpse of his beloved in any way he can, while still outside her home. Mordechai of Neschiz was a Ukrainian Hasidic teacher, a disciple of both the Maggid of Mezritch and the Maggid of Zlotchov.

TEXT:
["My beloved is like a gazelle, or like a young stag. There he stands behind our wall, gazing through the window; peering through the lattice."

Song of Songs 2:9]
In the *midrash* [on the verse] "My beloved is like a gazelle" [it says that] just as the gazelle runs while looking behind itself, so too the Holy Blessed One [flees from Israel, because of our sins, while looking back out of divine love]. Hence [the phrase]: "There he stands behind our wall," that is to say, the Holy Blessed One stands and looks out for our salvation. "Behind our wall" – even though we ourselves have made a partition wall that separates us through our transgressions, nevertheless, the Holy Blessed One continually looks out, "gazing through the window, peering through the lattice" for whatever could benefit us.

Hence, '[The Eternal says:] "What iniquity did your ancestors find in Me, that they distanced themselves from Me?" (Jeremiah 2:5), that is, [God, as it were, says:] "they distanced themselves from Me, but there is no impediment on My side because I always want to bestow benefit."

Mordechai of Neschiz (d.1800), *Rishpei Esh* (Coals of Fire, Song of Songs 8:6) (Jerusalem, 1997), §163, p.83.

NOTE:
**In the *midrash*...** Actually, the passage referred to may be found in the Zohar II, 14a.

COMMENT: To many people, God (if God exists at all) is remote, far off, a figure of mythology no longer compatible with life in a high-tech world. R. Mordechai understands that a wall, a partition, exists between us and God, but with the voice of faith, he asserts that the reason for this lies with us. God, he says, is always concerned with us, watching just out of sight, as it were, but always ready to assist us with our personal and social challenges, if only we could make the effort to remove the wall we ourselves have constructed.

# [32] A Little Seclusion is Good for You

CONTEXT: Hayyim of Kosov was a Ukrainian Hasidic teacher in the early nineteenth century. Here the lover's desire to find his beloved in the Song of Songs is transmuted into the soul's desire to find God.

TEXT:
"A little after I passed them, I found the one my soul loves."

Song of Songs 3:4

If people distance themselves from those who frequent the squares and streets, they may be able to find the One whom their soul loves, that is, [they may be able to achieve] attachment (*devekut*) to the Blessed God. However, this would only be "a little," not a lot, for "many have done what R. Shimon bar Yochai did, but without success," for no one has permission to distance themselves from them totally.

Hayyim ben Menachem Mendel of Kosov, (1795-1844), *Torat Hayyim* (The Torah of Life) (Haifa: 2004), pp.129-130.

NOTES:
**Attachment (*devekut*)...** Mental attachment to God in all one's doings is a key goal of Hasidic prayer and life.
**"Many have done ..."** Talmud, *Berachot* 35b.

**What R. Shimon bar Yochai did...** In order to escape the Romans, he lived in a cave with his son Elazar for twelve years. See Talmud, *Shabbat* 33b and *Zohar Chadash, Ki Tavo*, (Munkacs, 1911) pt.1, fol.97b. It is said that during these years he composed the Zohar.

COMMENT: Those of a spiritual frame of mind may be tempted to seclude themselves from society, from others not so inclined. I recognize this temptation in myself. I am not the most sociable of people. Judaism has never really encouraged hermits, monks or nuns living in monasteries or convents. (Shimon bar Yochai's twelve-year seclusion seems to be a rare exception, and that was imposed on him by political and military considerations.) The rabbi of Kosov suggests that a little seclusion is fine, even important, for connecting with the divine, but too much should be avoided. For what does attachment to God really mean if it is not made manifest in our behavior towards others?

# [33] Lip-Sync

CONTEXT: Mordechai of Neschiz, a Hasidic teacher of the third generation, discusses congruence (or the lack of it) in prayer and Torah study.

TEXT:
"Your lips are like a crimson thread."

Song of Songs 4:3

That is to say, like the crimson thread that was a sign to the Israelites: if it turned white their sins were atoned for. Similarly, you can now test yourself with "your lips." When you speak of Torah matters or prayer while thinking of vain things, it is a sign that you are not serving the Blessed God. The truth is that each person imagines that "the way of a person is right in their own eyes" [Proverbs 21:2] But, if there is a solution for all the deeds you [attempt to] do for the sake of heaven, in your Torah [study] and prayer, [it is to consider yourself] obligated to think only of God's name. Yet, this is certainly not the truth [of what occurs], for truly you serve yourself and not the Blessed God.

But the essence of the solution lies [in the concept of] exile, for knowledge is in exile, and we do not have the intelligence to serve the Blessed Creator of All [properly]. On the contrary, [we pray] "Draw near to my soul; redeem it" (Psalm 69:19). Each person, in their individuality, according to the intelligence that the Blessed God has granted [them], should strengthen and encourage themselves each day to be a true penitent, not to be a *tzaddik*; i.e., grasp hold of God's Torah one level [at a time]. The [other] way has no life in it at all; only, you must always consider all your actions and return to God each day with renewed vitality. Do not trust yourself [completely], but be in awe and fear, for perhaps you are one of those of whom people say "[To the wicked God says:] What right have you to declare My statutes" (Psalm 50:16).

Mordechai of Neschiz (d.1800), *Rishpei Esh* (Coals of Fire, Song of Songs 8:6) (Jerusalem, 1997), p. 55.

NOTES:

**If it turned white...** This refers to the rabbinic legend that on Yom Kippur a red thread was tied to the door of the Temple in Jerusalem. If it turned white, it was a sign that the scapegoat had reached the wilderness, thus taking away the people's sins. This is based on Talmud, *Yoma* 68b (=Mishnah, *Yoma* 6:8).

**"The way of a person..."** Each of us tends to self-justification, imagining that our thoughts during prayer and study are pure.

**Obligated to think only of God's name...** during prayer and study. Moshe Isserles (c.1530-1572) in his commentary on the *Shulchan Aruch* suggests this as a great overarching principle of Torah (*Orach Hayyim* 1:1).

**A true penitent, not to be a *tzaddik*...** We should aim to be repentant, not to become a Hasidic leader. *Tzaddik* normally means a righteous person, but in the social context of the Hasidic movement, it means a charismatic leader. I think the text is not trying to discourage us from aiming for righteousness; rather, it is encouraging humility.

**The [other] way has no life in it at all...** Our transition to righteous, spiritual behavior must be gradual. Attempting to do it all at once leads only to failure.

**Do not trust yourself [completely]...** Cf. *Pirkei Avot* 5:2. "Do not trust yourself until the day of your death."

COMMENT: This is a sermon urging profound self-examination. How dare we call ourselves religious if our hearts and minds are focused on other things than God, even when we addressing God in prayer or studying God's words in the Torah! Our spirituality means little if it does lead us to examine our innermost thoughts and desires, and if that in turn does not spur us on to greater efforts of self-purification and re-dedication.

## [34] The Righteous Feed God

CONTEXT: The Seer of Lublin, as Ya'akov Yitzchak HaLevi Horowitz, was known, was the disciple of the Rabbi Elimelech of Lyzhansk, himself a disciple of the Maggid of Mezritch. In his turn, the Seer, like his predecessors, taught a whole galaxy of Hasidic stars of the next generation, this time in Poland.

TEXT:
["I have eaten my honeycomb with my honey."

Song of Songs 5:1]
"He will not let go hungry – the Eternal – the soul of the righteous" [Proverbs 10:3]. The meaning is that the soul of the righteous does not allow the Eternal to go hungry, as it were, as it is said: "Israel sustains its Parent in Heaven." Thus, it is written: "I have eaten my honeycomb with my honey" (Song of Songs 5:1) – meaning, [I have] brought pleasure and enjoyment to the Eternal Blessed One, by virtue of which [God] gains power [to] "thwart the craving of the wicked."

Ya'akov Yitzchak HaLevi Horowitz, the Seer of Lublin (1745-1815), *Zot Zikkaron* (This is a Memorial, Exodus 17:14) (Jerusalem, 1992), p. 99.

NOTES:
**"He will not let go hungry – the Eternal…"** This is a very literal rendering of the verse from Proverbs. In its original setting, a more appropriate (and fuller) translation of the entire verse might be: "The Eternal will not let the soul of the righteous go hungry but thwarts the craving of the wicked."

**"Israel sustains its Parent in Heaven."** A quote from Zohar III, 7b, where the idea is that God is sustained by Israel's sacrifices, a notion already found in earlier *midrashim*. Sacrifices are not alluded to here, however.

**"Thwart the craving of the wicked"** … In the original, there is a further paragraph concerning the power of the *tzaddik*, the Hasidic leader, to feed his people through his spiritual connection to God, which I chose not to include here.

COMMENT: The Seer of Lublin tells us that the righteous bring joy and pleasure to God and thus, feed and sustain God. How does that work? Of course, he had in mind the power of the wonder-working Hasidic *tzaddik* or *rebbe*, who by virtue of his total attachment to God can bring about benefits for his followers. How are we, who are not Hasidim, to make sense of this? I would suggest that by the fact of being righteous, by the act of attempting to behave righteously and in ways that demonstrate (and in their turn, heighten) our spiritual awareness, we are feeding and sustaining God, as it were. When we behave in this way, we set back the forces of evil. The results may seem small, but we are not the ultimate judges of results.

# [35] Torah Binds Us to God in Love

CONTEXT: Mordechai of Chernobyl was the son of Nachum of Chernobyl, a student of the Maggid of Mezritch. Unlike his father, who was poor his entire life, Mordechai had a lavish life style and court.

TEXT:
["I am my beloved's, and my beloved is mine."

Song of Songs 6:3]
... The Torah unites the Community of Israel to the Infinite One, as is well known, [for] "the Holy Blessed One and the Torah and Israel are one," and the Torah is the intermediary between Israel and their Parent in Heaven. This is the mystical meaning [of the verse] "I am my beloved's, and my beloved is mine" (Song of Songs 6:3), for the Torah is represented by "I", as it says: "I am understanding; I have strength" (Proverbs 8:14). Hence, "I am my beloved's" – for the Torah binds Israel to the blessed Creator; "and my beloved is mine" – for "the Torah emerges from *Hochmah* (Wisdom)." And the Torah is capable of raising all levels, which is not the case without Torah. Even if you possess awe of the supernal, you could fall. But the Torah preserves you.

> Mordechai of Chernobyl (d.1837), *Liqqutei Torah* (Torah Gleanings) (Jerusalem, 2001), p. 128.

NOTES:
**"The Holy Blessed One and the Torah and Israel are one"** ... The reference to the Zohar is given in the text itself (as III, 73a), but it is incorrect. This is a manufactured quotation, in fact, a conflation of different statements in the Zohar, but very popular in Hasidic literature.
**The Torah is represented by "I", as it says: "I am understanding; I have strength" (Proverbs 8:14).** This chapter of Proverbs is presented as a speech by a personification of Wisdom, which the rabbis implicitly identified with Torah.
**"The Torah emerges from *Hochmah* (Wisdom)"** ... Zohar II, 85a.
**But the Torah preserves you.** Because of its divine origins, and the connection it provides to God, it has the power to tame the arrogance that might result from a belief that one has a proper relationship with God.

COMMENT: One can easily see the historical and cultural importance of Torah in maintaining the identity of the Jewish people, but this text emphasizes its spiritual importance. It serves as a bridge, a connecting link, between Israel and the divine. Where would the Jewish people, with our unique religious approach, be without Torah? With Torah, and all that it brings in its train, Jewish spiritual growth becomes possible and arrogance can be avoided.

## [36] The Flame of God Within

CONTEXT: Mordechai of Chernobyl was a prominent Hasidic rabbi of the third generation in the Ukraine.

TEXT:
["For love is fierce as death, passion is mighty as Sh'ol; its darts are darts of fire, a blazing flame."

Song of Songs 8:6]
You must begin by removing all the vanities of this world from your thought, by accepting upon yourself the yoke of God's divinity in a spirit of self-sacrifice, and by abandoning with a perfect heart every aspect of evil that is rooted within you, the stench of which has entered [within you] along with its fire that burns throughout your body. From that point onwards, you should take upon yourself the yoke of repentance by returning to the Blessed God at each and every moment in all the details of your service and with your strength, in order to continually accept into yourself renewed vital force (*chiyyut*), as mystically indicated [by the phrase] "and the living creatures (*chayyot*) ran and returned" (Ezekiel 1:14…). In this [way], you will be able to ignite the light of the soul (*neshamah*) and accept some of the light of the Infinite One, "the fire that consumes all fires," as Scripture says: "For the Eternal your God is a consuming fire" (Deuteronomy 4:24). The lamp of the soul receives "a blazing flame" (*shalhevet-yah*, literally, "the flame of YaH [God]"), through the love of the Blessed One [which may be experienced as] "darts of fire" (Song of Songs 8:6).

Mordechai of Chernobyl (d.1837), *Liqqutei Torah* (Torah Gleanings) (Jerusalem, 2001), p. 21.

NOTES:
**Vital force (*chiyyut*), as mystically indicated [by the phrase] "and the living creatures (*chayyot*) ran and returned" (Ezekiel 1:14)** … Like the living creatures of Ezekiel's vision of the divine chariot, our life force can go forth, but also return. This play on words is found frequently in Hasidic literature.
**"The fire that consumes all fires"** … A phrase found in Talmud, *Yoma* 21b and Zohar I, 50b; III, 138a.

COMMENT: Fire is a multivalent symbol in this passage. On the one hand, it refers to the process of self-cleansing and re-dedication to divine service, and on the other to divinity itself. But in fact, the two are the same: the purifying fire is God. When it burns within us, it renews our souls. A virtuous circle is created: we purify ourselves with our devotion and God purifies us, which in turn renews our devotion. The process is infused with love.

# THE SEVENTH DAY
# AND THE SONG OF THE SEA

## [37] True Freedom

CONTEXT: The following passage comes from one of the most popular and influential Jewish books of the seventeenth century, a work that discusses virtually every aspect of contemporary Judaism, by one of the great communal rabbis of the age. Here, Yeshaya Horowitz discusses the relative importance of Pesach and Shavuot.

TEXT:

When Israel were redeemed, they emerged into freedom below, but its supernal pattern, freedom from the *kelippot* ("shells"), they had not achieved at all. While, below, they were still afraid of the Egyptians, who were chasing after them until the seventh day of Pesach, above, their freedom was not achieved until the festival of Shavuot, "the time of the giving of our Torah." Thus, on Pesach, even though [God] had "chosen and raised us from among all tongues," this was not actually the case until the giving of the Torah.

Yeshaya HaLevi Horowitz (c.1570-1626), *Shnei Luchot HaBrit* (The Two Tablets of the Covenant, Deuteronomy 9:9,11) (Jerusalem: 1975), *Massechet Pesachim*, v. 1, p. 12a.

NOTES:

**The *kelippot* ("shells")** ... In the Lurianic scheme of Kabbalah, the shells represent the unredeemed forces that hold the sparks of divinity in thrall in the physical world.

**"Chosen and raised us from among all tongues"** ... A phrase from the *kiddush* (the sanctification for wine and bread) for festival evenings.

COMMENT: I remember one of my secondary school teachers scolding us students by telling us that freedom was not the same as license. I did not understand that at the time, but Horowitz seems to be making the same point. At Pesach, the Israelites achieved their physical freedom, but they were still slaves to fear. This they did not overcome until Pharaoh's men and chariots disappeared into the Sea. Yet, even then, their true freedom, their inner freedom, was not achieved until Shavuot when they submitted themselves to the discipline of Torah. Real freedom is not the right to do whatever one pleases; it is the right to work to make oneself a better a person and one's society a better place.

## [38] The Song of the Sea as Atonement

CONTEXT: *Chemdat Yamim* is extensive work of spiritual encouragement still studied in Hasidic communities. Its author is unknown but was probably a secret follower of the failed messiah Shabbetai Zevi. Its frequent exhortations to repentance (and lack of overtly heretical teachings) most likely made it immune to any anti-Sabbatian purges within the Ashkenazi Jewish world. As here, the author liberally sprinkles his text with biblical and other quotations.

TEXT:

Just as You forgave Your people the family of Israel at the Sea of Reeds for their sins by virtue of this Song, so too, our Parent, Author of mercy, have compassion on us, suppress our transgressions, and cast all our sins into the depths of the sea [see Micah 7:19] through the power of this Song which we sing now before You. Raise over us the light of the Holy Ancient One by destroying the evil of the decree of judgment against us, just as You destroyed the evil of the decree of judgment against our ancestors at the Sea of Reeds and You destroyed all the concealers and accusers who create a barrier between us and You. Shut up Satan's mouth and let him not accuse us. "May they be a chaff before the wind; may the angel of the Eternal chase them" [Psalm 35:5] "that Your beloved ones may be saved; save with Your right hand and answer me" [Psalm 60:7 and 108:7]. "Do it for Your name's sake..." [Jeremiah 14:7]. "May [the words of my mouth and the meditation of my heart] be acceptable [to You, my Rock and my Redeemer]" [Psalm 19:15].

Anon. (17th century), *Chemdat Yamim* (Most Precious of Days) (Jerusalem, 2004), v. 3, p. 260.

NOTE:

**Concealers and accusers...** Our author may have had demons in mind.
**Satan's mouth...** Satan in Jewish texts is usually God's prosecuting attorney, rather than the embodiment of evil.

COMMENT: The drowning of Pharaoh's army in the Sea was not simply God's victory over our oppressors. Following the *Chemdat Yamim*'s line of reasoning as presented in this prayer, it was also a divine triumph over our sins. May all our achievements direct us towards recognizing our sins and striving to overcome them. Viewed in this way, success can bring atonement just as effectively as fasting.

## [39] Two Kinds of Sustenance

CONTEXT: A descendant of the Ruzhyn Hasidic dynasty, R. Yisra'el of Sadagora frequently concluded his sermons with a prayer or benediction, as is the case here. (I have transliterated the conclusion from the original Yiddish.) Many of the talks in this work are dated. This was delivered the evening of the seventh day of Pesach, 29 April 1891.

TEXT:

It says: "Human sustenance is as difficult [to provide] as the dividing of the Reed Sea." I say: The dividing of the Reed Sea has already taken place. Similarly, there will certainly be sustenance. I say: May the Blessed God help every Jew achieve salvation regarding sustenance of the body and sustenance of the soul. *A guten yomtov! A guten yomtov!*

Yisra'el Friedman of Sadagora (1853-1907), *Or Yisra'el* (Israel's Light) (1997), p. 135.

NOTE:
**It says...** In the Talmud, *Pesachim* 118a.
***A guten yomtov!*** ... Yiddish. Literally, a good festival.

COMMENT: We know that Pesach was originally a harvest festival as much as a historical remembrance. R. Yisra'el's prayer suggests that it is a spiritual event as well. Our souls need nourishment as well as our bodies. What feeds the soul? Prayer and meaningful ritual, meditation and maintaining the awareness of God's presence in our lives. And this means overcoming the prevalent materialism in our society and in our hearts.

## [40] Towards a Superior Fear

CONTEXT: The Israelites are overcome with fear at the approach of Pharaoh and his men. Avraham of Sadagora was the son and principle successor to his father, Yisra'el of Ruzhin, who had moved to Sadagora in Austrian territory to flee from the Russian authorities in the 1840s.

TEXT:
"As Pharaoh drew near, [the Israelites caught sight of the Egyptians advancing upon them and became greatly frightened...]"

[Exodus 14:10]

The holy *Or HaHayyim* wrote that Israel was very afraid because of this, but I say that this was a fear of external things. Only afterwards is it written: "and the people feared the Eternal" [Exodus 14:31]. This was a superior fear. Thus, the Holy Blessed One said to Moses: "Speak to the Israelites that they may go" [Exodus 14:15] – i.e., that they may go from the fear of external things to a superior fear...

Avraham Ya'akov of Sadagora (d.1883), *Bet Yisra'el* (The House of Israel) (Piotrkov, 1913), pp. 97-98.

NOTES:
**The holy *Or HaHayyim*...** This Torah commentary by R. Hayyim ibn Attar of Morocco (1696-1743) is very popular among the Hasidim. In his comment on this verse, he argues that the Israelites' fear of Pharaoh and the Egyptians was meant to encourage them to turn in repentance to God.
**A fear of external things...** Of Pharaoh and his army, rather than of God. R. Avraham argues that the Israelites' fear of God only came later.
**"Speak to the Israelites that they may go"** ... In the biblical context, this of course means that they should go forward into the sea.

COMMENT: Does the fear of external things – anti-Semitism, terrorism, economic insecurity, disease, etc. – lead us to the fear of God? I would suggest that for most of us the answer is no. But perhaps it should. These kinds of things are largely beyond our personal control. When they threaten us, we need to dig deeper within ourselves for the emotional and spiritual resources to stand up against them. Surely, that is what the fear of God truly is: the inner strength to face adversity with hope but without arrogance.

# [41] Truth and Faith

CONTEXT: The city of Karlin, in modern Belarus, was home to a Hasidic dynasty founded by R. Aharon the Great (1736-1772), a disciple of the Maggid of Mezritch. This text is by the third leader of the group, the founder's grandson, also called Aharon.

TEXT:
["Then the people had faith in the Eternal and in Moses, God's servant. Then Moses and the people of Israel sang..."]

Exodus 14:31-15:1

At the end of the festival of Pesach, he spoke about the *midrash* on the verses "Then the people had faith in the Eternal... Then [Moses and the people of Israel] sang..."

44

[This *midrash* says:] "Great is faith, for on account of it, a person may inherit this world and the next. As a reward for faith, Israel was granted merit, the *Shechinah*, the Presence of God, rested on them, and they were able to sing the Song [of the Sea], as it is said, 'He had faith in the Eternal, and it was considered as righteousness' [Genesis 15:6] ..."

Then [R. Aharon] explained that *emet* (truth) and *emunah* (faith) are two things that are bound together and are the essence of everything. It is through faith that one comes to truth, and through truth that one comes to faith.

Then he said that the faith of the heart belongs to every descendant of Israel, for they believe that there is a Creator Who causes everything to exist, Who oversees and guides all the worlds, but a strong faith like this, by which one can overcome and skip over many matters [that arise] in the heat of one's heart, is only available to those who turn from evil and repair their character traits.

Aharon (II) ben Asher of Karlin (d. 1872), *Bet Aharon* (Aaron's House) (Brody, 1875; reprinted Jerusalem, 1990), pp. 184-185.

NOTES:
**[This *midrash* says:]** What follows is a quotation from *Midrash Mechilta, Beshallach* §6.
**"He had faith in the Eternal..."** The subject of the verse is the patriarch Abraham.

COMMENT: As I write these words in mid-2018, I realize that I have never understood the intimate connection between truth and faith or trust as I do now. In an era where major main stream western politicians regularly lie in the face of established or easily verifiable facts, it is clear that there is a serious erosion of faith taking place: faith in politicians, faith in free media, faith in democracy. The Karliner's emphasis is elsewhere, though. His concern is faith in God, but he says that true faith is only accessible to those of upright moral character. These points are not unconnected. If politicians want us to have faith in the democratic process, they need to demonstrate that they are of good moral character, and we, on our part, need to hold them to those standards and try to observe them in our own lives.


# [42] Our Ancestors and Us

CONTEXT: Like much biblical poetry, the Song of the Sea displays a fair amount of parallelism, that is, two successive phrases that mean much the same thing. The verse at the start of this text is an example. But the Moroccan commentator ibn Attar follows normal rabbinic practice is

45

treating the two phrases as if they indicated different things.

TEXT:
"The Eternal is my strength [and might, and has become my deliverance. This is my God whom I will glorify; my ancestor's God whom I will exalt]."

[Exodus 15:2]

Look here, the order for those who stand before God in order to sing, praise and pray is to begin with things that have been directed to oneself by God, and afterwards, those things that have been directed to one's ancestors by God. Thus, we find that the men of the Great Assembly decreed that the beginning of the first paragraph of the *Amidah* should have [the word] "our God" first and then [the phrase] "and God of our ancestors...."

Hayyim ben Moshe ibn Attar (1696-1743), *Or HaHayyim* (The Light of Life) (Jerusalem: A. Blum, 1994), pt. 2, p. 69

NOTES:
**The men of the Great Assembly...** A legendary group of scholars in the Persian or Hellenistic period who are credited with the arrangement of the main prayers of the Jewish liturgy. Their identities are largely unknown, but Ezra the scribe is supposed to inaugurated the group.
**The first paragraph of the *Amidah*...** Traditionally known as the *Avot* ("Fathers, Ancestors"). The *Amidah* (Standing) prayer is a central feature of the three statutory daily services: Morning, Afternoon and Evening. In similar fashion, the verse quoted begins with "my God" and then proceeds to "my ancestor's God."

COMMENT: I recently read a history of China. It was fascinating, interesting as a human story, but I had no real emotional or personal connection to it. This is not surprising, given my cultural background. But Jewish history is different, or should be, for Jews and those who would be Jews. Being Jewish should be personal but with a strong connection to what Jews have achieved and endured in the past. Hence our prayer to "our God and God of our ancestors."


# [43] Because of the Song

CONTEXT: The closest disciple, and our main source for the teachings of the great kabbalist R. Yitzchak Luria, the Ari, Hayyim Vital here discusses the importance of heavenly song in lifting human spirits.

TEXT:
"My strength and song [is of] the Eternal."

Exodus 15:2

This verse is said at the beginning of the Song [of the Sea] because the souls [of the Israelites] flew [out of their bodies], but when they heard the sound of the Song, the Holy Blessed One opened their ears so that they could hear the singing of all the supernal hosts, and because of this, their souls returned to them, as our sages have said. Hence it says, "My strength and song of the Eternal" – meaning, the power and strength that I had was because of the Song of the Eternal. The explanation is: By virtue of the songs that I heard from heaven, which [the angels] sang for the sake of the Eternal, "God has become my salvation," so that I was saved from death.

Hayyim Vital (1542-1620), *Liqqutei Tanakh veTa'amei HaMitzvot* (Gleanings on the Bible and the Meanings of the Commandments) (Jerusalem: Yeshivat Kol Yehudah, 1970), p. 140.

NOTES:
**"My strength and song [is of] the Eternal"** ... The JPS translation reads: "The Lord is my strength and might," while a footnote suggests the alternative "song." The translation and word order I have given (which varies from that in the previous passage) is consonant with the interpretation that follows.
**As our sages have said...** Zohar II, 45a.

COMMENT: I cannot speak to the benefits of hearing the angelic choirs. I cannot honestly say that I have heard them. But I know that singing, especially communal singing, can lift the spirits of those who are depressed or anxious, and help us all to face the future with hope and determination.


## [44] Your Own God Before Your Ancestors'

CONTEXT: In a conversation with his father, the fiery Menachem Mendel of Kotzk comments on why he chose to join the Hasidic movement. It was already some decades old, but still the subject of controversy.

TEXT:
["This is my God whom I will glorify; my ancestor's God whom I will exalt."

Exodus 15:2]

His father R. Leibush went [to Lublin] after him and cried over him: why was he letting go of the customs of his ancestors to find shelter with the Hasidim. He replied: "This is my God whom I will glorify" and afterwards "my ancestor's God whom I will exalt."

Found in Ya'akov Yitzchak, the Holy Jew (Yehudi) of Pshische (1765-1814), *Nifl'ot HaYehudi* (Wondrous Tales of the Yehudi) (Piotrkov, 1908), pp. 52-53.

NOTES:
**His father R. Leibush...** There are at least two other versions of this story. This is the only one that mentions the name of the other participant in the conversation. The young Menachem Mendel had gone off to study with the Seer of Lublin. His father felt that this amounted to departure from traditional Judaism.

COMMENT: Since the Enlightenment, that period in eighteenth century Europe when our modern liberal values were created, most people in western society have come to believe that religion is a private affair. That was certainly the view of the Founding Fathers of the United States, and broadly speaking, the view of the British political and judicial system, despite the fact that the Church of England is an established church. Mendel of Kotzk agrees that religion is personal in the first instance. Without that personal connection, why would anyone in our society join a religious organization? There are no political, and few social, pressures to do so. We have to start with ourselves. When we have made our own connection to the divine, we may be ready to truly join with others to form a community.

# [45] Our War Fought with Divine Force

CONTEXT: The Song of the Sea, Exodus chapter 15, is the main Torah reading for the seventh day of Passover, on the grounds that this extraordinary event occurred on that day. Elimelech was a grandson of R. Yisra'el, the Maggid of Koznitz, and the founder of his own Hasidic dynasty in the Polish town of Grodzisk.

TEXT:
["The Eternal [is] a man [of] war, the Eternal [is] God's name."

Exodus 15:3]

This may be explained [as follows]: There is no vital force in the world, not even the vital force in humans, except that which comes from the Blessed One. Even if a person has the merit to do something for the Blessed One, that too comes only from the Blessed One. But the essential point is that human beings need to see that they may enter into the state of willing for the Blessed One.

Hence it says "the Eternal – a man": [i.e., a human being] is from the Blessed God.

"War, the Eternal is God's name" – i.e., that the war that every Jewish person [is engaged in is for] "The Eternal God's name," that is to say, that one may enter into the state of willing for the Blessed One. Understand!

Elimelech ben Hayyim Meir Yechiel of Grodzisk (1824-1892), *Imre Elimelech* (Elimelech's Sayings) (n. p., 1876), p. 99.

NOTES:
**"The Eternal [is] a man [of] war..."** While reading the passage that follows, it is important to remember that the words "is" and "of" which are required in English are not present in the Hebrew.

COMMENT: For Elimelech of Grodzisk, everything comes from God, including that vital force that not only gives human beings life but also their ability to exercise their will. In that case, surely choosing to exercise our will for evil is just as valid a decision as choosing good. But that fails to take account of God's will. Although a person's decision to try to do God's will by spiritual commitment also comes from God, nevertheless, we ought to strive to align our will with God's as far as possible. That is the path to spiritual self-fulfilment for ourselves and for our wider community. Achieving this is certainly a struggle, a war, but with God as our greatest ally we can succeed.

# [46] "Deep Within Me"

CONTEXT: The Song of the Sea contains several examples of unusual or ambiguous words. *V'anveihu* is one. The great commentator Rashi offers two possible interpretations of this word: "I will glorify God" or "I will make a dwelling for God." Reb Mendel of Kotzk takes the second as his starting point.

TEXT:
"This is my God whom I will glorify (*v'anveihu*)."

Exodus 15:2

[*V'aNVeihu*] is a term [meaning] a home (*NaVeH*) or a dwelling.
[Thus,] I will make a dwelling for God in me, within me, in my midst.

Menachem Mendel of Kotzk (1787-1859), *Sefer Amud Ha'Emet* (The Book of the Pillar of Truth) (Bnei Brak, 2000), p. 46.

COMMENT: The Kotzker, it seems, never did anything half-heartedly. According to the many tales told about him, he was passionate and vehement in everything he did. And demanding of his followers, but most of all, of himself. In one brief sentence, with a message reinforced with three prepositions, he urges us to make space for God within ourselves, a space where ego is kept at bay and God alone reigns.

# PESACH FOR THE FUTURE

## [47] Pesach: A Message for the Future

CONTEXT: Meir ibn Gabbai was of the generation of the exiles from Spain, but very little is known of his life. This passage comes from his work presenting a kabbalistic perspective on Jewish prayer.

TEXT:
The exodus from Egypt is a guarantee and forecast of all the good things that we are going to receive in the End; it is the great evidence for the future world renewed for us....

Meir ibn Gabbai (1480–after 1540), *Tola'at Ya'akov* (O Worm, Jacob, Isaiah 14:14) (Jerusalem, 1996), p. 102.

COMMENT: Once again we are reminded that Pesach is not just about the past. It is not even about our present attitudes and behaviors. It is about our hope for the future. If in ancient times the Israelite slaves could be freed from an apparently hopeless situation in which back-breaking labor and oppression were everyday occurrences, then there is hope for all those who are oppressed today. If it happened once, it can happen again. The enemy of what is is the hope of what might be, inspired by what has happened before.

## [48] Pesach as Template

CONTEXT: This teaching is from the Naftali Zevi of Ropshitz, who studied with a variety of teachers, chiefly with Elimelech of Lyzhansk.

TEXT:
>    In the future, when the future redemption will have become the essence and the Exodus from Egypt secondary, we will still mention the miracles of the Exodus from Egypt, because it was the Exodus from Egypt that would make the future redemption possible.
>    Naftali Zevi Horowitz of Ropshitz (1760-1827), *Zera Qodesh* (Seed of Holiness) (Jerusalem, 1971), v.2, p.34a.

NOTE:
**When the future redemption will have become the essence...** This is based on a discussion in Talmud, *Berachot* 12b.

COMMENT: *Pesach Mitzrayim*, the Passover of Egypt, or the first Passover, was an event in our most ancient Jewish past. Where would we be without it? There would have been no Judaism, no Christianity, no Islam. But that is all in the past. What sustains us in the present? The hope of the future. Pesach provides that. Old spirituals song by black slaves in the American South, like O Mary, Don't You Weep and Go Down Moses, understood that. We may need to learn it again. Pesach provides a template for all liberations, until the final, messianic redemption.

# THE COUNTING OF THE OMER

## [49] A Period of Preparation

CONTEXT: On the second night of Pesach we begin the counting of the *omer*. An *omer* was a sheaf of grain brought as an offering in the Temple on each of the forty-nine days between Pesach and Shavuot. Here the *rebbe* of Pshische discusses the spiritual significance of counting off the days of the *omer*.

TEXT:
>    The days of *Omer*-period are for the purpose of repairing one's qualities, because "ethical behavior precedes Torah." That is, people should purify themselves during these weeks so that the words of the Torah might be able to enter into them.

51

Simchah Bunam of Pshische (1765-1827) in Yo'etz Qayyam Qadish Rokotz, *Siach Sarfei Qodesh* (The Conversation of the Holy Serafim) (Lodz, 1931), pt.1, p.14.

NOTE:
**Ethical behavior precedes Torah...** *Vayikra Rabbah* 9:3. Ethical behavior began with Adam and Eve; Torah only with Moses.

COMMENT: The counting of the *omer* should not be just a nightly ritual carried out with no extra thought. Nor is it simply a reminder that Shavuot is coming. It is an opportunity to examine ourselves, our inner thoughts and feelings, so that, when Shavuot finally arrives, we may be better prepared to accept the Torah anew.

# SHAVUOT

The giving of the Law at Mount Sinai, by Gustave Doré.

## [50] The Time of the Giving of the Torah

CONTEXT: The Kotzker *rebbe* was a reluctant leader, and this often expressed itself in anger at those who insisted on following him. He only accepted the leadership after his friend and teacher Simchah Bunam of Pshische died.

TEXT:

Look here, the Men of the Great Assembly arranged the text of the prayers for us, [including the words] "the time of the giving of the Torah." We must be precise about why they did not arrange [for the text to read] "the time of the receiving of the Torah," along the lines of what [our sages] have taught us: "Moses received Torah...."? Our teacher, Rabbi Simchah Bunam of Pshische said that the Torah was merely given then in the month of *Sivan* and [that thus this giving] is connected with [a particular] time, while the same is not true of the receiving of it, for which every day is the [right] time....

But we may further say that the giving of the Torah was equal for all, but that the receiving was not equal, but that each individual receives only what they are capable of understanding.

Menachem Mendel of Kotzk (1787-1859), *Ohel Torah MeHaRabbi MiKotzk* (The Torah Tent of the Rabbi of Kotzk) (Lublin, 1909), pp.46-47.

NOTES:

**The Men of the Great Assembly...** A shadowy group of (presumably) scholars who are traditionally credited with laying the foundations of Judaism, as opposed to the Biblical Israelite worship. They seem to have flourished in the Persian and Hellenistic periods. According to the Talmud (*Berachot* 33a), they ordained the prayers and blessings to be said by Jews.

**"Moses received Torah..."** The opening words of the Mishnah tractate, *Pirkei Avot*, the Ethics of the Fathers. If Moses is credited with receiving Torah, why not the rest of us?

COMMENT: Tradition says that the Torah was given on 6 Sivan millennia ago. But when was it received? This is not a historical query, but a personal one. At one level, we receive it whenever we choose to. All we need is an open mind and an open heart. We receive it on multiple occasions; innumerable opportunities to receive present themselves almost every day. And the receiving is not a once-and-for all, like receiving money, for example. We can receive Torah again and again. The only limit is our capacity to absorb it.

54

# [51] Why is It "Our Torah"?

CONTEXT: The following apparently derives from a Hasidic source, as do many of the teaching in the anonymous work from which it is drawn. It deals with a common liturgical phrase describing Shavuot.

TEXT:

In the book *Da'at Moshe* (Moses' Knowledge), [the author] wrote to explain why our liturgy says [that Shavuot is] "the time of the giving of our Torah"? It need only have said: "the time of the giving of the Torah." Why "our Torah"? Because each and every one of Israel receives their portion of Torah according to the repair and fitness of their actions. Hence, "the time of the giving of our Torah," because the giving of the Torah to each was according to the fitness of their deeds.

Anon., *Sefer Ta'amei HaMinhagim uMkorei HaDinim* (The Book of the Reasons for Customs and the Sources for Laws) (Brooklyn, NY, 1944), pt. 3, p. 163.

NOTES:

**In the book *Da'at Moshe*...** Probably a reference to a book by Moshe Eliakim Beri'ah, son and successor of the R. Yisra'el, the Maggid of Koznitz. I have not been able to gain access to this work.

**"The time of the giving of our Torah"** ... This phrase occurs at several points in the prayer book for the pilgrim festivals.

COMMENT: Torah has to be acquired through effort. Clearly, effort has to be expended in listening to Torah readings and sermons, attending classes, reading books, etc. But this is intellectual effort. Our source comes to remind us that our moral efforts are also important, perhaps more important. What good is our learning if we continue to behave unfairly, oppressively, unthinkingly?

# [52] Why We Eat Milk Products on Shavuot

CONTEXT: Zevi Elimelech of Dinov wrote a two-volume Hasidic classic on the festivals. The following is an extract from his extended discourse on Shavuot. He studied with a number of rabbis, including the Seer of Lublin, R. Ya'akov Yitzchak.

TEXT:

The custom of our ancestors, which is [equivalent to] Torah, is to eat milk [foods] on the festival of Shavuot. It seems to me that the reason is that milk represents *Hesed* (Lovingkindness) [indicated by its] white color, and hence [the biblical phrase] *L'hagid Baboker CHasdecha* ("telling of Your lovingkindness in the morning," Psalm 92:3), where the opening letters [of these three words spell] *CHaLaV* (milk).

> Zevi Elimelech of Dinov (1785-1841), *Benei Yissachar* (The Sons of Yissachar, I Chronicles 12:33) (Jerusalem, 1983), v.1, p. 134c.

NOTES:
**The custom of our ancestors, which is [equivalent to] Torah...** *Tosafot, Menachot* 20b and frequently.
**Eat milk [foods] on the festival of Shavuot...** This is codified in *Shulchan Aruch, Orach Hayyim* 494:3, in a comment by Moshe Isserles.
**Milk represents *Hesed* (Lovingkindness) ...** As stated in Moshe Cordovero's *Pardes Rimmonim* Gate 23, Chapter 8. Of course, mother's milk can also be a symbol of love.
***CHasdecha...*** Incorporating the word *Hesed*.

COMMENT: When I was a congregational rabbi, it seemed that every year I had to explain to people that I don't like cheesecake. To my lovely English congregants, it felt ever so slightly not quite Jewish. Still, there it is. But the custom is to eat dairy products on Shavuot, not necessarily cheesecake. So, really, I have other, perfectly kosher options. (Blintzes!) Still, what does this diary food represent? For the Dinover it is a symbol of God's love, here parallel to a mother's love. As children of the divine, surely, we need to feel our Parent's love.

# [53] Repairing Thought

CONTEXT: Menachem Mendel of Rymanov was a disciple of Elimelech of Lyzhansk, and a key figure in Polish Hasidism.

TEXT:
... Every human deed comprises three aspects: thought, speech and action. Thought alone is insufficient because we are not able to [fully] understand a person's motives, and no one knows the secrets of another's awareness and will. Similarly, with deeds, it is impossible to discern why and with what aim someone acts in a certain way. It is speech that brings them together, for it is only in this way that the thought that is recognizable within the deed is [actually] revealed. Corresponding to this, we have been given three pilgrimage festivals, each one of which offers a special time for repairing these three aspects. For example, the festival of Shavuot: all of its [special] observances are mental: accepting the yoke of the Kingdom of Heaven, the Torah and the *mitzvot*, and attaching oneself to God. On Sukkot, action is repaired, for all its [special] observances

relate to active *mitzvot*... And the festival of Pesach comes to repair speech, [because we are obliged] to relate the story of the exodus from Egypt and the praises of God...

> Menachem Mendel of Rymanov (d.1815), *Menachem Tziyyon* (Comforter of Zion) (Jerusalem, 1998), p. 56.

NOTE: **On Sukkot ... all its [special] observances relate to active *mitzvot*...** Namely, dwelling in a *sukkah*, waving the *lulav*, processing around the synagogue.

COMMENT: If the Jewish festivals are to be meaningful to us, they need to speak to our deeper selves, as well as our social selves. The Rymanover suggests that our three pilgrim festivals address three levels of our selves: the physical, social and mental. In fact, they each address all three aspects, but in each case the emphasis is different. For me, Shavuot is primarily mental, and spiritual. Ultimately, it's about committing oneself to Torah.

## [54] In Him and In It

CONTEXT: Little is known of the life of Meshullam Heller of Zbarazh in Galicia. He is primarily known for the work from which the following comes, a pamphlet spelling out the Hasidic approach to life and worship.

TEXT:
> ... Shabbat, Pesach, Shavuot and Sukkot, every one of them contains joy and pleasure in the Eternal One on those precise days, for that is what is written in the Zohar on the verse: "This is the day that the Eternal has made; let us be happy and rejoice in it/him (*vo*)" (Psalm 118:24). [The Zohar says:] "'in it' – on that day; 'in him' – in the Holy Blessed One, and both are one thing."
> Now, there is no need to explain either way: those who do not understand will not benefit by having it explained... For it is impossible to explain hidden things. Everyone knows what they know, and no more. And whoever understands, knows by himself. "'In it' – on that day; 'in him' – in the Holy Blessed One, and both are one thing." The joy of the day that we experience on it is the illumination and attachment to the Eternal One, and it is a commandment incumbent upon us to celebrate it. The joy of [observing] the commandment is actually, truly that, as is written in the *Tur*, on the laws of festivals, that we have not been commanded to rejoice over foolishness, but over that joy that the service of the Blessed Creator brings.

> Meshullam Feibush HaLevi Heller of Zbarazh (d. 1785), *Yosher*

*Divrei Emet* (Upright Words of Truth, Ecclesiastes 12:10) (Bnei Brak, 2004), p. 156.

NOTES:

**What is written in the Zohar…** Zohar III, 105a.

**"Rejoice in it/him (*vo*)"** … *Vo* can bear either translation. The Zohar suggests either is possible, or both. R. Meshullam says both, simultaneously.

**And whoever understands, knows by himself…** No amount of theorizing is a replacement for experience. This may be true in many areas of life, but is a frequent refrain when mystical experience is being discussed.

**In the *Tur*…** This is the Jewish law code the full name of which is *Arba'ah Turim* (Four Rows) by R. Ya'akov ben Asher (1268-1340). The reference is to the *Hilchot Yom Tov* §529.

COMMENT: There is an old joke about a man who talked all the way through the morning service. The rabbi asked him why he talked to his friend throughout, without praying. He replied: "My friend comes to talk to God. I come to talk to my friend." A friend of mine said the social and religious aspects of synagogue attendance are ultimately the same thing. At some level, perhaps they are, but I would suggest that talking to one's friend is the same as talking to God only if one is conscious of doing both. Similarly, here. Rejoicing on the festivals, enjoying oneself in celebration, is only the same as rejoicing with God if we are conscious of doing so.

## [55] Pesach and Shavuot

CONTEXT: Although Eliyahu HaKohen HaIttamari was a well-known preacher whose sermons are still studied today, he also compiled the anthology cited below, and arranged items by subject alphabetically. (Unfortunately, he stopped after the letter *kaf*.) The text given below is derived from a teaching in the *Shelah*: Yeshaya HaLevi Horowitz (c.1570-1626), *Shnei Luchot HaBrit* (The Two Tablets of the Covenant, Deuteronomy 9:9,11) (reprint of 1863 ed.; Jerusalem: 1975), *Parashat HaChodesh*, v. 2, p. 53d. However, R. Eliyahu has paraphrased (rather than quoted) Horowitz, and I have chosen this version because its focus is actually different from that of the original.

TEXT:

The exodus from Egypt was like *kiddushin* (engagement) for Israel, and it has been taught that a man, or his agent, may bring about *kiddushin*. Of God [it is written]: "I will pass through the land of Egypt" (Exodus 12:12). And of the agent it is written: "God sent an angel and brought us out [of Egypt]" (Numbers 20:16). But the giving of the Torah was [like] *nissu'in* (marriage), which can only be done by oneself. Hence it says: "[God] spoke with you face to face [at the mountain]" (Deuteronomy 5:4) ...

Eliyahu ben Shlomo Avraham HaKohen Ha-Ittamari of Izmir (d.1729), *Midrash Talpiyot* (Jerusalem, 1996), v. 2, p. 778.

NOTE:

**Kiddushin** (engagement)...*nissuin* (marriage) ... The traditional Jewish wedding ceremony consists of two parts, which are normally done one after the other today, but which in the past were often separated by months or even years. In the metaphoric case before us, seven weeks. The first consisted of the groom giving the bride a token (nowadays a ring) which she accepts in front of witnesses. According to law, neither of them has to be present. *Kiddushin* can be brought into effect by their duly appointed agents. The second (*nissu'in*) consists of the reading of the *ketubah* (marriage contract) and the recitation of the *Sheva Berachot* (Seven Wedding Blessings), for which both bride and groom must be present.

COMMENT: Ever since the prophet Hosea in the eighth century BCE, the relationship between Israel, the Jewish people, and God has frequently been described as one of mutual love like that of a loving couple, although their relationship can be stormy. Here that loving metaphor is enriched with symbols from Jewish marriage ritual and two of our pilgrim festivals. Pesach and Shavuot are connected by their history, with the revelation at Mount Sinai following on from the liberation from Egyptian slavery. Maybe the bottom line here is: God's love is all around us if we could but see it. Specifically, it is in our history, our festivals and our rituals.

# THE TEN COMMANDMENTS

## [56] Moses Still Speaks

CONTEXT: R. Aharon of Karlin was the second of that name, grandson of the founder (also called Aharon) of Karlin Hasidic dynasty. The opening verse is in the traditional Torah reading for the first day of Shavuot.

TEXT:
["Moses would speak and God would answer him with a voice."

Exodus 19:19]

"Moses would speak (*y'dabber*)" is an expression [employing the] future [tense], because in the future, in each generation, he will speak with each individual who comes to be cleansed and to accept the holy Torah. Moses speaks with them because the "Moses is spread throughout every generation." "And God would answer him with a voice" – by making the voice enter and unite with the word.

Aharon (II) ben Asher of Karlin (d. 1872), *Bet Aharon* (Aaron's House) (Brody, 1875; reprinted Jerusalem, 1990), p. 222.

NOTES:

**"Moses would speak (*y'dabber*)"** ... To grammarians, this verbal form is known as the imperfect. While it has a wide range of meanings in Biblical Hebrew, in modern usage, it most often refers to future events.

**"Moses is spread throughout every generation"** ... Based on *Tikkunei HaZohar* §69, 114a.

**By making the voice enter and unite with the word...** There is a clear difference between random sounds and articulated words. In order to communicate specific ideas, sounds must be transformed into words. There may also be a kabbalistic message here: "Sound/voice" represents the *Sefirah* of *Tiferet*, while "word" indicates *Malchut*. Positive energies are released into the word when these two are in union.

COMMENT: Moses still speaks – to anyone who would listen. Broadly speaking, it appears to me that Moses speaks to us in two different, though interrelated, ways. One the one hand, Moses the prophet who confronts Pharaoh encourages us to confront injustice wherever we find it. On the other, Moses the lawgiver leads us towards religious observance and ethical behavior. All we need to do is hear his voice – and act.

# [57] Torah for the Future

CONTEXT: Naftali Zevi of Ropshitz, a student of the Maggid of Mezritch and others, discusses the introductory verse to the text of the Ten Commandments.

"Then God spoke all these words, saying (literally, to say)."

[Exodus 20:1]

On the face of it, the word "to say" is superfluous, but the explanation follows the lines of the saying of our rabbis on the verse "May he kiss me (*yiS HaKeini*) with the kisses of his lips" [Song of Songs 1:2] that there are words that it is a *mitzvah* to say and there are words that "water (*maS HiKin*) the mouth" and close it [preventing it] from speaking. Hence, the saying "A new Torah will come forth from Me" [Isaiah 51:4]. There will not be another Torah, but the meaning is that things that are "closed" will be revealed now. The giving of the Torah on Mount Sinai was a preparation for the future. Hence, it says that these words were "to say" and to be revealed in the future.

Naftali Zevi Horowitz of Ropshitz (1760-1827), *Zera Qodesh* (The Seed of Holiness) (Jerusalem, 1971), v.2, p.44b.

NOTES:

**The word "to say"** ... *Lemor*, in Hebrew. In the Bible, it normally introduces a direct quotation. The Ropshitzer takes it hyper-literally.

**The saying of our rabbis...** Talmud Yerushalmi, *Avodah Zarah* 15a.

**"A new Torah will come forth from Me"** ... as interpreted in *Vayikra' Rabbah* 13:3.

COMMENT: The text of the Torah is complete, finished, unchanging, eternally fixed. The interpretation of Torah is always incomplete, unfinished, ever new, always developing, eternally growing. Its interpretation is limited only by human imagination.

## [58] Becoming a Vehicle

CONTEXT: R. Mordechai of Chernobyl was the second of that dynasty. Here, as part of a longer passage dealing with spiritual leadership, he comments on faith and devotion.

TEXT:

First, a person must know and trust with perfect and robust faith that there exists a God Who is One, singular and unique, Who brought about everything that exists out of nothing, a faith derived both from tradition and from experience, as it is written: "Know the God of your father and serve God" (I Chronicles 28:9). In this verse, there are two types of faith.

On top of this faith in the Blessed God, a person burning for divine service must give their soul for this, because this [is the meaning of the Talmudic teaching that] "'I [am the Eternal your God]' (Exodus 20:2) and 'You shall have no [other gods]' (Exodus 20:3) were both heard [directly] from the mouth of Mighty One (*ha-GeVuRah*)." Jewish people must exert (*lehaGBiR*) themselves over the material side, subduing it and purifying it. [By doing so,] one is illuminating one's spiritual being through one's physical being, and becoming a vehicle (*merkavah*) for the Blessed One. [Thus,] "I [am the Eternal your God]" (Exodus 20:2) and "You shall have no [other gods]" (Exodus 20:3) encompass the entire Torah and its fulfilment.

Mordechai of Chernobyl (d.1837), *Liqqutei Torah* (Torah Gleanings) (Jerusalem, 2001), p. 12.

NOTES:
**"From the mouth of Mighty One (*ha-GeVuRah*)"** ... Talmud, *Makkot* 24a. It seems likely that R. Mordechai has the *Sefirah* of *Gevurah* in mind here. It represents the attribute of restriction on both the divine and human levels. Hence, the sentence that follows.

**Becoming a vehicle (*merkavah*)...** Literally, a chariot. In rabbinic literature, the patriarchs are described as a chariot; cf. *Bereshit Rabbah* 47:6 and elsewhere.

COMMENT: Faith that remains in one's head is not true faith, but arrogance and self-delusion. True faith means transforming oneself into a vehicle for God through self-discipline and kindness towards the less fortunate. It means avoiding treating oneself or anyone else as an idol to be worshipped and slavishly followed. True faith means following God alone.

## [59] Through the Four Elements

CONTEXT: Moshe Cordovero, one of the most influential kabbalists of Safed, here employs a bit of *gematria* (numerology) and the medieval notion of the four (or five) elements to elucidate the revelation at Sinai.

TEXT:
[At Mount Sinai,] the Holy Blessed One spoke to Israel through every aspect of existence in order to demonstrate to them that there is nothing but God. Therefore, God spoke to them through the Throne of Glory (*KiSSei' hakavod*), when saying "I (*'aNoCHI*) am the Eternal your God" [Exodus 20:2]. *KiSSei'* has the same numerical value as *'aNoCHI*. God spoke with them through the angels, as it says: "And all the people saw the voices" [Exodus 20:15] – "voices" refers to angels, as it is written: "For a flying thing from heaven shall carry the voice" [Ecclesiastes 10:20].

God spoke with them through heaven, as it is written: "From heaven God made you hear the divine voice" [Deuteronomy 4:36]. God spoke with them through the earth, as it is written: "And on the earth, God showed you God's great fire" [Deuteronomy 4:36]. God spoke with them through all four elements, in order that they might see that within each and every element there is nothing but God. And through all of these aspects, God said: "I am the Eternal your God" [Exodus 20:2].

> Moshe Cordovero (1522-1570), *Shi'ur Qomah* (The Measure of the Height) (Jerusalem, 1999; Warsaw, 1883), *Torah*, chapter 42, p. 46.

NOTES:
**The Throne of Glory (*KiSSei' hakavod*)** ... God's heavenly throne. Here, it probably represents the quintessence, the spiritual substance that, it was believed, constituted the heavens.
***KiSSei'* has the same numerical value as *'aNoCHI*...** *KiSSei'* = 20 + 60 + 1 = 81; *'aNoCHI* = 1 + 50 + 20 + 10 = 81.

COMMENT: Modern science has long since disposed of the theory of the four terrestrial elements and the heavenly quintessence. Nevertheless, I was impressed with Cordovero's notion that revelation is to be found transmitted, as it were, by all the elements of the universe. What could be more inspiring than the idea that everything that is points to God? And not just to God as Creator of all, but also to God as the source of ethics and morality, as epitomized by the Ten Commandments.

# EZEKIEL'S VISION

## [60] The Living Creatures Ezekiel Saw

CONTEXT: The traditional *haftarah* for the first day of Shavuot is Ezekiel 1:1-28 & 3:12. This is the first part of the extraordinarily detailed vision that this most visionary of the biblical prophets had at the side of a canal while exiled in Babylonia. R. Mordechai of the Ukrainian town of Chernobyl, the second of that dynasty, makes use of a frequent Hasidic play on words on verse 14. This is part of the description of the *Chayyot* (Living Creatures), those fantastic four-faced entities that seem to guard the divine chariot in Ezekiel's vision. But now, with only a slight change of vowels, *CHaYYOT* is being read as *CHiYYUT* (life force). This text forms part of a discussion on the leadership of the *tzaddik*, here called the complete or perfect human being.

TEXT:

 First, a person must realize and truly believe that there is one, unique and unified God Who has brought all creatures and worlds, upper and lower, into existence, [Who is] without end or limit; Who fills all worlds and surrounds all worlds, is above all worlds, beneath all worlds, and in the midst of all worlds. [God] is the essential life-force (*CHiYYUT*) of every soul and living creature (*CHaYYOT*). Should God's life-force be removed for even one moment, [all] would be left like a body without a soul.

 Why was the obligation placed upon a complete human being to remember the outpouring of divine life-force at each and every moment, according to the saying of the Scriptures: "Every soul (*neshamah*) shall praise the Eternal" (Psalm 150:6), on which our rabbis have commented: "with each and every breath (*neshimah*)"? Because the soul wants to leave the body at each moment, but the Blessed One, out of the abundance of divine compassion and love, makes the soul return, as mystically described [in the phrase]: "And the living creatures (*CHaYYOT*) run to and fro" (Ezekiel 1:14).

  Mordechai of Chernobyl (d.1837), *Liqqutei Torah* (Torah Gleanings) (Jerusalem, 2001), pp. 8-9.

NOTES:

**In the midst of all worlds ...** See *Tikkunei HaZohar*, Introduction 5a, 6b; Zohar III, 225a.

**[God] is the essential life-force (*CHiYYUT*) of every soul and living creature (*CHaYYOT*) ...** See Hayyim Vital's *Etz Hayyim* (Tree of Life), Gate 3, Chapter 3.

**[All] would be left like a body without a soul ...** *Tikkunei HaZohar*, Introduction 17a.

**On which our rabbis have commented ...** *Bereshit Rabbah* 14:9.

**"And the living creatures (*CHaYYOT*) run to and fro" ...** See *Midrash Tehillim* 62:3 where the soul is said to be obliged to praise God in return for its presence in the body. The verse from Ezekiel is not quoted there, however.

COMMENT: Religious leadership is not confined to rabbis, or cantors, or even synagogue officers. Each of us has the potential to be a religious leader, and often the actuality as well, at least among our social circles, and perhaps beyond. Mordechai of Chernobyl reminds us that in Judaism religious leadership should be rooted in a concept of God that fills our consciousness and informs our behavior. Anything less is just self-seeking. It is why, he suggests, we have, and retain until our death, that most precious of divine gifts: our soul.

# THE BOOK OF RUTH

## [61] Who was Boaz?

CONTEXT: It is customary to read the Book of Ruth during the morning service on the second day of Shavuot, perhaps because Ruth's acceptance of Torah on a personal level mirrors Israel's acceptance at Mount Sinai. With the verse in question, we are introduced to her future husband. Elazar of Worms was one of the key figures of the Hasidei Ashkenaz movement in medieval Germany. In his commentary on the Torah and the Five Megillot, he loves to "deconstruct" the Hebrew of the biblical text in multiple ways.

TEXT:
"…Whose name was Bo'az."

Ruth 2:1

Through the strength (*B'oZ*) of Torah. Or, alternatively, *Bo'az* [means] "strong" (*'aZ*), and it is written: "Who is strong? Those who subdue their inclination." *Bo'az* – it is written: "A wise person is strong (*Be'oZ*)" (Proverbs 24[:5]), which is applied to Bo'az. *Be'oZ*, with strength. *Bo'aZ* [could also be spelt with a *vav* as] *BO'aZ*, [and understood as two words] *bo 'az*, "in him is strength," for within him is strength and might. *Bo'aZ* – he abandoned (*'aZaV*) his inclination.

Elazar ben Yehudah of Worms (c.1160-1237), *Perush HaRokeach* (The Torah Commentary of the "Pharmacist") (Bnei Brak, 1986), v.5, pp.187-188.

NOTES:
**"Who is strong? …"** Pirke Avot 4:1.
**Applied to Bo'az…** In Ruth Rabbah 6:4.

COMMENT: If Ruth is an example of loyalty to her family and to a faith into which she had not been born, then, in Elazar's view, Boaz is a model of inner strength born of immersion in Torah and his own innate qualities. It is this that makes him respectful of his workers, and most of all, of Ruth, who as both widow and foreigner was among the most vulnerable in his society. May Boaz be an example to us.

## [62] Benefiting the Heart

CONTEXT: The Zohar is the classic sourcebook of the kabbalistic tradition, arranged as a *midrash* commenting on verses of the Scriptures. It purports to be the work of second-century rabbis from the Land of Israel, but has been shown to be a product of the late thirteen century Spain.

TEXT:
["Then Boaz ate and drank, and his heart benefited."

Ruth 3:7]

Rabbi Yose began by saying: "Then Boaz ate and drank, and his heart benefited" (Ruth 3:7). What does "and his heart benefited" [mean]? [It refers to the fact that] he said a blessing over his food, and furthermore, there is a great secret here, for whoever says a blessing over food benefits the heart, as it is written: "To you, my heart says..." (Psalm 27:8) and it is written: "[God is] a rock, my heart [and my portion forever]" (Psalm 73:26).

Zohar II, 218a.

NOTE:
**"His heart benefited"** ... The JPS translation has: "[he was] in a cheerful mood."

COMMENT: How can one's heart benefit from the saying of a blessing over food? Clearly, we are not talking about cardiovascular health issues here, or even contentment after a hearty meal. "Heart" often has the meaning of "mind" in traditional texts. I would suggest that reciting blessings before and after eating connects that simple and necessary act with spirituality and divinity, reminding us of our dependence on an essentially benign universe. Surely that can bring a certain reassurance and calmness of spirit.

## [63] Limbs of the *Shechinah*

CONTEXT: A disciple of both Dov Baer of Mezritch and Yechiel Michal of Zlotchov, Ze'ev Wolf of Zhitomir in the Ukraine was an important teacher in his own right, and often critical of other Hasidic leaders.

TEXT:
"Meanwhile, Boaz had gone up to the gate and sat down there..."

Ruth 4:1

...Boaz was a righteous man in his generation, and a righteous person's entire self and development throughout life is [devoted] only to raising the "limbs" of the *Shechinah*, the Divine Presence, from being clothed (*hitlabbeshut*) [in] the lower levels [of existence]. This is what Scripture testifies to [when it speaks] of his righteousness: "Boaz had gone up" and raised "the gate" – a symbol of the *Shechinah*, known as "the gate of the Eternal" [Psalm 118:20] – and he raised her to Primordial Thought [= *Hochmah*] ...

Ze'ev Wolf of Zhitomir (d.1800), *Or HaMe'ir* (The Illuminating Light) (Warsaw, 1883), pt.4, p.16c.

NOTES:

**Limbs of the *Shechinah*...** I.e., the manifestations of the Presence of God in the world.

**Being clothed ...** The Hebrew term here, *hitlabbeshut*, means something like: the state of being clothed or dressed. In an erotic symbol, the righteous person is tasked with revealing the divine presence that is normally, modestly, concealed.

**"The gate" – a symbol of the *Shechinah*...** As *Malchut*, the lowest of the Ten *Sefirot*, the *Shechinah* is the gateway to the nine higher *Sefirot*.

COMMENT: R. Ze'ev Wolf of Zhitomir presents Boaz as the archetype of the *tzaddik*, usually a righteous person, but in a Hasidic context, the inspired teacher or *rebbe*. Perhaps they are the same thing here, for Boaz is depicted as raising the lower levels of existence (the limbs of the *Shechinah*, or *Malchut*) to higher realms. Surely that is the aim of all spirituality: to raise the mundane to the spiritual or (what amounts to the same thing) bring the spiritual into the mundane.

# VIEWS OF TORAH

## [64] Refinement

CONTEXT: Ya'akov Tzemach came from a family of Portuguese Jews who had had to convert to Christianity, but became a Talmudist and Kabbalist, as well as a key popularizer of the kabbalistic ideas of Isaac Luria.

TEXT:
The Torah was given to refine Israel. Therefore, everyone must be engaged with it so that all Israel may be refined by it.

> Ya'akov ben Hayyim Tzemach (died after 1665), *Nagid Umetzaveh* (Telling and Commanding, Isaiah 55:4) (reprint of 1880 ed.) (Jerusalem: 1965), p.82.

COMMENT: The festival of Shavuot celebrates the giving of the Torah, but what is the purpose of the Torah? We might be inclined to list, among its many purposes, the conveying of our most ancient Jewish heritage, history and practices, but Torah must be more than this if Judaism is to survive. Torah, a term which here encompasses its multifarious developments over the centuries, is, Jacob Tzemach suggests, intended to refine us: to make us better, more moral, more spiritual, as individuals and as a people. And each individual who undertakes this sacred task benefits the entire Jewish people. Perhaps that is the real message of Shavuot.

## [65] Preface to Torah

CONTEXT: Another contribution from the troubled *rebbe*, Menachem Mendel of Kotzk in Poland (1787-1859), this time from a book that draws together short sayings from numerous rabbis associated with the school of Pshische-Kotzk.

TEXT:
I heard in [Menachem Mendel of Kotzk's] holy name: "Ethical behavior (*derech eretz*) preceded (*KaDMah*) Torah." Just as a person can know the essence of book from its preface (*haKDaMah*), so too ethical behavior. One can recognize the essence of a person's Torah from their ethical behavior. Understand!

> Yo'etz Qayyam Qadish Rokotz (ed.), *Siach Sarfei Qodesh* (The Conversation of the Holy Serafim) (Lodz, 1931), pt.1, p.66.

NOTE:
**"Ethical behavior (*derech eretz*) preceded Torah..."** *Vayikra Rabbah* 9:3. Ethical behavior began with Adam and Eve; Torah only with Moses.

COMMENT: Jews who behave badly – especially those who purport to be religious – reflect badly on all of us. The greater our religious commitment, the greater should our commitment to ethics and morality be. But I am aware that the preface to a book is usually written after the book itself. Does the Kotzker wish to imply that Torah study must come first? That would surely undermine the point he is making! In my experience, that is not always the case. Sometimes the desire to behave ethically leads to Torah study. But the main thing is that our behavior should reflect, rather than contradict, our Torah learning.

## [66] Why the Torah Was Not Given in a Valley

CONTEXT: R. Yitzchak of Vorki, near Warsaw, was a disciple of Simchah Bunam of Pshische and friend to numerous other Hasidic leaders, including Menachem Mendel of Kotzk.

TEXT:

     Why was the Torah given at Mount Sinai? The Torah was given at Mount Sinai because it was the lowest of the mountains, as it says in the Talmud: "'[High and holy is the place where] I dwell, and with one who is contrite and humble...' (Isaiah 57:15) – for the Holy Blessed One left all the mountains and valleys alone, but made the [divine] Presence (*Shechinah*) dwell on Mount Sinai..." See there. But in that case, why wasn't the Torah given in a valley? It seems that the explanation is that [as for] those who are truly empty and lacking in everything, it is no wonder if they aren't haughty. But those who have something within and are not haughty, they are praiseworthy!

     Yitzchak of Vorki (d.1858), *Bet Yitzchak* (Isaac's House) (Jerusalem, 1992), p.145.

NOTE:
**As it says in the Talmud...** *Sotah* 5a.

COMMENT: If, as the Talmud says, the Torah was given on Sinai because it was the lowest of the mountains, and the choice of it would teach humility, surely the selection of a valley would have made the point even more forcefully! No, says the Vorker *rebbe*. Perhaps it is easy to be humble when you have nothing to say, when you feel inadequate. There is no virtue in this, except the recognition of the truth of the situation. Being humble when you do have something to say, when you feel that you can contribute, when you have self-esteem and confidence, that is true humility, because then you have something to be humble about. We have to shoulder our responsibilities, but not be arrogant about doing so.

     But I wonder: sometimes those with the least to say actually say the most, unhampered by knowledge, perhaps unaware or even unconcerned that they lack the knowledge. Surely, if they kept quiet, that too would be real humility.

## [67] The Divine Flame

CONTEXT: Although considered part of the Zoharic corpus, *Tikkunei HaZohar* (Zohar Repairs) is somewhat later than the main body of the Zohar, and probably by a different author. It offers more than seventy interpretations of the opening verse of Genesis.

TEXT:

Israel is the wick, the Torah is the oil, the *Shechinah* (the Presence of God) is the flame.

*Tikkunei HaZohar* §21, p. 60b.

COMMENT: What is the role of the Jewish people in history? What is the purpose of Torah in Jewish life? How can we make the presence of God manifest? These questions have been around since Judaism began. I find this mystical metaphor highly suggestive. If we pursue it, it becomes clear that our role is to bring God's presence to bear on life, that the Torah is the tool we have been given, and which we have developed, in order to achieve that task.


## [68] Whose Torah?

CONTEXT: The prayer below forms the conclusion of the sermon that Yisra'el of Sadagora, a descendant of the Maggid of Mezritch, delivered on the first day of Shavuot (= June 5) 1889. It was R. Yisra'el's habit to end each sermon with a prayer.

TEXT:

[The Torah] is called "the Torah of Moses" (Malachi 3:22). May the Blessed One help us to bring about a divine revelation in the world and fulfil through us the verse "In plain sight they shall see [the return of the Eternal to Zion]" (Isaiah 52:8). Then may each person receive their portion in the Torah through the purification of their own character. Then [the Torah] will be called "the Torah of the Eternal."

Yisra'el Friedman of Sadagora (1853-1907), *Or Yisra'el* (Israel's Light) (1997), p. 169.

NOTE:

**"The Torah of the Eternal"** ... This phrase is found eleven times in the Hebrew Bible.

COMMENT: For us, "the Torah of Moses" and "the Torah of the Eternal" are simply two expressions meaning the same thing. For R.

Israel, they represent two stages of spiritual development, mediated by the *tzaddik*, the Hasidic *rebbe*, symbolized by Moses. Most of us who become religious find that we have been inspired by other religious people, perhaps our parents, friends, teachers, or rabbis. I would suggest that that is the stage of "the Torah of Moses," when our spiritual understanding is very much shaped by that person who first influenced us in that direction. Later on, we may achieve the stage of "the Torah of the Eternal," where our understanding has grown past what we gleaned from our first teacher. Now, perhaps we can serve God directly, as ourselves, and thus, make the Torah our own.

## [69] An Interpretation of Our Very Own

CONTEXT: The details of Naftali Hertz Bacharach's life are very thin, but his book is without doubt one of the weirdest in kabbalistic literature, a genre known for its strange books. It presents a mixture of deep kabbalistic interpretation, mythology and magic, all described in rich and colorful language.

TEXT:
...To whomever engages with the "dew" of the Torah, like the Ari, and his like, the "dew" of the Torah gives life, by telling one the secrets of the Torah that touch upon one's soul (*neshamah*), for the sum total of all the souls (*neshamot*) is six hundred thousand, i.e. six hundred thousand seven-branched trees of light, all of which are known by the name of the *Guf* (body). The remaining [future] generations are [further] branches, and the Torah includes the souls of all Israel, mystically identified with *PaRDeS* and *Atzilut, Beri'ah, Yetzirah,* and *Asiyah.* Therefore, corresponding to them are six hundred thousand interpretations of the plain meaning (*peshat*), six hundred thousand interpretations of the allegorical meaning (*remez*) and proof, six hundred thousand interpretations of the aggadic meaning (*derash*), and six hundred thousand interpretations of the kabbalistic meaning (*kabbalah*), and so on. For there is no soul that is not composed of all of them. Hence, with every interpretation the root of a soul of Israel comes into being. In the messianic future, each one will read and know the Torah according to the interpretation that pertains to the root by which they were created, and similarly, in paradise. Each soul (*neshamah*) includes many interpretations, but the soul Moses our teacher included all six hundred thousand interpretations, [all of which] he knew.

Thus, each night, when the soul departs at the moment of sleep, those who are worthy to ascend [to heaven] to read there the interpretation that pertains to their root. But there is a difference, for on a given night, a certain verse may be particularly illuminated by one's soul, while on another night, another verse. It is all according to one's deeds.

Naftali Hertz ben Ya'aqov Elchanan Bacharach, (17th century), *Emeq HaMelech* (The Valley of the Sovereign) (Amsterdam, 1653), pt.2, p.42a.

NOTES:

**The "dew" of the Torah...** This expression is derived from Talmud, *Ketubbot* 111b: "For it is written in Scripture: 'For your dew is as the dew of light...' One who makes use of the light of the Torah will the light of the Torah revive." In the original context, this probably referred to the learning that one derives from the study of Torah. For Bacharach, it means kabbalistic interpretation, as the reference to the Ari makes clear.

**Like the Ari...** R. Isaac Luria (1534-1572), perhaps the greatest kabbalist of Safed.

**Six hundred thousand...** The number of Israelites that are supposed to have emerged from Egyptian slavery and traversed the wilderness. See Exodus 38:26 and Numbers 1:46.

**The remaining [future] generations...** I.e., those who live after the Exodus.

**Six hundred thousand seven-branched trees of light...** I.e., the bodies of each of them represent the seven lower *Sefirot*, symbolized by the *menorah*, the seven-branched candlestick.

**The *Guf* (body)...** A heavenly repository of souls destined to be sent into this world. See Talmud, *Yevamot* 62a & 63b and *Niddah* 13b.

**PaRDeS...** Meaning, orchard, but here, as frequently in later medieval literature, an acronym for the four levels of interpretation listed by Bacharach: *Peshat, Remez, Derash* and *Sod*. He uses the term *Kabbalah*, rather than *Sod*.

**Atzilut, Beri'ah, Yetzirah, and Asiyah...** The four realms or worlds, according to the kabbalistic scheme of Isaac Luria and others. In descending order, they are: *Atzilut*, Emanation, the world closest to the *Ayn Sof*, the Infinite; *Beri'ah*, Creation, the realm of the Throne of Glory and the archangels; *Yetzirah*, Formation, where the other, lower angels dwell; and *Asiyah*, Making or Action, this physical universe that we inhabit.

**The root of a soul...** In the higher worlds.

COMMENT: Once again, we see that Torah study is not the same as the study of other texts, or at least, it shouldn't be. In Naftali Bacharach's deeply mystical view, Torah study can be intensely personal and spiritual. Somewhere, in the spiritual realms or in the hidden recesses of our minds (which may be the same thing), there is an interpretation of Torah that belongs only to us, an interpretation that no one else can arrive at. We may not even recognize it when we come upon it, or rather, when it comes upon us. That revelation may have to wait for the messianic age to come. But in the meantime, we have to keep studying, thinking, and looking, precisely because it is unique to us.

## [70] A Parent's Letter to a Beloved Child

CONTEXT: R. Ya'akov Yosef of Ostrog, in Ukraine, a poor *maggid*, or preacher, was also known by the acronym, Rav Yeivi. This is a lovely example of his preaching skills.

TEXT:

Once on Shavuot, he spoke about the saying of the sages that *'aNoCHI* ("I") is an anagram for *'ana' Nafshi K'tavit Y'havit* ("I Myself wrote it [and] gave it"). This may be explained on the following analogy: A sovereign had an only child who was accomplished in all the levels befitting the child of a sovereign. The sovereign loved the child as their own soul, but it is the way of kings to send their children to faraway places to learn wisdom. So, the sovereign's child went away for a long time. After some time had passed, the sovereign wrote his beloved child, and while writing, an even greater love was awakened in the sovereign's heart. So, [the sovereign] put all desire, attachment and all strength into the letter. Then the letter reached the beloved child. As [the child] was reading it, [the child] actually felt the love of the parent's soul, for it had been put into the letter. Hence, the Holy Blessed One said: *'aNoCHI*, [i.e.] *'ana' Nafshi K'tavit Y'havit* – "I have put Myself into the Torah." And in it you will feel the divinity and love of the Holy Blessed One for Israel, and through it you will actually be bound up with the Holy Blessed One, like a parent to their child.

Ya'akov Yosef of Ostrog (d. 1790) in Hayyim ben Yeshayahu Liebersohn of Berditchev (ed.), *Tzeror HaHayyim* (The Bundle of Life, I Samuel 25:29) (Bilgorai, 1913), p. 28.

NOTES:
**The saying of the sages ...** Talmud, *Shabbat* 105a.
***'aNoCHI* ...** The opening word of the first of the Ten Commandments: "I am the Eternal your God" (Exodus 20:2).
***'ana' nafshi k'tavit y'havit* ...** This is in Aramaic, the primary language of the Talmud. The object of this sentence is the Torah.

COMMENT: As a parent and grandparent, I appreciate the practical intricacies of raising children. It's about setting limits, but not too strictly. It's about giving them freedom without making them feel alone. But through it all, it's about giving them the feeling that they are loved. Perhaps the Torah is like that. God gives us freedom, sets limits for us, and loves us, no matter what.

## [71] Seductive Torah

CONTEXT: This text comes from an anthology of short teachings of numerous rabbis of the schools of Pshische, Kotzk, Ger and others. This one in particular comes from the mouth of the fiery Rabbi Menachem Mendel of Kotzk.

TEXT:
Furthermore, I heard in the holy name of that it says in the Zohar, "Whoever labors (*miSHtaDaL*) in Torah…" – the meaning is: One must be seduced by the Torah, for on the verse: "If a man seduces a betrothed maiden…," Targum Onkelos translates ["seduces" as] *yeSHaDeL*. Understand this well, for it is very profound!
Menachem Mendel of Kotzk (1787-1859) in Yo'etz Qayyam Qadish Rokotz (ed.), *Siach Sarfei Qodesh* (The Conversation of the Holy Serafim) (Lodz, 1931), pt.1, p.66.

NOTES:
**"Whoever labors (*miSHtaDaL*) in Torah…"** This seems to be quoted from memory here, but there two possible sources: Zohar II, 124a ("…labors in the divine name") and Zohar II, 161b ("…sustains the world").
**"If a man seduces a betrothed maiden…"** This is also quoted from memory, but the reference seems to be to Exodus 22:15 ("If a man seduces a virgin…").
**Targum Onkelos…** The classic translation of the Torah into Aramaic. It often appears alongside the original in *chumashim* printed with commentaries.

COMMENT: I remember what it was like to be in love, and later, to be engaged. I couldn't spend enough time with my beloved (and after 40+ years of marriage, I still feel much the same). Our engagement (pun intended!) with Torah should be like that. To me, my wife is not just some random woman. To the committed Jew, the Torah should not be just some random book, like any other. That is what the Kotzker demands of us when he says we should be seduced by it.

## [72] How to Keep the Whole Torah

CONTEXT: Yisra'el of Ruzhyn was a descendant of the Maggid of Mezritch and founder of the Ruzhyn-Sadagora dynasty. He asks how it is possible to keep the entire Torah, given that it contains a great many commandments. The result formed part of his sermon for the night of Shavuot 1861.

TEXT:
It says: "'You shall love your neighbor as yourself' [Leviticus 19:18]. This is the principle of the entire Torah." And yet, it is only a commandment between one person and another. So how can we come to the other commandments through this one? The fact is that when people contemplate only the spiritual, that "the whole earth is full of God's glory" [Isaiah 6:3], and that spiritually, the root of [all] souls is one, and [then] turn and attach themselves to the root, they immediately fulfil the entire Torah, because the root includes all.

Yisra'el Friedman of Ruzhyn (1797-1850), *Bet Yisra'el* (The House of Israel) (Piotrkov, 1913), pp. 108-109.

NOTES:
**The principle of the entire Torah...** According to Rabbi Akiva, see *Sifra* 89b on this verse.

**Only a commandment between one person and another...** So, what about all those commandments that deal with relations between human beings and God?

COMMENT: I wish I had a penny for every person I have met in my rabbinic career who said that they did not have to go to shul or be observant of Jewish festivals and Shabbat because ethics was the most important thing, not ritual. Of course, at one level, they are correct. But ethics can become very shallow if not grounded in, and supported by, something deeper. Spirituality can be the deep soil upon which ethics can thrive.

## [73] Torah as Weapon

CONTEXT: Hayyim Yosef David Azulai, the great traveler and bibliophile, gave a sermon on 2 Sivan [= 22 May], 1784, on what is sometimes known as *Shabbat Kallah*, the Bride's Shabbat, just before Shavuot. This title derives from the notion that Shavuot represents the wedding of God and the Jewish people. What follows is a small portion of that sermon.

TEXT:
"Remember (*Zichru*) the Torah of Moses, My servant, which I commanded him…"

Malachi 3:22

The [letter] *zayin* of *Zichru* is written large [in many Hebrew bibles]. Perhaps the meaning is that Torah is a great weapon (*keli zayin*), both in this world and in the world-to-come.

In this world it saves [us] from slavery, as we have been taught: "Only those who are engaged with the Torah are [truly] free." Also, it is through Torah that we are saved from the inclination towards evil, which can poison all things, as it has been said: "[The Torah is] a perfect remedy."

In the world-to-come, it will protect the soul (*neshamah*) when it departs, as it is said: "When you lie down, it will guard you" (Proverbs 6:22).

Thus, the *zayin* was written large in order to teach [us] that Torah saves [us] from suffering, and those who have Torah within have a divine weapon [to protect] them.

Hayyim Yosef David Azulai (1724-1806), *Hadrei Vaten* (Innermost Parts) (Jerusalem, 1990), p.235.

NOTES:
**"Only those who are engaged …"** A statement to this effect is found in an extra-Talmudic tractate *Kallah Rabbati* chapter 8.
**"A perfect remedy"** … Talmud, *Kiddushin* 30b.

COMMENT: We don't often think of books as weapons, and yet, they can be very powerful indeed: changing lives, overthrowing governments. In American history, Harriet Beecher Stowe's Uncle Tom's Cabin is said to have contributed to the ultimate abolition of slavery, for example. But surely the most powerful literary weapon of all, at least in the West, has been the Torah. It inspired not only Jews, but Christians and Muslims as well, and helped to precipitate the Protestant Reformation, the American revolution, etc., etc. But it is first and foremost a spiritual blueprint for how to be devoted to God and not be subservient to others.

# [74] A Secret Treasure

CONTEXT: Mordechai of Neschiz was a Ukrainian Hasidic teacher who had studied with the Maggid of Mezritch and the Maggid of Zlotchov.

TEXT:

    The Torah is called "a secret treasure," because the treasure is that the Blessed One's Name is hidden within it.

    "[Beloved are Israel, for to them was given a precious instrument;] still greater was the love that made known to them that they were given the precious instrument [by which the world was created]" – i.e., the holy Torah – "as it is written, 'For I give you good doctrine; do not forsake my Torah' (Proverbs 4:2)."

    But [Mordechai of Neschiz] said [still greater] was that it was made known to them Who had given them this precious instrument.

    Mordechai of Neschiz (d.1800), *Rishpei Esh* (Coals of Fire, Song of Songs 8:6) (Jerusalem, 1997), p. 71, §§132,133.

NOTES:

**The Blessed One's Name is hidden within it...** A common notion in kabbalistic literature. Its most extreme form may be Nachmanides' statement, in his introduction to his Torah commentary, that the Torah consists entirely of God's name.

**"A secret treasure"** ... Talmud, *Shabbat* 88b.

**"Beloved are Israel..."** Quoted in the name of Rabbi Akiva in Mishnah, *Pirkei Avot* 3:18)

COMMENT: What are the origins of Torah? Clearly, it arose in a particular set of ancient historical circumstances, and has been interpreted and re-interpreted over the intervening centuries. But to the religious Jew, these facts are secondary to the belief in the Torah's divine origins. Without that belief, Torah study would just another form of literary archaeology, like studying the Iliad or the Odyssey. With that belief, Torah becomes a source of inspiration, a path to the divine within and beyond oneself.

## [75] An Image of Humanity and of God

CONTEXT: Menachem Nachum, student of the Maggid of Mezritch and preacher at Chernobyl in Ukraine, is here building on an ancient notion that the Torah contains 613 commandments in two categories: 248 positive and 365 negative.

TEXT:

    In the Torah there is a spiritual structure of 248 spiritual limbs, i.e., the 248 positive commandments, and of 365 spiritual sinews, i.e., the 365 negative commandments. In human beings too, there are 248 limbs and 365 sinews. Now, humanity was created in the image of God, but to understand this, it is relevant to note that there can be no physical representation of God. Instead, the meaning is that God is in the image of the Torah, for the Torah is [itself] called "God" in concentration, for the Blessed One has concentrated divinity into the Torah in order that people, bounded and finite though they may be, might attach themselves to the Blessed One, the unbounded and infinite. So, human beings are created in the image of the God of the Torah which is a spiritual structure of 248 positive commandments and 365 negative commandments. Thus, the perfect human being is one who is one with the image, that is, their physical structure is one with the spiritual structure of the Torah, the supernal human being. And when such people move a physical limb, they move and awaken a supernal limb. Such a person is called a perfect human being, in accordance with the saying: "But human beings walk about in the image" (Psalm 39:7), i.e., whoever goes about with the image, that is, is one with the image, [that person] is called a perfect human being. But, when they fail to perform a certain *mitzvah*, or commit a transgression, they are missing one limb or one sinew, and are no longer perfect...

> Menachem Nachum of Chernobyl (1730-1797), *Me'or Eynayim* (The Light of the Eyes) (n.p., 1952), p. 98.

NOTES:

**248 spiritual limbs...** The idea that the Torah is composed of 613 commandments, 365 negative commands corresponding to the days of the solar year and 248 positive ones corresponding to the (supposed) parts of the human body, is found initially in Talmud, *Makkot* 23b. In the hands of subsequent generations of kabbalists, this notion became extended and developed to strengthen the analogy between the Torah and the human body. Relating the 365 negative commands to the solar year was replaced by a connection with the (supposed) number of sinews in the body.

**It is relevant to note that there can be no physical representation of God.** I.e., do not take the notion of humanity in the image of God literally.

**Torah is [itself] called "God" in concentration...** This radical statement is based on the teachings of Menachem Nachum's teacher, Dov Baer of Mezritch.

**The supernal human being...** The person who embodies the Torah, and thus the 613 commandments, also embodies the Ten *Sefirot*, themselves configured as a model of humans below.

COMMENT: At our best, we humans can bring true divinity to bear in the world, in so far as we embody the Torah in our lives. Because doing so means that we also, as it were, embody God. But because we are "only" human, we may sin. This not only affects our psychological and

78

social realities, but also diminishes the extent to which we had truly represented God on earth.

## [76] Torah as Spiritual Advice

CONTEXT: Meshullam Feibush of Zbarazh was a second-generation Hasidic teacher, having studied with the Maggid of Mezritch and the Maggid of Zlotchov. Here he discusses the point of the Torah's legal material that is no longer of practical value. Why continue to study it?

TEXT:

For our entire Torah, the Written and the Oral, contains nothing, not even a single letter, that does not pertain to the service of the blessed Eternal One. It was given for that reason, and is called "Torah" because it teaches (*morah*), as if it were saying: "This is the way; walk it!" [This applies] even to the laws of finance and other legislation, that seem as if they have no practical significance. "If it is empty, it is from you." But those who serve the Eternal wholeheartedly have secrets of Torah revealed to them. And what are those secrets? How to derive advice for the service of the Blessed Creator from all the 613 commandments, even those which it is impossible to observe in themselves, like those that are dependent on being in the Land [of Israel] or other commandments. Hence, the Zohar's saying: "The 613 commandments? – The 613 kinds of advice." That is to say, they give human beings advice on how to cleave to the Creator...

> Meshullam Feibush HaLevi Heller of Zbarazh (d. 1785), *Yosher Divrei Emet* (Upright Words of Truth, Ecclesiastes 12:10) (Bnei Brak, 2004), p. 108.

NOTES:

**The Written and the Oral...** Since rabbinic times, Jews have distinguished between the Written Torah (the Five Books of Moses, plus the rest of our Bible) and the Oral Torah (now embodied in the Mishnah, Talmud and other written sources).

**"If it is empty, it is from you"** ... An interpretation of Deuteronomy 32:47 ("For it is not a trifling [literally, empty] thing for you" JPS) found in Talmud Yerushalmi, *Pe'ah* 1:1. If you think a text is worthless, it is because you have not grasped it by applying yourself to it sufficiently.

**613 commandments...** An idealized number made up of 365 negative commands corresponding to the days of the solar year, plus 248 positive commands corresponding to the (supposed) parts of the body; Talmud, *Makkot* 23b.

**The Zohar's saying...** Zohar II, 82b.

COMMENT: Since Israel was exiled from its Land by the Romans in the year 70 C.E., large portions of Jewish law have been in abeyance, suspended in the absence of a Temple with its priestly hierarchy and system of sacrifices. In addition, agricultural rules could not be observed outside of the Land. In our time, this category of no-longer practical legislation includes laws of damages and other financial provisions, since we accept the jurisdiction of non-Jewish courts in these matters. What is the point of studying those parts of the Torah today? For Meshullam Feibush of Zbarazh, they offer spiritual lessons for all time. For example, perhaps the sacrifices of animals and produce might inspire us to generosity and self-sacrifice. Perhaps the priesthood might offer examples of dedication that we might follow. And the financial provisions? Perhaps they offer models of how we should conduct ourselves in our financial affairs. But for Meshullam Feibush, the real point is that, with creative thinking, they can provide us with spiritual advice.

## [77] The Torah as God's Name

CONTEXT: Nachmanides (known in Hebrew as RaMBaN, R. Moshe ben Nachman) was one of the great medieval Bible commentators and a kabbalist. He was Catalan, had a key role in his community and was a confidant of the king of Catalonia (now part of Spain), but he had to flee the country for the Land of Israel after successfully defending Jewish against Christian attacks in debate. This is an extract from the introduction to his Torah commentary.

TEXT:
We possess an authentic tradition (*kabbalah*) that the entire Torah consists of names of the Holy Blessed One, that the letters may be divided into names in another manner, as you may imagine by way of example, for the verse "In the beginning" [Genesis 1:1] may be divided into other words, for instance: *BeRei'SHYT BaRa' 'eLoHIM* ("In the beginning God created") might have its letters re-distributed [to read] *BeRo'SH YiTBaRei' 'eLoHIM* ("At first, *'elohim* were created"). The entire Torah is like this, [even] apart from the combinations and numerical values (*gematriot*) of the names... For the writing was continuous, with breaks between words, so that it was possible to read it according to the way of names or to read it according to our [usual] reading as Torah and commandments. It was given to our teacher Moses according to the reading of it as commandments, but the reading of it as names was orally transmitted to him.

Moshe ben Nachman (Nachmanides) (1195-1270), *Perush Al-HaTorah* (Commentary on the Torah) (Jerusalem: Levin-Epstein), Introduction.

NOTES:

**Authentic tradition (*kabbalah*)...** The word *kabbalah* comes from a root meaning "to receive;" hence, tradition, that which is received from previous generations. In modern Hebrew, it means a receipt.

***BeRo'SH YiTBaRei' 'eLoHIM...*** The last two letters of *BeRei'SHYT* have simply been removed and added to *BaRa'*.

**"At first, *'elohim* were created"** ... *'Elohim* most commonly means "God," but it is plural in form and may mean "gods." In a kabbalistic context, it refers to the *Sefirot*. Ramban is not normally explicit about kabbalistic ideas, but the point is clear: Before the start of the creation process, the Ten *Sefirot* emerge out of (the unnamed) *Ayn Sof*, or the Infinite, Unknowable God. (These words do not appear in all printed versions of Ramban's commentary.)

COMMENT: What is Torah? This is a recurrent question for Jews who would be religious. It is many things, but at its heart it is a manifestation of God in Jewish life. With all its developments, it is our go-to text to learn about God and how to live a spiritual life in God's world. Referring to it as one extended name of God is, for me, a metaphor that tries to plumb the huge significance it has for us Jews. Where would we be without it? It is almost as if it were, itself, God.

## [78] The Torah as Mystical Body

CONTEXT: Azriel of Gerona was one of a small group of early kabbalists who flourished in Catalonia, prior to the publication of the Zohar in the late thirteenth century. He was a disciple of Isaac the Blind, the first scholar we know of who made Kabbalah his specialty. This is from Azriel's most important work.

TEXT:

Since the Torah is called a Name, and it restores the soul [Psalm 19:8], it contains *parashiyot*, chapters (*perakim*) and spaces, namely the open and closed *parashiyot*, so that it resembles a complete structure, just as a human being has hand- and foot-joints and [bodily] segments (*perakim*). Just as there are organs upon which the soul depends and organs upon which it does not depend, although there is neither addition nor diminution in the creation of the body, so too there are *parashiyot* in the Torah and the Scriptures that seem to those who do not know the

81

meanings of their interpretation as if they were fit to be burnt, and to those who have attained to the knowledge of their interpretation that they are the principles (*gufei*) of the Torah. So, those who omit a single letter or a single vowel of them is as if they had omitted the complete body. And there is no difference between [the text on] the chieftains of Esau [Genesis 37:15-19] and the Ten Commandments, for it is all one thing and one structure.

> Azriel of Gerona (early 13th century), *Perush Ha'Aggadot LeR. Azri'el* (R. Azriel's Commentary on Aggadot) (Isaiah Tishby, ed.) (Jerusalem: Mekize Nirdamim, 1945), pp. 37-38.

NOTES:

**The Torah is called a Name...** Nachmanides (in the introduction to his Torah commentary) had taught that the entire Torah is one great name of God. See the previous passage.

*Parashiyot...* In this context, the paragraphs into which the Torah text is divided, rather than the weekly Torah readings.

**Chapters (*perakim*)...** Or, segments.

**Spaces, namely the open and closed *parashiyot*...** If a paragraph of the Torah is followed by a space that ends with the start of the next paragraph on the same line, it is considered closed. If the next paragraph begins on the next line, it is called open.

**There are organs upon which the soul depends...** I.e., where damage to them would result in death.

**The principles of (*gufei*)...** Literally, bodies of the Torah.

COMMENT: Modern Biblical scholarship (like much of modern science) is given to analysis, that is, breaking things down into their constituent parts. So, modern scholars of the Bible tend to break the Torah down into four strands of tradition, and smaller sections by topics, in order to isolate them and try to set them into their original historical context. Jewish tradition viewed the Torah differently, holistically if you will, and R. Azriel of Gerona presents a mystical approach to this notion. For Jewish purposes, the whole is more important than the parts.

# [79] Torah as a Mirror

CONTEXT: Avraham Abulafia, the great teacher of prophetic *kabbalah*, a meditational path designed to attain prophecy, also composed commentaries on each of the Five Books of the Torah, though only four are extant. This comes from his commentary on the Book of Numbers.

TEXT:

[People] must inquire into the understanding of Torah so that they may know themselves in it, like those who look into a mirror in order to see their face, themselves and the other within it, and from there those who look into it will ascend to the contemplation of the blessed Creator.

> Avraham ben Shmuel Abulafia (1240-after 1291), *Mafteach HaSefirot* (The Key to the Numbers) (edited by Amnon Gross) (Jerusalem, 2001), p. 34.

COMMENT: Studying Torah from a religious or spiritual perspective means always asking ourselves, what does this have to do with me? With us? It is personal and communal, not academic or simply entertaining. Viewed from this angle, Torah does become like a mirror in which we see our flaws and those of our community. And looking at Torah and ourselves in this way can, in turn, lead us to God.

## [80] How Humanity Sustains the World

CONTEXT: The central text of the Kabbalah is the Zohar. It is frequently steeped in symbolism that is sometime difficult to decipher, but this piece is quite straightforward. It deals with the cosmic significance of the Torah.

TEXT:

Rabbi Hiyya began by quoting, "Who can tell of the mighty acts of the Eternal, and who can proclaim God's praises?" [Psalm 106:2]. Come and see! When the Holy Blessed One desired to create the world and sought to do so, [God] looked into the Torah, and created it, so that for each and every thing that the Holy Blessed One created in the world, God had looked into the Torah and created it, as it is written: "I was beside [God] like a confidant (*'amon*), a source of delight every day" [Proverbs 8:30]. Do not read *'aMON* (confidant), but *'uMaN* (artisan).

When God wanted to create humanity, the Torah spoke in [God's] presence: If people are created, they will in the end sin, and You will have to judge them, and the work of Your hands will come to nothing because they will not be able to bear Your judgment. The Holy Blessed One replied: Before creating the world, I prepared repentance.

At the moment of making the world and creating humanity, the Holy Blessed One said to the world: O world, O world, you and your laws can only be sustained through the Torah, and therefore, I have created humanity within you so they can occupy themselves with it. And if not, I will return you to chaos.

Everything is sustained because of humanity, as it is written: "I made the earth, and created humanity upon it" [Isaiah 45:12]. The Torah constantly calls to humanity that they might occupy themselves and exert themselves in it, but no one inclines an ear.

Come and see! Whoever exerts themselves in the Torah sustains the world, and each and everything in its proper form.

Zohar I, 134a-b.

NOTES:
**Rabbi Hiyya began...** The real Rabbi Hiyya lived c. 200 C.E., but the Zohar is a product of a band of kabbalists who lived in the late thirteenth century.
**[God] looked into the Torah, and created it...** According to *Bereshit Rabbah* 80:1.
**I was beside [God]...** The speaker is Wisdom, identified with Torah by the rabbis.
**Do not read 'aMON (confidant), but 'uMaN (artisan)...** *Bereshit Rabbah* 1:1.
**Before creating the world, I prepared repentance...** See Talmud, *Pesachim* 54a.
**O world, O world, you and your laws...** See Talmud, *Avodah Zarah* 5a.

COMMENT: For kabbalists, as for the rabbis before them, the Torah is a pale reflection of divine wisdom. Here it is the blueprint from which the world was created, as well as a guide for righteous human behavior. And our failure to behave righteously can lead to the destruction of the world. How prescient this text feels as we confront the real and present danger of climate change! Perhaps it offers us a way forward, too.

## [81] Religious and Secular

CONTEXT: It has been said that R. Pinchas of Koretz was a master of the aphorism. He was a younger contemporary of the Ba'al Shem Tov, but probably independent of him rather than a disciple. His teachings emphasize modesty and inner devotion.

TEXT:
He said: What is [the meaning of] "In all your ways, know [God]" ([Proverbs] 3:6)? When the Holy Blessed One gave the Torah, the whole world was filled with Torah, as it is said: "As I live, for the whole earth is filled with the glory of the Eternal" (Numbers 14:2[1]). And the Torah and the Holy Blessed One are one. Now, there is nothing that does not have the Torah of the Eternal in it, and this is [the meaning of the verse]

'In all your ways...' Anyone who says that words of Torah are one thing, and ordinary matters another denies [God].

> Pinchas of Koretz (1726-1791), *Imrei Pinchas* (Pinchas' Sayings) (Tel Aviv: Arnberg, 1974), §187, pp.51-52.

NOTES:

**"In all your ways, know [God]"** ... This verse has the status of a slogan or motto in Hasidic literature, embodying as it does the concept of *avodah be-gashmiyut* (worship through corporeality). JPS: "In all your ways, acknowledge Him."

**The whole world was filled with Torah...** An extraordinary statement. Perhaps based on the *midrash* that the entire world became silent when the Torah was given at Sinai (*Shemot Rabbah* 29:9). Alternatively, in the same *midrash* collection (5:9), we find that God's voice reverberated throughout the world. But the Koretzer goes beyond these in suggesting that Torah became a permanent aspect of reality, rather than a sound or a silence that might fade away or be overtaken with time.

**The Torah and the Holy Blessed One are one...** This phrase in Aramaic, often with the addition of Israel, is said in Hasidic literature to be a quotation from the Zohar, but in fact, it does not occur there. The closest to our version seems to be: "The Torah is nothing but the Holy Blessed One" (Zohar II, 60a).

COMMENT: If God is one, as the *Shema* affirms, then the universe which stems from God must itself be one. And any encounter with anything within that universe is an encounter with God. And if, as the Koretzer asserts, Torah and God are the same, then every encounter is also an encounter with Torah. Being aware of God as we navigate our way through life, meeting its challenges, is the same as being aware of Torah, of the obligations we owe to ourselves, to each other, our community and our society, and our shared world. Everything and everyone we encounter needs our respect as a manifestation of God. Everything and everyone we meet is an opportunity to learn Torah. It is all one. And to imagine that it is not is to miss the biggest picture of all.

# TISHA B'AV

The people mourning over the ruins of Jerusalem. By Gustave Doré .

# [82] Contrasting Opposites

CONTEXT: Yisra'el of Ruzhyn, a central figure in nineteenth century Hasidism despite not being a great scholar, was also a direct descendant of the Maggid of Mezritch. The following is from an address he gave during the Three Weeks in the run-up to Tisha b'Av, a period known as *Bein HaMeitzarim*, "between the straits" (Lamentations 1:3). As he frequently did, he ends with a prayer.

TEXT:
There are spiritual forces of greatness, and spiritual forces of smallness, and it is impossible for there to be greatness unless there is smallness first. There is right and left. Why is [a thing] called right? Because [if] there is a corresponding left, the right may be recognized as such. The Blessed One set [the world up] so that there should be "evening and it was morning: one day" [Genesis 1:5]. Evening represents darkness, and morning light, for the darkness is included in the light, and powers [of judgment] are included within those of kindness. May there be great kindness and compassion upon all Israel. Amen.

Yisra'el Friedman of Ruzhyn (1797-1850), *Irin Qadishin* (Holy Angels) (n.p., 1885), pt. 1, p. 68.

NOTES:
**Spiritual forces of greatness, and spiritual forces of smallness...** *Mochin*, literally, brains of greatness and brains of smallness. In their original Lurianic context, these refer to differing states of the *Sefirah* of *Tiferet*; in Hasidism, they refer to different psychological states: effusiveness vs. a more subdued state. In both systems of thought, there is a dialectic relationship between them, as each will tend to give way to the other.
**Darkness is included in the light...** Ultimately, even the negative derives from the positive.

COMMENT: Many years ago, before I found my way to Judaism, let alone Kabbalah and Hasidism, I had a very good friend who told me that his aim in life was to reconcile opposites. I'm not sure what he meant by that, but Kabbalah (and Hasidism in its wake) aims to do the same. The Tree of the Ten *Sefirot*, the attributes that make up God's personality (as it were) and the chain of being that stretches between God and ourselves, is made up of right and left branches, representing lovingkindness on the right and strictness on the left, with a central branch that aims to balance and reconcile the opposites. That central branch is characterized by beauty, justice and compassion. The Ruzhyner's statement above follows in this tradition. If we seek compassion in the world, for ourselves and for others, we must begin by reconciling our own opposites within us: our anger with our love, our selfishness with our selflessness, and so forth. If we can achieve this inner beauty, we can truly begin to spread such beauty beyond ourselves.

## [83] *Shabbat Chazon* – The Sabbath of Vision

CONTEXT: Each Shabbat during the Three Weeks between the seventeenth of *Tammuz* and the Ninth of *Av* has its own special *haftarah* or reading from the Prophets. Unlike most *haftarot*, these three are not related to the Torah portion they accompany, but to this period of mourning. The third is called *Chazon* ("Vision") from its opening word and gives its name to this Shabbat just before Tisha b'Av. Yisrael of Ruzhyn was the great-grandson of the Maggid of Mezritch, and had a very large following. He was a great believer in the power of the *tzaddik*, the Hasidic *rebbe*, to bring about real changes in life through spiritual activities.

TEXT:
["The vision (*chazon*) of Isaiah son of Amotz…"
                                                            Isaiah 1:1]
I heard from his holy mouth that he asked why [people] call this Shabbat *Shabbat Chazon*. He said that on this Shabbat one can see what will happen in the world. With regard to prophecy, when the prophets see something [bad] concerning Israel, that thing has already reached the [lower] attributes, as it says in the holy Zohar: "There are those who see concerning the hands and those who see concerning the feet" – and this refers to the [lower] attributes. Therefore, they are not able to sweeten the thing further, nor negate it. … As soon as the prophets see the thing, they say to Israel that they do not have the power to negate it, because it has already occurred among the attributes. However, a sage is superior to a prophet, for "the sage has eyes in his head" [Ecclesiastes 2:14]. When [a sage] sees something [bad] it is still in the "head," above the [lower] attributes. This is because the sage is at the level of Nothingness, and therefore, he sees [that bad] thing at that level of Nothingness as well. Therefore, [the sage] can sweeten and negate [that bad thing]. Then he concluded: What does he see when he sees Nothingness? Only that he sees nothing.

Afterwards he said: When there are judgmental forces [arrayed] against Israel I am ill and depressed, but when Israel experiences compassion, I am healthy and happy. For righteous people feel all types of change that occur in the world in their own body, whether from compassion to judgment or from judgment to compassion….

Yisrael Friedman of Ruzhyn (1797-1850), *Irin Qadishin* (Holy Angels) (n.p., 1885), part 1, pp. 66-67.

NOTES:

**The [lower] attributes...** The lower seven *Sefirot*, from *Hesed* (Lovingkindness) to *Malchut* (Sovereignty).

**Concerning the hands...** Meaning, the *Sefirot* of *Hesed* (Lovingkindness) and *Gevurah* (Might), corresponding to the right and left hand, respectively.

**Concerning the feet...** The *Sefirot* of *Netzach* (Victory) and *Hod* (Majesty), symbolized by the right and left leg or foot. (This Zoharic passage seems to be quoted from memory. It is similar in content to Zohar I, 265b, §45 – but incorrectly labelled §48 in standard editions.)

**Sweeten the thing further, nor negate it...** If the prophets were above the world of the *Sefirot*, they could overrule decisions taken in that realm.

**A sage is superior to a prophet...** As stated in Talmud, *Bava Batra* 12a. The Ruzhyner has in mind the Hasidic *rebbe*, the *tzaddik*, or even himself.

**In the "head," above the [lower] attributes...** Our rabbi interprets "head" as indicating the three upper *Sefirot* of *Keter* (Crown), *Hochmah* (Wisdom) and *Binah* (Understanding), which correspond to the head, or perhaps simply as *Keter* or *Hochmah*; *Keter* is frequently identified as Nothing in kabbalistic literature, while *Hochmah* is given this designation in the teachings of the Maggid of Mezritch, the Ruzhyner's ancestor. This Nothing is not no-thing, but everything in potential. From this vantage point, the sage can sweeten or override any negative energies from below.

COMMENT: This passage seemed to jump out at me from the page of the book as I was searching for a sermon idea for *Shabbat Chazon* in 2014. The Three Weeks had seen another round in the seemingly interminable tragedy played out between Gaza and Israel, as well as the spectacular and frightening success of Islamic State militants across Iraq and Syria, accompanied by massacres of Yazidis, Christians and Shia Muslims. As I watched each day's news unfold during this period I could not restrain my tears. When I read the Ruzhyner's sermon on *Chazon*, especially his last paragraph, I knew that my tears were not in vain, but formed part of the path of the righteous – may we all be included among them. May peace and justice emerge from tragedy.

# [84] The Prince in Exile

CONTEXT: The exile of the Jewish people is an underlying theme of the Three Weeks and of Tisha b'Av. If we had not been exiled, the list of the tragedies we have had to endure would have been shorter. The *CHIDA*,

Hayyim Yosef David Azulai, renowned kabbalist and book lover, presented this parable as an introduction to a sermon on *parashat Devarim*, the weekly Torah reading that always falls on the Shabbat just prior to Tisha b'Av.

TEXT:

There once was a prince whose father made him ruler over a third of his kingdom, apart from the father's royal throne. But he transgressed the laws of his father and set aside all his rulings, hating those who loved [his father] and loving those who hated him. On many occasions, the king sent many noblemen to persuade him and to remind him that, since [the king] would act justly, the counselors would join together against him. If he did not repent, there would be bitterness in the end. But [the prince] would not listen. So, a decree came from the king and his counselors to drive away the king's son, and to lay waste and despoil all that he owned, so that he would be left a wanderer, "wandering about for bread, [saying] 'where is it?'" [Job 15:23]. [O listeners!] say that the prince would always remain sorrowful and sighing. Let no joy come upon him!

The meaning is clear: How can we be happy and how can we eat a meal in friendship? This is certainly due to a lack of knowledge.

Hayyim Yosef David Azulai (1724-1806), *Chadrei Vaten* (Innermost Parts) (Jerusalem, 1990), p. 284.

NOTES:

**The meaning is clear...** So clear, the *CHIDA* thinks, that he does not offer an explanation.

COMMENT: The point of the parable is perhaps not as clear as the *CHIDA* suggests. The father is God, the prince, the Jewish people, and the king's counselors are the biblical prophets. The sin that led to our expulsion from the Promised Land was nothing short of rebellion, siding with God's enemies. When we think of how we were driven out, how can we be happy? If we focus on that, Tisha b'Av becomes real for us. But I was especially intrigued by the last sentence quoted above. What ignorance is the *CHIDA* referring to? What ignorance keeps us captive and wandering? Surely, he means the ignorance of the role God plays in our lives behind the scenes and should play in our awareness.

## [85] It's All Our Fault

CONTEXT: Yeshaya Horowitz was rabbi in Prague and Krakow, and author of a seventeenth century Jewish bestseller, of which this is an extract.

TEXT:
On the subject of Tisha b'Av: ... From the Prophets, the Writings, and from the words of our rabbis [found] in the Talmud, *midrashim* and the Zohar, the great duty of mourning for the destruction of the Temple and for the exile is clear. The reason for this is because of the honor of the *Shechinah* (the Presence of God) "As a result of our sins, we were exiled from our land," and it is as if the *Shechinah* is in exile. The serving girl has disinherited her mistress, the enemy from the side of the "shell," the Other Side, has won; and the glorious House of the Eternal has been burnt down. There is no burnt offering nor [other] sacrifice. Prophecy has ceased, along with the holy spirit, and the spirit of uncleanness has spread abroad. The people of the Eternal, the Israelite nation, are given over to plague, famine, hunger, captivity and despoiling, and even today they are in the midst of the nations like a lamb among wolves, and in shame and reproach. All this is a profanation of [God's] name. Woe to us, for our ancestors have sinned, and we have not cleansed ourselves of this. It still stands! We weep because we brought this all about. By taking into our hearts this fasting, weeping and mourning, and by arousing our hearts to cry out: "Return to us, O Eternal, that we may return" [Lamentations 5:21], may [this] cloud be removed and dispelled, that is, may the "shell" be diminished, and may we be purified from the power of distress and regret.

Yeshaya HaLevi Horowitz (c.1570-1626), *Shnei Luchot HaBrit* (The Two Tablets of the Covenant, Deuteronomy 9:9,11) (reprint of 1863 ed.; Jerusalem: 1975), *Massechet Ta'anit*, v. 1, p. 46a.

NOTES:
**"As a result of our sins, we were exiled from our land"** ... The opening words of a prayer found in the Additional Service (*Musaf*) for the three Pilgrim Festivals (Pesach, Shavuot, Sukkot) and the High Holy Days (Rosh Hashanah and Yom Kippur).

**As if the *Shechinah* is in exile...** The notion that the *Shechinah* accompanies Israel throughout our exile goes back to rabbinic literature, and beyond, to Ezekiel's vision of the chariot of God departing from Jerusalem (Ezekiel chapter 10). Exile is thus not simply a matter of Jewish powerlessness and human suffering, but of alienation from the divine in the world.

**The serving girl has disinherited her mistress....** The serving girl represents the forces of evil, the mistress is the *Shechinah*.

**The enemy from the side of the "shell," the Other Side....** The metaphoric terms "shell" and "the Other Side" both refer to evil forces within the divine economy of the universe.

**The glorious House of the Eternal....** The Temple in Jerusalem.

COMMENT: A friend of mine complains that Tisha b'Av is overly focused on our Jewish tragedies, and ignores our responsibility for them, and even more so, our involvement of the tragedies of others. I admit that this seems to be strong tendency at work in the modern Jewish community, as if our sufferings in the twentieth century might justify whatever action we may take in our own defense. Horowitz' comments, along with those of many others since the book of Lamentations itself, suggest that we too must bear some responsibility for the persecution we suffer. We have been too callous of the rights of others, but most of all, we have ignored the divinity within our enemies. To this extent, the *Shechinah* remains in exile, even though many Jews are at home in our ancestral land.

## [86] The Orphan and the Widow

CONTEXT: Levi Yitzchak of Berditchev in the Ukraine was a disciple of the Maggid of Mezritch, and the subject of some of the loveliest and most popular tales in Hasidic literature. He was also a considerable scholar.

TEXT:

Nowadays, Zion is called an orphan and the Kingdom of the House of David is called a widow now during the exile. Therefore, everyone who has compassion upon orphan and widow is worthy of seeing the consolation of Zion and of the Kingdom of the House of David upon its foundation.

Levi Yitzchak of Berditchev (1740-1809), *Qedushat Levi* (The Holiness of Levi) (Munkacs, 1829), p. 83c.

COMMENT: In our time, we have a Jewish State, something that the Berditchever could only have dreamed of. Yet, the isolation and vulnerability of the Jewish people to which he alludes has not come to an end. Instead, it is projected onto the international stage. But this teaching comes to remind us that Jewish salvation does not ultimately depend solely on international negotiation, but on a myriad of small acts of kindness. Indeed, human salvation does too.

## [87] From Mourning to Rejoicing

CONTEXT: Although the Three Weeks are a period of communal mourning, they contain a promise of redemption and rejoicing: The Messiah is to be born on Tisha b'Av, according to rabbinic teaching. (See the *midrash Esther Rabbah*, Introduction 11 and elsewhere.) Yisrael of Ruzhyn was the great-grandson of the Maggid of Mezritch, and founder of a Hasidic dynasty that continues down to our own time. The speaker is his son and successor, R. Avraham of Sadagora.

TEXT:

My father and master said that he understood the festivals from the Three Weeks. And I say that the Three Weeks are like precious stones that grow under mountains of darkness. Even though they partake of darkness, they nevertheless contain light. When our righteous messiah comes, and "the light of the moon will be like the light of the sun" [Isaiah 30:26], then the Three Weeks will be festivals, for the Three Weeks correspond to the Three Pilgrim Festivals. The Blessed One knows the truth, because in my younger days, when I had strength, I felt a new light on each of the days of the Three Weeks. And the truth is what our sages say: "Whatever the Merciful One does is for the good." The reference is to the Three Weeks. Even though they indicate descent for Israel, nevertheless, "whatever the Merciful One does is for the good."

Yisrael Friedman of Ruzhyn (1797-1850), *Irin Qadishin* (Holy Angels) (n.p., 1885), pt. 1, p. 68.

NOTES:

**They nevertheless contain light...** Hence, precious stones sparkle.

**The light of the moon will be like the light of the sun ...** As this verse is interpreted in Talmud, *Pesachim* 68a & *Sanhedrin* 91b.

**The Three Pilgrim Festivals...** Pesach, Shavuot and Sukkot.

**"Whatever the Merciful One does is for the good" ...** A quotation from Talmud, *Berachot* 60b.

COMMENT: Tragedy is never far away, even in our comfortable homes. Illness and death can strike our loved ones or ourselves without warning. (I was particularly conscious of this fact as I was writing this during the coronavirus pandemic of 2020.) Reports of diseases, climate degradation, civil wars and international crises fill our news media. The events of the Three Weeks and Tisha b'Av seem to be played out every day before our very eyes. The Ruzhyner urges us never to lose hope, nor abandon our messianic dreams. Though we may not see, there is always light to be found in even the darkest places. We need to maintain our faith that, despite appearances to the contrary, "whatever the Merciful One does is for the good."

# [88] In Great Concealment

CONTEXT: Pinchas of Koretz was a younger contemporary of the Ba'al Shem Tov, possibly his disciple, but with an independent approach to Hasidism.

TEXT:
Wherever there is great distress, there is a revelation of the divine in great concealment. Nighttime, in all circumstances, is of the mystical nature of judgment, and particularly at midnight, for that was when the miracle of the slaying of the first-born occurred. Balaam the wicked possessed within himself one particle [of the prophecy] that Moses our teacher had, [but] in a state of great concealment. Also, on the ninth of Av, when the Temple was destroyed, there was present a particle of redemption [in great concealment]. Thus, the Messiah was born on the day. Similarly, in the case of a pregnant woman, as long as she has no birth pangs she cannot give birth. It seems to me that he also said that [the following] appears in the *Tikkunei HaZohar*: "When troubles come, in place of troubles rescue will come to Israel." And this [is the meaning of] the question *Mah Nishtanah*.

Pinchas of Koretz (1726-1791), *Imre Pinchas* (Pinchas' Sayings) (Tel Aviv: Arnberg, 1974), §692, p. 134.

NOTES:
**The slaying of the first-born occurred...** The last of the ten plagues that resulted in the liberation of the Israelites from Egyptian slavery. See Exodus 11 & 12. According to Exodus 12:29, this took place at midnight.
**Balaam the wicked...** The non-Jewish prophet hired to curse the Israelites, according to Numbers 22-24. He is frequently called "wicked" in rabbinic literature, and considered the equal of Moses, according *Bemidbar Rabbah* 14:20.
**Thus, the Messiah was born on the day...** That the Messiah was or will be born on 9 Av is asserted in *Bemidbar Rabbah* 13:5 and elsewhere.
**In the *Tikkunei HaZohar*...** Introduction, p. 70b.
**The question *Mah Nishtanah*...** The opening words of the so-called Four Questions in the Passover Seder: "Why (or, How) is this night different from all other nights?" The Koretzer is suggesting that what distinguishes the first night of Passover from other nights of the year is precisely the fact that redemption from Egyptian slavery began at the moment of the terror that accompanied the death of the firstborn.

COMMENT: Tragedy brings grief and anguish certainly, but, Rabbi Pinchas implies, opportunity as well. But his approach is not that of a Polyanna, seeing only good in the world. I believe that he recognizes that

94

we must work through our grief if we are to realize the opportunity that it presents. No event is so terrible that no good may come of it. Tragedy may unite communities and teach valuable lessons, and ultimately bring redemption.

# LAMENTATIONS

## [89] The Alphabet of Hope

CONTEXT: The opening word of Lamentations, which gives its name to the book in Hebrew, is *eichah* (alas). Its opening letter is *alef*, the first of the alphabet. In fact, it is the start of one of three single alphabetic acrostics in the book; there is also a triple acrostic, where each letter of the Hebrew alphabet is assigned three verses. Menachem Mendel of Kotzk's grandson, the editor of the earliest collection of his sayings, begins his discourse by quoting Rashi (Rabbi Shlomo Yitzchak, 1040-1105), the greatest and most popular of the medieval commentators on the Bible.

TEXT:
"Alas! (*eichah*) Lonely sits the city..."

Lamentations 1:1

In [the commentary by] Rashi, it is written: Jeremiah wrote the Book of Lamentations. It is the scroll that [King] Jehoiakim burnt in the fire in the brazier [Jeremiah 36:23]. There are three alphabetic acrostics in it, [namely]: "Alas! (*eichah*) Lonely sits..." [chapter 1], "Alas! (*eichah*) The Eternal has shamed...." [chapter 2], and "Alas! (*eichah*) The gold is dulled..." [chapter 4]. To this he added "I (*ani*) am the human being..." [chapter 3], which [contains] a triple alphabetic acrostic, as it is said: "...and many similar words were added to them" (Jeremiah 36:[32]). [So that there are] three corresponding to three.

[The Kotzker's comment begins here:] [Here is] the reason why Jeremiah took pains to put Lamentations into alphabetic order. We might say that when Jeremiah saw the destruction [of the First Temple], and the great influx of holiness that was withheld from us, he almost thought that it was impossible for Israel and the world [to continue] to exist, until his soul almost failed with the tremendous grief. [It would have failed,] had it not been for [the fact] that he saw the residue of the alphabets that we have [within us] in their [various] combinations, as described in the *Sefer Yetzirah*. Then in his mind he found for us a residue of the Torah, and this was a comfort to him. This is truly the reason why we call this month by name of *Menachem Av*. And this is also the reason why the confession is an alphabetic acrostic.

Menachem Mendel of Kotzk (1787-1859), *Ohel Torah MeiHaRabbi MiKotzk* (The Torah Tent of the Rabbi of Kotzk) (Lublin, 1909), p.70.

NOTES:

**Jeremiah wrote the Book of Lamentations...** This is the traditional view as expressed in numerous places in the Talmud and *midrashim*.

**It is the scroll that [King] Jehoiakim burnt...** Although this story is told in Jeremiah 36, the scroll Jehoiakim burnt is identified with Lamentations only in Talmud, *Moed Katan* 26a.

**Three corresponding to three...** The three chapters with single acrostics correspond to the one chapter with a triple acrostic.

**The great influx of holiness that was withheld from us...** In rabbinic and medieval Jewish literature, the Temple is frequently considered to have been a channel for divine influence to enter the world.

**The *Sefer Yetzirah*...** The Book of Formation, an enigmatic text of uncertain provenance, often considered the earliest book of Kabbalah. It depicts a world in which all things are divinely produced through combinations of the letters of the Hebrew alphabet. Human beings are also so constituted.

**Then in his mind he found for us a residue of the Torah...** In meditation, the prophet came to the realization that Torah still remained in the hearts of the people. Since the Torah is eternal, "this was a comfort to him."

**Why we call this month by name of *Menachem Av*...** The name of this month is actually *Av*, but it is the custom to call it as *Menachem Av* when announcing it during the Torah service on the Shabbat just before the New Moon at the first of the month. *Menachem* means comforter, while *Av* in Hebrew is spelled *aleph-bet*, "alphabet;" hence the phrase may be understood as: "the alphabet is a comforter."

**The confession is an alphabetic acrostic...** The reference is to the *Ashamnu* ("We are guilty"), a confession in alphabetic order recited on Yom Kippur and other occasions during the year.

COMMENT: Tragedies are an inevitable part of life. We cannot avoid them. Tisha b'Av is our primary occasion for confronting the many tragedies of our Jewish history. But, the Kotzker maintains, the Hebrew alphabet, and all the literature that flows from it, continue to offer us hope and comfort to see us through any tragedy towards better days, even to the messianic age.

# [90] Breakage and Nothingness

CONTEXT: The Maggid (Preacher) of Mezritch, in Ukraine, was a considerable scholar who effectively became the successor to the Baʿal Shem Tov as leader of the nascent Hasidic movement. The theme of "becoming nothing" is one to which he regularly returns.

TEXT:
"Her gates have sunk into the earth."

[Lamentations 2:9]

Explanation: When something is at the level of "nothing," breakage does not apply to it, because "breakage" only applies to something that is an attribute or a vessel. Thus, if a people make themselves nothing, as a result of attachment to the Creator, [it is] like a nobleman who, although the greatest of all the nobility of the kingdom, is a child in his own eyes when standing before the king. He wants no honor paid to him because of his greatness and nobility, as would be the case if he were at home on his own. For then [people] would pay him honor, and would be ashamed and frightened in his presence. However, when he is before the king, he and all his attributes are nullified because of his awe and shame in the presence of the king. Hence [Scripture says]: "Have sunk into the earth" – that is, make themselves nothing, like the earth, nothing in their own eyes. "Her gates" – that is, the attributes. And when you have no attributes at all "breakage" cannot apply to you.

Dov Baer, Maggid of Mezritch (died 1772), *Maggid Devarav LeYaʿakov* (Telling His Words to Jacob, Psalm 147:19) (Brooklyn: Kehot Publication Society, 1972), §80, p. 29.

NOTES:
**When something is at the level of "nothing" ...** The concept of nothingness has a long history in Kabbalah. Essentially, it relates to the *Sefirah* of *Keter*, which is the nothingness from which all existence flows (although the Maggid associates it with *Hochmah*, instead). *Shevirah* ("breakage") refers to the cosmic catastrophe which, according to the Lurianic scheme, resulted in the shattering of the vessels of the seven lower *Sefirot*, from *Hesed* to *Malchut*. Thus, "breakage" does not relate to the three upper *Sefirot*. But as is often the case in Hasidism, the Maggid has applied kabbalistic terminology to human psychology.

COMMENT: What does "breakage" mean at a psychological level? I would suggest it refers to the inner turmoil and trauma that we experience virtually every day: worry, doubt, inner conflict and concerns. The Maggid posits a mental state that is above such issues, a state of nothingness characterized by a total lack of ego, of self-seeking, and even of self-consciousness. If we can attain such a state, through prayer and meditation, we can look down, as it were, on all that troubled us and understand how trivial it all really is.

## [91] Affliction and the Birth of the Messiah

CONTEXT: Uri of Strelisk was a disciple of Shlomo of Karlin who later became a Hasidic leader in his own right, though without establishing a court. He was known as the *Seraph* ("burning angel") because of his ecstatic approach to prayer. In chapter 3 of Lamentations, the poet seems to take a more personal view of the tragedy of Jerusalem's destruction.

TEXT:
"I am a man who has seen affliction under the rod of [God's] wrath."

Lamentations 3:1

It was superfluous to say "who has seen affliction." However, the intention is [as follows]: It is well known that at the conclusion of Tisha B'Av the Messiah is to be born. Hence, it is written: "I am the man who has seen affliction" – that is to say, who has seen the Messiah being born, for he is called "afflicted and riding upon a donkey" (Zechariah 9:9). "Under the rod of [God's] wrath" – that is to say, they have seen that there is none like our God, and as it is written: "Sing to the Eternal, God's pious ones… for God's anger is but for a moment" (Psalm 30:5[-6]) – that is to say, when the Temple was destroyed, meaning at the conclusion of Tisha B'Av, when [God's] wrath was great, as it is written: "When the Eternal afflicted me on the day of wrath" (Lamentations 1:12). "When [God] is pleased, [there is] life" [Psalm 30:6]. At that moment, the Messiah was born, for they say that his name is in the portion of life. Hence, it is written: "who has seen affliction" – i.e., the birth of the Messiah; "under the rod of [God's] anger" – present at the moment that [God] struck with "the rod of [God's] anger." "Words spoken by the wise bring grace" [Ecclesiastes 10:12].

Uri ben Pinchas of Strelisk (the Seraph) (d. 1826), *Sefer Imrei Qadosh* (The Book of the Sayings of a Holy Man) (Netanya, 2001), pp. 83-84.

NOTES:
**It was superfluous to say "who has seen affliction" …** The text need only have said: I am a man under the rod of [God's] wrath. Therefore, there must be some other, hidden meaning to this phrase.
**The Messiah is to be born…** Talmud Yerushalmi, *Berachot* 2:4.

**"Words spoken by the wise bring grace"** ... This quotation is often added to the end of Hasidic sermons, as if to say, go away and think about this.

COMMENT: As I write (March 2020), more and more countries are limiting travel and social interactions in an effort to control and slow down the progress of coronavirus COVID-19. With its knock-on economic and social effects, this is a crisis the like of which we have never seen in living memory. It seems to be a global tragedy unfolding in slow motion. And although the illness itself is relatively mild, many people will die. But perhaps the picture is not all gloomy. Maybe out of this a new sense of global interdependence will arise, and a new, more co-operative human society emerge. Uri of Strelisk's message seems to be pointing in the same direction.


## [92] Narrow Places

CONTEXT: Yisra'el of Koznitz was a renowned scholar of Jewish law, as well as a maker of amulets and a Hasidic *rebbe*. Here he quotes his main teacher, Dov Baer, the Maggid of Mezritch, successor to the Ba'al Shem Tov.

TEXT:

My teacher... Rabbi Dov interpreted [the verse] "All her pursuers overtake her in narrow places" (Lamentations 1:3). Those who pursue holiness will attain it in extremely narrow places.
Yisra'el ben Shabbetai Hapstein, Maggid of Koznitz (1733-1814), *Sefer Avodat Yisra'el* (The Book of Israel's Service) (Jerusalem, 1998), p. 340.

COMMENT: Holiness is a demanding mistress. It may lead us to take on practices we never contemplated before, and to give up others to which we have long been accustomed. In my twenties, I gave up certain foods entirely, and began to eat others only if kosher. I took up daily prayer and study, and numerous other *mitzvot*. It was not easy to change my life, but I have never looked back since. Change is always difficult, but never impossible, if we want to badly enough.


## [93] Longing for the Messiah

CONTEXT: Little is known of the life of the author of this piece, R. Yisra'el of Bopoli. His grandfather was Nachum of Chernobyl, and his book is a recognized source of his teachings and those of others, including, as here, Dov Baer, the Maggid of Mezritch (d.1772), his grandfather's teacher.

TEXT:
It is said in the name of the great and holy preacher of Mezritch on the verse: "Bring us back, O Eternal, to You and we will return; renew our days as of old" [Lamentations 5:21]. He explained that the dispute between the Holy Blessed One and the Community of Israel is well known. For the Holy Blessed One says, "'Return O, backsliding children, to Me" [Jeremiah 3:14,22]; "Return to Me and I will return to you." [Malachi 3:7].' That is, that first there must be an awakening from below, from the Community of Israel, and then "[God] will again have compassion upon us" [Micah 7:19]. While the Community of Israel says: "Bring us back, O God of our salvation" [Psalm 85:5] – meaning, that there has to be an awakening from below beforehand to bring them back to the Blessed One, to redeem them from exile and to gather them from among the nations. Then they will return to God with a perfect heart and repair their deeds. It was for this that Jeremiah came to bring them back to the Blessed One [in] an eternal repentance when he said: "Bring us back, O Eternal, to You" – first, and then "and we will return." Look here, the truth is that first there must be an awakening from below. Concerning all this, "renew our days as of old" means, just as it was before the creation of the world, when there was no creature in the world, there was only an awakening from above, so too, [should this be the case] for the purpose of the Coming [Messianic] Future. For [God] had looked and perceived as far as the end of all generations, and had seen the pleasure that would come to [God] through the service of Israel, the holy nation. Thus, [God] made it that even now the glory of Your sovereignty could be revealed upon us quickly. And there we will serve You with awe "as in ancient times" [Malachi 3:4]. "Words spoken by the wise bring grace" [Ecclesiastes 10:12]. And may Your peace increase.

Yisra'el ben Avraham of Bopoli (?) (d. 1847), *Ateret Yisra'el* (Israel's Diadem) (Shanghai, 1957; reprint of Zhitomir, 1867), p.105.

NOTES:
**The dispute between the Holy Blessed One and the Community of Israel...** What follows is based on *Eichah Rabbah* 5:21.
**An awakening from below...** Employing kabbalistic terminology. The relationship between God and the Israel exemplifies, and is paralleled by, the interaction between the *Sefirot* of *Tiferet* and *Malchut*, known as the Holy One, blessed be He, and the Community of Israel. When Israel prays and cries out before God, when *Malchut* beseeches *Tiferet*, that is an

awakening from below. When God responds, when *Tiferet* unites with *Malchut*, that is an awakening from above.

**That Jeremiah came...** He is the traditional author of Lamentations.

**Before the creation of the world... there was only an awakening from above...** Since there were no creatures before Creation, the impulse for creation could only have come from above, from God. The plea is for God to do the same with respect to the messianic age.

**"Words spoken by the wise..."** This quotation often concludes Hasidic sermons as encouragement to heed the teachings they contain.

COMMENT: Longing for the Messianic Age has been a part of Judaism since perhaps the time of the Biblical prophet, Isaiah. Each age, with its problems and disasters, has re-awakened that longing. In this passage, the Maggid of Mezritch seems to have eschewed the bottom-up approach to bringing the Messiah. Our prayers and supplications just won't do the job, he suggests. Only a decision from God, a top-down approach, if you will, will bring the desired result. Modern Jewry takes a very wide variety of positions on the arrival of the Messianic Age. Some have given it up altogether, others (notably Lubavitch) suggest that it has already begun. Most, I suspect, relegate it to the background of their religious life. Tisha b'Av, with its tearful commemorations of the tragedies of Jewish history, asks us once again to consider it. Are there things we can do to hasten its arrival? Or is it all up to God? Perhaps it is an unattainable goal, but (I would suggest) essential to aim for nonetheless, if we are to create a better world.

# ROSH HASHANAH

The creation of light. By Gustave Doré.

# [94] The Head of the Year

CONTEXT: Even though we normally translate "Rosh Hashanah" as "the Jewish New Year," the term literally means "the Head of the Year." Is there any hidden message to be derived from this choice of words? R. Yisra'el of Sadagora was a descendant of the Maggid of Mezritch, the second leader of the Hasidic movement, and himself the founder of a dynasty that continues to the present day. Many of his sermons are dated. This passage forms part of the address he gave on the second night of Rosh Hashanah in 1887.

TEXT:

...He said: [Why do we call this holiday] Rosh Hashanah? [Because] every person should apply the "head," i.e., the brain, to the heart. That is, [everyone should] contemplate [and] examine themselves with regard to their actions, from the beginning of the year until the end of the year. Hence [the holiday is called] Rosh Hashanah ("the head of the year"), for everyone should prepare themselves and apply the "head," i.e., the brain, to the entire year.

Yisra'el Friedman of Sadagora (1853-1907), *Or Yisra'el* (Israel's Light) (1997), p. 228.

COMMENT: Rosh Hashanah, for the *rebbe* of Sadagora, is about applying the mind to the past and the future, allowing our minds to rule over our emotions. Only in this way, can we consider our lives with any hope of objectivity. Only in this way, can we truly engage in the repentance which is the hallmark of this period of the year.

# PRAYER

## [95] How to Lead High Holy Day Services

CONTEXT: Moshe of Kobrin, now in Belarus, was fatherly figure who tended to teach in parables and short pithy sayings.

TEXT:

Once he was asked: How should the leader of the service go up to pray before the Ark on the High Holy days? A parable: There was a king who was angry with a certain province, and considered punishing the people. All of the inhabitants of the province gathered together and said, "Who will go to appease the king for us, to ask for our lives?" But they could find no one in the entire province who would go to ask for mercy from the king, because they all feared for their lives lest, while speaking to the king, they spoke badly and offended the king's honor, thus rendering their lives forfeit to the king. But there was a man among them who was a criminal and a rebel against the kingdom, and he knew in his soul that his head already was forfeit to the king. So, he said, "I will go and seek compassion on your behalf, because I know that my soul is already forfeit to the king, and if I find favor in the king's eyes, then the whole province will certainly find favor in the king's eyes!" In this way, and with this intention, should the leader of the service approach the Ark on the High Holy Days to ask and to pray on behalf of the congregation.

Moshe ben Yisra'el Polier of Kobrin (1784-1858), *Amarot Tehorot* (Pure Sayings, Psalm 12:7) (Warsaw, 1910), pp. 31-32.

COMMENT: At first blush, one might have thought that the main qualities one would look for in someone to lead High Holy Day services would be fluency in Hebrew and skill in prayer leadership. Moshe of Kobrin puts paid to that. The most important quality, in his view, is humility. The best prayer leader is the one who can really pray as if they mean it. All other qualities are secondary.

## [96] Overcoming Arrogance

CONTEXT: A central feature of every Jewish service since the time of the Mishnah has been the *Amidah* (Standing Prayer), also known as the *Shemoneh Esreih* (Eighteen Benedictions) or *HaTefillah* (The Prayer). Though recited every day, the central paragraphs vary depending on the occasion. The passage below considers one of the key phrases of the *Amidah* for Rosh Hashanah. Moshe Hayyim Efraim of Sudylkov was a grandson of the Ba'al Shem Tov, the founder of modern Hasidism. A shy retiring man, he is famous for the book of sermons of which the following is an extract.

TEXT:
"For the rule of arrogance shall pass away from the earth," that is to say that it alludes to those people who seem to be righteous in their deeds, but their hearts are not right within them. Hence, it says: 'for the rule (*memshelet*) [of arrogance] shall pass away,' where *memshelet* indicates a semblance (*mashal*) and appearance of arrogance, that is, of a worthless person. In this way, we are praying that arrogance should not seem like good, but on the contrary, there should be a distinction between light and darkness, then all the inhabitants of the world shall know and understand this. May it be God's will that this occurs soon. Amen.

Moshe Hayyim Efraim of Sudylkov (d.1800), *Degel Machaneh Efraim* (The Flag of the Camp of Efraim, Numbers 2:18) (Jerusalem, 1963), p. 263.

NOTES:
**"For the rule of arrogance..."** From the third paragraph of the *Amidah* for Rosh Hashanah.
**Where *memshelet* indicates a semblance (*mashal)...** Both Hebrew words come from the root *m-sh-l* which can mean 'to rule' or 'to compare, offer a parable.'

COMMENT: In the hands the Sudylkover, a prayer that was originally aimed at unjust foreign authorities under whom Jews lived has now become a prayer against deceit in all areas of life. In this world, it is often difficult, if not impossible, to distinguish between truth and falsehood, between sincerity and deceit. And though we must strive mightily to make that distinction, things may only become clear in the messianic age.

# The *Akedah*/Binding of Isaac

## [97] Where He Was

CONTEXT: Yitzchak of Vorki was a Hasidic leader in Poland, a former disciple of Menachem Mendel of Kotzk. Here he comments on a verse from the traditional Torah reading for the first day of Rosh Hashanah. It describes the birth of Isaac and the subsequent expulsion of Abraham's other son Ishmael and his mother Hagar from Abraham's camp.

TEXT:
"For God heard [the cry of the boy] where he was."

Genesis 21:17
    It says in the *midrash*: "Said R. Simon: The ministering angels jumped up to indict him. They said to [God], You are raising a well to a man who will in the future try to kill Your children with thirst! [God] replied, I judge a person only where he is at the moment. Hence the text says, "where he was." As if to say that Ishmael was judged only with respect to the present. So too, we ask the Holy Blessed One should see us according to our deeds during the days of Rosh Hashanah and Yom Kippur, not the past nor the future, but according to the present.
    Yitzchak of Vorki (d.1858), *Bet Yitzchak* (The House of Isaac) (Jerusalem, 1992), pp. 146-147.

NOTES:

**In the *midrash*...** *Bereshit Rabbah* 53:14.

**Raising a well...** In Genesis 21:19, God makes a well appear that saves Ishmael's life.

**Who will in the future try to kill Your children with thirst...** According to *Tanchuma*, *Yitro* §5 and *Eichah Rabbah* 2:4, this occurred in the aftermath of the destruction of the Temple by the Babylonians in 586 B.C.E.

COMMENT: On the High Holy Days, we go to *shul* and (hopefully) pray and study like pious Jews, but if we are honest, we know that we are not that good the rest of the year. Still, wouldn't it be nice if God could judge us the pious, caring, concerned individuals we appear to be on those Days of Awe? And wouldn't it be even nicer if we could be what we appear to be on the High Holy Days all year long?

# [98] Sanctification

CONTEXT: Kalonymos Epstein was a Hasidic Torah commentator, a disciple of Elimelech of Lyzhansk in Poland. His commentary also includes discussions of issues raised by the main festivals, as here.

TEXT:

[In the Talmud we read:] "Said R. Abbahu: Why do we blow a ram's horn? The Holy Blessed One said: Blow a ram's horn before Me in order that I may remember the binding of Isaac son of Abraham on your behalf, and credit it to you as if you had bound yourselves before Me." ...

It is not appropriate for a person to seek martyrdom in practice, as happened to R. Akiva who was killed for the sanctification of God's name. However, you should prepare yourself with all your strength to sanctify the Eternal. And whoever is truly and joyfully prepared for this is considered by the blessed God as if they had actually done it. This is the interpretation of [the sentence]: "that I may remember the binding of Isaac on your behalf and credit it to you as if you had bound yourselves before Me" – meaning, after you have proclaimed your God as sovereign over you and you are prepared to sanctify God's name and to undergo martyrdom, [God] will remember the binding of Isaac on your behalf, even though you have not been burned in practice. "And I will credit it to you as if you had bound yourselves before Me" – [meaning,] whole-burnt offerings are made in practice, and you do not have to engage in the act itself.

Kalonymos Kalman HaLevi Epstein (d.1823), *Ma'or VaShemesh* (Lamp and Sun, Psalm 74:16) (Warsaw, 1876), *Rimẓei Rosh Hashanah*, pt. 5, pp. 34d, 35a.

NOTES:
**"Said R. Abbahu..."** Talmud, *Rosh Hashanah* 16a. The notion seems to be that the near-martyrdom of Isaac will stand to Israel's credit in hard times to come.
**As happened to R. Akiva...** This story is told in Talmud, *Berachot* 61b. The Hebrew expression for martyrdom is *kedushat ha-shem*, literally, the sanctification of the Name [of God].

COMMENT: Our Jewish martyrs are too numerous to mention. Over the centuries, countless Jews have gone to their deaths at the hands of others for their Jewish faith, or simply because they were Jews. To be a martyr is a terrible, if noble, calling. May we and our children never know such things. However, the term "martyr" doesn't really do justice to the Hebrew phrase *kiddush ha-shem* ("the sanctification of God's name"). In fact, it covers a whole range of actions of which martyrdom is only the pinnacle. Any actions that we undertake that raise the positive profile of the Jewish people and of Judaism may be *kiddush ha-shem*. What matters, as our text suggests, is we be ready to undertake them whenever they may become necessary and that we do those actions with all our strength in the service of the Holy One.

## [99] Abraham Binds Isaac for Sacrifice

CONTEXT: The Zohar, the central text of the kabbalistic tradition, discusses the binding of Isaac in several places. This is perhaps the most straightforward of those discussions.

TEXT:
This is why Abraham bound Isaac: In order to include Strict Judgment within himself, that the Left Side might be included within the Right, and the Right rule over the Left. It is for this [reason] that the Holy Blessed One commanded Abraham to sacrifice his son to Strict Judgment and to take hold of him. [God] did not command Isaac, but Abraham. This is [why] it occurred. This one is in Strict Judgment and this one in Lovingkindness, but both are one and each is contained in the other.
Zohar II, 257a.

107

NOTE:

**In order to include Strict Judgment within himself...** In kabbalistic symbolism, Abraham represents the *Sefirah* of *Hesed*, Lovingkindness, the Right Side of the sefirotic tree, while Isaac stands for *Gevurah*, Strength (but also known *Din*, Strict Judgment) on the Left Side.

COMMENT: I confess that I have never really understood why the tradition chose Chapters 21 and 22 of Genesis as the readings for the first and second days of Rosh Hashanah respectively. Both stories are deeply troubling. The first opens with the long-awaited birth of Isaac, Abraham's son with Sarah, but also includes the expulsion from the camp of the hand-maid Hagar and Ishmael, Abraham's older son born of Hagar. The second focuses on how Abraham very nearly slaughtered Isaac as an offering at God's behest. What on earth are we meant to learn from these dreadful tales of a dysfunctional family?

Inspired by the Zohar passage above, I wonder if we are not meant to understand these stories in psychological terms. Perhaps, we are being presented with two approaches to dealing with the evil within ourselves. Ishmael is frequently presented in our tradition as a violent man, based on Genesis 16:12 ("He will be a wild ass of a man"), while, as we have seen, Isaac represents *Gevurah/Din*, the divine source of evil in the world. Viewed in this light, perhaps the expulsion of Ishmael stands for the attempt to expel our evil, to project it outwards onto others. It is doomed to failure. Its result can only be destruction. The Zohar's reading of Chapter 22 suggests another course: to try to understand that the impulse for the evil we do comes from within us – not from outside, that we have to embrace that impulse, and make it submit to the love that also dwells within.

# REPENTANCE

## [100] A Question of Free Will

CONTEXT: Natan of Nemirov was a devoted follower of Nachman of Bratzlav. While the latter still lived, Natan made notes of everything he said, and after his teacher's death, collected sayings and stories from others who had known him. Here he shares a second-hand report before offering his comment on it.

TEXT:

I heard that once someone asked him: "What is the meaning of free will?" He answered him with simplicity, saying that free will is simply something within human power. If one wants to do something, one does it. If one doesn't want to do something, one doesn't.

I noted that this [teaching] was very necessary, because there are many people who are very confused about this. Since they are accustomed to behaving and acting in certain ways since their youth, they therefore imagine that they have no free will and that they are unable to change their behavior. But in truth, this is not so! For surely every person always has free will in everything, and can do what they want. Understand these words well!

> Natan of Nemirov (1780-1844) in Nachman of Bratzlav (1772-1811), *Liqqutei Moharan* (Collected Sayings of Our Teacher, the Rav, Rabbi Nachman) (Jerusalem: Meshech HaNachal, 1986), pt. II, §110, p. 42b.

COMMENT: Much ink and paper has been expended in attempting to reconcile the concepts of human free will and God's foreknowledge. Some thinkers have denied the existence of free will, declaring it to be an illusion; yet, Judaism in general and the High Holy Days in particular depend on the notion that human beings can freely decide to do good or evil. Without free will the call to repentance makes no sense. Nachman of Bratzlav cuts through all the theology and goes straight for the psychological and practical. Free will just is; we make choices every day. Work on that!

## [101] The Cause of Sin

CONTEXT: The author of this passage was a grandson of the Ba'al Shem Tov, the reputed founder of the Hasidic movement, and often quotes him in his own writings on the Torah.

TEXT:

I heard from my grandfather that the word *CHeT'* (sin) has a silent *'alef* [at the end], and the reason is that one who commits a transgression has forgotten the Ruler (*'aluf*) of the universe.

> Moshe Hayyim Efraim of Sudylkov (d.1800), *Degel Machaneh Efraim* (The Flag of the Camp of Efraim, Numbers 2:18) (Jerusalem, 1963), p. 225.

NOTE:

***CHeT'* (sin) has a silent *'alef...*** Spelled *CHet-Tet-'alef*, but the *tet* has no vowel, effectively leaving the last letter totally unpronounced.

COMMENT: I would suggest that most of our sins are not deliberate. Most of us are not trying to be mean or selfish, but our emotions and insecurities can get the better of us, leading us into behavior that in a calmer setting we would not indulge in. Perhaps, remembering that we are God's creatures dwelling in God's universe could keep us from behavior that we will regret later.

## [102] Where Does Repentance Begin?

CONTEXT: Moshe of Kobrin was a rabbi in what is now Belorus, and was known for his homespun approach to spiritual teaching. His prayer here is recorded in Yiddish.

TEXT:
Once, at the time of the [*shofar*] blowing, he was only in charge of [the reading from] the Zohar and the blessings, as was customary. In a loud voice he said, "Ruler of the universe, have mercy on Jewish souls. Open their hearts that they might undertake repentance for Your sake."
Moshe ben Yisra'el Polier of Kobrin (1784-1858), *Amarot Tehorot* (Pure Sayings, Psalm 12:7) (Warsaw, 1910), p. 31.

NOTE:
**The Zohar...** Many traditional High Holy Day *machzorim* (prayer books) offer one or two readings from the Zohar to be recited just before the blowing of the *shofar* on Rosh Hashanah. These may be found in Zohar, III,98b-100b, in the main text or the *Ra'ya Mehemna* ("Faithful Shepherd") section on the same pages.

COMMENT: For the Kobriner, repentance begins with an open heart, and that is a gift from God. With an open heart, we can begin to understand the bad that we do, and then maybe find the steps we need to undertake to put it right and avoid it in future. If our hearts are closed, we are condemned to make the same mistakes over and over.

## [103] Repentance is Like a Mother

CONTEXT: Rosh Hashanah inaugurates the period of the Jewish year known as the Ten Days of Repentance. Mordechai of Neshchiz was a Hasidic teacher in Ukraine, and a disciple of both the Dov Baer, Maggid of Mezritch and Yechiel Michal, Maggid of Zlotchov.

TEXT:

"Repentance is called the supernal mother." On this, the holy *gaon*, the holy one of Israel and its light, head of the *Bet Din* of the holy community of Neshchiz said: Why is it called this? Because, just as a small child hides under the skirts of their mother to hide from a scolding poised above them, so too do those who return in repentance hide with her from those who would accuse them of the treachery they have committed. And then they would be rescued from any punishment.

Mordechai of Neschiz (1752-1800), *Rishpei Esh* (Coals of Fire, Song of Songs 8:6) (Jerusalem, 1997), §161, p.82.

NOTES:

**"Repentance is called the supernal mother"** ... Zohar III, 278b. In the context of the Zohar, this is a reference to the *Sefirah* of *Binah* (Understanding). On the one hand, one of its designations is *Imma* (Mother), as opposed to *Hochmah* which is known as *Abba* (Father). On the other hand, *Binah* is also known as *Teshuvah* (Repentance) since we need to understand what we have done before we can repent of our sins.

**The holy *gaon*....** A term normally reserved for exceptional scholars.

**The *Bet Din*...** Rabbinic court.

COMMENT: A child's misbehavior does not disappear when the child runs to its mother and embraces her. The child is protected, and yet, the wise mother still chastises the child, but gently, encouraging the little one to say sorry. Our sins do not disappear when we repent, but their nature is transformed, and so are we. We become better, purer, more spiritual.

## [104] Mutual Trust

CONTEXT: In the Jewish religion, *emunah*, usually translated as "faith," plays a central role. But faith may not be the best way to understand this term. Perhaps more useful would be "trust." But is "trust in God" the only spiritual understanding of this central concept? Yisra'el of Sadagora, a descendant of the Maggid of Mezritch and leader of one of the largest Hasidic groups in the nineteenth century, spoke the following as part of a sermon he delivered the year on the second night of Rosh Hashanah 1886.

TEXT:

...In truth, it all depends on trust, for Israel trusts that the Holy Blessed One will forgive their sins, while the Holy Blessed One trusts that Israel will repent and correct their deeds...

Yisra'el Friedman of Sadagora (1853-1907), *Or Yisra'el* (Israel's Light) (1997), p. 227.

COMMENT: That God has faith seems a paradoxical, radical, perhaps even nonsensical statement. But maybe the meaning is that, if we follow R. Yisra'el's interpretation, then *emunah* (faith) becomes reciprocal. Perhaps the lesson derives from our human relationships. Our deepest commitments are often to those we trust and who trust us in return. Our faith/trust in God is pointless, unless God, as it were, can depend on us to try to do the right thing.

## [105] Repentance through Unity

CONTEXT: Aharon II (his grandfather, the founder of the Karliner dynasty, was also called Aharon) brought his community to the height of its influence in Lithuania.

TEXT:
On the evening of Rosh Hashanah he said that it is impossible to accept this holy day except through friendship (*Rei'ut*), as it says: "It is a day of blowing (*teRu'ah*) [the *shofar*] for you" [Numbers 29:1]. It is only possible to accept it through unity and friendship. Hence it is written, "On [day] one of the seventh month" which alludes to [the notion] that everything is through oneness. Hence, it is written: "On that day, the Eternal will be one and [God's] name one" [Zechariah 14:9]. For it is certain that there is no doubting [God's] oneness and there is no need to say that everything is through oneness. Take care to understand.

Then he said: It is only through joy and calmness of mind, for it is through joy that the mind is purified, and the essence of repentance is [achieved] through a pure mind.

Aharon (II) ben Asher of Karlin (d. 1872), *Bet Aharon* (Aaron's House) (Brody, 1875; reprinted Jerusalem, 1990), p. 263.

NOTES:
**"On [day] one of the seventh month" ...** Apparently, a misquotation of Leviticus 23:24 or Numbers 29:1. The point is that both verses say "one" rather than "the first," though it is frequently translated that way.

COMMENT: Much of our High Holy Day liturgy seems intended to instill in us the fear of God. The Karliner points us in a different direction, towards unity on the social and spiritual levels, and this too is an important element of Rosh Hashanah and Yom Kippur. We come together in our communities in perhaps the most intensive and spiritual experiences of the Jewish year. Perhaps it is only through this powerful mix that we can enter into the spiritual clarity of which he speaks here. In Judaism, social unity is conducive to spiritual unity.

# THE *SHOFAR*

## [106] In All Our Limbs

CONTEXT: After the death of his friend and teacher, Simchah Bunam of Pshische in 1827, Menachem Mendel of Kotzk set up as a *rebbe* in his own right in the town of Tomashov (Tomaszow) before settling in Kotzk two years later. He was a great believer in passion in religious observance.

TEXT:
On the first Rosh Hashanah in Tomashov, before the blowing of the *shofar*, our rabbi said: [The blessing speaks of God who] "commanded us."

[This means:] This commandment should enter into all our limbs, so that one who hears it will be moved by it when remembering it forty years from now!

Menachem Mendel of Kotzk (1787-1859), *Sefer Amud Ha'Emet* (The Book of the Pillar of Truth) (Bnei Brak, 2000), pp. 178-179.

COMMENT: We live in a world of noise and sound of all kinds. Sound is everywhere, and amplified in comparison with what earlier generations experienced. There is so much noise on our city streets and in our homes that it is sometimes difficult to recognize which of them might be important. The sound of the *shofar* is meant to be different. We should feel it penetrating into our very being, as it were. It should move and inspire us, cutting through the noise that fills our lives to the center of our being.

## [107] The *Shofar* and Fear

CONTEXT: Pinchas of Koretz, in Ukraine, was a younger contemporary of the better known Ba'al Shem Tov. His teachings are often presented in the form of conversations or oral reports.

TEXT:
It is said in the name of Sa'adia Gaon that the *shofar* [is meant] to produce fear. Therefore, small children are afraid of the sound of the

*shofar*, but not of [other] musical instruments. Thus, it is appropriate to feel fear, and as soon as one does so, the *Shechinah* (Presence of God), is elevated. Hence, [the verse]: "God ascends with [the *shofar*] blast" [Psalm 47:6].

Once he spoke in the synagogue before the [*shofar*] blowing and brought the crowd to extreme tears. When he returned home, he said to us that the reason was this: We speak before the [*shofar*] blasts in order to make the people listen. When someone listens, their soul is gathered to themselves, [the *shofar* blower] takes their souls and with them, blows on the *shofar*, thus elevating their souls. And he said to us that one cannot explain this to others, because it is higher than words, as if one wanted to show a person [something], but could only show it with the head or the hand. This is similar. A person who is ill, while in pain, cannot say how they hurt, but [can only] moan in a sound without words [like] ah! Similarly, the *shofar* is a sound without words. Then he said, "If I had only entered this world to make this matter known, it would have been sufficient."

Pinchas of Koretz (1726-1791), *Imre Pinchas* (Pinchas' Sayings) (Tel Aviv: Arnberg, 1974), §571, p. 115.

NOTES:
**Sa'adia Gaon…** Sa'adia ben Yosef Al-Fayyumi (892-942) was an early medieval Jewish philosopher, renowned scholar and *gaon*, head of the academy, of Pumbedita in Babylonia, modern Iraq. This teaching in his name may be found in David ben Joseph Avudarham, *Sefer Avudarham* (Amsterdam, 1726), pp. 100a-b.
**"God ascends with [the *shofar*] blast" [Psalm 47:6]** … This Psalm is recited just before the blowing of the *shofar* in the Torah service on Rosh Hashanah. The Hebrew for "ascends" is often understood as "is exalted," or the like.

COMMENT: *Shofar* blower and congregation are in a symbiotic relationship. Each needs the other. The congregation needs to hear the *shofar* to fulfil their obligation on Rosh Hashanah; the *shofar* blower needs the congregation because making the *shofar* heard is itself a *mitzvah*. What point would there in the blowing of the *shofar* with no one to hear? Hence, the blower's blessing "Blessed are You… who makes the *shofar* heard." But beyond this, as R. Pinchas suggests, the *shofar* is a wordless cry, a deep sigh of pain, that raises our souls and unites us with God in an embrace that is beyond the capacity of words to express.

## [108] Not Even Poverty

CONTEXT: R. Zusya of Hanipol, a disciple of the Maggid of Mezritch, is most well-known nowadays for the lovely, even simple, stories told about him. In them, he usually appears as one of God's fools.

TEXT:

Once on the day of Rosh Hashanah, before the blowing of the *shofar*, our teacher R. Zusya ran out of his house of study and immediately went outside. There, in the middle of the street, he met a poor lad, homeless and abandoned, nearly naked, barefoot and hungry. The rabbi said to the lad, "Are you not jealous of the Gentile lad coming towards you who has all good things, food, drink and nice clothes?" The lad replied, "Let him have what he has! I, with the help of God, am a Jew and I trust in God." Immediately, [the rabbi] went back to the house of study and began to declare the merits of Israel before the *shofar* blowing. He cried out and said, "Ruler of the universe, who is like Your people Israel? This poor hungry lad lacks everything. Yet he accepts it all. He does not want to change his faith." By declaring the merits of Israel, the gates of mercy were opened for all Israel.

(Meshullam) Zusya (Zusha) of Hanipol (d. 1800), *Butzina Qadisha* (The Holy Lamp) (Lodz, 1931), p. 35.

COMMENT: How fervent is our commitment to Judaism? Rosh Hashanah often serves as a reminder of how much we have let our commitment slip over the past year. Will it also inspire us to take our commitment more seriously in the year just begun? The boy in the story would not give up his Jewish identity for riches or security. What things get in our way?

## [109] Stimulating God

CONTEXT: Many texts are devoted to expounded the meaning of the three sequences of *shofar* notes that go to make up the blowing of the *shofar* on Rosh Hashanah. *Sefer HaQanah* is an anonymous kabbalistic text from the late fourteenth century, but attributed to the R. Nechunyah ben HaQanah, an ancient scholar quoted in the Mishnah. The book presents itself as a dialogue between student and teacher.

TEXT:

[My teacher] said to me: My son, listen and pay attention to the point of Rosh Hashanah, and afterwards, you may speak. Know that the Holy Blessed One directs [God's] creatures through the divine attributes, whether strict judgment or compassion. This is [what is meant by the phrase] "He browses among the lilies" [Song of Songs 2:16,6:3]. The lilies [represent] the supernal *Vav* which alludes to the six extremities. When [God] has compassion on the creatures, it is through one of the routes of compassion, namely *Hesed* (Lovingkindness), but at a time of [divine] anger, it is through one of the routes of strict judgment (*din*), namely *Pachad* (Fear).

This is [the meaning of] the blowing of the *shofar* from which emerges either strict judgment or compassion: *teru'ah* and *shevarim* are strict judgment; *teki'ah* is compassion. So, we stimulate the Holy Blessed One's attributes, to make [God] treat us well....

> Anon. (14th century), *Sefer HaQanah* (The Book of [Nechunyah ben] HaQanah) (Jerusalem, 1998), p. 159.

NOTES:

**The supernal *Vav*....** Of the four-letter unpronounced divine name of *YHVH*. *Vav* has a numerical value of six.

**Which alludes to the six extremities....** Meaning, the six *Sefirot* from *Hesed* to *Yesod*, clustered around *Tiferet*. "He browses among the lilies" thus means that divine energies from above focus on one or the other of these six *Sefirot*, particularly, *Hesed* or *Gevurah*.

**Namely *Pachad* (Fear)....** An alternative designation for *Gevurah* (Strength), also known as *Din* (Strict Judgment).

**The blowing of the *shofar* from which emerges either strict judgment or compassion....** At one level, the *shofar* sounds represent the opposite branches of the sefirot tree, which produce either positive or negative effects below.

***Teru'ah* and *shevarim* are strict judgment; *teki'ah* is compassion...** Of the three sequences of *shofar* blasts, *teki'ah* is the most common. Thus, the three represent both sides of the sefirotic tree and their reconciliation, but we hope to stimulate *Hesed*, rather than *Gevurah*.

COMMENT: Life is uncertain. Good fortune can transform into bad in an instant. If we are religious, we acknowledge our ultimate dependence on God. If we are inclined towards Kabbalah, we recognize that the world and the divine are in a symbiotic relationship: what we do here affects the divine realm of the *Sefirot*, and that, in turn, impacts on the world here. Viewed from this perspective, hearing the *shofar* with proper concentration thus becomes a recognition that all comes from God, and a prayer that good things will predominate.

# [110] Blasts of Love

CONTEXT: There are three distinct sequences of notes for the blowing of the *shofar* on Rosh Hashanah, known as *tek'iah, shevarim, teru'ah*. These are blown in set patterns at four points during the morning and additional services. R. Levi Yitzchak of Berditchev was a great scholar and student of the Maggid of Mezritch. He was famous for his love of ordinary Jews.

TEXT:

"*Tek'iah, shevarim, teru'ah, teki'ah*" – *TeKi'ah* is a term indicating "love," as in the expression "if he [accidentally] had sexual intercourse (*niTKa'*) with his sister-in-law," for love comes from the Holy Blessed One first, through Israel, for Israel serves God in truth and love. Then, when Israel serve God in love, they shatter (*meSHaBeRim*) the inclination towards evil which wants to lead Israel to evil (*lehaRea'*), but Israel shatters it. Hence, *SHeVaRim TeRu'ah*, shattering the inclination towards evil that wants to lead Israel to evil. After that, more love comes from the Holy Blessed One. Hence, [we have] *teki'ah* at the end.

> Levi Yitzchak of Berditchev (1740-1809), *Qedushat Levi* (The Holiness of Levi) (Munkacs, 1829), p. 94b.

NOTES:

"***Tek'iah, shevarim, teru'ah, teki'ah***"... At each of the four points in the traditional Rosh Hashanah morning and additional services, these are the first four sequences that are blown.

"***TeKi'ah* is a term indicating "love," as in the expression "if he [accidentally] had sexual intercourse (*niTKa'*) with his sister-in-law...**" Both *TeKi'ah* and *niTKa'* seem to come from the same Hebrew root *T-K-'*, meaning "to blow [a horn]" or "to insert." The quotation is based on Talmud, *Yevamot* 54a. It is interesting that even an incestuous (and therefore forbidden) relationship is seen as indicating love.

**They shatter (*meSHaBeRim*) the inclination towards evil...** The name *SHeVaRim* suggests a link with the root *SH-V/B-R* meaning 'to break, shatter.'

**Which wants to lead Israel to evil (*lehaRea'*)...** The word *lehaRea'* seems to suggest a connection with *TeRu'ah*, though grammatically speaking, the roots of both words are quite different.

COMMENT: For the Berditchever, the sequence "*Tek'iah, shevarim, teru'ah, teki'ah*" indicates, God's love for Israel (*teki'ah*), which when reflected by Israel in acts in love towards God, destroys the inclination towards evil (*shevarim teru'ah*), and this results in more love from God. In other words, these four represent the ideal reciprocal relationship between God and the Jewish people. We are always the objects of divine love.

117

When we reflect that love back to God (and to God's creatures), we subdue that part of us that would do evil through selfishness, and stimulate yet more love. We thus create a virtuous circle of love and goodness.

## [111] Becoming a Divine Instrument

CONTEXT: Hearing the *shofar* (ram's horn) blown on Rosh Hashanah is perhaps the most distinctive feature of this festival. Traditionally, it is blown at four points during the service: once during the Torah service, and three times during the *Musaf* (Additional) service. Each of these occurrences consists of a series of three different sounds, which will be discussed below. Dov Baer, the Maggid (Preacher) of Mezritch, succeeded the Ba'al Shem Tov as leader of the nascent Hasidic movement in late eighteenth century Ukraine. From his teachings, it is clear that he was a considerable kabbalist as well as a powerful and influential teacher.

TEXT:

A parable before the *shofar* blasts: There was a great and splendid monarch who sent the royal children to hunt for game, but the children strayed from the path, and called out. Perhaps their father would hear, but there was no reply. So, they said to themselves, Perhaps, we have forgotten our father's language, and therefore, he does not hear our cry. Therefore, let us cry out in a loud voice without words. So, they designated one of their number to cry out, and admonished him: Realize and understand that we are all dependent on you.

Here is the meaning: The Holy Blessed One has sent us to elevate sparks of holiness, but we have strayed from our Parent. Perhaps we have forgotten our Parent's language, so that we are unable to pray [properly] with words. So, we send you, our *shofar* blower, to awaken mercy for us in a loud sound without words. Realize and understand that we are all dependent on you.

Nevertheless, hold yourself as naught, because you are like a drum made of skin, with holes, and it is because of the holes that it becomes a musical instrument. Does the skin pride itself that the musical sound comes from it? So, should it be with you. Thought, speech and all attributes rest within you, as within a vessel. How can you take pride in that? By yourself you are nothing! You contain only negative attributes, and you are obligated to elevate them to the Holy Blessed One, Who may pass judgment against them - God forbid – and clothe you in the shells, as it were – God forbid – may God preserve us! But if it enters your mind that you are serving God, then you are worse than before.

118

Dov Baer, Maggid of Mezritch (died 1772), *Torat HaMaggid* (The Preacher's Teaching) (edited by Israel Klepholtz) (Tel Aviv: Pe'er HaSefer, 1969), v. 2, p. 8.

NOTES:

**Sparks of holiness....** According to the kabbalistic teachings of R. Yitzchak Luria, as a result of a cosmic catastrophe known as "the breaking of the vessels," there are sparks of divinity scattered throughout the world awaiting liberation through our prayers and observances.

**But if it enters your mind that you are serving God....** The true service of God is totally devoid of thoughts of self.

COMMENT: Sometimes we use our piety as a means towards greater status in our community, or towards enhancing our notions of self-worth, but for the Maggid of Mezritch, this is a trap. We need to take our egos out of the equation, for if we use piety in these ways, we are really serving ourselves, and not God.

# YOM KIPPUR

The Holy of Holies, lithograph by J.R. Jones.

# [112] Praise and Criticism

CONTEXT: Although this saying, attributed to the founder of the modern Hasidic movement, is not directly on the theme of Yom Kippur, I felt it addresses a central question of this day, namely: where does responsibility for our failures and achievements lie?

TEXT:
From the Ba'al Shem Tov: If people want to praise, let them praise the Holy Blessed One. But if they want to criticise, let them criticise themselves. For one who praises acknowledges unity and is honoured; the contrary is true of one who belittles and criticises, for [such a person] is separated from unity.

Yisra'el ben Eliezer, Ba'al Shem Tov (1700-1760), *Keter Shem Tov* (The Crown of a Good Name, Pirkei Avot 4:13) (Brooklyn: Kehot Publication Society, 1972), §54, pt.1, p.8a.

COMMENT: Some people have a habit of blaming others for their own failings: their partners, colleagues, fate, God. And many of us give ourselves credit for things we have accomplished that may be the result of other people's efforts more than our own. The Ba'al Shem Tov teaches us a spiritual way of accepting blame, and giving credit where credit is really due.

# [113] Trusting Ourselves

CONTEXT: R. Nachman of Bratzlav was the only leader of this Hasidic group that has continued to this day without a centralized leadership. Along with Chabad (Lubavitch), Bratzlav Hasidism specializes in outreach to other, non-Hasidic Jews.

TEXT:
On the subject of avoiding a spiritual fall as a result of many mistakes and the damage that one has caused through one's actions, [Rabbi Nachman] spoke and said: "If you believe you can damage [things], then believe that you can repair [them]."

Nachman of Bratzlav (1772-1811), *Liqqutei MOHaRaN* (Collected Sayings of Our Teacher, the Rav, Rabbi Nachman) (Jerusalem: Meshech HaNachal, 1986), pt. II, p.42b, §112.

COMMENT: The Day of Atonement seems to be fixated on sin in all its forms. If we do not take care, it can leave us depressed, with a sense of guilt and futility. R. Nachman asks us to believe that just as our sins are real, so too is our ability to overcome them and put them right. Surely, that is the ultimate message of this holiest of days.

## [114] Subduing the Will

CONTEXT: Nachman of Bratzlav was the great-grandson of the Ba'al Shem Tov and probably one of the most original thinkers in the history of Hasidism.

TEXT:
"Your eyes saw my unformed substance; [in Your book were written all] the days that were formed [for me, and one of them was His]."

Psalms 139[:16]

Every day is a formation in its own right. "And one of them is His" [i.e., God's] – this is Yom Kippur, as explained by Rashi. This is the fast that gives life to all the days [of the year], for Yom Kippur is the sum total of all days. Of it, it is said: "On this very day, you shall afflict your souls." This refers to the will, as it is written in the Zohar... "[this is] to join together every body and soul and to submit on this day, and that their will will be with the Holy Blessed One..." For the soul is an aspect of the will, and the essential thing is: to make the will submit. Hence, "on this very (*eTZeM*) day" – through the internal essence (*aTZMiyyut*) of the day which includes all days "shall you afflict [your souls]."

Nachman of Bratzlav (1772-1811), *Liqqutei MOHaRaN* (Collected Sayings of Our Teacher, the Rav, Rabbi Nachman) (Jerusalem: Meshech HaNachal, 1986), pt. 1, §179, p. 109.

NOTES:
**"And one of them is His" [i.e., God's]** ... This is the interpretation demanded by Rabbi Nachman's comment. The JPS translation (2003) says that the meaning of this phrase is "uncertain."
**Rashi...** The great medieval Bible commentator, 1040-1105.
**"On this very day, you shall afflict your souls"** ... A conflation of Leviticus 16:29 and 23:28.
**"To join together every body and soul..."** Based on Zohar III, 68b.

COMMENT: At one level, Yom Kippur is like any other day. The sun rises and the sun sets. Life goes on. But for most Jews, even many who are not particularly religious, Yom Kippur is different. It is a day dedicated to prayer and to thinking about our lives. In that sense, perhaps it does include all days, as R. Nachman suggests.

122

# FASTING

## [115] Why We Fast

CONTEXT: Little is known of the life of Meir ibn Gabbai. He probably lived in Turkey and was perhaps the most important writer of Kabbalah between the expulsion from Spain (which he may have experienced) and the rise of the mystics of Safed. The work from which this passage derives is devoted to discussions on prayer.

TEXT:

The essential secret of fasting is, above all, [that you are] an altar established to atone for your sins. By diminishing eating and drinking, your fat is diminished, and you offer that diminution in your prayer before God. Thus, when towards evening, when weakness in the limbs is overpowering you, a fire burning in your foundations is kindled, not extinguished, to consume and diminish your fat and blood.

Meir ibn Gabbai (1480–after 1540), *Tola'at Ya'akov* (O Worm, Jacob, Isaiah 14:14) (Jerusalem, 1996), p. 124.

NOTE:

**Foundations...** This might refer to the four "elements" of medieval thought: earth, air, fire and water. All four were thought of as present in all physical entities in various combinations.

COMMENT: In English, the word "sacrifice" has connotations of giving something up for a higher cause. In Hebrew, one of the key words for sacrifice is *korban* from the root meaning "to approach." Here, I believe, both concepts are in play. Fasting on Yom Kippur, for ibn Gabbai, is about sacrificing something of ourselves, of our bodies in fact, in order to approach God in a more elevated and devoted way than we may do the rest of the year.

# THE EVENING SERVICE

## [116] Lie No More

CONTEXT: Some communities have the custom of reciting psalms before the *Kol Nidrei* (All Vows), the opening ritual of this holiest day of the Jewish year. In the literature that emerged from the Hasidic community founded by Pinchas of Koretz, a younger contemporary of the Besht, "the Rav" always indicates R. Pinchas himself.

TEXT:
Concerning the Rav: Once, on the eve of Yom Kippur, everyone was shouting and carrying on a great deal as [they chanted] psalms before Kol Nidrei. The Rav turned towards the people and said: "What is going on? You are shouting, but the words are not ascending, because all year long you tell lies. So how words rise from [your] mouth like this...? And how can I speak to you in this way? Because I am engaged in this very thing!"
Then he explained that there is nothing more difficult to completely give up than this, and yet you can. Therefore, take upon yourselves [the obligation] not to tell lies, then there will be an ascent of the *Shechinah*, and your prayers will ascend.
Pinchas of Koretz (1726-1791), *Imre Pinchas* (Pinchas' Sayings) (Tel Aviv: Arnberg, 1974), §616, p. 122.

NOTES:
**"And how can I speak to you in this way? ..."** What gives me the right to speak to you like this? Like you, I am trying to avoid lies. A remarkably honest statement from the rabbi.
**Then there will be an ascent of the *Shechinah*, and your prayers will ascend...** In the Lurianic Kabbalah, the *Shechinah* (another name for the lowest of the *Sefirot*, usually called *Malchut*), must ascend to meet her "lover," the *Sefirah* of *Tiferet*, in order to achieve cosmic union that produced positive benefits for the world. Avoiding lies will produce spiritual benefits, both cosmic and personal.

COMMENT: We cannot know if our prayers really "ascend," but we can tell if they seem to flow from our lips. Yom Kippur is meant to be a trying time, not just in terms of fasting, but in terms of delving into our behavior and attitudes without excuses. And the fact is, as R. Pinchas says, we are all prone to lying, if only so-called "white" lies, where our intentions are good, but our words are still false. Perhaps the way to avoid white lies is to refrain from speaking at all. Not easy!

# [117] Changing Nature

CONTEXT: The traditional Yom Kippur service is punctuated with many *piyyutim*, liturgical poems of medieval origin inserted at certain points. *Ki Hinneh KaChomer* ("As clay in the hand of the potter") is sung during the service on the eve of Yom Kippur. Its author is unknown.

Hayyim of Kosov succeeded his father Menachem Mendel as leader of the Hasidim of Kosov.

TEXT:
"As clay in the hand of the potter... so are we in Your hand, O You who show kindness...." For Israel has the power to change nature with their potential, just as they wish, if they do God's will. For this is the purpose of creation: [it was done] for the sake of Israel and for the sake of Abraham our father by way of [the interpretation of] *hibar'am* ("when they were created"). Hence, "as clay in the hands of the potter, so are we" – we have it in our power to change nature, because [God] "shows kindness" from the beginning of creation. Thus, Jeremiah says: "Like clay in the hand of the potter, so are you in My hands, O house of Israel" [Jeremiah 18:1], for they have the power to change nature, but only if they do God's will.

Hayyim ben Menachem Mendel of Kosov (1795-1844), *Torat Hayyim* (The Torah of Life) (Haifa: 2004), p. 210.

NOTES:
**"As clay in the hand of the potter..."** The opening words of this *piyyut* for Yom Kippur evening. But R. Hayyim turns the meaning of the poem on its head by understanding it as if it meant that we are like the potter, rather than the clay!

**For the sake of Israel...** The notion that Creation came about for Israel's sake may be found, for example, in *Bereshit Rabbah* 83:5.

*Hibar'am* **("when they were created")** ... From Genesis 2:4: "These are the generations of heaven and earth when they were created." According to a *midrash* recorded in *Bereshit Rabbah* 12:2, HiBar'aM alludes to Abraham (*'aVRaHaM*) because both contain the same consonants.

**"Shows kindness"** ... *Notzer chesed*, another phrase from the *piyyut*.

COMMENT: In Hayyim of Kosov's day, the notion that we have the power to change nature must have seemed utterly revolutionary, perhaps even unbelievable. In our times, we have discovered that we have indeed changed nature, and not always for the better. We have learned to control and even eradicate many diseases, for example, but we are destroying the environment. But did the Kosover foresee this? Probably not. His intention was undoubtedly spiritual, rather than materialistic. If we can change our spiritual lives so that we care for each other with more concern and interest, we will change the world for the better. Our potential for changing the physical world is not exhausted; our potential for changing the spiritual world is largely untapped.

# CLEANSING

## [118] Clean Before the Eternal

CONTEXT: Shalom of Belz, known as *Sar Shalom* (Prince of Peace), was the founder of the Belz Hasidic dynasty, once powerful in Poland and still continuing today. He was a disciple of the Seer of Lublin. Here he comments on a verse that occurs in the traditional Torah reading for Yom Kippur morning, and is frequently repeated throughout the day.

TEXT:
"For on this day, atonement shall be made over you to cleanse you; from all your sins before the Eternal you shall be cleansed."

Leviticus 16:30

A question [may be posedhere] because it should have said "[atonement shall be made] *for* you." We must say that if someone sins they do not just harm their soul, but [cause harm] in all the upper worlds. Hence it says: "atonement shall be made over you," for as soon as you create an opening [the size] of the eye of a needle for repentance, [then] you are repairing whatever harm you have done, even in the worlds that are above you, and the upper worlds will aid you by "cleansing you from all your sins," then "before the Eternal you shall be cleansed;" that is to say, first it is incumbent upon you to return in perfect repentance for any harm you caused, and then, help will be granted from above [for you] to be made clean before the Eternal.

> Shalom Rokeach of Belz – Sar Shalom (d. 1855), *MaHaRaSH MiBelza* (Our teacher, the rabbi, Shalom of Belz) (Israel Klepholtz, ed.) (Bnei Brak, 1987), pt. 2, pp. 74.

NOTE:
**"[Atonement shall be made] *for* you"** ... Rather than *"over* you," as the text literally says. He answers his question with reference to the upper worlds of kabbalistic thought.

COMMENT: Our actions, for better or for worse, have an impact well beyond their immediate sphere. Physical and material damage may be made good, but psychological damage may remain. How much thought do we give to the spiritual damage our negative actions, or inaction, may cause?

# [119] Sins into Merits

CONTEXT: Leviticus 16 is the primary Torah reading for the morning of the Day of Atonement, but the verse quoted below (v.30), is repeated throughout the day in every occurrence of the *Amidah*. R. Yisra'el of Ruzhyn, a descendant of the Maggid of Mezritch, moved his headquarters to Sadagora in Hungary after suffering persecution by the Tsarist regime in Russia. Most of his sermons are dated. This was delivered on the night of Yom Kippur, 1903.

TEXT:
"For on this day atonement shall be made for you to cleanse you; from all your sins before the Eternal you will be cleansed."

Leviticus 16:30

[I shall interpret] along of the lines of what R. Zevi of Berditchev said about [our sages'] teaching "The first thing is to assess your transgressions." For when Israel repent out of love, "premeditated sins are considered merits." So, they search out their transgressions in order to turn them into merits.

Hence [it says]: "For on this day atonement shall be made for you to cleanse you," punctuated with an *etnachta*, "from all your sins before the Eternal you will be cleansed" – that is, when you repent out of love, and awaken the [divine] attribute of compassion, then "from all your sins you will be cleansed," for your premeditated sins will be turned into merits....

Yisra'el Friedman of Sadagora (1853-1907), *Or Yisra'el* (Israel's Light) (1997), p. 246.

NOTES:
**R. Zevi of Berditchev...** A younger contemporary of the *rebbe* of Sadagora, died 1934.
**"The first thing is to assess your transgressions"** ... Quoted from the *Midrash Tanchuma*, *Emor* chapter 23.
**"Premeditated sins are considered merits"** ... A quotation from Talmud, *Yoma* 86b.
**Punctuated with an *etnachta*...** This is the name of one of the *ta'amim* or *neginot*, the signs indicating the punctuation and chanting of biblical texts in printed editions. *Etnachta* marks the end of a clause, and acts rather like a semicolon. Hence, R. Yisra'el's comment dividing the verse in two.

COMMENT: Why do we repent? Perhaps we are afraid of consequences if we don't. Perhaps we just feel guilty and this seems an easy way out of our guilt. R. Yisra'el suggests that we repent out of love. If we hurt someone we love, we don't just feel bad and let it go. We want to do something to say sorry and make it up if we can, because we love that person and want to restore things to the way they were. Our relationship with God should be like that. We should repent because we love God and really want to put our relationship right again.

# CONFESSION OF SINS

## [120] Why is There No Answer?

CONTEXT: At the end of each of the five occurences of the *Amidah*, the five sets of benedictions that make up the liturgy of Yom Kippur, there are a series of confessions of sin. One of these, perhaps the longest is a list of sins for which we ask forgiveness, each beginning with the word *al chet* ("for the sin of…") or *ve'al chet* ("and for the sin of…"). Another presents us with an alphabetic acrostic beginning with *Ashamnu* ("we are guilty"). Simchah Bunam, perhaps the most modern of nineteenth century Hasidic leaders, asks: why are all these prayers for forgiveness not answered?

TEXT:
 Why, on Yom Kippur, do we recite so many confessions and *al chet*s without being answered or being informed that the Eternal has set aside our sins? But when King David said that he had surely sinned, he was immediately told by Nathan the prophet, who said: "the Eternal also sets aside your sin" (II Samuel 12:13). Because King David had said "I have sinned" [meaning] "I have sinned, so do with me according to Your will," and he accepted the judgment upon himself lovingly, because "You, O Eternal, are righteous" – this was true repentance. Therefore, he was immediately forgiven.
 This is not so of us. As soon as we say: *Ashamnu* ("we are guilty") we imagine in our souls that [the Eternal] will certainly forgive us, and when we say: *Bagadnu* ("we have acted treacherously") we think that by this everything good will have to come to us. And therefore, this is not perfect repentance.
 Simchah Bunam of Pshischa (1765-1827), *Midrash Simchah* (Jerusalem: Mossad HaRYM Levin, 1988), v. II, p. 233.

COMMENT: On his death-bed, the great French philosopher Voltaire, not a traditional Christian believer, was asked if he thought that God would forgive him for his sins. He is said to have replied, "Oui, c'est son métier!" ("Yes, it's His job!"). Simchah Bunam would not have considered this proper repentance. For him, repentance eschews arrogance. It involves throwing ourselves entirely on God's mercy.

## [121] Choosing Your Sin

CONTEXT: On Yom Kippur, each of the five occurrences of the *Amidah* is followed by confessions of sin, of which the *Al Chet* ("For the sin we have committed before You by...") is one of the best known. Pinchas of Koretz was a popular Hasidic leader in Ukraine. He was younger than the more famous Ba'al Shem Tov, and may have been marginally influenced by him.

TEXT:

On the subject of the *Al Chet* [prayer], he explained that there are many [of the individual confessions] among them that just [involve] a simple movement.

"[For the sin we have committed before You] by hardheartedness." In its plain meaning, this applies only to [the giving of] charity, but [actually it applies] in all things....

"[For the sin we have committed before You] by confessions of the mouth." The meaning is: we say the confession only with our mouth, but the heart is not engaged with it.

"[For the sin we have committed before You] by turning the neck, by glancing with the eye." This just [involves] a turning movement or a seeing.

Then he said that in his opinion, it would be good for each person to choose one *Al Chet* in any case, and take a strong grasp on that, for all of them are too difficult to take proper care over....

Pinchas of Koretz (1726-1791), *Imre Pinchas* (Pinchas' Sayings) (Tel Aviv: Arnberg, 1974), §622, p. 123.

NOTES:

**On the subject of the *Al Chet*....** This confession consists of a list of statements each beginning with the words *Al Chet* ("For the sin...").

**Just [involve] a simple movement...** Actually, R. Pinchas comments more widely on this prayer than this opening sentence suggests.

**In all things...** Hardheartedness may manifest as an unwillingness to be charitable, but it can infect our entire being and influence all our actions.

**But the heart is not engaged with it...** On the surface this sentence of the *Al Chet* addresses the issue of hurtful words, but the Koretzer takes it to mean hypocrisy, the gap between the words we say and the things we do.

**A turning movement or a seeing...** Even simple movements like these can be sinful depending upon the circumstances and our motives. Turning the head and looking with lustful eyes, for example.

COMMENT: The *Al Chet* presents us with a formidable list of sins for which we seek divine forgiveness. For a few of these, the Koretzer demonstrates their deeper significance. I was particularly struck by the final suggestion of this piece. The full list may seem impossible to ever atone for adequately. R. Pinchas tells us to focus on one, and be truly repentant for that. Attempting to address the entire range of sins may merely disperse our spiritual energies too thinly.

## [122] Sin & Repentance Have No End

CONTEXT: Yitzchak of Vorki was a disciple of Menachem Mendel of Kotzk. Here he puts forward his view of the alphabetic acrostics that form such an important part of our confessional prayers on this holiest of days.

TEXT:
"We are guilty. We have acted treacherously. We have stolen..."

Why is this confession, along with the *Al Chet* prayer, arranged alphabetically? That people may know when to stop. If they were not arranged in the way, we would not have known when to stop feeling remorse, because sin has no end, and repentance has no end. But the alphabet has a beginning and an end.

Yitzchak of Vorki (d. 1858), *Bet Yitzchak* (The House of Isaac) (Jerusalem, 1992), p. 146.

NOTES:
**"We are guilty. We have acted treacherously. We have stolen..."** The first three words of the alphabetic confession: *Ashamnu, Bagadnu, Gazalnu...*
**The *Al Chet* prayer...** This confession is not so obviously alphabetic. The relevant letters occur only towards the end of each line. In fact, it is a double acrostic.

COMMENT: It can become very easy to be overwhelmed by our sins. There seem to be so many of them that sensitive souls can feel weighed down by them. They are a constant feature of the lives of anyone who attempts to live by an ethical code, because we cannot fail to fail sometimes. And each sin requires repentance. There would seem to be no end to this cycle, and depression may ensue. Alphabetic confessions, in

130

Yitzchak of Vorki's view, may help us to set limits to our yearly fixation with our sins and assist us in setting them aside so we can move on.

## [123] Insincere Confession

CONTEXT: Yeshaya Horowitz was a communal rabbi in Prague and Krakow, and author of one of the most comprehensive and popular Jewish books of his era.

TEXT:

It is certain that someone who confesses then slides back, then does not break their heart within them at the moment of confession, [such a person] experiences double punishment, for it is as if they had gloried – God forbid – in what they had done and as if they had said: Who is my ruler? This is the meaning of what is written in the *Al Chet* ("For the sin...") prayer: "For the sin which we committed before You for confessions of the mouth" – that is to say, it was in the mouth, but not in the heart...

> Yeshaya HaLevi Horowitz (c.1570-1626), *Shnei Luchot HaBrit* (The Two Tablets of the Covenant, Deuteronomy 9:9,11) (reprint of 1863 ed.; Jerusalem: 1975), *Massechet Yoma: Hilchot Teshuvah*, v. 1, p. 65b.

NOTE:
*Al Chet* (**For the sin...**) ... A double acrostic confession where each line begins with the words *Al Chet* (for the sin) or *Ve'al Chet* (and for the sin).

COMMENT: Each of the five services that constitute the liturgy for Yom Kippur includes confessions of sin. What is their purpose, if not to help us bring to mind our wrongdoings? And if reading them does not achieve that, and make us realize that we have something to repent for, then what good are they? They only work if we pay attention and open our hearts to the meaning of their words.

## [124] Emptying the Vessel

CONTEXT: In this teaching, the founder of the Belz Hasidic dynasty considers what confessing our sins on Yom Kippur might achieve.

TEXT:
"Behold, I am like a vessel full of shame and confusion."
> [From the end of the Yom Kippur *Amidah*]

Perhaps this may be interpreted positively, for all the transgressions that we commit are not because the power of evil is impressed upon our bones, but [that power] is only like something that fills a vessel. So, it is possible to empty it and leave the vessel as before. Similarly, we have the power from You to expel revolting things from the midst of us, and to cleanse and purify ourselves. Then we may serve You with a perfect heart as in days of old.

> Shalom Rokeach of Belz – Sar Shalom (d. 1855), *MaHaRaSH MiBelza* (Our teacher, the rabbi, Shalom of Belz) (Israel Klepholtz, ed.) (Bnei Brak, 1987), pt. 2, p. 75.

NOTE:
**As in days of old...** A phrase from Malachi 3:4 meaning, in Israel's ancient past.

COMMENT: We may be forgiven for imagining that Yom Kippur is a sad, dour occasion. There is so much emphasis on our sins and our failures, and even our martyrs. Frequently, we are made to consider the unfathomable spiritual distance that separates us from our God, a distance made greater by those very sins and failures. And yet for all its apparent negativity, the Day of Atonement is really a joyful festival (or should be). The essential message of it is that if we truly repent we can be released from all our sins. The Belzer has taken one particularly negative phrase from one of the confessions that mark this day and turned it on its head. Far from making us depressed at how sinful to the core we are, he encourages us to consider that if we are filled with sin now, we can empty ourselves of those sins. We are not bad people, but good people who have done bad things.

## [125] Why the Confessions are in the Plural

CONTEXT: Yehudah of Regensburg was the first great teacher of the Hasidei Ashkenaz, the pietists of thirteenth century Germany. This passage is from the primary text of that group, attributed to him.

TEXT:
It is written: "We have sinned, we have done wickedly" (Daniel 9:15). He [Daniel] includes himself with the totality, for all Israel are responsible for each other, as it is said of Achan: "And that man did not perish alone in his iniquity" (Joshua 22:20). Thus, we have to beseech [God] in the plural: "Forgive us, our Parent, for we have sinned." And when we recite the confession, we say: "For the sins for which we deserve stoning, burning, beheading or strangulation." And even though a person

may be aware that they have not personally done this, they are nevertheless obligated to recite the confession in this way, because all Israel are responsible for each other. Furthermore, it is so that a guilty person should not be ashamed to recite the confession.

> Yehudah ben Shmuel HeHasid of Regensburg (d.1217), *Sefer Hasidim* (The Book of the Pious) (Reuben Margoliot, ed.) (Jerusalem: Mossad HaRav Kook, 1957), §601, p.391.

NOTES:
**All Israel are responsible for each other…** Talmud, *Sanhedrin* 27b.
**Achan…** The story of Achan is told in Joshua 7. It is a tale of a man who took spoil from a Canaanite town that had been put under the ban, i.e., everything within it was to be destroyed. As a result, he and his entire family were executed in punishment. Hence, its relevance to the notion of mutual responsibility among Jews.

COMMENT: On Yom Kippur, are we being asked to utter false confessions to things we have not done? It would appear so, yet the confessions are in the plural for a reason. It's all about joint responsibility. As members of a faith group, or a society, what one does affects us all.


# *AVODAH* – THE HIGH PRIEST'S SERVICE


## [126] A Goat for Azazel

CONTEXT: This teaching comes from the *Ra'ya Mehemna* (Faithful Shepherd) section of the Zohar. The shepherd is meant to be Moses, and the author offers kabbalistic interpretations of the commandments contained in the Torah. Here, he deals with the command for the High Priest to designate a goat (the scapegoat) for Azazel, apparently a demon, and send it out to wilderness bearing the sins of the people on Yom Kippur. (This injunction is found in the traditional Torah reading for Yom Kippur morning, Leviticus 16, and forms a central theme of the *Musaf* (Additional) Service.)

TEXT:
This commandment (44) is for the High Priest to perform the service on that day as required by sending the goat to Azazel. The secret of this… is in order to separate him [Azazel] from the holy people and [so that he will] not to search out their sins before the Sovereign, so that he should not accuse them. For he has no power or authority unless the

anger from above is dominant. And by that gift he is turned into an advocate for them...

Zohar, *Ra'ya Meheimna*, III,63a.

NOTES:

**Unless the anger from above is dominant...** This anger stems from the *Sefirah* of *Gevurah* (Strength), also known as *Din* (Strict Judgment). *Gevurah* can turn to anger when rules are not strictly adhered to, and that anger can become the dominant influence coming into this universe from the realm of the *Sefirot*. This in turn gives authority to negative forces, such as the demon Azazel, to punish.

COMMENT: I find this a most extraordinary passage. It would appear that our author views the goat for Azazel as a gift, an offering, to a demon. Normally, of course, offerings to demons are strictly forbidden! (See Leviticus 17:7 "that they may offer their sacrifices no more to the goat-demons(!)" – JPS translation.) Perhaps we need to view this from a psychological perspective. Maybe Azazel represents that part of ourselves that is prone to act wickedly, selfishly, unthinkingly. We cannot remove it from ourselves, banish it to the wilderness. But we can acknowledge its presence within us, and maybe occasionally, carefully, give it its due, the better to control it. Trying to repress it totally only means that it will break out more destructively at inappropriate times.

## [127] Saying the Name Explicitly

CONTEXT: The *Musaf* (Additional) Service on the Day of Atonement rehearses the progress of the High Priest in ancient times as he made confession on behalf of himself, the Levites and priests, and the entire people. R. Kalonymos Kalman was one of the primary Hasidic teachers in Galicia, and the first in Krakow. He was a disciple of Elimelech of Lyzhansk, among others, and the book from which the following is taken is a central Hasidic text. Mainly framed as a Torah commentary, it also includes discussions on the festivals, as here.

TEXT:

"When the priests and the people who were standing in the courtyard heard the honourable and awesome Name emerge explicitly from the mouth of the High Priest in holiness and purity, they would bow, prostrate themselves and fall on their faces... And even he would pray with intention, in accordance with those reciting the blessing, by concluding with the Name... And say to them 'you shall be cleansed'."

[Leviticus 16:30]

We have to consider why it was only on Yom Kippur that [the people] would prostrate themselves when they heard the Name from the mouth of the High Priest. In the Temple, did they not hear the Four-Letter Name [pronounced] as it is written from the mouth of the High Priest [on all other days of the year]? So, why did they not bow [on those other days]? We also need to know why the word "explicitly" [is employed]. It seems superfluous, for it is well known that in the Temple they would make mention of the Name only explicitly. So, it would have been sufficient for [the text] to have said: "the honourable and awesome Name emerge from the mouth of the High Priest…"

But the fact is that on other days of the year, even though the righteous are performing unifications (*yichudim*) and the worlds are ascending, nevertheless, the light of *Keter* (Crown) is not revealed – except at Yom Kippur. For then the light of the Supernal Crown is revealed to them and shines over them [throughout] the whole day. And it cleanses Israel on that day, as it is said: "For on that day atonement will be made for you to cleanse you… before the Eternal you shall be cleansed (*tit-haru*)" [Leviticus 16:30]. The word *TiT-HaRU* alludes to *Keter* because its letters have the numerical value of 620, the same as that of *Keter*. Therefore, many kabbalists are of the opinion that one should say the *Kedushah* [that opens with the word] *Keter* in the morning service on Yom Kippur. Thus, [on] all [other] days of the year there was no bowing when the Name was explicitly pronounced because there was no great unification at all. But on Yom Kippur, when the High Priest mentioned the honourable and awesome Name with intention in order to draw down the light of *Keter*, [there was]. Therefore, [we] have to bow because of the greatness of its holiness and the power of its brilliance which is beyond conception. Hence, [this is] the explanation [of the words] "[when they] heard the honourable and awesome Name emerge explicitly from the mouth of the High Priest" – i.e., they heard the Name from the mouth of the High Priest [spoken] with the intention of drawing down the [light of] the Supernal Crown. The word *MFoRaSH* (explicitly) alludes to *Keter*, because *MFoRaSH* and *KeTeR* have the same numerical value. And so, they bowed, because it would not have been possible [to stand] without bowing [and] falling on their faces because of the greatness of the holiness and the power of the brilliance of the Supernal Crown which is beyond conception.

And it says after this: "And even he would pray with intention, in accordance with those reciting the blessing, by concluding with the Name…" – that is to say, by unifying the Name with this intention: to draw down the holiness of *Keter*. Hence, he says "shall you be cleansed" – i.e., when he said "shall you be cleansed" to them he was intending to draw down the light of the holiness of the Supernal Crown that it may shine upon them. [And this is] alluded to in the word *tit-haru*, as mentioned above.

Kalonymos Kalman HaLevi Epstein (d.1823), *Ma'or VaShemesh* (Lamp and Sun, Psalm 74:16) (Warsaw, 1876), *Rimzei Yom HaKippurim*, pt. 5, p. 38c.

NOTES:

**"When the priests and the people…"** A direct quotation from the *Musaf* for Yom Kippur, itself quoted from Mishnah, *Yoma* 6:2.

**Four-Letter Name [pronounced] as it is written…** Utilizing its actual letters YHVH with its proper vowels, rather than substituting the word *Adonai* as we do. Mishnah *Sotah* 7:6 tells us that in the Temple the priests would pronounce the name as written, but not outside its precincts.

**The righteous are performing unifications (*yichudim*)…** This refers to the kabbalistic practice of mentally combining divine names in order to produce positive effects in the sefirotic realm.

**The worlds are ascending…** I.e., each of the four worlds of kabbalistic theory are entering into higher, more spiritual realms as a result of the *yichudim* the righteous perform.

**The light of *Keter* (Crown) is not revealed…** *Keter* is the highest, most remote, of the Ten *Sefirot*. Normally, it is too remote for us to access, but the especially holy nature of Yom Kippur may permit us to gain access to its light, its influence.

**And it cleanses Israel on that day…** The light of *Keter* cleanses Israel of all its sins because it represents God's absolute and unalloyed compassion.

**Its letters have the numerical value of 620, the same as that of *Keter*…** *TiT-HaRU* = 400 + 9 + 5 + 200 + 6 = 620; *KeTeR* = 20 + 400 + 200 = 620.

**The *Kedushah* [that opens with the word]** … The *kedushah* is the third section of the *Amidah*. The Sefardi version for the morning service opens with the words: "A crown (*keter*) do the heavenly host of angels above, and Your assembled people Israel below, give to You." Many kabbalists and Hasidim have adopted so-called *Nusach Ari* prayer books which incorporate many Sefardi elements.

***M'FoRaSH* and *KeTeR* have the same numerical value…** *M'FoRaSH* = 40 + 80 + 200 + 300 = 620.

COMMENT: On the scale of holiness, Yom Kippur is the highest ranked of all our festivals, higher even than Shabbat. From a kabbalistic perspective, therefore, it would make sense for it to be represented by the highest of the *Sefirot*, Keter. (R. Kalonymos was not the first to make this connection.) And the *Avodah*, the service of the High Priest, is the highest point of this highest day. If we follow the line of reasoning presented here, we are being encouraged to seek the highest spiritual level, the level of *Keter*, from which to view our lives and our society. At this level, there is total inclusivity and absolute compassion. May we retain those lessons as we return to the world at the end of Yom Kippur.

# SUKKOT

Wood Carvings of Sukkot Customs - Dated 1 January 1662.

# [128] The Festival of the *Sukkah*?

CONTEXT: Zevi Elimelech of Dinov was a key Hasidic *rebbe* in Galicia and Hungary in the nineteenth century, having been a disciple of a number of great *rebbes* including Menachem Mendel of Rymanov. This passage comes from his magnum opus.

TEXT:

This festival is called "the festival of *sukkot* (booths)" in the Torah (Leviticus 23:34), because of the commandment that is carried out on this festival. But how are we to understand why it is referred to by the plural term Sukkot, and not with the singular [as] the festival of *Sukkah*? ... Our rabbis have taught... that even the righteous do not all have similar faces, [let alone personalities]. Therefore, the festival is known by a plural term, the Festival of Sukkot, because no *sukkah* is like another...

Zevi Elimelech of Dinov (1785-1841), *Benei Yissachar* (The Sons of Yissachar, I Chronicles 12:33) (Jerusalem, 1983), v. 2, pp. 39d-40a.

NOTE:
**Our rabbis have taught...** *Bemidbar Rabbah* 21:2.

COMMENT: For years I had a hand-made wooden frame on the patio in my garden, and each year, after Yom Kippur, my wife and I (and the children when they were at home) would decorate it. It was quite unique, I'm sure. Then I noticed that the wood was rotting, and at a more advanced age, I no longer had the energy to re-build it. So, we bought a *sukkah* kit: a metal frame with canvas covers. Not quite so unique, any more, as there are probably thousands of these around the world. Still, we make sure to personalize it. Especially with art work by our grandchildren. A *sukkah* isn't just a *sukkah*; it's a personal, family or communal expression of our faith and devotion. And thus, each one is as unique as those who build and decorate it.

# [129] The Season of Our Rejoicing

CONTEXT: Written by a secret follower of failed messiah Shabbetai Zevi, this anonymous work on the festivals still retains great popularity in Hasidic circles.

TEXT:

In the evening, when the Festival [of Sukkot] is sanctified, the righteous rejoice happily before God, and revel in joy because this pilgrim festival is the time for rejoicing, for our prayer book calls it *z'man simchateinu*, "the season of our rejoicing." It is fitting for everyone to set aside any kind of anxiety or sadness, and to gird themselves with joy and a good heart. As a result, the Place of Joy will be aroused above...

> Anon. (17th century), *Chemdat Yamim* (Most Precious of Days) (Jerusalem, 2004), Sukkot, chapter 4, p. 375.

NOTES:

***Z'man simchateinu...*** This term occurs in the *Amidah, kiddush* and *Birkat HaMazon* (Grace after meals) for Sukkot.

**The Place of Joy...** Probably the *Sefirah* of *Malchut* (Sovereignty), identified as the *Shechinah*, the Presence of God.

COMMENT: Joy is a much-underrated emotion. The United States Declaration of Independence proclaimed the right to the "pursuit of happiness," but sometimes the pursuit gets in the way of happiness. Joy is a central element in kabbalistic psychology, and many writers encourage us to experience it, particularly on Shabbat and festivals. Sukkot is singled out in this regard because it is the only one of the festivals where the Torah commands us to rejoice in three places (Leviticus 23:40, Deuteronomy 16:14.15). We often think of joy as personal or social, but the *Chemdat Yamim* urges us to consider its cosmic dimension. Our joy may reverberate up to, or in harmony with, the *Shechinah*.


# THE DATE OF THE FESTIVAL


## [130] The Timing of Sukkot

CONTEXT: Sukkot comes hot on the heels of Yom Kippur, with just four days in between. Why so soon? *Sefer HaPeli'ah* is an anonymous kabbalistic work presented in the form of a dialogue between a student and a teacher, both unnamed, but traditionally the latter is identified as the mysterious teacher of the Mishnah period, Nechunyah ben HaKanah.

TEXT:

> I said to [my teacher], "Why does Sukkot come [almost immediately] after Yom Kippur?"
>
> He replied, "[Yom] Kippur atones for Israel's transgressions, and as for Sukkot, what does it teach? Whether I say it [stands for] the supernal wisdom or the lower wisdom, it is [represented by] a house, and a house offers shelter; hence [Scripture] says that Sukkot should be after Yom Kippur. That is to say, after [the people] have received atonement, they are fit to take refuge in the shelter of the Holy Blessed One, as it

says: '[One who dwells in the secret of the Most High] may take refuge in the shelter of the Almighty' (Psalm 91:1)."

> Anon. (14th century), *Sefer HaPeli'ah* (The Book of Wonder) (Jerusalem, 1997), p. 107a.

NOTES:
**The supernal wisdom (*Hochmah*) or the lower wisdom (*Hochmah*)...** The upper Wisdom is the *Sefirah* of *Hochmah*, the lower is *Malchut*.
**Wisdom ... is [represented by] a house...** See Proverbs 9:1 "Wisdom has built her house."

COMMENT: True joy is not the same as laughter or levity. It comes from a much deeper place within us, or, in kabbalistic terms, from a higher plane, in the realm of the *Sefirot*. And to attain to true joy, our anonymous teacher suggests, we need first to cleansed of our sins. Through our repentance and atonement, we come to dwell "in the secret of the Most High." If we have achieved this at Yom Kippur, we can attain the true joy that Sukkot represents.

## [131] Happy are We After Yom Kippur

CONTEXT: Meshullam Feibush Heller was an early Hasidic leader, having studied with a number of teachers, including Dov Baer, the Maggid of Mezritch. This is passage is from his main work.

TEXT:
> Happy are they, and "happy are we, how good is our portion" that the Blessed God has chosen us and granted us amazing advice about each thing in its time, for after these days [of Rosh Hashanah and Yom Kippur] have passed, the festival of Sukkot begins. It is as our sages have said...: "His left hand under my head" (Song of Songs 2:6) – from Rosh Hashanah until Yom Kippur, and from Yom Kippur until Sukkot "his right hand embraces me" (Song of Songs 2:6) ...
> The fact is that after the supernal judgments, known as the "left hand," against us have been sweetened up above, the joy of the Blessed God may be revealed to us, for the root of joy is in the beginning of the purification of the soul before the Blessed God through repentance. However, at the time of repentance, the thing was hidden, because the heart was broken, but later on, the pleasure and joy are revealed. Hence, [the prayers refer to] "the festival of Sukkot, the time of our rejoicing."

Meshullam Feibush HaLevi Heller of Zbarazh (d. 1785), *Yosher Divrei Emet* (Upright Words of Truth, Ecclesiastes 12:10) (Bnei Brak, 2004), pp. 168-169.

NOTES:
**"Happy are we, how good is our portion"** ... A phrase quoted from the Morning Prayers and Blessings.
**As our sages have said...** See Zohar III, 214b.
**The supernal judgments, known as the "left hand"** ... The *dinim* (judgmental forces) stem from the *Sefirah* of *Gevurah* and the other *Sefirot* on the left side of the Tree. These forces have been "sweetened" above through our sincere repentance.

COMMENT: Sometimes our emotions need to catch up with reality. We occasionally experience a time lag between our social and personal lives and our emotions. Old angers and frustrations can linger long after their causes have been dealt with. On the other hand, joy may be delayed following the cause of that joy. This is what the *rebbe* of Zbarazh is suggesting. Yom Kippur is meant to be a joyous occasion, but we may be so intent on delving into our sins and our repentance that we may miss the joy that comes from knowing that our sins are forgiven. That, our teacher proposes, is the point of Sukkot, just a few days later.

## [132] Still in Yom Kippur Mode

CONTEXT: Rafael of Bershad was the main disciple and successor of Pinchas of Koretz. Here we get a brief glimpse into his personality. (The context in the book from which this passage comes indicates that the speaker is Rafael, not Pinchas.)

TEXT:
For three days after Yom Kippur, the aura of Yom Kippur remains, and thus, because of the aura of Yom Kippur, the Holy Blessed One [continues to] forgive the transgressions of Israel. Then on the eve of the festival, [we] are busy with the *sukkah* and *lulav*, and therefore, the first day of the festival is the first day of the [new] reckoning of transgressions. Then he said that we should believe that for three days after Yom Kippur he did not hear what [people] said to him. He did not hear as if they were speaking to a piece of wood!

In Pinchas of Koretz (1726-1791), *Midrash Pinchas* (Pinchas' Interpretation) (Jerusalem, 1971), p.48.

COMMENT: So, it appears that Rafael of Bershad was so moved and uplifted by the Yom Kippur experience that he was unable to engage in normal conversation until Sukkot. This put me in mind of the story in the *Shivchei HaBesht* (In Praise of the Ba'al Shem Tov), the earliest collection of Hasidic tales to be printed. The Ba'al Shem Tov was unable to talk with people about ordinary matters because of his total attachment to God, until he learned how to combine the two, and remain attached even while speaking of mundane matters. Although Hasidism is very much centered on the community, there is a recognition that spirituality seems to require a degree of social isolation from time to time. Perhaps there is a lesson here for those of us who are addicted to our online devices.

## [133] Even the Days Before are Special

CONTEXT: Yom Kippur is the tenth day of Tishri; Sukkot begins on the fifteenth. What is the status of the eleventh, twelfth, thirteenth and fourteenth of the month. On the surface, they are just ordinary weekdays. To the anonymous author of *Chemdat Yamim*, they are more than that.

TEXT:
The early [sages] said that the four days between Yom Kippur and the festival of Sukkot should be remembered and observed as sanctified days, for they are sanctified by heaven in several ways: first, by virtue of being the days between two holinessess, the holiness of Yom Kippur and that of Sukkot, and thus, they are like *chol ha-mo'ed*, the intermediate days of a festival. And secondly, because on them, every person of Israel is involved with holiness, with the commandments of *sukkah*, *lulav* and the four species, and these activities bring a person to remember the Eternal their God, to cleave to God, and to rejoice in a spiritual way in serving the Eternal with joy and a good heart...
Anon. (17th century), *Chemdat Yamim* (Most Precious of Days) (Jerusalem, 2004), v. 3, p. 334.

NOTE:
**The early [sages]...** It is not clear to whom our author is referring, or even if there is a genuine source for the statement that follows.

COMMENT: If, as the *Chemdat Yamim* says, the days between Yom Kippur and Sukkot are not really ordinary, it raises a question (at least in my mind): Are there any really ordinary days for religious people, for those of us seeking spirituality? Surely all our "ordinary" days are sandwiched between other, "holy" days, just like these days between Yom

Kippur and Sukkot. It is up to us to infuse our "ordinary" days with holiness too.

## THE *LULAV*

## [134] The Lesson of the *Lulav*

CONTEXT: The waving of the *lulav* (the palm frond), with the rest of the Four Species (*etrog* – citron, *aravot* – willow and *hadas* – myrtle), on each of the seven days of Sukkot is one of the primary *mitzvot* of this festival. Moshe ibn Machir was a kabbalist and head of a *yeshiva* near the kabbalistic center of Safed in the sixteenth century. His book was instrumental in spreading kabbalistic ideas and practices throughout the Jewish world.

TEXT:

The commandment of the *lulav*. The object of this *mitzvah*, and the intention of it, is to unify the Name of Heaven with all your heart and with all your soul. Thus, *LULaV* [can be divided into two words and read as] *LO LeV* ("he has a heart"), that you may be wholehearted [in devotion] to your Heavenly Parent. And just as the *lulav* has all its leaves joined into one so that it all makes one bundle, with division [but] in total unity, so too should a person join together all their ideas and thoughts and turn all toward one place, and not to turn their thoughts here and there. Hence, [Scripture] says: "Be wholehearted with the Eternal your God" [Deuteronomy 18:13]. That is to say, let all your thoughts be turned towards one place, and in this way, you will be wholehearted and complete in your service and awe [of God] …

Moshe ibn Machir, *Seder HaYom* (The Order of the Day) (Warsaw, 1876), p.91.

NOTE:

**Toward one place…** Perhaps, an oblique reference God; a rabbinic term for God is *ha-makom*, the Place.

COMMENT: Our minds are constantly flitting from one object to another, with thoughts popping in and out, sometimes unexpectedly. We are so easily distracted, blown off course. Just take a brief moment to notice what is going on in your head and you will know this to be true. But all religious and spiritual traditions are united in their belief that true spiritual work can only be accomplished if we can concentrate our minds and focus our thoughts. Ibn Machir presents the *lulav* as a symbol of this desirable concentration and focus.

## [135] The Embrace of God

CONTEXT: Shneur Zalman of Liady was the founder of the movement we know as *Habad* or Lubavitch Hasidism. This passage comes from his collected sermons, rather than his more philosophically-inclined opus, known as the *Tanya*. Here he discusses the meaning of the *sukkah* and the practice of waving the *lulav* with its four species in the six directions, each day during Sukkot (apart from Shabbat).

TEXT:

Through this supernal repentance there is revealed from the depths of the heart on Sukkot an aspect of "and his righthand embraces me" [Song of Songs 2:6, 8:3]. For the supernal right hand is an aspect of the great love that is high above reason and revealed knowledge, and gives light below when the heart is open, that there might be no separation from the Blessed One. Hence, "embraces me," the way one embraces a friend so that he should not leave. [And this occurs] through the *sukkah* which is like a shade, as in the verse: "The Eternal is your shade [at your righthand]" [Psalm 121:5], and through the shaking of the *lulav*, for the four species that make up the *lulav* allude to the Four-Letter Divine Name. So, [when] we wave [the *lulav*] we bring [the divine name] to mind – for everything that occurs [comes] to the heart in order that it may be illumined and revealed in the human heart. Hence, we shake [the *lulav*] in the six directions, up, down and the four compass points, because the Blessed God is one in heaven and on earth and in the four directions, and because God is "the place of the world," as it says: "Look, here is a place with Me" [Exodus 33:21]. We have to continuously cause that aspect of oneness to enter the heart, so the Eternal may [truly] be one, dwelling and revealed within it, that there may be one in one...

> Shneur Zalman of Liady (1746-1813), *Liqqutei Torah* (Torah Gleanings) (London: Kehot Publication Society, 2002), Sermons on *Shmini Atzeret*, p. 87, col. a-b, §3.

NOTES:

**Through this supernal repentance...** In the previous paragraph, Shneur Zalman discusses how on Yom Kippur repentance enters the deepest regions of the human heart, i.e. mind. This in turn produces the love that is symbolized by the embrace of God and the soul, alluded to in the Song of Songs.

**For the supernal right hand...** A reference to the *Sefirah* of *Hesed*, Lovingkindness.

145

**To the Four-Letter Divine Name...** Unpronounceable, transliterated as *YHVH*.
**Everything that occurs [comes] to the heart...** Everything we experience contains spiritual lessons.
**We shake [the *lulav*] in the six directions** ... Because the Blessed God is one in heaven and on earth ... As taught in the Talmud, *Sukkah* 37b.
**God is "the place of the world"** ... *Bereshit Rabbah* 68:9, where the verse that follows here is quoted in support.

COMMENT: At first sight, waving the *lulav* seems a bizarre practice, but Shneur Zalman of Liady suggests that it serves as a reminder of God's presence in all things, and that underlying all multiplicity is a divine unity. For him, this is not a merely a philosophical or theological position. On the contrary, it must enter the heart; we have to assimilate it and make it part of ourselves. The unity of God is there to be experienced and lived, not merely thought about.

## [136] External and Internal Light

CONTEXT: Mordechai of Chernobyl succeeded his father Nachum, a disciple of the Maggid of Mezritch, and founder of what became a large and disparate dynasty of Hasidism down to our own day. Here, he discusses the kabbalistic significance of the two most unique features of this festival, dwelling in the *sukkah* and waving the *lulav*. (The text is peppered with references of Hayyim Vital's *Peri Etz Hayyim*, and another compendium of *kavvanot*, kabbalistic meditations on rituals, which I have omitted.)

TEXT:
This is the secret of the *sukkah* and the *lulav*. The *sukkah* [represents] the "surrounding light" ... while the *lulav* represents the "internal light." The *sukkah* is the surrounding light, according to the phrase "and spread over us the shelter (*sukkah*) of Your peace," where "over us" indicates the surrounding light. The *LULaV* is the internal light [because its letters spell] *LO LeV* ("he has a heart") ... Thus, [many people] have the custom of waving the Four Species in the *sukkah*..., in order to unite the aspect of the internal light with that of the surrounding light. Similarly, even when we wave them in the home, the space that remains between the *lulav* and the wall represents the surrounding light... Then when you are attached to the heart [i.e. concentrating], you should intend to make the illumination of the surrounding light enter into the internal light, so that a unification of the surrounding light and the internal light may be born...

Mordechai of Chernobyl (d.1837), *Liqqutei Torah* (Torah Gleanings) (Jerusalem, 2001), p. 179.

NOTE:

**The "surrounding light" ... the "internal light."** ... These represent two complementary forces at work in the kabbalistic universe. The first, said to be greater, represents the transcendent divine power that encompasses all things, while the second refers to divine energy concentrated within finite beings.

**"And spread over us..."** From the service for the Eve of Shabbat.

COMMENT: The surrounding light suggests God's creative presence throughout the universe, while the internal light brings to mind the notion of divinity within oneself. Divine transcendence on the one hand, divine immanence on the other. Viewed in this way, the Chernobyler urges us to understand that in fact these two are one, and that the twin practices of Sukkot, dwelling in the *sukkah* and waving the *lulav*, together symbolize that oneness. Surely, that is implied by the central Jewish religious teaching of the unity of God. Whether in nature, in history, or in the depths of our soul, all that we perceive is the activity of the one God.

## [137] The Message of Sukkot

CONTEXT: The book *Chemdat Yamim*, written by a Sefardi supporter of the failed messiah Shabbetai Zevi, proved very popular in Ashkenazi communities as well. It provides many kabbalistic prayers, meditations and moral lessons on the festivals of the Jewish year.

TEXT:

The essential point of the commandment of the four species and the waving [of them that] comes on this holy festival is that it [the festival] is entirely filled with forces of kindness, intended to conquer the forces of judgment that have been dominant from Rosh Hashanah to Yom Kippur.

Anon. (17th century), *Chemdat Yamim* (Most Precious of Days) (Jerusalem, 2004), v. 3, p. 354.

NOTES:

**Forces of kindness...** In Hebrew, *chasadim*, the forces that stem from the *Sefirah* of *Hesed*, Lovingkindness.

**Forces of judgment...** *Dinim*, the forces that stem from *Gevurah* (Strength), also known as *Din*, Strict Judgment.

COMMENT: Hasidim use the terms *chasadim* ("forces of kindness") and *dinim* ("forces of judgment") to describe what they see as divinely influenced emotional states that we all regularly go through. We may experience a feeling of well-being, happiness, and this is the result of the forces of kindness, while sadness, depression, and so forth are the result of the forces of judgment. These are not just individual or group feelings; the festivals tend to induce these feelings in us. The Ten Days of Repentance are days of judgment, when we consider the highest moral and spiritual goals Judaism sets for us, and how far short of them we have fallen. Sukkot, on the other hand, is a week-long festival that celebrates God's kind acts, specifically, the autumn harvest and Israel's successful passage through the wilderness between Sinai and the Promised Land.

There is a deeper message here that the *Chemdat Yamim* is alluding to. The two types of forces that the author refers to are not confined to the Tishri festivals. We experience each of them from time to time, but they all stem from the same divine Source, and although their relative strengths constantly fluctuate, they tend towards balance. And balance is a key goal of the kabbalistic approach to Jewish practice, if not of Judaism itself.

## THE *SUKKAH*

## [138] Doing the Opposite

CONTEXT: The anonymous author of *Chemdat Yamim* discusses the question of why, when autumn weather looms, we go to sit out in our *sukkot* when the rational thing might be to stay indoors. Though written by a follower of false messiah Shabbetai Zevi, this book remains popular in very Orthodox circles.

TEXT:

Every person should concentrate on this when sitting in their *sukkah*, and inform the members of their household: that we leave our homes for the *sukkah*, whereas it is the practice of everyone else for each person to enter their homes from their [summer] shelters because of the cold that takes over in the [second] half of *Tishri*. But we do the opposite in order to fulfil the command of the blessed Creator....

Anon. (17th century), *Chemdat Yamim* (Most Precious of Days) (Jerusalem, 2004), *Sukkot*, chapter 4, p. 391.

COMMENT: Why do we perform slightly "crazy" rituals like going out to sit in the *sukkah* when its windy or even rainy? It raises the question: Is religion rational? At its heart, it is not. It asks us to go beyond rationality and simply trust. Sitting in the *sukkah* during the festival is a *mitzvah*. Let's just do it.

## [139] The Air of the *Sukkah*

CONTEXT: This teaching is by the founder of the Belz community. He studied with numerous Hasidic rabbis before setting up on his own.

TEXT:

    The purpose of the *sukkah* is [to teach] that the blessed God surrounds us on all sides, in every place, even outside of the Land [of Israel] through the holiness of the Temple, on all four sides, above and below – hence the [four] walls, its floor and the covering. And thus, the air of the *sukkah* is the air of the Land of Israel.

    Shalom Rokeach of Belz – Sar Shalom (d. 1855), *MaHaRaSH miBelza* (Our teacher, the rabbi, Shalom of Belz) (Israel Klepholtz, ed.) (Bnei Brak, 1987), pt. 2, pp. 77.

COMMENT: For the Belzer *rebbe*, sitting in the *sukkah* is an object lesson in the omnipresence of God. And since Jewish tradition suggests that the experience of the presence of God is most available in the land of Israel (see Talmud, *Ketubot* 110b: "Whoever lives outside of the Land [of Israel] is like one who has no god"), then being in the *sukkah* is like being in Israel. Does this put the primary emphasis on being in the Land? Or on being in the presence of God wherever we are geographically?

## [140] The Mystery of Faith

CONTEXT: This text comes from the section of the Zohar known as the Faithful Shepherd (*Ra'ya Mehemna* in Aramaic), a unit that offers kabbalistic analysis of the commandments of the Torah.

TEXT:

"You shall dwell in *sukkot* for seven days...."

Leviticus 23:42

    This commandment (45) is to dwell in a *sukkah*. This teaches us that this is in order to show that Israel dwells in the mystery of faith, without any fear at all, for the Accuser has been separated from them already. And anyone who is in the mystery of faith may dwell in a *sukkah*, as we have been taught in the Scriptures "all the native born in Israel shall dwell in *sukkot*" (Leviticus 23:42). Whoever is in the mystery of faith, and of the seed and the root of Israel "shall dwell in *sukkot*." And this mystery has been mentioned in many places.

Zohar, *Ra'ya Mehemna*, III,103b.

NOTES:

**This commandment (45)** ... Of the 613 commandments said to be in the Torah.

**Accuser has been separated from them already...** By virtue of Yom Kippur.

COMMENT: The Zohar calls the *sukkah* "the shade of faith." Why should the *sukkah* represent faith or trust in God? On the physical plane, and in England especially, it is quite likely to rain during Sukkot. So, going out into the *sukkah* to eat (sleep?) is an act of faith, especially if clouds are gathering in the sky. On a deeper level, the *sukkah* represents our trust in God's concern for our future, as individuals, as a people, as a species. The world is full of problems and pitfalls, personal, global and every level in between. Yet, we try to go forward. So, what keeps us going on through whatever crises happen to befall us, if not some kind of faith, in God, in the future, call it what you will? The *sukkah*, with the shade of its branches giving us a degree of shelter from the elements, represents that trust. Trust in God cannot prevent bad things from happening, any more than the *sukkah* can keep off a downpour, but it can help us to stay just a bit dryer so we can survey our troubles from a more universal perspective.

For some people, faith seems to be a tightly closed box which nothing is allowed to enter. Now, the *sukkah* has to have walls, and may have four, but only needs two-and-a-bit. And the *sukkah* has to have a roof of plant material (no longer growing), with holes no bigger than three hand's-breadths across, yet it is traditionally recommended that we able to see the stars through the roof on a clear night. (Recommended, but not required – contrary to popular belief!)

So, if the *sukkah* represents faith, then is it recommending a faith that is full of holes, an incomplete faith? Some people may see this as a threat. To me, this suggests that faith must be open. Faith must never be allowed to dissolve into dogma, must never be permitted to become dull and insensitive. The light of the spiritual luminaries, both Jewish and non-Jewish and the winds of change that blow through the world, must be allowed to enter into, and even challenge, our faith. In this way, we make it stronger and deeper.

# [141] A Broken Vessel

CONTEXT: Avraham, the *rebbe* of Trisk (Turiysk, 1806–1889), was the fifth son of Mordechai of Chernobyl, and like most of his brothers, became a *rebbe* in his own right. Avraham Ettinga (or Ettinger, 1874–1924) of Dukla was a scion of a famous rabbinic family and a genealogical researcher. This comes from a collection of sayings and stories that he edited.

TEXT:

Once on the evening of the festival of Sukkot, when R. Avraham, the *rebbe* of Trisk was going on his way to the *sukkah*, he remained standing at the threshold of the *sukkah* for a long time without entering. The people who stood beside him saw and were surprised. The rabbi opened his mouth and said: "As I approached the *sukkah*, a thought occurred to me. This is not right. In the High Holy Day prayer, I said '[a human being is] like a broken clay pot' – i.e., a human being is compared to a clay vessel. In that case, how am I permitted to enter, when according to the law, it is forbidden to bring a clay vessel to the *sukkah*, into the midst of the *sukkah*. But our sages have said that a clay vessel cannot lose [its uncleanness] unless it is broken. Therefore, we broke our hearts before the fearsome and awesome God, and "a broken and contrite heart [God] will not despise." Then he entered the *sukkah*.

Avraham Ettinga (ed.), *Imrei Tzaddikim* (Sayings of the Righteous) (Lvov, 1929), p. 33.

NOTES:

**This is not right...** *Gadol*, literally, great.

**"Like a broken clay pot"** ... From the extended poem *Unetanneh Tokef*, recited in the Musaf (Additional) Services of Rosh Hashanah and Yom Kippur.

**It is forbidden to bring a clay vessel to the *sukkah*...** Presumably, because it might result in uncleanness being introduced into the *sukkah*.

**A clay vessel cannot lose [its uncleanness] unless it is broken...** Talmud, *Avodah Zarah* 34a, based on Leviticus 15:12.

**A broken and contrite heart [God] will not despise...** Based on Psalm 51:19.

COMMENT: Sukkot, in all its observances, is first and foremost about joy: joy in the autumn harvest, joy in wilderness survival, joy in divine providence over the Jewish people. It can be very difficult, if not impossible, to be joyful when we are worried about our past deeds or feeling guilty. The *rebbe* of Trisk suggests that it is our very act of repentance on Yom Kippur that opens us to the possibility of real joy in our *sukkah*. For, if we have observed Yom Kippur properly, all our guilt should have been cleansed from within us.

## [142] Divine Help and Freedom

CONTEXT: Pinchas of Koretz was an independent Hasidic teacher who may have been influenced by the Ba'al Shem Tov, but perhaps only marginally.

TEXT:

*SUKKaH* is an anagram of *Somech V'ozer Kol Ha-nof'lim* ("Who supports and helps those who have fallen"). And all those who lower themselves and seem as if they had fallen, the Holy Blessed One helps them, stands them up and strengthens them with [God's own] right hand. But this applies only to those who are nothing in their own eyes, as it is said in the *Gemara*.

And *SuKKaH* is a term of authority, from the word *n'SiCHut* ("principality"). And thus, we sit in the *sukkah*, "in the shadow of faith," because we sit as princes [in] a world of freedom, like someone who has won a battle and has his weapons in his hand – [namely,] the *lulav* and *etrog* – and is afraid of no one.

Pinchas of Koretz (1726-1791), *Imre Shefer* (Graceful Sayings, Genesis 49:21) (Piotrokov, 1910), §18, p. 5.

NOTES:

**As it is said in the** *Gemara*… Talmud, *Eruvin* 13b: "Those who lower themselves, the Holy Blessed One raises."

**"In the shadow of faith"** … See Zohar I, 257b & III, 103a and elsewhere.

**His weapons in his hand…** That is, has not been wounded.

COMMENT: The Koretzer here presents two different, but perhaps complementary interpretations of the *sukkah*. On the one hand, it represents God's care for the fallen, the suffering, though he restricts divine providence to those who have achieved a high degree of selflessness. (This is characteristic of the Reb Pinchas, and goes back as far as Maimonides' *Guide to the Perplexed* III, 51.) On the other hand, the *sukkah* suggests to him a victorious warrior sitting in his tent, confident in his hard-won freedom after the battle. Perhaps the warrior is confident because the awareness that by virtue of selfless devotion to duty he has the support of a powerful Ally.

# [143] An All-Encompassing *Mitzvah*

CONTEXT: Perhaps the most westernized of the Hasidic rabbis of his day, Simchah Bunam of Pshische considers the physicality of the *sukkah*.

TEXT:

Our holy Rabbi used to say: There is nothing as lovely as the commandment of the *sukkah*, for people enter the *sukkah* with all their limbs, with their clothing and their shoes, [right] into the midst of the commandment – which is not the case with other commandments.

Simchah Bunam of Pshische (1765-1827), *Midrash Simchah* (Simchah's Interpretation) (Jerusalem: Mossad HaRYM Levin, 1988), v.2, p.233.

COMMENT: Despite the centrality of Torah study in all its forms, Judaism was never meant to be a purely cerebral undertaking. On the contrary, study was always intended to lead to practice, practice that would involve all the levels of our being. To this extent, Simchah Bunam may be said to place entering the *sukkah* during the festival at the pinnacle of Jewish activity in fulfilment of Torah, since no other *mitzvah* is so all-encompassing.

# [144] The Walls of the *Sukkah*

CONTEXT: By tradition, a *sukkah* should have four walls, but two complete walls and a part of a third may suffice. In his popular magnum opus, Yeshaya Horowitz, author of the most popular book of his time, considers the spiritual significance of this configuration.

TEXT:

I have received a tradition that draws a hint from the word *SuKKaH* from which one can explain the laws of the sides of the *sukkah*. The best way of [fulfilling] the *mitzvah* is with four sides, but one has fulfilled [one's duty] from the start with even three sides, and the rule is that two and a bit [is sufficient]. The four sides allude to the four "walls" ...: repentance, prayer, charity and Torah, and corresponding to this is [the letter] *Samech* which surrounds and encompasses on all sides. However, there are Jews who are not learned in Torah, or who do not have the capacity to understand; they take hold of "three sides," which are the three walls of repentance, prayer and charity. Corresponding to this is [the letter] *Kaf* of the word *sukkah*, which offers a surrounding in three directions. However, there are sometimes those who are unable to hold fast to even three, because they are not learned in Torah and are too poor to give charity. They can still hold fast to two sides, the two "walls" of repentance and prayer, for this every Jewish person can fulfil. And as for the extra third "bit," this is for giving a bit [of charity], as our sages have taught: "Even a poor person who has to take charity must give a little charity." This corresponds to the letter *Hay* of *sukkah*, which has two full sides and a bit of a third.

> Yeshaya HaLevi Horowitz (c.1570-1626), <u>Shnei Luchot HaBrit</u> (The Two Tablets of the Covenant, Deuteronomy 9:9,11) (reprint of 1863 ed.; Jerusalem: 1975), *Bayit HaGadol*, v.1, p.27c.

NOTES:

**The best way of [fulfilling] the *mitzvah* is with four sides...** See Moses Isserles' comment in the *Rema* on *Shulchan Aruch*, *Orach Hayyim* 630:5.

***Samech* which surrounds and encompasses on all sides...** For the benefit of those who do not know Hebrew, it is important to note that, depending on the font, the letter *Samech* can be round, oval, or very nearly square. ***Kaf...*** resembles three sides of a square open to the left. ***Hay ...*** This letter is formed by a line above, joined to another descending on its right, plus a shorter third stroke that does not connect to the top on the left.

**"Even a poor person who has to take charity..."** See Talmud, *Gittin* 7b.

COMMENT: Everyone should be welcome in your *sukkah*. If we follow Horowitz' reasoning, then the very shape of the *sukkah* spells that out for us, for it represents in a graphic way different types of Jews: rich and poor, ignorant and learned, perhaps even those who are committed to living their Jewishness and those who are not. Being in the *sukkah* places few demands upon us.

## [145] God's Hidden Love

CONTEXT: The word *sukkah* comes from a Hebrew root that means to cover. Here, the early Hasidic teacher, Menachem Nachum of Chernobyl explores the spiritual significance of this.

TEXT:

> Sukkot comes from the root *SaCHaCH*, i.e. that which covers (*m'SaKeCH*) a thing and hides it, for the Holy Blessed One created the universe with divine love in order to reveal divinity to that which had been created. Hence the verse: "For I have said: The universe [is built by love; Your faithfulness shall You establish in the heavens" (Psalm 89:3)].

"For I have said: The universe" – I have said that the universe should come into existence so that love may be built, so that there should be a structure for love to be revealed through the universe. Before the creation of the universe, there was no structure for love. It was above the structure, with no possibility of reaching it. But, it is the nature of the good to do good, not, as has been said, because [God] had to create the worlds out of necessity in order to do good; rather, [God] created out of true love, [the kind of] love people perform for the dead, that is, of levels of the needy that have nothing at all of their own...

> Menachem Nachum of Chernobyl (1730-1797), *Me'or Eynayim* (The Light of the Eyes) (n.p., 1952), p. 142.

NOTE:
**[The kind of] love people perform for the dead...** See Rashi on Genesis 47:29: "The love that one performs for the dead is true love because [the one who does it] seeks no repayment." Based on *Bereshit Rabbah* 96:5.

COMMENT: In the view of Menachem Nachum of Chernobyl, the *sukkah* represents the "structure" of divine love that permeates the universe, yet is hidden from our gaze. The *sukkah*, as it were, makes that love visible. It is a love freely bestowed, an unconditional love, because there is no expectation that we could ever repay God for all that we receive from the divinity. The mere thought of it should fill us with awe.

## [146] The *Sukkah* as a Symbol of Divine Wisdom

CONTEXT: As the name of his book indicates, Recanati offers kabbalistic understanding of the Torah's 613 commandments. He was an Italian kabbalist who, according to legend, acquired his knowledge in a miraculous way, but little is known for certain of his life.

TEXT:
The commandment to rest on the first day of the festival of Sukkot, and on the eighth day, and to make a *sukkah*: [The *sukkah*] alludes to the supernal Wisdom (*Hochmah*), which is like a *sukkah* for the Holy Blessed One. It is the home of the paths of all the [next eight] *Sefirot*, because it encompasses all...

> Menachem ben Binyamin Recanati (late 13th-early 14 centuries), *Sefer Ta'amei HaMitzvot* (The Book of the Meanings of the Commandments) (London, 1962), p. 76a-b.

NOTE:

**The home of the paths of all the [next eight]** *Sefirot...* The *Sefirot* from *Binah* to *Malchut* are said to emerge from the *Sefirah* of *Hochmah*, also known as *Reshit*, the First.

COMMENT: We all know that the *sukkah* is meant to represent the forty years of wandering in the wilderness that the Israelites endured after they left Egyptian slavery. The Torah says as much. But what is the mystical significance of the *sukkah*? What spiritual principle may it be said to embody? For Recanati, the answer is divine wisdom, the *Sefirah* of *Hochmah*, from which all things emerge.

## [147] A Temporary Dwelling Made Permanent

CONTEXT: R. Yisra'el of Sadagora was a member of the Friedman family, *rebbes* of the Ruzhyn dynasty, descendants of the Maggid of Mezritch.

TEXT:
A *sukkah* is called a "temporary dwelling." I say: "A temporary dwelling" [means that] when people think about doing *teshuvah* (repentance), they are already penitents. (*Az a mentsch tiht un tracht in teshuvah iz er shoyn ein ba'al teshuvah.*)
May the Blessed God help make that "a permanent dwelling," that is, that this repentance should be permanent for the entire year. May the Blessed God help each individual of Israel to have faith and to do *teshuvah* permanently. Then salvation will be forthcoming for the totality of Israel.
Given in 1889 by Yisra'el Friedman of Sadagora (1853-1907), *Or Yisra'el* (Israel's Light) (1997), p. 250.

NOTE:
**A *sukkah* is called a "temporary dwelling"** ... Talmud, *Sukkah* 2a.

COMMENT: After three days of preparations for Sukkot, I find that all thoughts of Yom Kippur have receded into the distance, even though it has only just passed. In the Sadagora *rebbe's* view, the *sukkah*, which is intended purely is a dwelling purely for the duration of the festival, symbolizes repentance. We "dwell" in repentance only temporarily, perhaps only during Yom Kippur itself. But what would happen if our repentance could be permanent? if we could bring our minds back to God throughout the year? It would make us more religious, certainly, perhaps more spiritual, and as he suggests, might that not produce wider effects in the world?

# ECCLESIASTES / *KOHELET*

## [148] Why Do We Read Ecclesiastes?

CONTEXT: Within the Hebrew Bible, there is a group of five books known as *megillot*, little scrolls, each of which is read on a particular occasion during the year. It is the custom of read Ecclesiastes (*Kohelet*, in Hebrew) on the intermediate Shabbat of Sukkot, or on Shmini Atzeret if there is no intermediate Shabbat. But why? The controversial *rebbe* of Isbica, disciple of the Kotzker, offers his suggestion.

TEXT:
> King Solomon produced the book of Ecclesiastes in his old age, and I heard that this is why we read it during Sukkot. Not because he disparaged the joy of this world, but because from it we can derive the strength and essence of true joy through the disparagement of all matters of this world. This alone is my portion...
>
> Mordechai Yosef Leiner of Izbica (1814-1878), *Mei HaShiloach* (The Waters of the Shiloach [Isaiah 8:6]) (Bnei Brak, 1995), v. 2, p. 248.

NOTE:
**King Solomon produced the book of Ecclesiastes in his old age...**
According to *Shir HaShirim Rabbah* 1:10.

COMMENT: I love the book of Ecclesiastes. Its author, traditionally identified as King Solomon, is so wonderfully fed up with the world and all its vanities. It makes me feel that it is alright for me to be fed up and cynical too, sometimes. After all, this author was, and yet his book was put into the Bible! For the Izbicer *rebbe*, the book's purpose to teach us to detach ourselves from the things of this world. They will all pass away, as we ourselves will too. So, let us not invest too much of our emotions in them. Detached in this way, when we find that our feelings are no longer tied to material things, the path to true joy may open before us.

## [149] Inclusive Words

CONTEXT: Pinchas of Koretz was an early Hasidic teacher in late eighteenth century Ukraine. His relationship with the Ba'al Shem Tov, the founder of modern Hasidism, is unclear.

TEXT:
"The words of Kohelet, son of David, King of Israel."

Ecclesiastes 1:1

Rashi explains [that he was called *KoHeLet*] because all of his words were [spoken] at a public assembly (*haKHeL*). For all expressions of words of holiness and prayer include all the worlds, angels and souls and the like. Thus, each person should see that [their] every expression includes them too. All of King Solomon's words [were spoken] in this way, for they included within them all the souls of Israel, the angels and the like, for *SHeLoMoH* (Solomon) is the same letters as *LeMoSHeH* (of Moses) as is well known, and all of his words were [spoken] in public assembly. And if people act in this way, so that all their words are thus, they will be exalted over all creatures. And this is the explanation of "the words of Kohelet."

Pinchas of Koretz (1726-1791), *Midrash Pinchas* (Pinchas' Interpretation) (Jerusalem, 1971), p. 48.

NOTES:
**King of Israel...** The *Midrash Pinchas* says "of Israel," but Ecclesiastes actually says, "in Jerusalem."

**Rashi explains...** Based on *Kohelet Rabbah* 1:2, itself based on I Kings 8:1.

**For all expressions...** From this point onwards, we hear the words of the Koretzer.

**[Spoken] in public assembly...** As Moses' words were. See Deuteronomy 31:12, the commandment of *Hakhel*.

COMMENT: How can our words "include all souls of Israel, angels and the like"? Surely, through our sensitivity, our awareness of the great variety of needs and fears that exist among our people and beyond. It is about inclusivity, about opening our hearts to truly hear those who are different from us. To hear that is to hear the voice of the angels, the voice of God.

# [150] By Contrast

CONTEXT: In this part of Ecclesiastes, the author considers the difference between the wise and the foolish. Ya'akov Yosef of Polonnoye was a prolific writer and preacher, and primary disciple of the Ba'al Shem Tov.

TEXT:
'[Wisdom is superior to folly, and] light is superior to darkness.'

Ecclesiastes 2:[13]

That is, the superiority of light is recognized because of darkness, and likewise, a wise person [is recognized] because of fools. Similarly, the superiority of the righteous is recognized because of the wicked. And pleasure is recognized because of blows and suffering, and the superiority of awareness because of forgetfulness. One therefore becomes a throne for the other... This being so, however, idolaters could make a mistake and think that since [evil is] a vehicle for [good], then everything is actually one unity. This is not true, since there is a separation...

Ya'akov Yosef of Polonnoye (died c.1782), *Tzafnat Pa'neach* (Joseph's Egyptian name, Genesis 41:45) (Brooklyn, N.Y.: A. Laufer, 1991), pp. 366d-367a.

NOTE:
**Since there is a separation...** As hinted at by the verse from Ecclesiastes.

COMMENT: Does Ya'akov Yosef really wish to deny that there is a higher, overarching oneness that unity good and evil? That would seem to contradict his master's view that all things are the manifestation of God, of divine energies. Perhaps he would say that it is only from the divine point of view that good and evil may seem elements of a single unity, but that from our limited human perspective they are distinct and separate. I am reluctant to speak of God's point of view, but maybe the reason for the contrast we see between good and evil is to encourage us to pursue the good and eschew the evil. In other words, good and evil present us with a never-ending test of our humanity.

# [151] God's Hands

CONTEXT: Much of Ecclesiastes chapter 9 is concerned with advice on making the best of life. Here, the founder of the modern Hasidic movement reflects on what it means to be a Jew. The verse he chose seems to be a particular favorite of the Ba'al Shem Tov's, as we find it frequently interpreted in his name.

TEXT:

"Whatever your hand (*YaDcha*) finds to do, do with all your strength."

Ecclesiastes 9:10

Meaning: One should raise people of action (*asiyah*) to thought, so that a Jew (*YUD*) may be called *YaDO*, [God's] hand.

Yisra'el ben Eliezer, Ba'al Shem Tov (1700-1760), *Keter Shem Tov* (The Crown of a Good Name, Pirkei Avot 4:13) (Brooklyn: Kehot Publication Society, 1972) §49, pt. 1, p. 14.

NOTES:

**People of action (*asiyah*) to thought...** The Besht may simply mean that active people should be encouraged to become more contemplative, or he may also have in mind that we inhabit the lowest, most physical of the kabbalistic Four Worlds, the Realm of *Asiyah*, and need to be encouraged to try to live on a more spiritual plane.

**A Jew (*YUD*)...** In Yiddish, both the name of the Hebrew letter *yod* and the word Jew would be pronounced *Yid*. Both *YOD* and *YaDO* contain the same three consonants.

COMMENT: What does it mean to be a Jew? For many it means, first and foremost, Jewish survival. For others, it includes Jewish culture. For still others, it remains a religious and spiritual path. The Besht clearly agrees with the latter view. As expressed here, he views being Jewish as a holy task: to act as God's hands, doing good wherever and whenever we can, without thought of reward or favor.

# [152] Extraneous Thoughts

CONTEXT: In chapter 11, the author of Ecclesiastes contrasts the wise and the foolish. The Maggid of Koznitz was an important teacher in the third generation of the Hasidic movement.

TEXT:

"Dead flies turn the perfumer's ointment fetid and putrid, [so a little folly outweighs wisdom]."

Ecclesiastes 10:1

These are the extraneous and evil thoughts that rage over the world...

Yisra'el ben Shabbetai Hapstein, Maggid of Koznitz (1733-1814), *Sefer Avodat Yisra'el* (The Book of Israel's Service) (Jerusalem, 1998), p. 353.

NOTE:

**Extraneous ... thoughts...** Technically, these are thoughts that enter our minds when we are attempting to concentrate on prayer or Torah study.

COMMENT: The Hasidic movement has always placed great emphasis on intention, often suggesting that even good deeds done with self-seeking motives are impure or even invalid. At one level, this passage is of part of that approach. On the other hand, even a cursory glance at politics in our time suggests that many a worthy project has been fouled by self-seeking and mindless hatred.

## [153] The Whole of Humanity

CONTEXT: R. Ze'ev Wolf of Zhitomir, one star in a constellation of future Hasidic masters who gathered around their teacher, the Maggid of Mezritch, here discusses the penultimate verse of Ecclesiastes. (Traditionally, it repeated after the last verse, in order end on a positive note.)

TEXT:

"The end of the matter, when all is said and done: Be in awe of God and observe God's commandments, [for this is the whole of humanity]."

Ecclesiastes 12:13

Our rabbis were stirred [by the phrase] "this is the whole of humanity" [to say that] the entire world was created only to command this... The entire world, from top to bottom, from individual creatures and inanimate objects, everything that comes under the generality of Existence, all of it was created only to command this. The meaning of the term "command" is that we are commanded, as a form of service, for divinity is clothed in everything in the world...

Ze'ev Wolf of Zhitomir (d.1800), *Or HaMe'ir* (The Illuminating Light) (Warsaw, 1883), pt.5, p. 43d.

NOTE:

**The entire world was created only to command this...** The awe of God. See Talmud, *Berachot* 6b: "R. Elazar said: The whole world was created only for this."

COMMENT: I have a non-Jewish friend who phones me from time to time to ask me religious and spiritual questions. Often, he tells me of his encounters with evangelical Christians who tell him that God speaks to them, and would speak to him too, if he but asked. He has tried to test this by asking God to speak to him in words, and when nothing happens, he is disappointed! I have tried to tell him of teachings, like that by Ze'ev Wolf of Zhitomir, that perhaps God speaks to him through all that is, through the challenges and pleasures of life, and that he might "hear" this voice if he could only open his mind to the possibility. Perhaps everything that occurs to him contains a hidden command, to be kinder, say, stronger or more thoughtful. Sadly, he doesn't seem to understand what I mean. But perhaps you do.

# WATER-DRAWING

## [154] The Ceremony of the Water-Drawing

CONTEXT: Menachem Mendel of Vorki succeeded his father Yitzchak as leader of his Hasidic community. Their teachings are primarily found in the same text. The Talmud (in tractate *Sukkah* chapter 4 & 5) describes the libation of water (and wine) that was offered each day during Sukkot in the Temple in Jerusalem. It was said to have been a time of great rejoicing like no other.

TEXT:
The [ceremony of the] water-libation [performed in the Temple] during the Festival … was done with great preparation. So why is a commandment apparently as important as this not written in the Torah? Because the Holy Blessed One wanted to leave room for Israel to understand this out of their own insight (*sechel*).
Menachem Mendel of Vorki (d.1868) in *Bet Yitzchak* (Isaac's House) (Jerusalem, 1992), p.154.

NOTE:
**Not written in the Torah…** The Talmud itself declares this ceremony to be "a law from Moses on Sinai" (*Sukkah* 34a, 44a), i.e., an ancient law for which there is a strong oral tradition, but no scriptural warrant.

COMMENT: The laws and practices of Judaism do not require us to give up our intellectual autonomy. On the contrary, we are expected to apply our minds to them, rather than simply accepted them as hallowed by tradition.

# SHMINI ATZERET &
# SIMCHAT TORAH

The festival of Simchat Torah by Bernard Picart, between 1723 and 1743.
This depicts the Portuguese Synagogue in Amsterdam.

# JOY & DANCING

## [155] Joining Together on Simchat Torah

CONTEXT: Of all our pilgrim festivals, Simchat Torah seems deliberately designed to encourage participation by as many people as possible. Almost anyone can dance with the Torah scrolls. No expertise is required, not even the ability to read Hebrew (or dance!). And many congregations try to ensure that everyone possible is called to recite the blessings over the Torah readings. The Ruzhyner *rebbe*, descendant of the Maggid of Mezritch and founder of a major Hasidic dynasty offers a reason for this inclusivity. (Traditionally, of course, outside of Israel, Simchat Torah corresponds to the second day of Shmini Atzeret.)

TEXT:

He talked about the Jewish custom of joining every one of the children of Israel together on Shmini Atzeret and Simchat Torah, whether learned in Torah or ordinary folks, and rejoicing together on Simchat Torah. For in the *midrash*, which the Rashi also quotes, there is a parable of a king who made a banquet [for his children for a certain number of days, but when the time came for them to go,] he said: "Your separation is difficult for me. Stay with me one more day."

He said: The meaning of "separation" is that if there were to be any separation among you, that would be difficult for me. Therefore, on this day, we join together and drink and eat together in love and affection.

In [the light of] this, what is written in the Talmud is correct: "A non-Jew came before Shammai and Hillel and said, 'Convert me [to Judaism] on condition that you can teach me the entire Torah [while standing] on one leg.'" [The questioner's] intention in this [matter] was [that] for all the festivals and appointed times that Israel observes there is a reason for it in the Torah: Passover is in memory of the exodus from Egypt; Sukkot is "because I made the Israelites dwell in *sukkot*" [Leviticus 23:43]; and thus [for] all the appointed times, but for Shmini Atzeret there is no reason in the Torah! Thus, the non-Jew was suggesting that they have no reason for the festivals; Israel just do what they do. Hence, the non-Jew said to teach him the "entire Torah" – that is, [because] I have looked through the entire Torah and have not found a reason for one [pilgrim] festival, namely the festival of Shmini Atzeret, which is called a festival in its own right. So, I am bewildered about this festival. And Hillel replied: "Whatever is hateful to you, do not do to anyone else" – because this festival exists because "your separation is difficult for me," as mentioned above. For [on this occasion,] Israel is joined together, and fulfilling [the commandment of] "you shall love your neighbor as yourself" [Leviticus 19:18].

Yisra'el Friedman of Ruzhyn (1797-1850), *Bet Yisra'el* (The House of Israel) (Piotrkov, 1913), pp. 28-29.

NOTES:

**In the *midrash*, which the Rashi also quotes...** See Rashi on Leviticus 23:36, and his comment on Numbers 29:36; based on Talmud, *Sukkah* 55b.

**If there were to be any separation among you...** In the original parable, the separation was between the people and the king (God), but in the hands of the Ruzhyner, it is between the people themselves.

**Written in the Talmud...** *Shabbat* 31a.

**A festival in its own right...** As opposed to simply the last day of Sukkot. This point is made in Talmud, *Pesachim* 93a and frequently in rabbinic literature.

COMMENT: I have always taught that the ritual of Simchat Torah was devised to celebrate the end and beginning of the annual reading of the Torah, because the study of Torah is not only a *mitzvah* but also a pleasure. And of course, it is that, but perhaps Israel of Ruzhyn is also correct when he says that the whole point of the celebration is to bring the Jewish people together, regardless of their level of learning, simply to celebrate being Jewish and the Torah which lies at the center of their group identity.

## [156] Investing Joy in Torah

CONTEXT: Sukkot is called *z'man simchateinu*, the season of our rejoicing, and in the liturgy, this term is applied to Shmini Atzeret/Simchat Torah as well. During the week-long festival we rejoice in our ancestors' safe progression through the wilderness between the Exodus and the entry into the Promised Land. We rejoice in the autumn harvest and its produce. Now, at the very end of this period we have Simchat Torah. How does it fit with all the rest? This text seems to be quoted in the book *Sefat Emet* by Menachem Mendelof Kotzk's loyal disciple Yehudah Leib Alter of Gur, but I found it in a small anthology of the Kotzker's sayings.

TEXT:

Why Simchat Torah? Because all the days of Sukkot are days of joy, so now the Israelites should invest their joy in the Torah.

Menachem Mendel of Kotzk (1787-1859), *Emet MiKotzk Titzmach* (May Truth Spring from Kotzk) (Bnei Brak, 1961), §493, p. 157.

COMMENT: Joy is a wonderful emotion. It can be brought on by so many events: a gift, a great achievement, a happy event, something to celebrate. Sukkot might be said to focus mainly on physical things, but Jews who wish to celebrate their Jewish identity need to focus on the central role that Torah has always played in the construction of that identity. And, according to the Kotzker, Simchat Torah is the primary occasion for that.

## [157] Processing the Scrolls in the Evening

CONTEXT: Many communities have the custom of parading the Torah scrolls around the synagogue seven times on the Eve of Simchat Torah. This is quite unusual. Normally, such parades occur only at morning services, and then there is only one circuit before and after the reading. Alexander ben Moshe Süsskind was a Lithuanian recluse and kabbalist from Grodno, most famous for this book on prayer and the holy occasions of the Jewish calendar.

TEXT:
After the *Amidah* for this evening [of Simchat Torah], it is the custom in throughout the dispersion of the Israel, a holy people, to adorn the Torah Scrolls with crowns and to process with them for seven circuits. This is a custom and a reparation (*tikkun*)... And it has already been mentioned in [kabbalistic] books that the [spiritual] level of the person who behaves with all types of joy before the Torah Scrolls in this way is great, awakening the upper realms with joy and mighty gladness. Whoever takes care to act with joy in the Torah on this day may be assured that Torah will never cease among their descendants.
Alexander ben Moshe Süsskind (died 1793), *Yesod VeShoresh Ha'Avodah* (The Foundation and Root of Worship) (Jerusalem, 1978), p. 258.

NOTE:
**This is a custom and a reparation (*tikkun*)...** Süsskind is suggesting that this practice somehow adds to the mystical repair of the world. He points us towards Zoharic and kabbalistic literature in his support, but without providing details.

COMMENT: Torah is serious business. It is our earliest history, our most sacred laws, an opportunity to interact with the divine, the ultimate object of all Jewish study. Does that mean it must only be approached with solemnity, and not joy? Is it too holy to allow for any frivolity? Clearly not! It must be approached with joy, and Simchat Torah is our primary opportunity each year to display our joy in the Torah.

## [158] Synagogue Crawl

CONTEXT: This text originates in a popular work by an anonymous scholar who was a secret follower of the failed messiah Shabbetai Zevi. Despite what it says, it is doubtful that the author heard this story directly from Hayyim Vital, the primary disciple of the great kabbalist, R. Yitzchak Luria, known as the Ari, the Lion.

TEXT:
Our teacher, R. Hayyim Vital testified about his teacher the Ari as follows: "I saw that my teacher used to go before the [Torah] scrolls dancing and singing songs and praises, and would go around with them on the seven circuits with great joy with all his strength. Afterwards, people would walk to another synagogue where they began later, and my teacher would do the seven circuits with the scrolls again, going around with them, dancing and singing with great joy. And then, if another synagogue began [even] later, he would do the same and finish up there. This [would go] on all night, but by day, I did not see him [do this]."
Anon. (17th century), *Chemdat Yamim* (Most Precious of Days) (Jerusalem, 2004), *Sukkot*, chapter 8, p. 458.

COMMENT: Based on this tale, it seems that the Ari took the notion of rejoicing on Simchat Torah very seriously indeed. He was apparently capable of dancing all night in celebration! No wonder he didn't do it at the morning service too!

## [159] Its End and Its Beginning

CONTEXT: Zevi Elimelech of Dinov was a Hasidic rabbi and kabbalist whose most famous work explores the deeper meaning of the festivals. He called it *The Sons of Issachar* because he believed himself to be a descendant of that son of the patriarch Jacob.

TEXT:
... On this day there is no limit to those who may come up [to recite the blessings] for the reading of the Torah, since the illumination of

167

this day is that of the generalized surrounding light upon the Torah – automatically, there is no limit or calculation. Thus, you may understand the custom we observe of concluding the Torah on this day and immediately beginning with *Bereshit* (Genesis) – its end is embedded in its beginning – for there is [really] no conclusion or limit. Understand this teaching well.

On Shmini Atzeret, which is the day of Simchat Torah, we conclude the Torah with the letter *lamed* and begin with the letter *bet*, so that that day may see a complete union of the Holy One, blessed be He, and the Community of Israel.

Zvi Elimelech of Dinov (1785-1841), *Benei Yissachar* (The Sons of Yissachar, I Chronicles 12:33) (Jerusalem, 1983), v. 2, pp. 55b-c.

NOTES:

**No limit to those who may come up...** See *Shulchan Aruch, Orach Hayyim* 669, note by Moshe Isserles.

**The generalized surrounding light...** Divine energy as diffused throughout the universe, as opposed to the internal light confined within a given individual.

**Its end is embedded in its beginning...** A phrase recycled from *Sefer Yetzirah* (3:7), where the Ten *Sefirot*, rather than the Torah, are meant.

**The day of Simchat Torah...** The text gives the source for this idea as Zohar III, 256b.

**We conclude the Torah with the letter *lamed* and begin with the letter *bet*...** The last word of the Torah (Deuteronomy 34:12) is *Yisra'el* (Israel) and the first word of Genesis is *B'reishit* ("in the beginning"). The identification of these two letters with the *Sefirot* whose names follow seems to be an innovation of the *B'nei Yissachar*.

**The Holy One, blessed be He...** I.e., the *Sefirah* of *Tiferet* (Beauty).

**The Community of Israel...** symbolizing the *Shechinah*, the *Sefirah* of *Malchut* (Sovereignty).

COMMENT: By applying the phrase "its end is embedded in its beginning," Zevi Elimelech of Dinov has signaled the endlessness of Torah. On Simchat Torah, we participate, as it were, in its endlessness, and in doing so, bring about joy in the spiritual realms. The Torah is not a finite book. Of course, it arose at a particular time and place, under a particular set of historical circumstances, yet we Jews have endowed it (or, professed to see it endowed with) an infinite divine power. It is from this power that the Jewish people have always derived our inner strength. Another cause to rejoice on Simchat Torah, surely!

## [160] Reciprocity and Blessing

CONTEXT: What follows is a sermon given on Simchat Torah 1886 by the *rebbe* of Sadagora, Yisra'el Friedman, just before the Torah scrolls were taken on their seven circuits of the synagogue. In it, he links the first line of the Torah portion that is unique to the day, *V'zot HaBerachah* ("This is the blessing"), with the opening line of the second scroll, Genesis 1:1 (*Bereishit*, "In the beginning, God created...").

TEXT:

The point about Simchat Torah is that the totality of Israel rejoices in the Torah, and the Torah rejoices in this, that Israel has kept the commands of Rosh Hashanah, Yom Kippur and Sukkot. This is the essence of joy.

"And this is the blessing that Moses gave to descendants of Israel" (Deuteronomy 33:1) – "In the beginning God created the heavens and the earth" (Genesis 1:1). This is the great blessing, and the essence of the blessing is that Israel knows and believes that "in the beginning God created..." where "in the beginning" [relates to the verse]: "The beginning of wisdom is the awe of the Eternal" (Psalm 111:10); "God created" – that they know that there is a God, that the Holy Blessed One created and guides the world. This is the essence.

"This is the blessing" – "In the beginning," for this is the essence of the blessing: that each and everyone realizes that they have so far achieved nothing in their [divine] service, and that they are still at the start of their service, and at the beginning.

"And this is the blessing that Moses gave to descendants of Israel." It has been said that Moses our teacher pleaded before God [as follows]: "May the *Shechinah* (the presence of God) rest upon their work of their hands." Hence [the text says:] "And this (*v'zot*)" – alluding to the *Shechinah*, along the lines of the verse "with this (*zot*) shall Aaron enter the holy place" (Leviticus 16:3). Hence, "And this is the blessing" – i.e., that [God] should bless them that the *Shechinah* rest upon the work of their hands; "that Moses the man of God gave to descendants of Israel" – i.e., that God should be over Israel, that is, the *Shechinah* should rest upon them, as mentioned above. [Thus, it says] *v'zot*, with an extra [unnecessary] *vav* [at the start], for this is the essence of the blessing.

Delivered on Simchat Torah in 1885, before the Torah-circuits, by Yisra'el Friedman of Sadagora (1853-1907), *Or Yisra'el* (Israel's Light) (1997), pp.267-268.

NOTES:

**The blessing that Moses...** The Torah adds the words "the man of God" but these are missing in the text of the sermon at this point, though supplied later.

**It has been said...** In the *midrash* anthology *Yalkut Shimoni, Berachah* §950.

**"And this (*v'zot*)" – alluding to the *Shechinah*...** This connection is made in Zohar II, 290b. Actually, *zot* is frequently taken as symbolic of the *Shechinah*.

COMMENT: R. Yisra'el begins by asserting the reciprocal nature of Simchat Torah: we rejoice in the gift of Torah and the Torah, as it were, rejoices over our observance of the festivals just passed. He then draws two lessons from the convergence of *V'zot HaBerachah* and *Bereishit*. First, that our true blessing as Jews is our faith that God created and guides the world, and secondly, that whatever our service of God, we are always just beginning. How can this be a blessing? Surely, it can be a cause of frustration and a sense of futility. However, it can also reassure us that, no matter our past mistakes, we are all still learning. We must not be too hard on ourselves. Lastly, the *rebbe* uses an old kabbalistic symbol to affirm the help of the *Shechinah* in our endeavors, for this is the true nature of blessing: that the Presence of God go with us.


# RAIN


## [161] Praying for Rain


CONTEXT: After *Musaf*, the Additional Service, on Shmini Atzeret, we begin to pray for the winter rains by adding the words *mashiv ha-ruach umorid ha-gashem* ("causing the wind to blow and the rain to fall") in the second paragraph of the *Amidah*. This practice continues until the first day of Pesach, when communities switch to *morid ha-tal* ("causes the dew to fall") or omit the phrase entirely. Here, one of the greatest and most forceful figures in the Galician and Hungarian Jewish community offers a kabbalistic explanation of the difference between these two practices.

TEXT:

Our rabbis said: "The Congregation of Israel said in God's presence '[God] will come like rain to us' (Hosea 6:3), and the Holy Blessed One said, 'I will be like dew to Israel' ([Hosea] 14:6)." It seems to me that the difference between dew and rain is that rain is an awakening from below [since] "There is not a single drop from above which does not correspond to two drops [of tears] from below." On the other hand, dew is awakening from above. Therefore, during the festival of Pesach, which was an awakening [achieved] without action on our part, but [which was] only "in haste," as is well known, we pray for dew. However, on the festival of Sukkot [when] awakening [occurs] by our own actions, [namely,] repentance, good deeds and *mitzvot*, we pray the prayer for rain.

> Zevi Elimelech of Dinov (1785-1841), *Benei Yissachar* (The Sons of Yissachar, I Chronicles 12:33) (Jerusalem, 1983), v. 2, p. 55b.

NOTES:

**Our rabbis said...** Talmud, *Ta'anit* 4a.

**An awakening from below...** As opposed to an awakening from above. The question is: Where does the spiritual impetus originate? From people below or from the divine realms above?

**"There is not a single..."** The text credits Talmud, *Ta'anit* 28b, but the quote is actually from Zohar, *Ra'ya Mehemna*, III, 247b.

**Only "in haste"** ... I.e., without preparation. This phrase occurs twice in the narratives of the Exodus for Egypt: Exodus 12:11 & Deuteronomy 16:3.

**As is well known...** See Hayyim Vital (1542-1620), *Peri Etz Hayyim* (The Fruit of the Tree of Life) (Jerusalem, 1980), Gate 21, Chapter 1, p.494.

COMMENT: I find the twin, dialectic concepts of "awakening from above" and "awakening from below" quite fascinating. There are some things we achieve in life apparently without effort, as if they had dropped down from heaven like rain. For example, falling in love, being conceived by our parents, our birth and the gift of life itself. Might this be awakening from above? Other things, perhaps, most things, require our effort, our work, our sweat and perhaps our prayers. Awakening from below? And it would seem that life is made up of the intertwining of these two threads. We are both blessed and challenged every day.

# CHANUKAH

Mattathias appeals to the refugees (I Maccabees 2:42-70). By
Gustave Doré - Doré's English Bible, Public Domain.

## [162] Increasing our Divine Service

CONTEXT: Hayyim Yosef David Azulai (known by the acronym *CHIDA*) was an Italian kabbalist, a fundraiser for *yeshivot* in the land of Israel, and a great bibliophile and bibliographer, as well as a preacher. This comes from a book of his sermons, and is concerned with the meaning of Chanukah as (Re-)Dedication. It is so called because Maccabees re-dedicated the Temple in Jerusalem after it was defiled by soldiers of the Seleucid ruler, Antiochus IV Epiphanes.

TEXT:

The king's servant who receives specific acts of kindness from the king, beyond [those of] all the rest of the king's servants, must certainly render greater service than the others, and increase service. And what will reconcile the servant to his master, demonstrating to him that he recognizes his kindnesses, if not demonstrating that his service is perfect? Just as the king increases his acts of kindness towards him with specific acts beyond those offered to other servants, so too is [the servant] obliged to demonstrate a greater [and] more specific service to the king than the others...

Especially during the days of Chanukah (Dedication), when, in essence, troubles came upon us because of the neglect of [divine] service, it is appropriate that we increase our service...

Hayyim Yosef David Azulai (1724-1806), *Hadrei Vaten* (The Innermost Parts) (Jerusalem, 1990), pp. 80a, 81a.

NOTE:

**Troubles came upon us because of the neglect of [divine] service...**
The sacrificial service in the Temple could not take place for three years (167-164 BCE) while the Seleucids controlled it.

COMMENT: Our modern celebration of Chanukah tends to center on candles and presents. There is nothing wrong with that, but we sometimes miss the deeper meanings, like loyalty to our people, and beyond that, loyalty to God. We give thanks for the miracle of the oil, but sometimes neglect the miracle of the restoration of the service and re-dedication of the Temple. Today, our service to God is personal and communal, but we may need to devote ourselves to it with more rigor lest it get stale.

## [163] Chanukah and a Good New Year

CONTEXT: This is part of a sermon delivered by Yisra'el of Sadagora, a key figure in Hasidism in his time, on the fourth night of Chanukah 1885.

TEXT:

The righteous men of old said that on Chanukah a person can, through prayer, procure a good year from the Creator – more so than on [other] holidays.

I say that on all the [other] holidays the "awakening" [proceeds] from bottom to top, whereas on Chanukah it [proceeds] from top to bottom. It is like a king. When he sits [on his throne] in his palace, and someone comes before him with a request, the king will treat him according to strict justice and will examine him closely [to determine] if he deserves to have his request fulfilled. But when the king is travelling, and someone comes before him with a request, the king does not examine him closely about the appropriateness of the action he is asking for, and even if he does not deserve to have his request fulfilled, he will grant it out of obligation (*mitzvah*) and compassion.

Look here, Chanukah is indicated by "a commandment (*mitzvah*) is a lamp;" Shabbat and [other] festivals by "the Torah is light." Chanukah is indicated by "a commandment is a lamp" – that is, on Chanukah a person may be saved by the blessed Creator out of obligation (*mitzvah*) and compassion, even though one may not deserve it. But, the [other] festivals and Shabbat are called "Torah is light." Therefore, on those occasions, the blessed Creator acts toward that person according to the Torah and [strict] justice.

Yisra'el Friedman of Sadagora (1853-1907), *Or Yisra'el* (Israel's Light) (1997), p. 40.

NOTES:

**The righteous men of old…** I have been unable to locate a source of this teaching. Is this perhaps an indication of the influence of the Christian New Year?

**The "awakening" [proceeds] from bottom to top…** I.e., the impetus for salvation comes from us, from our prayers.

**On Chanukah it [proceeds] from top to bottom…** I.e., the impetus for salvation comes from God.

**Look here…** The analysis that follows is based on Proverbs 6:23: "For a commandment is a lamp; Torah is light."

COMMENT: Does God have an obligation to preserve the Jewish people? Is it a *mitzvah* incumbent upon God to ensure our survival? Perhaps it is the thing the God has to do to fulfill the divine side of the Covenant that is said to exist between God and Israel. This notion has been a part of Jewish thinking since the Torah itself, but, especially since the Holocaust, under serious question. It would appear that Chanukah, the celebration of the unexpected miracle of the defeat of the many by the few, is an example of God's performance of the divine *mitzvah* mentioned above, but can we still believe in it today? Perhaps we need to bear in mind that, despite our horrendous losses, the Jewish people as a whole survived the Holocaust.

## [164] Chanukah, Education, Creation

CONTEXT: Here Yeshaya Horowitz, a major scholar, communal rabbi and popular author of his day, discusses the meaning of the word Chanukah and its root. (This author is so famous that later generations have referred to him as the holy *SHeLaH*, a name formed from the opening letters of the title of his magnum opus, *SHnei Luchot HaB'rit*.)

TEXT:

Chanukah is [so-called] because the dedication of the [Second] Temple (*chanukat bet ha-mikdash*) occurred on it, and it alludes to the education (*chinuch*) of the world. For the world was created for the sake of Torah and the inception of the commandments (*mitzvot*), but the Hellenists wanted to abrogate the Torah and *mitzvot* from Israel. When the Hasmoneans won, Torah and the *mitzvot* were deemed to have won, and thus the world was being educated. Just as the world was created on the twenty-fifth of the month – for the world was created on the twenty-fifth of *Ellul*, and when people say that the world was created in Tishri, this refers only to the creation of humanity; the beginning of Creation was on the twenty-fifth of the month – so too Chanukah [begins] on the twenty-fifth of the month [of *Kislev*]. And just as the beginning of creation was "Let there be light," so too is the commandment of Chanukah concerning lights. Just as the first light was hidden and not available for use, so too these lights are forbidden for our use.

Yeshaya HaLevi Horowitz (c.1570-1626), *Shnei Luchot HaBrit* (The Two Tablets of the Covenant, Deuteronomy 9:9,11) (Jerusalem: 1975), *Torah Shebichtav*, v. 2, p. 29a-b.

NOTES:

**The world was created for the sake of Torah...** A teaching variously expressed in rabbinic literature. See for example, *Esther Rabbah* 7:13 and Rashi on Genesis 1:1.

**Created on the twenty-fifth of Ellul...** See *Vayikra Rabbah* 29:1.

**The first light was hidden...** See *Bereshit Rabbah* 3:6

**Forbidden for our use...** The Chanukah lights should not be used for illumination or for kindling. They are only to be seen. See *Shulchan Aruch, Orach Hayyim* 673:1.

COMMENT: The holy *SHeLaH* utilizes the linguistic connection between Chanukah and *chinuch* to initiate a series of links between Chanukah and Creation. What might this mean for us? Political and military victory should be more than just a cause for celebration, and certainly not an opportunity for arrogance. It should inspire us to work towards higher goals, goals set out by Torah itself: justice, righteousness and concern for the less fortunate. And highest of all, it should re-connect us with life and creation. Chanukah should mean that in celebration we re-dedicate ourselves to the highest ideals of Torah and Judaism.

# THE MIRACLE OF CHANUKAH

## [165] Divine Concern for our Deeds

CONTEXT: The cantankerous *rebbe* of Kotzk discusses the brief Talmudic passage concerning the origins of Chanukah, and spells out a lesson for his own time.

TEXT:
In the *Gemara* ... [we read]: "On the twenty-fifth day of Kislev, the days of Chanukah [begin]. They are eight.... [For when the Greeks entered the Temple, they defiled the oils in it, and when the Hasmoneans prevailed against them and defeated them, they searched and found only one jug of oil which still had the seal of the High Priest on it, and it contained enough for only one day's lighting,] but a miracle was performed through it and they [were able to keep the Temple-*menorah*] alight for eight days. The next year they established a festival with *Hallel*-psalms and thanksgiving."
But [there is a] question: What is this great miracle of Chanukah? Do we not say every day: "[We thank You] for the miracles that are with us day by day and for Your wonders...."? Moreover, why was [no holiday] established because of the miracle of the [defeat of] the thirty-one kings ... or the miracle of [the defeat of] Sennacherib?
It seems that this may be explained [by the fact] that in truth the intention of the Greeks was not the destruction of bodies but "to make them forget Your Teaching and make them turn away from the laws You desire." And as it has been said in the words of our sages, "[The Greeks] would say: Write on the horn of an ox that you have no portion in the God of Israel." Now Israel experienced a great [spiritual] fall as a result of this, for they thought that the Holy Blessed One was not concerned about their deeds. And a miracle was performed for them, in that the Holy Blessed One made them find a small jug of pure oil which [the Greeks]

had not touched, in order that they might be able to observe the commandment of lighting the lamps [in the Temple], when in truth, according to law, they were exempt from [observing] this commandment, for "the All-Merciful exempts one who sins under compulsion."

But the Holy Blessed One showed them through this that, although in truth they were exempt, and were not in the category of those whose abrogate the positive commandments, nevertheless, from the side of God's concern for their deeds, the blessed One performed miracles for them, so that they might be able to keep the God's commandments even when they were exempt. For it is the deeds of their hands that [God] wants, and it was made clear to them by this means that the Holy Blessed One is concerned with their deeds. Certainly, one could not measure the greatness of the joy that was then established in their hearts because of this, for in truth, when people understand that the Holy Blessed One is concerned about their deeds, they desire to do God's will in full perfection. Consider [this well.]

Menachem Mendel of Kotzk (1787-1859), *Ohel Torah MeiHaRabbi MiKotzk* (The Torah Tent of the Rabbi of Kotzk) (Lublin, 1909), p.18.

NOTES:
**Gemara...** Talmud, *Shabbat* page 21b.
**Hallel-psalms...** Psalms 113-118.
**Do we not say every day: "[We thank You]"** ... In the penultimate paragraph of the *Amidah, Modim.* If there are miracles every day, why single out this one?
**The [defeat of] the thirty-one kings...** Who took the field against the Israelites, as described in in Joshua 12.
**[The defeat of] Sennacherib...** In II Kings 19. The forces of the King of Assyria laying siege to Jerusalem were struck down overnight, as predicted by the prophet Isaiah.
**"To make them forget Your Teaching..."** A quotation from the Chanukah prayer *Al HaNissim*, inserted into the *Modim.*
**"[The Greeks] would say, Write on the horn of an ox ..."** This is described in Talmud Yerushalmi, *Hagigah* chapter 2; *Bereshit Rabbah* 2:4; and *Tanchuma, Tazria* section 11.
**"The All-Merciful exempts one who sins under compulsion."** Talmud, *Avodah Zarah* 54a.

COMMENT: Hasidic sermons rarely mention contemporary events and issues directly. Instead they allow their listeners and readers to draw the implications for themselves. The Kotzker's message to his followers seems clear enough. He is warning them not to succumb to "enlightened" notion that God is somehow too remote for our individual deeds to matter in the divine scheme of things, that God doesn't care about what we do. The idea is not confined to the *Maskilim*, the Enlightened (that is, westernized) Jews of the Kotzker's time. It is still present among us, compounded by the common lack of belief or trust in God. But for those of us of a more spiritual bent and for those of us influenced by the growing clarion calls of the ecological movement against the climate crisis, the idea that every one of our deeds matters is gaining new traction.

## [166] The Miracle of Trust

CONTEXT: Simchah Bunam of Pshische was a key teacher in a radical re-interpretation of Hasidism in early nineteenth century, emphasizing authenticity and truthfulness in all things. Here he employs an old technique of using initial and final letters of the words of a Biblical text to spell out other words to make his point.

TEXT:
"*NachoN libO batuaCH bYHVH.* [*SamuCH libo, lo yiyra…*] (Their heart is set, trusting in the Eternal. Their heart is established; they shall not fear; they shall look [in triumph] on their enemies.)"

Psalm 112:7-8

The final letters of the words from *NachoN* to *SamuCH*, including *SamuCH*, are the letters [of the word] *CHaNuKaH*, while [letters of] the two words [at the beginning and end of the phrase], namely the letter *N* of *Nachon* and the letter *S* of *Samuch* spell *NeS* (a sign, miracle), that is, that the miracle of Chanukah came from this: That they trusted in the Eternal and so were worthy to "look [in triumph] on their enemies."

> Simchah Bunam of Pshische (1765-1827) in Yo'etz Qayyam Qadish Rokotz (ed.), *Siach Sarfei Qodesh* (The Conversation of the Holy Serafim) (Lodz, 1931) pt.3, p.52.

COMMENT: What is the miracle of Chanukah? The one day's worth of oil that lasted for eight days, until new supplies could be brought to the Temple in Jerusalem, as the Talmud suggests? That a small band of Jewish soldiers defeated the much more numerous Seleucid armies, as our *Al-HaNissim* prayer says? Perhaps, but for Simchah Bunam, the real miracle of Chanukah was the trust in God displayed by the Maccabees and their supporters. It was that trust that made them worthy of victory. How strong is our trust in God?

# [167] Not Because of the Oil

CONTEXT: *Chemdat Yamim* is an extensive anonymous work, compiled and composed by a secret follower of the failed messiah, Shabbetai Zevi. It has remained a popular text among Hasidic and ultra-orthodox groups to this day.

TEXT:

And just before the lamp of Israel was nearly extinguished, the Eternal One aroused the spirit of the priests of the Eternal, those who serve God and perform the divine will, "and inspired them to teach." [God] said: "Strengthen your weak hands, avenge the Eternal, [and] afterward you shall be gathered to your people]" (Numbers 31:2). [God] strengthened and encouraged the hands of the Hasmonean and his sons to be courageous among heroes, he and his sons, and the word went throughout the camp: "Whoever is for the Eternal, come to me!" So, all the elders of Israel gathered to him, everyone a warrior of mighty deeds whose heart the Eternal had touched to exact the vengeance of the Eternal – the zealotry of the Eternal acts in this way. They fought against [Antiochus] and drove him away; they followed and defeated him and his people, so that no one was left. When they returned [to Jerusalem], they gave praise and thanks to God, and vigorously undertook the maintenance of the Temple. The light of Israel burst into flame, and the land was made brighter by its glory, as in days of old. This alone would have been sufficient as memorial for the descendants of Israel as a miracle, to establish the eight days of Chanukah [be celebrated] with *Hallel* and thanksgiving. This is not as it enters most people's minds. [Most think] that they were established primarily because of the miracle of the cruse [of oil]. No holidays have been established with *Hallel* and thanksgiving because of a miracle that somehow overturned the natural order! On the contrary, they exist on account of a deliverance, as a result of some deliverance.

Anon. (17th century), *Chemdat Yamim* (Most Precious of Days) (Jerusalem, 2004), v. 4, p. 278b.

NOTES:

**Before the lamp of Israel was nearly extinguished...** by the Seleucid oppression.

**The priests of the Eternal...** Mattathias, instigator of the rebellion was of priestly stock.

**"And inspired them to teach"** ... A phrase borrowed from Exodus 35:34.

***Hallel...*** Psalms 113-118.

**The Hasmonean...** Mattathias. Hasmonean was his family name. After his death, leadership passed to the third of his five sons, Judah the Maccabee.

COMMENT: This account of the Chanukah miracle strikes me as remarkably modern and rational. To be fair, our anonymous author does not deny the miracle of the oil; he merely states that it is not the most important element of the story. We too need to keep our focus on the element of an extraordinary victory against seemingly impossible odds.

# THE CHANUKAH LIGHTS

## [168] The Significance of 36

CONTEXT: An early Hasidic rabbi and possible student of the Ba'al Shem Tov, Pinchas of Koretz frequently comments on folk customs and practices. Here he discusses the "coincidences" surrounding the number 36.

TEXT:

It says in the [books of] customs (*minhagim*) that one should light thirty-six candles on *Erev Shabbat* corresponding to the thirty-six hours that the first light shone; that is, the first person was created on *Erev Shabbat* [i.e. Friday]: hence twelve hours for *Erev Shabbat* plus twenty-four hours of Shabbat [itself]. Then it was hidden. My teacher said that this is the light of the thirty-six tractates of the Talmud and the thirty-six candles of Chanukah. (Once he said that the light was hidden in the thirty-six tractates.) Therefore, the miracle of Chanukah occurred because then the hidden light was revealed.

(Another time I heard from him that every Chanukah, at the time of the lighting of the candles, the hidden light is revealed, and that it is the light of the messiah.) I heard these words from his holy mouth on the night of the Shabbat that was the first one that he had prayed in his synagogue in the holy congregation of Ostrog. Later, when he entered the synagogue in the morning, he counted the candles that had been burning in the synagogue, and found exactly thirty-six, neither more nor less, and it pleased him greatly.

(It was also his custom during Chanukah, at the time of the lighting of the candles, not to close the [shutters of the] windows, in order that the candles should shine through the windows into the street "in order to publicize the miracle.") On all other nights he was very particular about closing the [shutters of the] windows at the start of evening.

Pinchas of Koretz (1726-1791), *Midrash Pinchas* (Pinchas' Interpretation) (Jerusalem, 1971), p. 2a.

NOTES:

**In the [books of] customs (*minhagim*)...** There are numerous such books, but I have been unable to locate the source of this practice.

**Thirty-six candles on Erev Shabbat...** In synagogue to provide lighting. (See the next paragraph of this text.)

**The thirty-six hours that the first light shone...** See *Bereshit Rabbah* 11:2. This spiritual light is hidden away for the righteous in the world-to-come, but the Koretzer suggests that it can be accessed now, in this world.

**The thirty-six tractates of the Talmud...** There actually sixty-three tractates, but in the Babylonian Talmud only thirty-six have *Gemara*, that is, later rabbinic expansions.

**The thirty-six candles of Chanukah...** Strictly speaking, there are forty-four, but eight (the *shamashim*) are used to light the others. The connection between the thirty-six lights of Chanukah and the thirty-six hours during which Adam had access to the hidden light goes back to at least the twelfth century. See *Sefer HaRokeach* (§227) by Elazar of Worms (c.1160-1237).

**The first one that he had prayed in his synagogue in the holy congregation of Ostrog...** R. Pinchas was forced to leave Koretz for Ostrog in 1770 as a result of altercations with followers of the Maggid of Mezritch.

**"In order to publicize the miracle"** ... It is traditional to put the *chanukiyah* (the Chanukah candelabrum) in a position where it can be seen from outside the home. Talmud, *Shabbat* 21a & Rashi.

COMMENT: I love this passage. It almost gives the feeling of being in Koretzer's presence. But I also like the notion of the hidden light which God stashed away for the righteous rather than leave it accessible to the wicked. A question that arises is: Can it be accessed today, in this world? R. Pinchas says yes. Historically, he says, it manifests in God's saving acts and again, liturgically, when we commemorate those acts. It manifests in our holy texts and again, when we study those texts. The light of primordial creation, the light of the messianic age, is attainable by us, today, in this world.

# [169] Why Do We Light Lamps?

CONTEXT: Avraham of Sochtchov lived in Poland in the late nineteenth and early twentieth century, and was a student and son-in-law of

Menachem Mendel of Kotzk before becoming a *rebbe* in his own right. The question he asks here has a much simpler traditional answer. We light lamps for Chanukah in remembrance of the miracle of the oil. But his answer goes deeper into the meaning of the festival.

TEXT:

Why was it decided to light lamps to commemorate the miracle of the candelabrum in the Temple, and [why] was it not decided to commemorate the other miracles that were performed at that time? Because it is written: "The commandment is a lamp and the Torah light" (Proverbs 6:23). Now the wisdom (*hochmah*) of the Greeks was dominant in those days, and they said that [their] wisdom went as far as the intellect [could go], and that what was beyond the intellect could be considered nothing. However, we, believers, the children of believers, think that the light of the Torah is beyond the intellect. Look here, "the commandment is a lamp" – it is from the One Who commands, from the Torah. Therefore, the Torah is higher than the intellect because the commandment receives [divine] influence from the Torah.

Look here, the candelabrum alludes to the light of the Torah, and in that case, this commandment by which we are enjoined to light the lamps of the candelabrum, [means that] there must be a higher light from which the candelabrum derives its [divine] influence. In this way, they [the Maccabees] defeated the Greeks, because they demonstrated to them that there is a higher light. Therefore, it was decreed that we should commemorate precisely this miracle, because this is how they defeated the Greeks.

Avraham ben Ze'ev Nachum Bornstein of Sochtchov (1839-1910) in Yo'etz Qayyam Qadish Rokotz (ed.), *Siach Sarfei Qodesh* (The Conversation of the Holy Serafim) (Lodz, 1931) pt.3, p.126.

NOTE:

**Believers, the children of believers…** See Talmud, *Shabbat* 97a & *Shemot Rabbah* 3:12.

COMMENT: Avraham of Sochtchov opposed all modern technological innovations and western ideas, and this is evident in his attack on "Greek wisdom." (*Hochmah* can mean "science" as well as "wisdom.") We may not share his opposition to these things, but if we are true religious seekers we must recognize that our science can only take us so far. And that things that lie beyond the scope of science may be some of the most important aspects of being human: the search for meaning and the hidden depths of spirituality.

## [170] The *Chanukiya* Symbolizes Humanity

CONTEXT: *Gallei Razayya* was written in the mid-sixteenth century, probably in Safed, by an unknown author and is primarily concerned with theories of the human soul, especially transmigration or reincarnation.

TEXT:

You should know the secret of these lamps [of Chanukah]. They are wonderful, and allude to supernal spiritual, holy and pure things. Just as [the lamps] give light below, so too do the [spiritual things] give light above and arouse divine influence and light in the supernal worlds, in order that they may be projected into the world of the intellect. Each lamp is a *mitzvah* in its own right, and therefore, [our sages] ordained that each lamp has a blessing in its own right.

Now a lamp is an object that is made up of three physical things and one spiritual thing. The vessel, the wick and the oil are the physical things, and the flame is the spiritual. Together they allude to earthly human beings who are made up of three [essential physical] things: the liver, the heart and the brain are the physical, [plus the soul, which is the spiritual].

Anon., *Gallei Razayya* (Heaps of Secrets), (Mogilev, 1792), p. 23b.

NOTES:

**Each lamp has a blessing in its own right...** Perhaps the reference is the view that each person in a household should have their own *chanukiyah*. See Talmud, *Shabbat* 21a.

**The vessel, the wick and the oil...** Candles only gradually replaced oil for use during Chanukah, and some people continue to hold that oil is more appropriate, given the miracle story.

COMMENT: The lamp is an ancient symbol for the soul. (See, for example, Proverbs 20:27: "The lamp of the Eternal is the human soul.") What might be the implications of such a notion? Among them might be the capacity of the human soul to shed light in darkness, to bring morality and spirituality to bear in conditions of hardship and ignorance. May God give us strength to shine brightly.

## [171] Seeing the Good

CONTEXT: Levi Yitzchak of Berditchev, in Ukraine, is one of the best loved Hasidic teachers. He founded no dynasty, but his teachings are preserved in *Kedushat Levi*, a volume of his sermons.

183

TEXT:
The principle is that on Rosh Hashanah and Yom Kippur, the Holy Blessed One remembers Israel for good, but on Chanukah Israel *sees* the good in their mind, i.e. in thought. For [the phrase] "the eyes of the community" [Numbers 15:24] is explained by Rashi as "the wise of the community." Therefore, Chanukah involves candles, that is, seeing. Then comes Purim, which relates to speech, since the *Megillah* is read aloud, and then Pesach, which relates to action, since *matzah* has to be eaten. Thus, Chanukah, which concerns seeing, occurs in the month of *Kislev*, whose permutation [of the Tetragrammaton] is *VYHH*, which may be found in the opening letters [of the words of the phrase] "the Canaanite inhabitants of the land saw" (*Vayar Yoshev Ha'aretz Ha-k'na'ani*) [Genesis 50:11].
Levi Yitzchak of Berditchev (1740-1809), *Qedushat Levi* (The Holiness of Levi) (Munkacs, 1829), p. 23a.

NOTES:
**"The wise of the community"** ... I imagine that this comment by Rashi is quoted from memory. In his commentary on Talmud, *Ta'anit* 24a, he says "the eyes of the community" means the elders.
**Whose permutation...** According to kabbalistic tradition, each month of the Hebrew year is assigned one of the twelve permutations of the letters of the Tetragrammaton (*YHVH*), which is then located in the opening letters of four consecutive words in the Hebrew Bible. That of *Kislev* is given as *VYHH*. (See Immanuel Chai Ricchi, *Mishnat Hasidim, Masechet Cheshvan v'Kislev*, chapter 1, mishnah 1.)
**"The Canaanite inhabitants of the land saw"** ... This re-connects *Kislev*, and therefore Chanukah, to seeing. What the Canaanites saw was Egyptian's mourning for Jacob.

COMMENT: I liked the idea of Chanukah as the festival of seeing. (The Chanukah lights are, in fact, only to be seen, and not to be used in any way.) Not only do we see the candles which form such an essential part of the holiday, but we can also "see" the power of God clearly in the Chanukah story. For the tale of how the Jewish people under Maccabean leadership defeated the far superior forces of the Seleucid Empire and cleansed the Temple is the only one of our ancient redemptive events to occur, as it were, in the full light of history. It is therefore the only one of which historians can posit a precise date: the first Chanukah occurred on 25 *Kislev* 164 BCE.

# [172] Kindling the Soul

CONTEXT: Avraham Ya'akov of Sadagora was the son and successor of Yisra'el of Ruzhyn, himself a descendant of the Maggid of Mezritch. The family had moved to Sadagora, in the Austrian Empire, from Ruzhyn to escape persecution in Tsarist Russia.

TEXT:

"Lighting [the Chanukah lights] is performing a *mitzvah*; [placing them where they can be visible outside is not]."

"It is not the place that honors the person, but the person who honors the place," for, at whatever place or level a person stands, if they do not kindle their soul with "the lamp of a *mitzvah* or the light of Torah" [Proverbs 6:23], they are nothing. But if they kindle their soul with the light of a *mitzvah* or the light of Torah, and repent, then the Holy Blessed One sends them life-force from a place that is much higher than the lowly place where they are standing. By joining with the lights [above], they draw divine influence into the world. Hence, the place does not honor the person, but the person honors the place. And thus, lighting is performing a *mitzvah*, but placing [where it is visible outside] is not.

Avraham Ya'akov of Sadagora (d.1883), *Bet Yisra'el* (The House of Israel) (Piotrkov, 1913), p. 65.

NOTES:

**"Lighting [the Chanukah lights] is performing a *mitzvah*...** Talmud, *Shabbat* 22b. This is not to say that we should not place the lights where they can be seen from outside. Only to suggest that it is not technically a *mitzvah*, and may be set aside under certain conditions, danger, for example.

**"It is not the place that honors the person..."** Talmud, *Ta'anit* 21b.

COMMENT: R. Avraham treats the lighting of the Chanukah lamp as a metaphor for spiritual enlightenment. In his view, our spiritual status as Jews, as human beings, at any given moment is achieved only through the study of Torah or the performance of *mitzvot*. Such study or observance must, in his words, kindle the soul. I think this means that it must be accompanied by appropriate enthusiasm and commitment. There are spiritual rewards for doing this, and our spiritual level is improved, but it should not be an excuse for self-congratulation or arrogance. Just as we are not unequivocally commanded to place our *chanukiyah* where it can be seen from outside our homes, so too we must not engage in Torah study or *mitzvot* in order to be seen to be religious. Any recognition that may accrue should be seen as purely incidental.

## [173] The Meaning of Not Using the Lights

CONTEXT: This brief extract comes from a book of sermons by the *CHIDA* (an acronym of his name Hayyim Yosef David Azulai) the distinguished eighteenth century Italian kabbalist, author, fundraiser and bibliophile.

TEXT:
     ... All the observances of Chanukah are intended to recall the commandments. [For example,] it is forbidden to utilize the light [of the *Chanukiyah*] because a commandment should be done for the sake of heaven, and "not for the purpose of receiving a reward."
     Hayyim Yosef David Azulai (1724-1806), *Hadrei Vaten* (Innermost Parts) (Jerusalem, 1990), p. 92a-b.

NOTE:
**"Not for the purpose of receiving a reward"** ... A phrase recycled from the Mishnah, *Pirkei Avot* 1:3.

COMMENT: Every night in Chanukah, after lighting the *menorah*, we recite the prayer *HaNerot Halalu* ("These lights..."). It reminds us the signs and the wonders that the lights commemorate, but also that we are not meant to make us of them, but only to see them. For the *CHIDA*, this becomes a symbol of the manner in which we should undertake all *mitzvot*, doing them for their own sake, and not for any ulterior motive or purpose.

## THE *AL HANISSIM* PRAYER

## [174] God's Name is Not Mentioned

CONTEXT: Yitzchak of Vorki was a disciple of several Hasidic masters, and a friend to Menachem Mendel of Kotzk. The prayer known as *Al HaNissim* ("For the signs") is recited in every *Amidah* and every *Birkat HaMazon* (Grace after Meals) during the eight days of Chanukah.

TEXT:
     Why is the Tetragrammaton not mentioned in the prayer *Al HaNissim* ("For the signs")? We must explain this in the same way [that we explain the fact] that the name of Moses is never mentioned in *parashat Ve'Atah Tetzaveh* ("And you shall command"). After the signs and wonders that Moses had done, he was so close to the Blessed God that it

186

was no longer necessary that he be called by name, but simply "you" (*Atah*), just as a child never calls their parent by their name.

Now, it seems to me that after the signs and wonders that the Blessed God had performed for Israel in the Hellenistic period, that Israel had become so close to God, as if they were like a child to the Holy Blessed One that they were no longer required to write the Tetragrammaton in *Al HaNissim* that pertains to the days of Mattathias, but only "And You" (*V'ata*): "And You in your great mercy stood by them…"

Yitzchak of Vorki (d.1858), *Bet Yitzchak* (House of Isaac) (Jerusalem, 1992), p.156.

NOTES:
**The Tetragrammaton…** The four-letter divine name transliterated as *YHVH*, but which we normally read as *Adonai*.
***Parashat Ve'Atah Tetzaveh…*** Exodus 27:20-30:10.
**Mattathias…** The instigator of the revolt against Antiochus, and father of Judah the Maccabee.

COMMENT: Can we ever feel so close to God that we no longer feel it necessary to call upon "God" in our private prayers? Could we just say "You"? Levi Isaac of Berditchev wrote a little song to God in Yiddish. Its most recurrent word is "*du*" (you). Hence its name, *A Dudele*. Perhaps this is a level that can be attained by anyone, everyone, but to refer to God only as "You" would be a *chutzpah*!

# [175] Chanukah and the World-to-Come

CONTEXT: Nachman of Bratzlav (Breslov) was the great-grandson of the Ba'al Shem Tov, and a uniquely gifted and creative teacher.

TEXT:
The days of Chanukah are days of thanksgiving, as it has been written: "And they established these days of Chanukah to thank, and to praise…" And days of thanksgiving are an aspect of the delights of the world-to-come, for this is the essence of the delight of the world-to-come: to thank and to praise [God's] great blessed name and to recognize the Blessed One, for in this way [we become] much nearer and closer to God. For all those who know and recognize the Blessed One most are nearest to [God]. All other things will be completely annihilated in the [messianic] future, according to the teaching that "All [sacrificial]-offerings will be abolished, except for the thank-offering" … In that future, nothing will be left except the aspect of thanks and thanksgiving, to give thanks, praise

and know the Blessed One, as it is written: "For the earth will be filled with the knowledge of Eternal as the waters cover the sea" (Isaiah 11:[9]) for this is all the delight of the world-to-come.

> Nachman of Bratzlav (1772-1811), *Liqqutei Moharan* (Collected Sayings of Our Teacher, the Rav, Rabbi Nachman) (Jerusalem: Meshech HaNachal, 1986), pt.2, §2:1, p.3a.

NOTES:
**As it has been written…** In the prayer *Al HaNissim* ("For the signs") recited in each *Amidah* and Grace After Meals during Chanukah.
**"All [sacrificial]-offerings will be abolished, except for the thank-offering"** … *Midrash Vayikra Rabbah, Tzav* 9 & *Emor* 27.

COMMENT: If giving thanks is a primary function of the messianic age, then Chanukah is a taste of that promised future. Is it possible that every time we express our thanks to God and to others that this too is a taste of the messianic days? It is certainly amazing how saying thank you can sometimes transform a difficult situation.

# THE *DREIDL*

## [176] The *Dreidl* and the Messiah

CONTEXT: In the literature stemming from the school of R. Pinchas of Koretz, the Rav always refers to Pinchas himself. His sayings seem to be drawn mainly from conversations rather than sermons.

TEXT:
Why is it customary to engrave [the letters] *Nun-Gimel-Hei-SHin* on the *dreidl?* The Rav said that this is an allusion to the *mitzvot* of Chanukah, namely kindling [the lights] and reciting *Hallel*. Thus, *Nun-SHin* [stands for] *Nerot Shemoneh* (Eight Lights) [and] *Hei-Gimel* [stands for] *Hallel Gamur* (Full Hallel).

Then he said: Since the custom of Israel is Torah, then just as there are seventy facets to the Torah, so too [there are seventy facets to a custom]. [Therefore, I can offer a mystical interpretation of the *dreidl*.] Thus, it seems to me that these four letters [on the dreidl] have the same numerical value as *MaSHIaCH* (Messiah).

> Pinchas of Koretz (1726-1791), *Imre Pinchas* (Pinchas' Sayings) (Tel Aviv: Arnberg, 1974), p. 129, §663.

NOTES:

**Nun-Gimel-Hei-SHin...** These stand for the words *Nes Gadol Hayah SHam* (a great miracle happened there), but also are the basis of the traditional dreidl game.

**Hallel Gamur (Full Hallel)** ... Psalms 113-118, as opposed to the so-called Half *Hallel*, which skips part of psalms 115 & 116.

**The custom of Israel is Torah...** A common saying of uncertain origin. Its earliest known occurrence is in Ramban's commentary on *Pesachim* 7b.

**The same numerical value...** *Nun-Gimel-Hei-SHin* have a numerical value of $50+3+5+300 = 358$. *MaSHIaCH* has a numerical value of $40+300+10+8 = 358$.

COMMENT: Chanukah is, of course, a celebration of the defeat of the enemies of the Jewish people and of the restoration of national independence. Traditionally, Jewish history is seen as a progression from the past, the age of the patriarchs, the Exodus and Giving of the Torah, towards the Messianic Era. From the Koretzer's perspective, Chanukah, with its redemptive elements, points towards the ultimate redemption. In hard times, we need to keep our messianic goal in mind.

## [177] The World is Like a *Dreidl*

CONTEXT: Nachman of Bratzlav, the great-grandson of the Besht and one of the most original minds in Hasidic history, had a devoted disciple called Natan of Nemirov. Nathan wrote down everything he heard his master say, and after Nachman's death, everything he could glean from others. The following comes from one of Nachman's recorded discourses.

TEXT:

In truth, you should know that the entire world is like the spinning top we call a *dreidl*. Everything returns and is changed: human to angel, angel to human, head to foot and foot to head, and similarly with everything that is in the world. All of them return and revolve and are changed this into that and that into this, from higher to lower and from lower to higher, but truly, at the root, all is one...

> Natan of (Nemirov) Breslov (ed.) (1780-1844), *Sichot HaRaN* (Conversations with the Rav, Rabbi Nachman) (Jerusalem, 1979), p. 26, §40.

COMMENT: In this passage, Nachman has transformed the humble *dreidl* from a child's toy into a metaphysical symbol. Life is just a constant flow of changes. In fact, the only thing that never changes is change. It is the only constant. Our lives can change irrevocably in an instant, for good or for ill. The truly spiritual person knows that behind all this change stands God, the Unchanging One around which all else revolves.

# PURIM

ESTHER ACCUSING HAMAN

For we are sold, I and my people, to be destroyed, to be slain, and to perish
Then Haman was afraid before the king and the queen.... (Esther 7:4, 6)

Esther accuses Haman (Esther 7:1-10), by Gustave Doré.

# [178] Physical or Spiritual?

CONTEXT: Yitzchak of Vorki was a disciple of the *rebbe* of Kotzk, Menachem Mendel. An audience with the *tzaddik* is an important part of Hasidic communal practice. Hasidim would bring their requests, often written, and await the rabbi's answer. The requests themselves often deal with "life, children and sustenance" (cf. Talmud, *Moed Katan* 28a).

TEXT:

Before the morning service on Purim, a certain wealthy man pushed in and entered into the presence of our holy rabbi with a note [requesting that the *rebbe* pray for] material things, but every word that was written there was interpreted by our rabbi as concerning spiritual matters, and in that manner, he read the note to the end. Then he said "Torah" on that note.

Afterwards, at his holy table, at the Purim meal, he related: "Before prayers, a certain wealthy man came to me with a note about material things, but he was actually in spiritual danger, for is it possible that today is a time for the fulfilment and acceptance of a request for physical things? So, I advised him that the entire subject of his note concerned spiritual matters."

Yitzchak of Vorki (d.1858), *Bet Yitzchak* (The House of Isaac) (Jerusalem, 1992), pp.158-159.

NOTE:
**Then he said "Torah"** ... He gave a brief sermonette.

COMMENT: Purim seems our most material of festivals. Where is the spirituality in the story where God is never mentioned, or in our indulgence in alcohol or *homentashen*? It raises the question of the difference between material matters and spiritual matters. We talk of these as if they were very distinct, but in fact, they overlap and intersect at multiple levels. Sometimes what we experience as material desires are really spiritual desires that we have not recognized as such. We want to acquire more and more objects, pile on ever more pleasurable experiences, try to associate ourselves only with the beautiful and rich, when all along what we really lack may be only a proper sense of our own self-worth.

# SHABBAT ZACHOR

## [179] The Lesson of *Zachor*

CONTEXT: Hayyim Yosef David Azulai (known as the *CHIDA*) was a rabbi, fundraiser, bibliophile and head of the kabbalistic community of Bet El in Jerusalem. *Hadrei Vaten* is one of several books of his collected sermons. *Shabbat Zachor* immediately precedes Purim and is so called because of the special *maftir* for the day (Deuteronomy 25:17-19), which begins with the word *Zachor* and prescribes the remembrance of the cowardly attack the Amalekites made against the Israelites (Exodus 17:8-15). (Haman is said to be a descendant of Amalek.)

TEXT:
Perhaps the following is the meaning of the command of remembering what Amalek did: *ZaCHOR* stands for *Zikkaron* (remembrance), *Kavod* (honor) *V'ahavat Rea* (and love of neighbor).
Hayyim Yosef David Azulai (1724-1806), *Hadrei Vaten* (Innermost Parts) (Jerusalem, 1990), p.152.

NOTE:
*ZaCHOR* **stands for...** The four letters of this word are here treated as a *notarikon*, an anagram.

COMMENT: What does the *CHIDA* mean when he offers this anagram? He doesn't explain it further. Perhaps *Zikkaron* means more than just remembering what Amalek did. Attacks on the Jewish people may be a frequent and recurrent feature of Jewish history (and the Jewish present), but we need to remember the positive aspects of Jewish life and culture, rather than focus on the negative. We must not let anti-Semitism define us. *Kavod* (honor) suggests that we should consider ourselves honored to be Jewish and proud of our rich heritage. And *V'ahavat Rea*, love of neighbor, points to ethical behavior as a primary means of living out that heritage.

## [180] Amalek Within

CONTEXT: Another passage discussing *parashat Zachor*, the extra *maftir* that is read on the Shabbat before Purim. This one is by a descendant of the Maggid of Mezritch and member of the powerful Ruzhyn dynasty of Hasidic teachers. Yisra'el of Sadagora delivered this sermon on *Shabbat Zachor* in 1886.

TEXT:
"Remember what Amalek did to you..."

Deuteronomy 25:17-19

[We] always need to remember what the inclination towards evil, symbolized by Amalek, has done to us. So, when a good thought enters [our] hearts, we should immediately use it to refine our speech and action, so the inclination towards evil, symbolized by Amalek, [and] representing forgetfulness in our hearts, should not come and spoil that good thought.

Yisra'el Friedman of Sadagora (1853-1907), *Or Yisra'el* (Israel's Light) (1997), p.105.

COMMENT: One of those jokes that is not really a joke says "just because you are paranoid doesn't mean they're not out to get you." We Jews are especially concerned about antisemitism, and with good cause, of course. We may be paranoid, but our history suggests that we have good reason to be. On the other hand, fixating on anti-Jewish hatred, as we sometimes do, is not healthy either. Yisra'el of Sadagora reminds us that the evil we experience does not come solely from outside, like the real Amalek did. It may be found within us, too – a psychological Amalek, if you will. This Amalek can never be defeated, but it can be controlled by our impulse towards good.

## [181] Haman, then Mordechai

CONTEXT: In this text, Ya'akov Tzemach, the last great kabbalist of Safed in the Galilee, discusses the odd custom of getting drunk on Purim as prescribed by the Talmud.

TEXT:
Regarding what our rabbis have said about becoming so drunk that you do not know [the difference between "Cursed be Haman" and "Blessed be Mordechai"], the point is that within the "shells" there is always a spark of holiness that sheds light within it, but that [the shell] annuls it. So, at first, you need to say "Cursed be Haman" to draw light down even to that spark, but you must not say it with any other intention when you are drunk, and your consciousness is already going, so that the intention should not – God forbid – be to illumine the shell [itself]. It seems to me that when we draw down the light of the "brain" of *Binah* into Rachel through the drinking of wine in great abundance, that there is a great illumination, so that she may possess the power to grant illumination even as far as that spark that is in the midst of the shell.

Ya'akov ben Hayyim Tzemach (died after 1665), *Nagid Umetzaveh* (Telling and Commanding, Isaiah 55:4) (Jerusalem: 1965), p. 139.

NOTES:
**Our rabbis have said ...** Talmud, *Megillah* 7b.
**Within the "shells" ...** In the kabbalistic scheme of Isaac Luria, "sparks" of divine light are held captive in "shells," the shards of the "vessels" broken in the process of emanation of the *Sefirot* and the creation of the universe. There, they await liberation through the meditation techniques undertaken by kabbalists.
**We draw down the light of the "brain" of** *Binah* **into Rachel...** *Binah* (Understanding) is third of the trio of the highest *Sefirot*, including *Keter* (Crown) and *Hochmah* (Wisdom), corresponding to the human brain. Rachel is a name given to *Malchut* (Sovereignty), also known as *Shechinah* (the Presence of God). This process is helped by consuming alcohol!

COMMENT: In this world, the kabbalists tell us, good and evil are totally intertwined, mixed up. We don't really need them to tell us that. If we are honest and sensitive, then we know that it is sometimes very difficult to differentiate between good and evil. We all know that murder is wrong, but what about killing in self-defense? In practice, we are often not choosing between good and evil, but between two unpalatable evils as we try to determine which is the least bad. Ya'akov Tzemach attempts to address these dilemmas in kabbalistic terms. He suggests that we must distinguish the holy spark within the evil from the evil itself. Haman, for all his murderous intent, is still a human being, and as such, worthy of our respect. But this is not the same as ignoring or condoning the evil that he does. On the contrary, we have to recognize that evil and move beyond it, towards good. Hence, we go from cursing Haman to blessing Mordechai.

# [182] A Hidden Miracle

CONTEXT: It is well known that God is never mentioned in *Megillat Esther*. Our prayer, *Al HaNissim* refers to miracles at Purim. Why is God not given credit? Levi Yitzchak of Berditchev, one of the best loved Hasidic teachers, shares the response of his teacher, the Maggid of Mezritch.

TEXT:
There are miracles that are hidden, as in the days of Mordecai and Esther, when there is no change in the natural order; instead, the miracle occurs within the natural order. Our master, Dov Berish said that this is why she is called Esther (*eSTeR*), because the miracle was hidden

195

(*behaSTeR*) within the natural order.

> Levi Yitzchak of Berditchev (1740-1809), *Kedushat Levi* (The Holiness of Levi) (Munkacs, 1829), p.114d.

NOTE:

**Our master, Dov Berish...** Dov Baer, the Maggid of Mezritch (died 1772), successor of the Ba'al Shem Tov and teacher of the next generation of Hasidic luminaries.

COMMENT: I have a friend who sometimes asks me: if there is a God, why do we not see miracles in the world today of the kind we find in the Bible? There may be many reasons one could offer, some more convincing than others, but for me, the key is in this comment from the Mezritcher Maggid. If we affirm God's existence and activity in the world, then perhaps miracles are happening around us all the time, but they are hidden, so unobtrusive as to be easily dismissed or taken for granted. The triumph of Esther and Mordechai over Haman looks like political maneuvers and machinations, but who is to say that this was not God at work saving God's people from destruction?

## *MEGILLAT ESTHER*

## [183] Why is This Little Book Called "The" *Megillah*

CONTEXT: In the Hebrew Bible, there are five *megillot* (small scrolls): Song of Songs, Ruth, Lamentations, Ecclesiastes, and Esther. But when we say "the *megillah*," without specifying we always mean *Megillat Esther*, the Book of Esther. The troubled and impassioned Kotzer *rebbe* offers his view.

TEXT:

> The reason why this book is called [the] *megillah* is because *megillah* is an expression of revelation (*hitgallut*).
>
> Menachem Mendel of Kotzk (1787-1859), *Sefer Amud Ha'Emet* (The Book of the Pillar of Truth) (Bnei Brak, 2000), p. 68.

COMMENT: On the surface, this seems a strange thing to say about a biblical book that does not even mention God. Menachem Mendel does not explain what he means, so we are left to speculate: In what sense is the scroll of Esther a revelation? What is being revealed here? Perhaps, paradoxically, the revelation is that there is no revelation, that salvation for the Jewish people arises not from divine intervention but through political maneuvering. There are no plagues, no angelic armies, no heavenly bodies stop their movements, nothing really extraordinary at all. In fact, it seems all very normal, but good triumphs over evil nevertheless. And that is a revelation for us, a model for us to achieve salvation in our time. Salvation, at least in the first instance, arises within the human heart, and who is to say that that in itself is not a revelation?

## [184] Naked Evil

CONTEXT: Ze'ev Wolf of Zhitomir, a disciple of the Maggid of Mezritch and the Maggid of Zlotchov, suggests a Kabbalah-based reason why King Ahasuerus demands that Queen Vashti appear before him and his courtiers naked. (The book of Esther does not say this explicitly; it is stated in Talmud, *Megillah* 14b.)

TEXT:
I heard in the name of the Ba'al Shem Tov who said [the following] on the verse, "When [people] say that King Ahasuerus ordered that Queen Vashti be brought before him but she would not come" [Esther 1:17]. The content of these words is holy because the *kelippot* (shells) only have existence if they are clothed in something. And since it says that the king ordered that Vashti be brought to him, it teaches [us] about the *kelippot* [on the side of evil], corresponding to Esther on [the side of] holiness. [It is] a *mitzvah* to bring the *kelippot* naked, without a garment. Therefore, she did not come, but refused to come, because she had no existence without intermediary clothing. This matter is profound, and not every mind can bear his holy words...
Ze'ev Wolf of Zhitomir (d.1800), *Or HaMe'ir* (The Illuminating Light) (Warsaw, 1883), pt.2, p.60.

NOTES:
**"When [people] say that King Ahasuerus ordered..."** These words are spoken by the King's minister Memucan as part of his speech advising him to divorce Vashti and find her successor. His main point seems to be that it would maintain male dominance throughout the empire.
**The *kelippot*...** In the Lurianic school of Kabbalah, these are the shells that contain and confine the sparks of holiness, preventing them from re-uniting with their Divine Source. Here, though, it is sufficient to think of them as representing the forces of evil.

COMMENT: I believe that most people do not deliberately choose to do evil. Rather, they do so because they have been persuaded (or persuaded themselves) that the evil is actually good or necessary. Using the

197

symbolism of Ze'ev Wolf of Zhitomir, the evil must be clothed in good in order for it be accepted. Rendering it naked would expose it for what it truly is, and that would nullify it in people's eyes.

## [185] The Jew and God

CONTEXT: A grandson of the Ba'al Shem Tov, Moshe Hayyim Efraim of Sudylkov, gives his commentary on the verse that introduces us to Mordechai for the first time. It is only one of two occurrences of the term *Yehudi*, Jew, in the Hebrew Bible. (The other is Zechariah 8:23.)

TEXT:
"There was a Jewish (*Yehudi*) man in Shushan the capital, and his name was Mordechai, son of Ya'ir, son of Shimi, son of Kish, a Benjaminite."
[Esther 2:5]
["A Jewish (Yehudi) man."] It is revealed and known that the name *Yehudi* derives from *Yehudah* (Judah), and that the letters of *YeHUDaH* contain the [divine] name of *YHVH*, [the name] which teaches [us that] God was, is and will be (*HayaH, HoVeH, v'YiHyeH*), and [the phrase] "there was a Jewish man" hints [at the notion] that [God] exists in every generation, always. And this aspect of [being] a Jew will not pass from among the Jews.
"And his name was Mordechai" – that is, the illumination of the divine aspect, [namely that of] "great lovingkindness" (*RaV HeSeD*), which has the same numerical value as *MoRDeCHaI*. Hence, in every generation there are righteous ones who are people of lovingkindness (*hesed*) who arouse "great lovingkindness" through their actions; that is, [they arouse] great lovingkindness which flows over all the worlds from *Ayn Sof* (the Infinite) without limit.
"Son of Ya'ir" – that is, [the lovingkindness] is taken from a place that illuminates with a pure and clear light.
"A Benjaminite (lit. son of the right hand)" – that is, he was the same as his name, [a man] of "great lovingkindness," from the side of the right hand. Hence, in every generation. Understand!
Moshe Hayyim Efraim of Sudylkov (d.1800), *Degel Machaneh Efraim* (The Flag of the Camp of Efraim, Numbers 2:18) (Jerusalem, 1963), p.139a.

NOTES:
**God was, is and will be (*HayaH, HoVeH, v'YiHyeH*)** ... The unpronounced and unpronounceable divine name *YHVH* is clearly related to the root *HaYaH* or *HaVaH*, meaning "to be."

198

Great Lovingkindness (*RaV HeSeD*), which has the same numerical value as *MoRDeCHaI*. *RaV HeSeD* = 200 + 2 + 8 + 60 + 4 = 274; *MoRDeCHaI* = 40 + 200 + 4 + 20 + 10 = 274. (The phrase r*av hesed* occurs 8 times in the Hebrew Bible, but is used there only of God.)

**A place that illuminates with a pure and clear light...** The name Ya'ir means "he will bring light." The place is probably the *Sefirah* of *Hochmah* (Wisdom), on the right side of the sefirotic tree, just above *Hesed*.

**The side of the right hand...** In the sefirotic system, the right hand symbolizes *Hesed*.

COMMENT: Moshe Hayyim Efraim takes Mordechai as a role model for the Hasidic *rebbe*, whose actions should emerge from *Hochmah*, divine wisdom and exhibit *Hesed*, Lovingkindness. Such people, he says, occur in every generation, and they serve as reminders to ordinary Jews of what being Jewish means. In my view, Mordechai should be seen as a role model for all Jews who would be religious or spiritual, not just Hasidic masters.

## [186] Singled Out

CONTEXT: Rabbi Menachem Mendel of Kotzk, known for his passion and fierce temper, discusses the deeper significance of what it means to be a Jew, based on the introduction to Mordechai in the *Megillah*.

TEXT:
"There was a Jewish (*Yehudi*) man in Shushan the capital, and his name was Mordechai, son of Yair, son of Shimi, son of Kish, a Benjaminite."

[Esther 2:5]

In the *Midrash Rabbah*, [it says]: "Why was he called a *Yehudi*? Was he not a Benjaminite? [But he was so called because] he affirmed the unity of the name of the Holy Blessed One against everyone in the world. [... Do not read *yeHudi* (Judahite or Jew), but *yeCHidi* (unique).]" Thus far the *midrash*.

But this is not clear, for isn't *Yehudi* what is actually written? It appears that by this the *midrash* is teaching us that whoever is alone (*yechidi*) is singled out to be attached (*davuk*) to the Unique One of the universe. This is what a Jew is...

Menachem Mendel of Kotzk (1787-1859), *Ohel Torah MeiHaRabbi MiKotzk* (The Torah Tent of the Rabbi of Kotzk) (Lublin, 1909), p.68.

NOTES:
**In the *Midrash Rabbah*...** *Esther Rabbah* 6:2. It is not uncommon for a *midrash* to suggest an apparent emendation of a biblical text in order to make a homiletic point.
**Was he not a Benjaminite?** ... *Yehudi* suggests a member of the tribe of Judah, rather than Benjamin. How could he be a member of both tribes?
***YeHudi* (Judahite or Jew), but *yeCHidi* (unique)...** In Hebrew, these two words sound nearly identical, and look very similar indeed, the only difference between them being a tiny bit of ink in one letter.
**Isn't *Yehudi* what is actually written?** ... What point is the *midrash* making when it suggests this emendation?

COMMENT: What does it mean to be a Jew? Of course, specific answers may vary depending on who is answering. We are all unique, yet at some level we share a common culture. What is it that unites us? that means that we identify with each other as Jews? For some it is that culture itself, and that is not wrong, but for me (and for the Kotzker) that culture is ultimately spiritual and religious. Even if we don't identify as religious Jews, our identity and history demand that we react and define ourselves in relation to Judaism as a religious tradition. Speaking very personally, my Jewish identity is very much bound up with my spirituality. It is precisely about being attached to God to the best of my endeavors.

# [187] Attached Only to God

CONTEXT: In Esther chapter 2 we are introduced to Mordechai, and then to his niece or cousin (the text is unclear), Esther. We are told that she is under his care, because she is an orphan. Here the Ba'al Shem Tov's grandson, Moshe Hayyim Ephraim of Sudylkov, endeavors to find a deeper significance to this description of the maiden who will save her people.

TEXT:
"For she had neither father nor mother."

[Esther 2:7]

[This may be explained] by way of [the verse]: "Hear, O daughter and see, incline your ear; forget your people and your father's house, and let the king be aroused by your beauty" (Psalm 45:11). That is, when you completely forget your people and your father's house, and attach yourself only to the blessed God, then "the king will be aroused by your beauty." "And a Tyrian lass (*bat tzor*)" [Psalm 45:12] – that is, the Torah, which is a balm (*tzor*) to you, that is, a [source of] healing, as in [the phrase] "is there no balm (*tzori*) in Gilead" (Jeremiah 8:22). See there. Hence, there is also an allusion [here, in the phrase] "for she had neither father nor mother." The enlightened will understand.

> Moshe Hayyim Efraim of Sudlykov (d.1800), *Degel Machaneh Efraim* (The Flag of the Camp of Efraim, Numbers 2:18) (Jerusalem, 1963), p.140a.

NOTE:
**"Hear, O daughter and see…"** Psalm 45, of which this is a part, seems to have been written for a royal wedding. Here, the king stands for God, and the bride is the soul.

COMMENT: This piece demands some thought. It suggests that spiritual healing, that is, true healing, requires that we put our family and ethnic relationships out of our minds and attach ourselves solely to God. This may seem a curious interpretation, given that Esther, rather than forgetting her people, risks death to save them. Perhaps the Sudlykover would reply that it was her reliance on God alone that gave her the courage to take that risk.

## [188] Two Kinds of Anti-Semites

CONTEXT: The author of this passage, Uri of Purisov, was a descendant of the Holy Jew of Pshische, and succeeded his father Ya'akov Zevi as leader of his community. He died in the Warsaw Ghetto, but this text was composed long before that. Here, he discusses a *piyyut*, a liturgical poem, recited in some congregations on Purim.

TEXT:
> Look here, on Purim people recite [the *piyyut* that begins] "Who sets the advice of the nations at nothing and frustrates (*vayaFeR*) the thoughts of the devious…" There are two types of those who are hostile to the Jews. There are those who are hostile without clever devices and deviousness, but only pursue [their goal] straightforwardly and explicitly. And there are those who follow a devious path, like the wicked Haman who sought out clever devices, making lots and casting *pur*. Now, of those who pursue without cleverness, as mentioned above, the Holy Blessed One pays back measure for measure, wiping out their advice without [further] cause, according to their simplicity. Hence, this [is the meaning of] "Who sets" (*heini*) – meaning, prevention (*hana'ah*), as [in the phrase] "her father (*heini*) prevents her" [Numbers 30:6]. "And frustrates the thoughts of the devious" – that is, of the masters of deviousness, like Haman the wicked – may his name be blotted out – who acted with

201

deviousness: "He cast *pur*, that is, lots" [Esther 3:7] The Holy Blessed One frustrated (*heifir*) his thought.

Uri Yehoshua Asher Elchanan of Purisov (1865-1941), *Imrei Yehoshua* (Joshua's Sayings) (Warsaw, 1929), p.47.

NOTES:

**"Who sets the advice of the nations at nothing..."** The opening line of the poem is based on Psalm 33:10: "The Eternal frustrates the advice of nations, sets at nothing the thoughts of peoples."

**Making lots and casting *pur*...** See Esther 3:7, quoted below.

**"Her father prevents her"** ... This Torah passage concerns an unmarried woman who takes a vow of which her father disapproves. He has the legal power to annul it and prevent her from fulfilling it.

COMMENT: The *rebbe* of Purisov tells us that there are two kinds of anti-Semites: those who are upfront and "in your face" about their hatred of us, and those who are more devious. These seem to be archetypal figures, always present, and always a threat. But the real threat comes when people of the second type come into power and influence, empowering and enlisting the aid of the first group. As I write (2019), this process seems to be underway in a number of the great Western democracies, and not only in relation to the Jews, but to all visible minorities: blacks, Hispanics, Muslims, immigrants, etc. Racists of the first type will always exist, but those who give them carte blanche can and must, like Haman, be driven from power.

## [189] Strict Judgment Tempered with Mercy

CONTEXT: With Haman overthrown, Mordechai is elevated to his position and, as a symbol of his new status, is allowed to wear royal apparel. For Moshe Hayyim Ephraim of Sudylkov, grandson of the Ba'al Shem Tov, and influential Hasidic author, this has kabbalistic significance.

TEXT:

There is another allusion: For it is well known that *Malchut* (Sovereignty, Kingdom) is an aspect of *Din* (Strict Judgment), along the lines of [the phrase]: "The law of the kingdom is the law" (*dina d'malchuta dina*). And *MoRDeCHaI* has the same numerical value as *Rav CHeSeD*, great lovingkindness. It is well known that the world would be unable to stand with the attribute of *Hesed*, lovingkindness, alone, because there would no punishment for the wicked. So, the attribute of *Din*, strict judgment, was joined with that of *Rachamim*, Compassion. This is alluded to [in the phrase, Esther 8:15]: "And Mordechai" – i.e., great lovingkindness; "went out from before the King" – the King beyond the kings of kings, the Holy Blessed One; "in royal apparel" – i.e., with the attribute of *Din*, an aspect of *Malchut*, joined with the attribute of *Hesed* and *Rachamim*. Understand.

Moshe Hayyim Efraim of Sudylkov (d.1800), *Degel Machaneh Efraim* (The Flag of the Camp of Efraim, Numbers 2:18) (Jerusalem, 1963), p.142a.

NOTES:
**"The law of the kingdom is the law"** (***dina d'malchuta dina***) ... A well-known principle of Jewish law, found multiple times in the Talmud.
**And *MoRDeCHaI* has the same numerical value as *Rav CHeSeD*, great lovingkindness...** *RaV HeSeD* = 200+2+8+60+4 = 274; *MoRDeCHaI* = 40+200+4+20+10 = 274.
**So, the attribute of *Din*, strict judgment, was joined with that of *Rachamim*, Compassion...** Based on the *midrash* in *Bereshit Rabbah* 12:15.

COMMENT: For Moshe Hayyim Ephraim, Mordechai's ascension to power in the Persian Empire represents the restoration of the perfect balance between strict justice and compassion that characterized God's act of creation of the world. In fact, it might be said that this restoration is exactly the aim of all kabbalistic meditation and of all righteous action. The world is in constant flux, and the forces of injustice easily take hold if good people's attention is elsewhere. Our life goal should always be the restoration of the primeval balance in our personal lives, in our society, in our environment.

# [190] A Thing and its Opposite

CONTEXT: It is quite clear from *Megillat Esther* itself that the name of this festival comes from the Persian word "*pur*," which means "lot". How do we know? Because the book itself feels the need to translate *pur* into Hebrew as *goral* (Esther 3:7 & 9:24). Elimelech of Grodzisk was a grandson of the Maggid of Koznitz and the father of Kalonymus Kalman Shapira of Piaseczne (1889-1943), known as the *rebbe* of the Warsaw ghetto.

TEXT:
'Therefore, they called these days Purim [after *pur*].'

[Esther 9:26]
[What follows is] based on our explanation that the essence of [divine] service is to unite the Attributes with Thought, and particularly during the days of Purim, when, as explained in [kabbalistic] books,

exalted awe is revealed below and everyone must join it with the Attributes. Then, automatically, one causes only Compassion and Lovingkindness to enter the world. For, within the Attributes there is an aspect of division, an aspect of good and evil. There are attributes of Compassion and Lovingkindness, and the opposite. When a person unites the Attributes, and they are annulled in Thought, they automatically cause Compassion and Lovingkindness only to be drawn from above. Hence, this is [the meaning of the phrase]: "They called these days." "They called" is a term for Thought, as explained in [kabbalistic] books. "Days" [also refers to] Thought, as is well known. And "these" (*ha'eileh*) [refers to] the Attributes, for six times six is the numerical value of *Ha'eiLeH*. That is, one draws the Attributes into Thought. And by this means, [we analyze] Purim into *PUR YM*. "*PUR* is the lot" [Esther 3:7, 9:24] – this teaches about a thing and its opposite, which [in turn] teaches about the Attributes, which [represent] the aspect of division, as mentioned above. But *YaM* (sea) [represents] *Binah* (Understanding), the world of Thought. That is, in this way, one draws compassion and lovingkindness from the world of *Binah* into the Attributes.

Elimelech ben Hayyim Meir Yechiel of Grodzisk (1824-1892), *Imrei Elimelech* (Elimelech's Sayings) (n. p., 1876), p.77a-b.

NOTES:

**To unite the Attributes with Thought...** This notion operates on two levels simultaneously. On the kabbalistic level, the Attributes are the seven lower *Sefirot*, from *Hesed* and *Gevurah* down to *Yesod*, while Thought refers to *Binah*, from which they all emerge and in which they are all unified. On the psychological level, the term "Attributes" refers to our emotions, particularly, our capacity for love (*Hesed*) and for strict judgment (*Din/Gevurah*). These opposites are reconciled in our higher thought processes, where Understanding (*Binah*) allows us to take a more balanced and nuanced view of our emotions.

**For six times six is the numerical value of *Ha'eiLeH*...** *Ha'eiLeH* has a *gematria* (numerological value) of $5 + 1 + 30 + 5 = 36$. There are six Attributes (*Hesed, Gevurah, Tiferet, Netzach, Hod and Yesod*), each of which itself contains six attributes; hence, thirty-six.

**This teaches about a thing and its opposite...** It is not clear how the lots in the book of Esther worked, but it appears that this may have been a binary process. That is, the taking of lots would result in a yes or no answer to whatever question is posed, in this case, Haman's choice of date for the pogrom against the Jews of the empire. Hence, the reference to a thing and its opposite. And opposites comprise the seven lower attributes.

**But *YaM* (sea) [represents] *Binah* (Understanding)...** *Binah* is frequently described as the sea from which all rivers (i.e., the lower *Sefirot*) flow. Hence, the two syllables of Purim indicate the reconciliation of opposites in Understanding.

COMMENT: We live in a world that is riven by divisions, often expressed in binary terms, despite the clear evidence that life is actually more complicated and much more nuanced that such binary thinking would allow. The book of Esther is itself an example of binary thinking: the bad Haman vs. the good Mordechai and Esther. Elimelech of Grodzisk asks us to look beyond conflict towards reconciliation, towards a greater level of understanding where compromise and peace become possible. May the day come soon!

## [191] Costumes on Purim

CONTEXT: Making and wearing costumes, i.e., disguising oneself, is a favorite part of Purim for many people, adults as well as children. In his Torah commentary (which appears in numerous collections), R. Kalonymos, a disciple of Elimelech of Lyzhansk and a *rebbe* in his own right, discusses the mystical significance of this unusual custom. He gives it a rather radical twist.

TEXT:
... The light of wisdom shines on all the worlds every Purim day, and each year on these days of Purim, the light of wisdom sparkles and shines on all the worlds more than on the Shabbat day. For on Shabbat, we change our clothes, because on Shabbat we are departing from the Tree of Knowledge [of Good and Evil] and adhering to the Tree of Life. The light of wisdom shines on Shabbat; therefore, we take off our weekday clothes, which are garments of *'or* (skin) and put on our Shabbat clothes, for on Shabbat we adhere to the Tree of Life, and *'or* (skin) is turned into *'or* (light). On Purim, the light of wisdom shines all day more than [it does] on Shabbat. Therefore, the custom is to put on strange clothing to demonstrate that by means of such clothing a person may cleave to the Tree of Life, if that clothing can be "repaired" by turning *'or* (skin) into *'or* (light)...

Kalonymos Kalman HaLevi Epstein (d.1823), *Ma'or VaShemesh* (Lamp and Sun, Psalm 74:16) (Warsaw, 1876), on Exodus 22:28.

NOTES:

**These days of Purim...** Not only Purim itself, but Shushan Purim, celebrated in cities in the Land of Israel that were walled in the days of Joshua, most notably, Jerusalem.

**On Shabbat, we change our clothes...** Dressing more nicely than we do the rest of the week, as a mark of respect for the holy day.

**The Tree of Knowledge [of Good and Evil] and ... the Tree of Life...** These feature in Genesis 3, of course, but here (as frequently in kabbalistic literature) they symbolize the world of conflict, on the one hand, and of resolution and unity, on the other.

**And *'or* (skin) is turned into *'or* (light)...** In Hebrew, the difference between these two words is their initial letters, both glottal stops. The first is spelled with an *'ayin*, while the second opens with *'alef*. This well-known word-play goes back to *Bereshit Rabbah* (20:12) on the verse: "And the Eternal God made garments of skin (*'or*) for Adam and his wife" (Genesis 3:21). In that *midrash* we are told: "In R. Meir's Torah there was found written, 'Garments of light (*'or*).'" These luminescent garments, symbolizing the first couple's innate, unblemished holiness, were presumed to have been replaced with ordinary ones of animal skins after they ate of the fruit of the Tree of Knowledge.

COMMENT: I find it extraordinary that R. Kalonymos suggests that Purim displays a higher level of wisdom than Shabbat. His reason for this seems to be that on Purim our change of clothing is more radical than on Shabbat. On the seventh day, we would traditionally wear clothing appropriate to our age, gender, financial position and social status, but on Purim anything goes. Moreover, he indicates that such clothing allows us to cleave to the Tree of Life, that is, to that realm that exists beyond the dichotomies of this world: beyond good and evil, light and dark, multiplicity and unity. In this realm, all is one in God. He doesn't say it, but getting drunk might help too!

# ORIGINAL TEXTS

## שבת

[1] איתא בזהר (יתרו דף פ״ח ע״ב) מהו שבת שמא דקוב״ה שמא דאיהו שלים
מכל סטרוי, עכ״ל, נראה לי לפרש, דהנה כ״ז אתוון דאורייתא הם, ובכל אות יש
בו חיות מן שם הנכבד הוי״ה ב״ה, ואם כן בכ״ז אותיות הם כח כ״ז הוי״ת
בגימטריא שב״ת, וזהו שיש לפרש מהו שבת שמא דקוב״ה שמא דאיהו שלים
מכל סטרוי, דהיינו מכל צד הכ״ז אתוון שבהם ברא הקב״ה את כל העולמות
בכח שמו יתברך המתפשט בהם, והנה ברא עולמות בששת ימים, והשבת הוא
כדמיון הנשמה והצורה לעולם, על כן נקרא שבת שמא דקוב״ה המחיה את
כולם, ולהיות שבת שמא דקוב״ה, אסור להזכירו במקום שאסור לדבר דברי
תורה, וידעתי ממדקדקים במעשיהם שנזהרו להזכיר שם שבת ללא צורך, והוא
נכון כיון שאמרו חכמי הזהר שהוא שמא דקוב״ה המשכיל יבין הדבר.

ר׳ צבי אלימלך מדינאב, ס׳ בני יששכר, כרך א׳, דף ב׳, עמוד א׳.

[2] סיפר כשהיינו צעירים אצל היוד הקדוש כשבא ש״ק א״ע מה זה
שבת, השטריימעל על הראש עושה שבת, הקאהל שאוכלין הוא שבת עד
שנתוודע לנו מה שבת והידיעה הזאת נתעכב אצלינו עד מוצש״ק, וזה פי׳ יום
קדוש הוא מבואו ועד צאתו:

ר׳ חנוך העניך הכהן מאלכסנדר, ס׳ חשבה לטובה, דף 46.

[3] בערב שבת בתפלת מנחה וקבלת שבת מעלין כל אותן הדיבורים והמצות
של כל השבוע, שאז הוא עליית העולמות.

ר׳ ישראל בן אליעזר, הבעל שם טוב, כתר שם טוב, סימן רצ״ט, דף
קע״ג.

[4] כל מה שקיבל כל השבוע תורה ומצות יש לה עליה בשבת ומשפיעים עליו
מלמעלה נשמה יתירה:

ר׳ חיים חייקא מאמדור, ס׳ חיים וחסד, דף 21.

[5] לא יאמר אדם בשבת אתפלל בכוונה ולא בחול, שלא יהא כעבדים
המשמשין את המלך וכהמלך עומד לפניהם מתדבקים [נ״א מחזקים] בעבודה,
וכשאין המלך לפניהם אין מזדרזין בעבודה, ואין זה עבד נאמן. אבל [עבד נאמן]
יודע לו באמונה שרע לו בלא המלך, וידחה כל המשמורות עד שיבא לפני המלך,
אע״פ שאין יכול לדבר לפניו ואין ראוי לבא לפניו, אעפי״כ יעשה כי רצונו כי
רחמנות גדול עליו עד מאד.

ס׳ צוואת הריב״ש, סימן פ״ה, דפ׳ 23-22.

207

[6] והנה בקדושת השבת נזכרו ג' קדושות והם קדושת המחשבה כמו שכתב במכילתא שבות ממחשבת העבודה. וגם קדושת הדיבור שהוזהרנו בו בשבת כמו שכתוב "ודבר דבר" [ישעיה נח,יג]. וגם קדושת המעשה כאשר בא בביאורה בכמה מקראי קדש באיסור המלאכות. והאיש הקדוש יהיה לו מושך מג' קדושות הללו יום יום בכולו או ברובו או במקצתו, וכל אדם אינו חייב אלא כשיעורו. והנה מתנאי קדושת המחשבה שיתקדש בו בו' ימי החול הוא לחשוב במחשבות קדושות ובפרט בעתות עסק התורה והתפלות, ויהיו כל מעשיו לשם שמים וליחד הדורות למעלה [תפארת ומלכות], ובעסק התורה והמצוות יחשוב, כי איננו פה עמנו עומד היום בעולם הזה, אפס בעולם הנשמות לפני השכינה, ובכן יטהר מחשבותיו.

ועיקר הדבר להיות חפץ בהתבודדות, אשר בזה מראה בנפשו כי אין לו קשר עם אנשי העולם הזה כמו שהוא אמת אחר פטירתו, ולכן תראה מעתה גירות בעה"ז שאינו רוצה להתדבק מחשבתו כי אם בצור עשהו שבו עתיד להתדבק עצמי אם יזכה ...

ס' חמדת ימים, כרך א', דף 30.

[7] הנה כמוטב תלתא מחש"בה ודב"ור ומעשה יתקדש כל איש הישראלי בששת ימי המעשה להקדיש ולהעריך הנשמה והרוח והנפש להמשיך עליו מאורי אור קדושת שבת הגדול. ואף אנשי המלאכה האביונים אשר עול המלאכה תכבד עליהם ואין הפנאי מסכים אליהם מקוצר רוח ומעבודה קשה על המחיה ועל הכלכלה בגלות החיל הזה, הנה בשעת התפלה שהם על כרחם פנויים ממלאכתם יזהרו לקדש מחשבותם ודיבורים ושאר חושיהם בעת ובעונה ההיא, כדי שאותה השעה או חצי שעה יהיו נקדשים בקדושת שבת ולא יפסיקו בתוך התפלה בדבור של באופן שלא יהא שום יום משולל מקדושת שבת, כי בהתקדש עצמם בששת ימי החול יוכלו בנקל לקבל אור פני קדושת שבת הגדול. ואי אפשר לקנות קדושת שבת אלא אם כן יתקדשו עצמם גם בימי החול, כי קדושת שבת היא קדושה עליונה מאד אור האצילות, ואי אפשר לאדם להשיגה מפני שהוא מלובש בו' ימי החול ששולטים בו ל"ט מלאכות. והמשילו זה לבגד שנפלו בו כתמים משמן וכיוצא שאם לא יורחץ וילובן כראוי לא יוכל לקבל, שום צבע וג"כ הוא משל לאדם היושב במקום חשך וצלמות שאם בפתע פתאום יצא לאור וקבל אור השמש בתוקפו יחשכו עיניו ולא יהנה ממתיקות האור. כן הבא לקבל אור שבת ונפשו מלוכלכת מזוהמת כתמי פשעיו שאין אור הנשמה שולטת בו...

ס' חמדת ימים, כרך א', דף 35.

[8] זאת התשובה השיב רבינו משולם נ"ע למינין שאינן מדליקין נרות בבתיהם בשבת מפני שאומר הפסוק (שמות ל"ה ג') לא תבערו אש בכל מושבותיכם ביום השבת והשיב להם כך: כתיב (בראשית ב' ג') ויברך אלהים את יום השביעי אין אנו יודעים במה ברכו אלא ממה שאנו רואים בקללות שקלל איוב את יומו

208

שקיללו בחשיכה שנאמר (איוב ג' ו') הלילה ההוא יקחנו אופל וגו' יקר לאור ואין (שם ט') מכלל שהברכה שבירך הקב"ה השבת היא אורה שהיא שלום הבית. וכל מה שאמר איוב בקללה יש לומר בהיפך גבי שבת לברכה באיוב (ג' ז') כתיב אל תבא רננה בו מכאן שיש לו לרנן בשבת בשירות ותשבחות.

ר' יהודה החסיד, ס' חסידים, סימן תתשמ"ז, דף תקע"א.

[9] ויגיל שמח לשמחת הכלה הבאה אלינו. "ותבא אליו היונה לעת ערב" וראוי לשמח אותה בכל דבר הבא על ידינו. ואם יש לו קטטה עם חבירו או עם אנשי ביתו, יעבור על כל פשע ולא יזכור שום עון ביום השבת אלא אהבה וחיבה ושלום וריעות. ולא יחלל קדושת השבת בכל דבר שהוא חול כי פוגם בזה קדושתו ומעלתו, כי קדושת השבת רומז לענין גדול אשר אין שם אלא מנוחה והשקט, "והרשעה כולה כעשן תכלה" ...

ס' חמדת ימים, כרך א', דפ' 167-168.

[10] 'שבת' לשון השבה, ששבו הברואים לשרשם, ... כמו התינוק שהולך אחר מעשה נערות ושוכח באביו, ואחר כך כשרואה את אביו, מחמת חשקו אליו משליך הכל ומתדבק בו ורץ אליו, מחמת שהוא נתח מנתחיו, כן כביכול כשה' יתברך מבהיק זיו הדרו אל הברואים, אז מגמת פניהם אליו בתשוקה גדולה... וזהו ענין השבת, שהוא השבה אל השרש, רצה לומר, השרש מאיר על הענפים, והענפים חושקים ומתענגים בו ונכנסים אליו, והוא אחדות עם ה' יתברך.

ר' משולם פייבוש הלוי העליר, מזבאריזא, ס' יושר דברי אמת, דפ' קמ"ט-ק"נ.

[11] ...עיקר יום השבת הוא להתדבק בהש"י על ידי תפלה ותורה, ולזה קורא בזוהר האי יומא יומא דנשמתין ולא יומא דקיימא דגופא, ר"ל שמאיר שורש הנשמות על הנשמות שבגופים והם נכספים אליו, וזה נק' תוספות שבנשמה יתירה וכ'ז נרגש לברי לבב.

ר' ישראל בן אליעזר, הבעל שם טוב, ס' כתר שם טוב, סימן ת"ב, דף 118.

[12] עוד ששמעתי ממנו פ' בא מ"ש בשבת זכר ליצ"מ כי עיקר שבת להיות למעלה מן הטבע היינו ביטול המידות לה' כמ"ש לך ה' הגדולה כו', וזה ג"כ יצ"מ שכ' בכל מכה וידעתם כו' שהביא ידיעה לישראל, זה שהבנתי ע"י דבריו ואיני זוכר כל הלשון אולי הי' קצת שינוי אך אני כן הבנתי:

ר' חנוך העניך הכהן מאלכסנדר, ס' חשבה לטובה, דף 5.

[13] ...אל"ר איזהו גדול יציאת מצרים או בריאת העולם א"ל בריאת העולם. א"ל נילף זכירה זכירה מי"מ דכתיב זכור את יום השבת וכתיב זכור את היום הזה אשר יצאתם ממצרים מה לשם ניסים ונפלאות שנעשו אף בשבת גדולות ונוראות שנעשו וא"כ נעשה אגדה לספר הבריאה ובכל ליל שבת נשב ונספר. אל"ב האם אינך אומר ויכולו בקידוש שלך ויכולו כולל כל הבריאה...

ס' הקנה, ענין לספר ביציאת מצרים, דף קנ"ג.

[14] שמעתי בשמו שבת וינפש כיון ששבת וי אבדה נפש והקשה שהי' צריך לומר זה הפסוק במו"ש ולא בערב שבת וגם מה שמזמרין אותו בניגון נאה וכו' וביאר כי מי שהוא חולה לגמרי אינו מרגיש בשום כאב כי אין לו אבר אחד בריא שאותו אבר ירגיש את הכאב אבל האדם הבריא ואבר אחד כואב לו כל האברים מרגישים בכאב האבר המיוחד וכדומה והאדם כל ימות החול הוא חולה כל איברי נפשו ואינו מרגיש כלל מטעם הנ"ל ובשבת שמתחיל קצת להתרפא אזי הוא מרגיש בכאב גודל כובד חולי נפשו וזהו כיון ששבת שמרגיש קדושת השבת ווי אבדה נפש שיודע ומרגיש מכאוביו וחליו:

אמר לו הרב הגדול מהר"צ בן הריב"ש שצריך האדם לעשות הכנות שיוכל לקבל קדושת השבת כמ"ש והכינו את אשר יביאו והוא השיב לו כי דבר הניתן מלמעלה ואינו יודע כלל איך וגם מה יותן לי איך אפשר לאדם להכין א"ע אליו רק שצריך לשמור א"ע מכל דבר רע וזהו בשני דרב יהודה כולי תנויי בנזיקין הוה לשמור א"ע מכל דבר המזיק לנפש:

ר' פנחס מקאריץ, ס' מדרש פנחס, דף' יד עמ' א'-ב'.

[15] שמעתי מדקדק הרב האיש האלקים קדוש ר' ישראל בעה"ש למה אנו אומרים זה בחתלת השבת שבת וינפש, כדר הגמרא וי אבדה נפש די לזה בשעתה במוצאי שבת, וידוע מה שתירץ ז"ל להוסיף לנו אהבה ושמחה משבת קודש בזכרנו כי אחרי כן תפסוק הנשמה יתירה גדולה של שבת כאשר האריך במשל ומליצה.

ר' יעקב יצחק הלוי הורוויץ, החוזה מלובלין, ס' זכרון זאת, דף קנ"ז.

[16] ובזה יובן וידבר ה' בהר סיני דבר אל בני ישראל כי תבואו אל הארץ ר"ל כמו במעמד הר סיני היו ארציות החומר מזוכך כמו זכות הנפש כך תראו שכשתבואו אל הארץ העליונה אשר אנ"י נותן לכם ושבתה הארץ ר"ל שגם ארציות החומר יהיה מזיכך כ"כ שיהי' קודש כמו הצורה והנשמה שהוא שבת לה' כי יש עולם שנה ונפש כמו שבכללות העולם יש חיצונית ופנימית זכמ"ש בכתבים ענין תוספת שבת יעו"ש. כן יש בשנה פנימיות וחיצונית שהם ו' ימי החול ושבת כי שבת נקרא הנפש והנשמה כמ"ש שבת וינפש ו' ימי החול הוא החומר. וכך יש באדם חומר וצורה והתכלית שיעשה האדם מחומר צורה ואז ושבתה הא"רץ שב"ת לה' והבן:

ר' יעקב יוסף מפאלנאי, ס' תולדות יעקב יוסף, דף' ת"ח-ת"ט.

210

[17] ושמרו בני ישראל את השבת לדורותם וג' בשבת כתיב לדרתם חסר לשון
דירה להורות כשנכנס שבת השכינה באה. וראה אם ערך ביתו בשלחן ומטה ונר
אמרה שכינה זו היא דירתי ואם לאו אומרת אין זה דירה של ישראל וכן גבי
מזוזה כתיב לדרתם חסר וכו'. (זהר במדבר)...

ר' ראובן האשקי, ס' ילקוט ראובני, חלק א' דף 156.


[18] ונראה לי דשמעתי בשם המגיד מו' מענדיל לתרץ קו' התו' במס' ביצה
(טו:) שהקשו על הא דאמרינן בש"ס עשה שבתך חול ואל תצטרך לבריות והוא
נגד הש"ס דאמרי' לוו עלי ואני פורע. וביאר ע"פ הש"ס אלמלא שמרו ישראל ב'
שבתתו וכו' (שבת קי"ח): למה דוקא ב' שבתות ולא שבת א' ופירש כי אדם
השלם צריך לשמור שבת בב' בחי' האחד בדברים נוגעים לגופו וב' לנשמתו
וביאר ע"פ משל למלך שנשבה בנו יחידו בשבי הקשה מכולם ועברו זמני זמנים
ותוחלתו נמשכה מלפדותו ולהשיבו אל אביו וברוב עתים ושנים הגיעוהו מכתב
אביו המלך לבל יתייאש שמה ושלא לשכוח נמוסי המלכות בין זאבי ערב כי עוד
ידו נטוי' להחזירו אל אביו ע"י כמה וכמה טצדקאות במלחמה או בשלום וכו'
ומיד שמח בן המלך שמחה גדולה אפס שהי' מגילת סתרים ואי אפשר הי' לו
לשמוח בגלוי מה עשה הלך עם בני עירו אל בית היין או שאר דבר המשכר והם
שמחו ביין שמחה גשמיות והוא שמח באגרת אביו וכו' וככל החזיון הזה הוא
ממש מצות עונג שבת אל הגוף שהוא החומר במאכל ומשתה כדי שיהי' פנאי
להצדיק לשמוח שמחה ב' שהוא שמחת הנשמה בדביקות הש"י כל היום לבל
יסיח דעתו מקדושת ומורא השבת ק"ו מתפילין וכו'.

ר' יעקב יוסף מפאלנאי, ס' תולדות יעקב יוסף, כרך א', דף של"א.


[19] סעודת שבת צריך להיות בהכנה, ולא לילך במהירות, אלא צריך ליישב
עצמו לפני מי הוא סועד הסעודה, ומי ציוה על סעודת השבת, וזהו הפי' אתקינו
סעודתא שהסעודה צריך להיות בהכנה:

ר' חנוך העניך הכהן מאלכסנדר, ס' חשבה לטובה, דף 45.


[20] אח"כ ילבוש בגדי שבת וילבוש חלוקו דוקא ביום ו'. ולא ימתין עד שבת
בבוקר. ושמעתי שדודי הק' מנעשכיז זצ"ל סיפר שכאשר נסתלק אבי הק' בא
אליו שליח דרחמנא שמכבדין אותו שיקבל שבת בהיכל של משיח והלך אחר
השליח וכאשר הגיע לפתח ההיכל ראה שם זקן נכבד עומד ומאיר ואינו הולך
לפנים ושאל אותו זקני הק' למה הוא אינו הולך לפנים והשיב שאין מניחין אותו
לפנים עד הבוקר לפי שהי' מנהגו תמיד שלא לבש כתונת לבן לכבוד ש"ק עד
הבוקר.

ר' מרדכי מלעכאוויץ בס' אילנא דחיי, חלק ב' (אור הנר) , דף 11.


211

# פסח

[21] ענין פסח שנמצא בדברי רבותינו ז"ל שהוא מל' פ"ה ס"ח ... והנה מלך ב"ו
המצוה לעבדיו לעשות כך וכך עודם מדברים עמו יש יכולת בידם לבקש הפוך
ציווי אבל כשכיבר עמהם והלכו מלפניו א"א להפוך דבריו אבל מידת הקב"ה לא
כמדת בשר ודם שאף שנאצלו האותיות ונבראו ונצטיירו ונעשו והגיע השתלשלות'
בעולם השפל הזה להעשות כך וכך יש צדיקים המהפכים מידותיו או אם יעשו
בניו תשובה אזי תיכף נתהפכו לצירוף אחר לעשות עם עמו לטובה אות דמין
המלך המדבר עם עבדיו בעודם לפניו מפני שמלא כל הארץ כבודו ולית אתר
פנוי מיני' וככחו אז כחו עתה וזהו פ"ה ס"ח רצה לומר פה המדבר כלומר אף
שכבר ברא כל העולמות הרי הוא בבחינת מדבר עם עבדיו ועודם לפניו.

ר' לוי יצחק מברדיטשוב, ס' קדושת לוי, דף ס"א עמוד ג'.

[22] פסח הוא דרועא ימינא דהיינו שבפסח נתגל' חסדים בעולם ופסח הוא
חיות של כל השנה דהיינו באותן חסדים שממשיכים בפסח באמצעות הסדר
ושאר דברים שעושין בפסח ולכן שנו חכמים במשנתם בפסע [בפסח?] על
התבואה דהיינו מזונות וכל העולם ניזון בחסדו הגדול ...

ר' מנחם נחום מטשארנאביל, ס' מאור עינים, דף 85.

[23] אמר בפסח שהי' להם אמונה ללכת במדבר לא זרועה ולא שאלו מהיכן
יתפרנסו הוא זמן אשר כל אחד יוכל לקבוע בלבו אמונה עכ"פ מאן דיהיב חיי
יהיב מזוני. ולא שהי' ראשם ולבם ברדיפות הפרנסה כמו בדורות הללו.
הי' צועק מה זה בדורות הללו משעבדים לעול פרנסה כל ימיהם וחייהם
הלא כל אחד ואחד יודע שהשי"ת הוא זן ומפרנס לכל הנבראים ומאן דיהיב חיי
יהיב מזוני הגם שנצרך לעסוק במר"מ אבל לא שיהי' ראשו ולבו שוקעין בו.

יועץ קיים קדיש ראקאץ, ס' שיח שרפי קודש, חלק א', דף 16.

[24] אלה מועדי ה' אשר תקראו אותם במועדם. הנה אנו אומרים מקדש ישראל
והזמנים. דבאמת אצלו ית' לא שייך זמן. דהוא ית' למעלה מן הטבע והזמנים. אך
מאהבת ישראל עמו אשר בחר בהם. ועבורם הוצרך לברוא את כל העולמות.
הוכרח גם כן לחדש הזמן. והנה בג' רגלים אז נמשך השי"י לתוך הזמן. ויש
התגלות אורו על הכנ"י. ובמה ממשיכין אותו כביכול לתוך הזמן. כשאנו מדבקים
א"ע אל ראשית המחשבה. אשר עלה ברצונו הפשוט לברוא הזמן בשביל ישראל
כמ"ש קודש ישראל לה' ראשית תבואתו. אנו ממשיכין ומזמנים את הקודש
לשכון בארצנו להיות כביכול נמשך ויורד לתוך העולמות. וזהו במועד שאנו
מזמנים את הקודש ובזה אנו ממשיכין אותו בתוך הזמן. ע"י שאנו מדבקים
עצמינו בבחי' הגבוהה למעלה מן הזמן ...

ר' אברהם יהושע העשל מאפטא, ס' אוהב ישראל, דפ' 180-181.

[25] המצוות שאנו אוכלים בפסח הם סגולה לנו שנתחזק באמונה ובסכות בחי'
מקיפין ע"ד שנותנין תחבושת וסמים לרפאות מבחוץ ובפסח אוכל מצות דוגמת
רפואה בפנים.

ר' נפתלי צבי הורוויץ מראפשיץ, ס' זרע קודש, כרך ב' דף ל"ד עמוד
א'.

[26] פוסקין מלומר גש"ם בחג הפסח. דהנה גשם הוא פרנסה והנה אכילת מצה
לחם עוני הוא סגולה לפרנסה כי מאכילת מצה הלזו נמשך פרנסה לכל השנה
ע"כ בפסח נידונין על התבואה ... ע"כ מצה לחם עני בגימ' גשם ...:

ר' צבי אלימלך מדינוב, ס' בני יששכר, כרך א', דף קי"ג, עמוד ב'.

[27] בפסח נידונין על התבואה (ר"ה טז.). כתיב (ירמי' ב,ג) קדש ישראל לה'
ראשית תבואתה. פסח הוא אמונה, שהקדוש ברוך הוא האמין להם לישראל
והוציאם ממצרים, והאמין להם כי אחרי זה ימנו מ"ט ימי הספירה ואחר כך
יקבלו את התורה. תבואתה, על דרך הכתוב (דברים לג, טז) תבואתה לראש
יוסף. וזהו בפסח נידונין על התבואה, היינו על דבר שיבוא אחר כך (חסר.)

ר' ישראל (פרידמן) מסאדיגורא, ס' אור ישראל, דף קי"ב.

[28] בשיר השירים אין יכולין להבין שום דבר, כי כל הכתובים קודש ושיר
השירים קודש קדשים והוא שכל הכתובים ממוצעים בין עולמות עליונים
לתחתונים, ושיר השירים ממוצע בין עולמות עליונים לאין סוף ב"ה ואין אנחנו
מבינים, ועוד אמר בלשון אחר, כל הנביאים היו מעלים עולם השפל לעולם
העליון ושה"ש מעלה עולמות עליונים לא"ס ב"ה.

ר' פנחס מקאריץ, ס' אמרי פנחס, סימן קצ"א דף נ"ב.

[29] אם אדם מתפלל ויש לו מחשבה אחרת אזי ח"ו הקליפה רוכבת על הדיבור
כי מחשבה רוכבת על הדיבור וזהו לסוסתי ברכבי פרעה. סוסים נקראים
הדיבורים וכשפרעה היינו המחשבה זרה רוכבת עליו אזי דמיתיך רעיתי יותר
טוב אלו שותק אבל דבר היוצא מהלב נכנס בלב. פי' בלב עליון ע"י ההבל
כידוע:

ר' ישראל בן אליעזר, הבעל שם טוב, צוואת הריב"ש, סימן ע"א, דף
21-22.

[30] ...חבצלת השרון שושנת, אילו הנשמות, וכתי' (ישעי' ל"ה ב') ותפרח
כחבצלת, וכתי' (הושע י"ד) ויפרח כשושנה...

ר' אלעזר מגרמייזא, פירוש הרוקח על המגילות, כרך א', דף קי"ב.

[31] במדרש דומה דודי לצבי (שיר השירים ב ט), מה הצבי הלזה כשהוא רץ
מביט לאחוריו כך הקדוש ברוך הוא, הנה זה עומד אחר כתלנו. רצה לומר,
הקדוש ברוך הוא עומד ומצפה לישועתינו 'אחר כתלנו' אף על פי שעשינו

213

בעצמינו כותל מסך המבדיל בעוונותינו, ועם כל זה הקדוש ברוך הוא מצפה תמיד 'ומשגיח מן החלונות ומציץ מן החרכים' בכל מה שאפשר להיטיב לנו. וזהו מה מצאו אבותיכם בי עול כי רחקו מעלי (ירמיהו ב ה), רצה לומר כי המה רחקו מעלי אבל אין המניעה ממני ח"ו כי רוצה אני תמיד להיטיב.

ר' מרדכי מנעשכיז, ס' רשפי אש, סימן קס"ג, דף פ"ג.

[32] כמעט שעברתי מהם [עד] [ש]מצאתי את שאהבה נפשי (ג' ד'). אם אדם מרחיק עצמו מאנשים שהם תמיד ברחובות ובשווקים, יוכל למצוא את שאהבה נפשו, דהיינו דביקות לשם יתברך ברוך הוא, רק שיהיה מעט ולא הרבה, כי 'הרבה עשו כרבי שמעון בר יוחאי ולא עלתה, (ברכות לה:), כי אינו רשאי להתרחק מהם מכל וכל.

ר' חיים מקאסוב, ס' תורת חיים, דפ' קכ"ט-ק"ל.

[33] כחוט השני שפתותיך (שיר השירים ד ג). רצה לומר, כמו חוט השני שהיה סימן לבני ישראל אם היה מלבין עוונותיהם מתכפרים (יומא סח ע"ב), כן עתה תוכל לבחון עצמך על ידי 'שפתותיך', כשאתה מדבר בדברי תורה ותפלה ומחשב בדברי בטלים, זהו סימן שאינו עובד לה' יתברך. כי אם [האמת] כמו שסובר האדם שדרך איש ישר בעיניו ויש לו תירוץ על כל מעשיו שעושה [שהם] לשם שמים, אם כן יתחייב שבתורתו ותפלתו לא יחשוב מאומה רק לשמו יתברך, אלא וודאי שאינו אמת, כי באמת עובד לעצמו ולא לה' יתברך.

רק עיקר התירוץ הוא, על ידי הגלות שהדעת הוא בגלות ואין לו שכל לעבוד הבורא הכל ברוך הוא, אסני קרבה אל נפשי גאלה (תהלים סט יט), כל איש בפרטיות לפי שכלו שחננו ה' ברוך הוא, יתחזק ויוסיף אומץ בכל יום להיות בעל תשובה ולא להיות צדיק, דהיינו להחזיק בתרותו על כל דרכיו ולשוב לפניו [יתב"ש] בכל יום ויום בחיות חדשה, ולא יאמין בעצמו, רק יירא ויפחד כי אולי הוא ח"ו מאותן שאומרים עליו מה לך לספר חוקי וגו' (תהלים נ טז).

ר' מרדכי מנישכיז, ס' רשפי אש, דף נ"ה.

[34] ...לא ירחיב - ה' - נפש צדיק. פירוש הנפש של הצדיק אינו מרעיב את ה' כביכול. כדאיתא ישראל מפרנסין לאביהם שבשמים. וכן כתיב (שיר השירים ה. ד) אכלתי יערי עם דבשי פירוש, גורם תענוג ונחת רוח לה' יתברך. על ידי זה יש לו כח, והוא בוגדים יהדוף.

וכן יש לומר, "לא ירחיב ה'", 'נפש צדיק". פירוש רצון הצדיק הוא שה' לא ירעיב לישראל, ועל ידי זה הות בוגדים יהדוף, מאחר שרצונו הוא כן, כי רצון יראיו יעשה (תהלים קמה. יט.). וכן פשוט, לא ירעיב ה' נפש צדיק, כי אדרבה נותן לו פרנסתו וכל צורכו, כדי שלא יהיה טרוד בטרחת פרנסה. שיהיה יכול להדוף הות בוגדים. לבטל גזירות, ולהמתיק דינין.

ר' יעקב יצחק הלוי הורוויץ, החוזה מלובלין, ס' זאת זכרון השלם, דף צ"ט.

[35] ...שהתורה מיחדת את כנסת ישראל לאין סוף ברוך הוא וברוך שמו,
כנודע קוב"ה ואורייתא וישראל חד אינון (זח"ג ע.ג.), והתורה היא ממוצע בין
ישראל לאביהם שבשמים. וזהו סוד (שה"ש ו ג) אני לדודי ודודי לי, כי התורה
היא בחינת אני, כמאמר (משלי ח יד) אני בינה לי גבורה. והיינו אני"י לדוד"י,
שהתורה מקשרת את ישראל להבורא ב"ה. ודוד"י ל"י, כי אורייתא מחכמה
נפקת (זח"ב פה), והתורה יכולה להעלות כל המדריגות, מה שאין כן בלא תורה,
אף אם יהיה לו יראה עילאה יוכל ח"ו ליפול, רק התורה משמרתו.
                                    ר' מרדכי מטשערנאביל, ס' ליקוטי תורה, דף קכ"ח.


[36] ...צריך האדם מתחילה לפנות ממחשבתו כל הבלי עולם הזה, ולקבל על
עצמו עול אלהותו ית"ש במס"נ, ולעזוב בלב שלם כל בחינת הרע הנשרש בקרבו
ונכנס צחנתו ובאשו בכולו בכל כל הקומה, ומעתה לקבל עליו עול התשובה
לשוב אליו ית"ש תמיד בכל עת ורגע, בכל פרטי עבודתו וכחותיו, בכדי לקבל
תמיד חיות חדש, בסוד והחיות רצוא ושוב (יחזקאל א יד), ע' קדו"ל משפטים
ד"ה ותחת רגליו) ובזה יוכל להאיר אור הנשמה, ותקבל אורה מאור אין סוף
ברוך הוא, אשא דאכלא כל אשא (ע' זח"ג קלח., זח"א נ:), כמאמר
הכתוב (דברים ד כד) כי ה' אלהיך אש אוכלה הוא, ונר נשמה מקבל אור
משלהבת י"ה על ידי אהבתו ית"ש כרשפי אש (ע' שיר השירים ח ו).
                                    ר' מרדכי משערנאביל, ס' ליקוטי תורה, דף כ"א.


[37] ...כשנגאלו ישראל ויצאו לחירות למטה, ודוגמתו למעלה חירות
מהקליפות, לא היה חירות לגמרי. אם למטה שהרי עדיין היו יראים ממצרים
כאשר באמת רדפו אחריהם עד יום שביעי של פסח, ואם החירות של מעלה
עדיין לא היה נגמר לגמרי עד חג שבועות זמן מתן תורתינו. נמצא בפסח אף
שנברר בנו ורוממנו מכל לשון, לא היה בעצם עד מתן תורה.
                                    ר' ישעיה הורוויץ, ס' שני לוחות הברית, מסכת פסחים, דף י"ב עמוד
                                    א'.


[38] ...וכשם שסלחת לעמך בית ישראל על ים סוף בעד חטאתם, בסגולת
השירה הזאת, כן אבינו אב הרחמן רחם עלינו וכבוש עוונותינו ותשליך במצולות
ים כל חטאתינו, בכח סגולת השירה אשר שרנו עתה לפניך, ונסה עלינו אור
עתיקא קדישא לקרוע רוע גזר דינינו, כמו שקרעת רוע גזר דין אבותינו על ים
סוף וקרעת כל המכסים והמקטרגים אשר הם מבדילים בינינו לבינך. חתום פי
שטן ואל ישטין עלינו. יהיו כמוץ לפני רוח ומלאך ה' דוחה, למען יחלצון ידידיך,
הושיעה ימינך וענני. עשה למען שמך וכו'. יהיו לרצון וכו'.
                                    ס' חמדת ימים, כרך ג' דף 260.


[39] איתא קשין מזונותיו של אדם כקריעת ים סוף (פסחים קי"ח עמ' א') אומר
אני, קריעת ים סוף הרי כבר היתה, וכמו כן בודאי צריך שיהיה פרנסה, אומר

215

אני, השי"ת (השם יתברך) יעזור שכל יהודי יוושע בפרנסת הגוף ופרנסת הנשמה. א גוטין יו"ט (יום טוב), א גוטין יו"ט.

יום שביעי של פסח, תרנ"א, ר' ישראל פרידמן מסדיגורא, ס' אור ישראל, דף קל"ה.

[40] ופרעה הקריב. באוה"ח הק' כתב שהי' לישראל יראה מזה ואומר אני שהי' יראה חיצוניות רק מה שאח"כ כתיב ויראו העם את ה' זהו יראה עלאה וזה שאמר הקב"ה למשה דבר אל בני ישראל ויסעו היינו שיסעו מיראה חיצוניות ליראה עלאה...

ר' אברהם יעקב מסאדגאארא, ס' בית ישראל (אמת ליעקב) דפ' 97- 98.

[41] במוצאי יו"ט של פסח אמר על מדרש של הפסוק. ויאמינו בי"י וגו' או [אז] ישיר וגו'. גדולה אמונה שבשבילה נוחל האדם העוה"ז והעוה"ב שבשכר האמונה זכו ישראל ושרתה עליהם שכינה. ואמרו שירה שנא' והאמין בי"י ויחשבה לו צדקה: ע"כ. פתח ואמר. אתי מלבנון כלה א'תי מ"לבנון ת"בואי. ר"ת אמ"ת. ת"שורי מ"ראש א"מנה ג"כ ר"ת אמת למפרע ותשורי הוא ל' ראיה ול' תשורה. וביאר כי האמת והאמונה הם ב' דברים קשורים זה בזה והם עיקר הכל וע"י האמונה בא אל האמת וע"י אמת בא לאמונה. ואמר כי אמונה בלב יש לכל בר ישראל שמאמין שיש בורא ממציא הכל ומשגיח ומנהיג כל העולמות אבל אמונה חזקה כזו שיוכל לעבור ולדלג על כמה ענינים בחום לבו זו אינו כי אם במי שהוא סר מרע והתקין מדותיו.

ר' אהרן מקארלין, ס' בית אהרן, דף 185-184.

[42] עזי וזמרת וגו'. הנה סדר העומדים לפני ה' לשורר ולשבח ולהתפלל הוא להתחיל בדברים המושכלים מה' אליו, ואחר כך במושכל מה' לאבותיו, וכמו שמצינו שתקנו אנשי כנסת הגדולה באבות אלהינו ואחר כך אלהי אבותינו...

ר' חיים בן משה אבן עטר, פירוש על התורה, חלק ב', דפ' 68,69.

[43] פסוק זה נאמר בראש השירה, כי פרחה נשמתן, ושמעו קול שירה, ופתח הקב"ה אזניהם ושמעו זמירות כל צבא מרום, וע"כ חזר נשמתן בהם כאמרז"ל. וז"ש עזי וזמרת יה, פי': כחי שהיה לי, היה ע"י זמרת י"ה. פירוש: ע"י אותן הזמירות ששמעתי מן מה"ש שאמרו לשם י"ה, שע"ז ויהי לי לישועה, ונושענתי מן המות.

ר' חיים וויטל, ס' ליקוטי תנ"ך, דף ק"מ.

216

[44] עוד שמעתי בשמו הק׳ וכו׳ עה״פ (תהלים קלט) גם חושך לא יחשיך ממך
ולילה כיום יאיר. הפי׳. אם אני יודע שהוא ממך, גם חושך לא יחשיך לי וכו׳.
והבן.

ר׳ מנחם מענדל מקאצק, ס׳ שיח שרפי קודש, חלק א׳ דף 88 סימן
תפ״ו.

[45] יבואר דהנה בודאי אין שום ענין חיות בשום דבר שבעולם וגם כל חיות
אדם. רק ממה שנשפע ממנו ית״ש. ואף אם אדם זוכה לעשות שום דבר אליו
ית״ש. גם זה הוא רק ממה שנשפע ממנו ית״ש. ורק העיקר מה שצריך האדם
לראות. הוא שיבוא לבחי׳ רצון אליו ית״ש וזהו ה׳ איש הוא מהשי״ת. מלחמה ה׳
שמו. היינו שכל מלחמת איש ישראלי הוא רק ה׳ שמו. ר״ל שיבוא לבחי׳ רצון
אליו ית״ש. והבן.

ר׳ אלימלך בן חיים מגראדזיסק, ס׳ אמרי אלימלך, דף 199.

[46] זה אלי ואנוהו (שמות ט״ו ב׳) לשון נוה ודירה, אעשה דירתו בי בתוכי
ובקרבי.

ר׳ מנחם מעמדל מקוצק, ס׳ עמוד האמת, דף מ״ו.

[47] והנה יציאת מצרים בטחון ובשורה לכל הטובות שאנו עתידים לקבל
באחרונה, והיא עדות גדול על העולם העתיד להתחדש עלינו:

ר׳ מאיר ן׳ גבאי, ס׳ תולעת יעקב, דף ק״ב.

[48] לעתיד שתהי׳ הגאולה העתידה ב״ב עיקר ויצמ״צ טפל אז נכיר גודל
הניסים של יצמ״צ שיצמ״צ הי׳ שיהי׳ יכול להיות אח״כ גאולה העתידה ב״ב.

ר׳ נפטלי צבי מרופשיץ, ס׳ זרע קודש, כרך ב׳, דף ל״ד, עמוד א׳.

[49] ימי הספירה המה לתקן המדות והוא שדרך ארץ קדמה לתורה היינו לתקן
עצמם בשבועות הללו שיוכלו ליכנס בעצמם ר״ת:

ר׳ שמחה בונם מפשיסחא בס׳ שיח שרפי קודש, חלק א׳, דף 14.


## שבועות


[50] הנה סידרו לנו אנשי כנסת הגדולה בנוסח התפלה, זמן מתן תורתינו, ויש
לדקדק מדוע לא סידרו זמן קבלת תורתינו כדרך ששנינו (אבות פ״א מ״א) משה
קיבל תורה, ואמר רבינו הק׳ הרבי רש״ב מפאארשיסחא זצוקללה״ה כי רק מתן
תורה הי׳ אז בחודש סיון ויש לה שייכות עם הזמן משא״כ הקבלה דכל יומא
ויומא זמני׳, עבדה״ק. וי״ל עוד כי נתינת התורה הי׳ שוה לכל אבל הקבלה לא
קבלוה בשוה רק כל אחד ואחד כפי עשך השגתו.

217

ר׳ מנחם מענדל מקאצק, ס׳ אהל תורה, דפ׳ 46-47.

[51] ובספר דעת משה כתב לבאר מה שאנו אומרים בנוסח התפלה זמן מתן
תורתינו. והי׳ די לומר זמן מתן תורה. מה תורתינו. שכל א׳(?) מישראל לפי
תיקון וכשרון פעולתו כן הוא מקבל חלק תורתו. וזהו זמן מתן תורתינו. שהוא
מתן תורה של כל אחד וא׳ לפי כשרון מעשיו.
ס׳ טעמי הנמנהגים ומקורי הדינים, חלק ג׳, דף 163.

[52] מנהג אבותינו תורה היא לאכול חלב בחג שבועות (שו״ע או״ח תצד ס״ג
בהג״ה), נראה לי הטעם (פרד״ס שער כג פרק ח) חלב רומז לחסד גוון לובן,
והנה (תהלים צב ג) להגיד בבקר חסדך ראשי תיבות חל״ב.
ר׳ צבי אלימלך מדינוב, ס׳ בני יששכר, כרך א׳, דף קל״ד עמוד ג׳.

[53] ...שכל מעשה בני אדם כלולים בשלש אמות, והם מחשבה דבור מעשה.
והנה במחשבה לבד אין די, כי לא יכולין להבין כוונת האדם, ואין אדם יודע
מטמוניותיו של חבירו מה בדעתו ורצונו. גם במעשה שלו עדיין אי אפשר להבחין
למה ועל מה הוא עושה כך. אכן הדבור הוא המזווגה, שעל ידו מתגלה מחשבתו
הנכרת בתוך מעשיו. ולעומת זה ניתן לנו שלש רגלים, שכל אחד מהם הזמן
ההוא מסוגל לתקן אחד מג׳ אמות הנ״ל. דהיינו שבחג השבועות, כל העובדות
במחשבה, לבקל עליו עול מלכות שמים ותורה ומצות, ולדבקה בו. ובסוכות,
נתקן המעשה, שכל עובדותיו במעשה המצות... וחג הפסח, בא לתקן הדבור,
לספר ביציאת מצרים ושבחו של מקום ...
ר׳ מנחם מענדל מרימנוב, ס׳ מנחם ציון, דף 56.

[54] ...שבת ופסח ושבועות וסוכות, כל אחד מהם השמחה והתענוג בהם בה׳
יתברך בעצם היום, שהוא מה שכתוב בזוהר (אמור קה, א) על פסוק (תהלים
קיח, כד) "זה היום עשה ה׳ נגילה ונשמחה בו", "בו ביומא, בו בקודשא בריך
הוא, וכולא חד [מלה]". ואין צריך לפרש, כי ממה נפשך, מי שאינו מבין זה אינו
מועיל לו לפרש. . . שאי אפשר לפרש ענין הנסתרות, דהיינו דבקות האהבה בה׳
יתברך, האיך הוא, כי הוא נסתר וכל אחד יודע מה שהוא יודע ולא יותר, ומי
שמבין [יודע] בעצמו. בו ביומא, בו בקודשא בריך הוא, וכולה חד, והוא שמחת
היום שיש לנו בו בו הארה ודבקות בו בה׳ יתברך, ועלינו הוא מצוה לחוגגה,
ושמחה של מצוה היא זו באמת לאמתו, כמו שכתב הטור סוף הלכות יום טוב
(סימן תקכט) שלא נצטוינו על שמחה של הוללות, כי אם אל שמחה שיש בה
עבודת היוצר ברוך הוא.
ר׳ משולם פייבוש הלוי העליר מזבאריז׳א, ס׳ יושר דברי אמת, עמ׳
קנ״ו.

218

[55] יציאת מצרים היה כמו קידושין לישראל ותנינן האיש מקדש בו ובשלוחו. בו ועברתי בארץ מצרים, ובשלוחו דכתיב וישלח מלאך ויוציאנו. אבל מתן תורה הוי נשואין דוקא על ידי עצמו. וזה אומרו פנים בפנים דבר ה'...

ר' אליהו בן שלמה אברהם הכהן האתמרי מאיזמיר, ס' מדרש תלפיות, כרך ב' דף' תשע"ח.

[56] משה ידבר ל' עתיד. כי עתיד הוא בכל דור ודור לדבר עם כל אחד ואחד בא לטהר ולקבל עליו התוה"ק. משה מדבר עמו כי אתפשטותא דמשה בכל דרא ודרא. והאלקים יעננו בקול. להכניס וליחד הקול בדיבור.

ר' אהרן בן אשר מקארלין, ס' בית אהרן, דף 222.

[57] וידבר אלקים את הדברים האלה לאמר לכאורה תיבת לאמר מיותר רק הפי' ע"ד מאמר רז"ל ע"פ ישקני משיקות פיהו שיש דברים שמצוה לאומרם ויש דברים שמשתיקין הפה וסותמים מלאמרם וזהו מ"ש תורה חדשה מאתי תצא הגם שבאמת הוא שלא תהא תורה אחרת רק הפי' שיתגלה דברים הסתומים עתה ומ"ת בהר סיני הי' הכנה על לע"ל וד"ז שאלו הדברים היו לאמר ולהגלות אותם לעתיד לבא.

ר' נפתלי צבי הורוויץ, ס' זרע קודש, דף מ"ד, עמוד ב'.

[58] תחילה צריך האדם לידע ולהאמין באמונה שלימה וחזקה, שיש אלוה מצוי אחד יחיד ומיוחד, שהמציא כל הנמצאים כולם יש מאין, הן מצד אמונת האבות, והן מצד אמונת הידיעה, כמאמר הכתוב (דה"א כח ט) דע את אלקי אביך ועבדהו, ויש בפסוק זה משמעות ב' האמונות.

ועל אמונתו ית"ש צריך האיש הנלבב לעבודתו, למסור נפשו על זה, כי זה אנכי ולא יהיה לך מפי הגבורה שמענום (מכות כד.), כי צריך איש הישראלי להגביר את עצמו על החומר להכניע בקומתו הגשמי ונעשה מרכבה אליו ית"ש, ואנכי ולא יהיה לך הם כלל כל התורה כולה, וקיומה.

ר' מרדכי מטשערנאביל, ס' ליקוטי תורה, דף י"ב.

[59] ...שדבר הקב"ה עם יש' מכל הבחי' שבמציאות להראות להם שאין זולתו ולכך דבר עמהם בכסא הכבוד ואמר אנכי ה' אלהיך אנכי עולה בחשבון כס"א ודבר עמהם מהמלאכים שנא' וכל העם רואים את הקולות והמלאכים הם הקולות דכתיב כי עוף השמים יוליך את הקול ודבר עמהם מן השמים דכתיב מן השמים השמיעך את קולו ודבר עמהם מן הארץ דכתיב ועל הארץ הראך את אשו הגדולה ודבר עמהם מכל ד' יסודות כדי שיראו שבכל יסוד ויסוד אין זולתו ומכל הבחי' האלו אמר אנכי ה' אלהיך.

ר' משה קורדאווירו, ס' שיעור קומה, עמ' 64.

[60] אשונה צריך האדם לידע ולהאמין באמת שיש אלו"ה אחד יחיד ומיוחד, שהמציא כל הנבראים ועולמות עליונים ותחתונים עד אין קץ ואין תכלית, ואיהו

ממלא כל עלמין ואיהו אסחר כל עלמין, ואיהו מלעיל כל עלמין, ואיהו מתחות
כל עלמין, ואיהו בתוך כל עלמין..., ואיהו עיקר החיות והנשמה לכל הנשמות
והחיות ...., וכד מסתלק חיותו אפילו רגע אחת היה נשאר הכל כגופא בלא
נשמתא...:

ומהאי טעמא חיוב מוטל על האדם השלם לזכור בכל עת ורגע על שפעת
חיותו ית"ש, כמאמר הכתוב כל הנשמ"ה תהלל י"ה (תהלים ק"נ ו') ודרשו
חז"ל... על כל נשימה ונשימה כו', כי הנשמה רוצה לצאת מן הגוף בכל רגע
ורגע, אך השי"ת ברוב רחמיו וחסדיו מחזיר חיות הנשמה, בסוד והחיות רצוא
ושוב (יחזקאל א' י"ד.)...
ר' מרדכי מטשערנאביל, ס' לקוטי תורה, דפ' ח-ט.

[61] ושמו בעז בעזו של תורה. ועוד בעז עז, וכתי' איזהו גבור חיל הכובש את
יצרו. בעז וכתי' (משלי כד) גבור חכם בעז, נדרש על בועז, בעז, בועז, בו עז, יש
בו עוז וגבורה, בעז עזב יצרו.
ר' אלעזר מגרמייזא, פירוש הרוקח, כרך ה', דפ' 187-188.

[62] רבי יוסי פתח ואמר (רות ג) ויאכל בעז וישת וייטב לבו. מהו וייטב לבו
דבריך על מזוניה ואוקמוה. ודא איהו רזא דמאן דמברך על מזוניא דא אוטיב
לליביה ומאן אוטיב כמה דכתיב (תהלים כז) לך אמר לבי. וכתיב (שם עג) צור
לבבי וגו'.
ספר הזהר, כרך ב', דף רי"ח, עמוד א'.

[63] ובועז עלה השער וישב שם והנה הגואל עובר אשר דבר בועז ויאמר סורה
שבה פה פלוני אלמוני ויסר וישב ... בועז איש צדיק בדורו וכל עצמו של צדיק
והשתדלותו כל ימי חיים חיותו כי אם להעלות איברי השכינה מהתלבשות
מדריגת התחתונים וזהו שמעיד הכתוב על צדקות הצדיק ובעז עלה והגביה
השער כנוי לשכינה הנקרא שער לה' והעלה אותם [צ"ל אותה] למחשבה
הקדומה ...
ר' זאב וואלף מזוטאמיר, ס' אור המאיר, חלק ד', דף ט"ז, עמוד ג'.

[64] התורה ניתנה לצרף את ישראל לכן צריך כל אחד לעסוק בה כדי שיצטרפו
כל ישראל בה.
ר' יעקב בן חיים צמח, ס' נגיד ומצוה, דף פ"ב.

[65] שמעתי בשמו הק'. דרך ארץ קדמה לתורה. אמר שדרך ארץ הוא הקדמה
לתורה כמו בהקדמת הספר יוכל אדם לידע מהות הספרין כמו כן הדרך ארץ
הוא הקדמה לתורה שניכר מתוך התנהגות דרך ארץ של אדם מהות תורתו.
והבן.
יועץ קיים קדיש ראקאץ, ס' שיח שרפי קודש, חלק א', דף 66.

[66] למה נתנה בהר סיני. התורה נתנה על הר סיני, משום שהוא נמוך שבהרים. וכן איתא בגמרא (סוטה ה.), אשכון ואת דכא ושפל רוח (ישעיה נז, טו) וכו', שהרי הניח הקב"ה כל הרים וגבעות והשרה שכינתו על הר סיני וכו', עיי"ש, ולכאורה למה לא נתנה התורה בבקעה. ונראה לפרש שמי שהוא באמת ריק ומחוסר כל, אין פלא שאינו מתגאה, אבל מי שיש בו משהו ואינו מתגאה, הרי הוא משובח.

ר' יצחק מווארקא, ס' בית יצחק, דף קמ"ה.

[67] ישראל אינון פתילה. אורייתא משחא. שכינתא שרגא.
תיקוני הזוהר, תיקון כ"א, דף ס' עמוד ב'.

[68] ...שנקרא תורת משה (מלאכי ג' כ"ב). יעזור השם יתברך שיהיה התגלות אלקות בעולם ויקויים בנו מקרא שכתוב (ישעיה נ"ב ח') כי עין בעין יראו וגו'. ואז יקבל כל אחד ואחד חלקו בתורה על ידי הזדככות מדותיו בעצמו, ואז יהיה נקרא תורת ה'.

ר' ישראל מסאדיגורא, ס' אור ישראל, דף קס"ח. (שבועות תרמ"ט יום א').

[69] ...העוסק בטל תור' כמו האר"י ודומתו טל תור' מחייהו לומר לו סודו' התור' הנוגעים בנשמתו בפי שבכללות כל הנשמו' הם ששים רבוא נשמות ס' רבוא אילנות של ז' ענפים של אור וכולם נקראים ע"ש הגוף ושאר הדורות הם ענפים והתורה היא כוללת כל הנשמו' של ישראל בסוד פרד"ס ואבי"ע ולכן יש כנגדם ס' רבוא פירושים בפשט וכנגדם ס' רבוא ברמז וראיה וכנגדם ס' רבוא בדרש וכנגד' ס' רבוא בקבלה וכן כיוצא בזה כי אין לך נשמה שאינה כלולה מכלם. ומכל פירוש נתהוה שורש נשמה א' מישראל ולעתיד לבא כל אחד ואחד יקרא וידע את התורה כפי הפירוש המגיע לשרשו אשר על ידו נברא וכן הוא כג"ע ויש נשמה כוללת כמה פירושים ונשמת מרע"ה היתה כוללת כל הס' רבוא פירושים וידע אותם. ולכן בלילה אחר צאת הנשמה בעת השינה הנה מי שזוכה לעלות הקורא שם אותו הפירוש המגיע אל שרשו אכן יש בחינת חלוקות כי בלילה זו מאיר יותר פסוק זה בנשמתו ולילה אחר פסוק אחר והכל כפי מעשיו ...

ר' נפטלי (הערץ) בן יעקב אלחנן (באכראך), ס' עמק המלך, דף מ"ב א'.

[70] פעם אחת אמר בשבועות על מאמר חז"ל (שבת דק"ה.) א'נ'כ'י ר"ת אנא נפשי כתבית יהבית ע"ד ההסבר אשר למלך אחד הי' לו בן יחיד והיה מושלם בכל המעלות כראוי לבן מלך והמלך אהב אותו כאהבת נפשו רק דרך המלכים לשלוח את בניהם למרחקים ללמוד חכמות ונסע הבן על זמן רב ובהמשך הזמן כתב המלך לבנו יחידו האהוב ובעת הכתיבה נתעורר בלב המלך עוד אהבה יותר גדולה וחשוקה ודביקות וכל כחו נתן בהמכתב וכאשר הגיע המכתב לבנו האהוב בעת הקריאה ממש הי' מרגיש נפש אהבת אביו כי הוא מונח

221

בתוך המכתב וזה אמר הקב"ה א'נ'כ'י אנא נפשי כתבית יהבית אני נתתי א"ע
בהתורה ובה תרגיש אלקית ואהבת הקב"ה לישראל ותקשור בה ממש עם
קוב"ה כבן אל אביו.
ר' יעקב יוסף מאוסטרהא, בס' צרור החיים, דף 28.

[71] עוד שמעתי בשמו הק' בזוה"ק איתא מאן דמשתדל באורייתא, הפי' ער
ווערט איבער רעדט דוירך דיא תורה. כי על הפסוק כי יפתה איש נערה בתולה.
תרגום אונקלוס ארי ישדל. והבן כי עמוק מאד.
ר' יועץ קיים קדיש ראקאץ, ס' שיח שרפי קודש, חלק א', דף 66.

[72] איתא ואהבת לרעך כמוך זהו כלל כל התורה כולו ולכאורה זהו רק מצות
שבין אדם לחבירו אבל שאר מצות איך יכולים לבוא עי"ז אך הענין הוא כשאדם
מסתכל רק ברוחניות כי מכה"כ וברוחניות שורש נשמות אחד ומחזיר ומדבק
עצמו אל השורש ממילא מקיים כל התורה כי בהשורש נכלל הכל.
ר' אברהם יעקב מרוזין, ס' בית ישראל, אמת ליעקב, דף 109.

[73] זכרו תורת משה עבדי אשר ציויתי וכו' זיין של זכרו גדולה, אפשר הטעם
לומר, שההתורה כלי זיין גדול, בין לעה"ז בין לעה"ב, בעה"ז ניצל משעבוד, כמו
ששנינו, אין לך בן חורין אלא מי עוסק בתורה, וגם על ידי התורה ניצל מהיצה"ר,
סמא דכולא, כמ"ש, סם תם, ובעה"ב, בצאת הנשמה תגן עליו, וכמ"ש, ובשכבך
תשמור עליך, ולזה נכתב זיין גדולה, לומר, שהתורה מצלת מהפורענות, ואשם
שיש בו תורה כלי זיינו עליו.
ר' חיים יוסף דוד אזולאי, ס' חדרי בטן, דף רל"ה.

[74] התורה נקראת חמדה גנוזה (שבת פח ע"ב). שהחמדה לשמו גנוז בתוכה.
חיבה יתירה נודעת להם שניתן להם כלי חמדה היינו התורה הקדושה כדכתיב
(משלי ד ב) כי לקח טוב נתתי לכם תורתי אל תעזובו (אבות פ"ג מי"ח). וקאמר
נודעת שיודע להם זה שנתן להם כלי חמדה.
ר' מרדכי מנשכיז, ס' רשפי אש, דף ע"א, סי' קלב, קלג.

[75] ...שבתורה יש קומה רוחניות מן רמ"ח איברים רוחניים היינו רמ"ח מ"ע
ושס"ה גידים רוחניים שהם שס"ה ל"ת ובאדם יש ג"כ רמ"ח אברים ושס"ה גידים
והנה האדם נברא בצלם אלהים ולהבין הענין וכי שייך לומר בו ית' שום תמונ'
ח"ו אך הפי' הוא בצלם של התורה שהתורה נקראת אלהים שהוא צמצום
שהש"י צמצם א"ע לתוך התורה כדי שיוכל האדם שהוא בעל גבול ותכלית לדבק
א"ע בהש"י שהוא בלי גבול ותכלית ולא היה באפשרי לדבק בו ית' לכן צמצם
הש"י עצמו לתוך התורה ואדם נברא בצלם אלהים של התורה שהוא הקומה
רוחניות רמ"ח מצות עשה ושס"ה ל"ת והנה האדם השלם הוא כשהוא א' עם
הצלם דהיינו מקומה גשמיות שלו הוא א' עם הקומה רוחניות של התורה אדם
העליון וכשמנענע' אבר גשמי מנענע ומעורר אבר העליון וזה נקרא אדם שלם

222

כמאמר אך בצלם יתהלך איש ר"ל מי שמהלך עם הצלם שהוא א' אם הצלם אז נקרא איש שלם אבל כשלא עשה איזה מצוה או עבר איזה עבירה הוא חסר אבר א' או גיד א' ואינו שלם...

ר' מנחם נחום מטשארנאביל, ס' מאור עינים, חלק א' דף 98.

[76] כי כל תורתנו כלה, שבכתב ושבעל פה, אין דבר אחד אפלו אות אחת יוצא לדבר אחר זולת לעבוד ה' יתברך, כי לזה נתנה, ונקרא תורה על שם שמורה לאמר זה הדרך לכו בה, ואפלו בדיני ממונות ושאר דינים, הדומים שאין נפקותא ועובדא מהם, אם ריק הוא מכם הוא (ע"פ דברים לב,מז, ...), אבל מי עובד ה' יתברך בשלמות, מגלין לו רזי תורה, וזהו הרזין, איך לקח עצה מכל תרי"ג מצות לעבוד בהם הבורא יתברך, אף על פי שאינם באפשר לקיימם בעצמם, כמו מצות התלויין בארץ ושאר מצות, וזה שקרא הזהר (יתרו פב,ב) את תרי"ג מצות - תרי"ג עיטין, רצה לומר, שנותנים לאדם עצה איך להתדבק ביוצרו.

ר' משולם פייבוש הלוי מזבאריזא, ס' יושר דברי אמת, דף ק"ח.

[77] ...יש בידינו קבלה של אמת כי כל התורה כולה שמתיו של הקב"ה שהתיבות מתחלקות לשמות בענין אחד כאלו תחשוב על דרך משל כי פסוק בראשית יתחלק לתיבות אחרות כגון בראשית ברא אלהים ברא אלהים וכל התורה כן מלבד צירופיהם וגימטריותיהן של שמות. . . שהיתה הכתיבה רצופה בלי הפסק תיבות והיה אפשר בקריאתה שתקרא על דרך השמות ותקרא על דרך קריאתנו בענין התורה והמצוה ונתנה למשה רבינו על דרך קריאת המצות ונמסר לו על פה קריאתה בשמות.

ר' משה בן נחמן (רמב"ן), פירוש על התורה, הקדמה.

[78] ...ולפי שהתורה נקראת שם והיא משיבת הנפש יש בה הפרשיות ופרקים והפסקות שהם פרשיות פתוחות וסתומות דוגמת בנין שלם, כמו שיש באדם קשרי יד ורגל ופרקים. וכמ' שיש איברים שהנשמה תלויה בהם ויש איברים שאין הנשמה תלויה בהם ואע"פ שאין תוספת ואין מגרעת בבריאת הגוף, כן יש פרשיות בתורה ומקראות שיראה למי שאינו יודע טעמי פירושם שהם ראוים לישרף ולמי שהשיג לדעת פירושם יראה שהם גופי תורה, והמחסר אות אחת או נקודה אחת מהם כמ' שהוא מחסר גוף השלם, ואין הפרש בין אלופי עשו ובין עשרת הדברות שהכל דבר אחד ובנין אחד.

ר' עזריאל מגירונה, פירוש האגדות, דפ' 73-83.

[79] צריך לעיין בהבנת התורה על דרך שיכיר אדם עצמו בה כמי שמעיין במראה לראות פניו ועצמו וזולתו בה, ומשם יעלה הרואה בה בעיון אל הכרת קונו ית'.

ר' אברהם אבולפיא, ס' מפתח הספירות, דף ל"ד.

223

[80] פתח רבי חייא ואמר. (תהלים ק"ו ב') מי ימלל גבורות יי' ישמיע כל
תהלתו. תא חזי כד בעא קב"ה וסליק ברעותא קמיה למברי עלמא. הוה מסתכל
באורייתא וברא ליה. ובכל עובדא ועובדא דברא קב"ה בעלמא הוה מסתכל
באורייתא וברא ליה. הדא הוא דכתיב (משלי ח' ל') ואהיה אצלו אמון. ואהיה
[קל"ד ע"ב] שעשועים יום יום. אל תקרי אמון אלא אומן .

כד בעא למברי אדם. אמרה תורה קמיה. אי בר נש יתברי ולבתר יחטי.
ואנת תידון ליה. אמאי יהון עובדי ידך למגנא. דהא לא יכיל למסבל דינך. אמר
לה קב"ה. הא אתקינת תשובה עד לא בראתי עלמא .

אמר קב"ה לעלמא בשעתא דעבד ליה וברא לאדם. א"ל עלמא עלמא.
אנת ונימוסך לא קיימין אלא על אורייתא. ובגין כך בראתי ליה לאדם בך בגין
דיתעסק בה. ואי לאו הא אנא אהדר לך לתהו ובהו .

וכלא בגיניה דאדם קיימא. הדא הוא דכתיב (ישעיה מ"ה י"ב) אנכי
עשיתי ארץ ואדם עליה בראתי. ואורייתא קיימא ומכרזא קמייהו דבני נשא בגין
דיתעסקו וישתדלו בה. ולית מאן דירכין אודניה .

תא חזי כל מאן דאשתדל באורייתא איהו קיים עלמא. וקיים כל עובדא
ועובדא על תקוניה כדקא יאות.
ספר הזהר, כרך א', דף קל"ד, עמ' א'-ב'.

[81] בכל דרכיך דעהו (ג, ו), אמר מה הפירוש, אלא כשנתן הקב"ה את התורה
נתמלא כל העולם בתורה שנאמר חי אני וימלא כבוד ה' את כל הארץ (במדבר
יד, כ), ואורייתא וקב"ה חד הוא, ועכשיו אין דבר שאין בו תורת ה', וזה בכל
דרכיך דעהו. האומר דברי תורה דבר אחד ומילי דעלמא דבר אחד הוא כופר.
ר' פנחס מקאריץ, ס' אמרי פנחס, סימן קפ"ז, דף' נ"א-נ"ב.


## תשעה באב

[82] הנה יש מוחין דגדלות ומוחין דקטנות וא"א להיות גדלות אלא א"כ יש
מתחלה קטנות. יש בחי' ימין ובחי' שמאל מפני מה נקרא ימין כי כנגדו בחי'
שמאל ניכר שהוא ימין. השי"ת יתן שיהיה ויהי ערב ויהי בקר יום אחד ערב בחי'
חושך ובקר בחי' אור. שיוכלל החושך באור ויכללו הגבורות בהחסדים שיהיה
רב חסדים ורחמים על ישראל אמן:
ר' ישראל מריזין, ס' עירין קדישין, בין המצרים, דף 68.


[83] שמעתי מפיו הקדוש ששאל למה קורין אותו שבת שבת חזון. ואמר כי
בשבת זה יכולים לראות מה יהיה בעולם. וענין נבואה היא כשהנביאים רואים
ח"ו דבר מה על ישראל רואים את הדבר כשכבר בא אל המדות כמו דאיתא
בזוה"ק אית דמסתכלין בידין ואית דמסתכלין ברגלין וזה ענין המדות. ולכך אינם
יכולים להמתיק הדבר עוד ולבטל הדבר.... תיכף כשראו את הדבר אמרו

לישראל שאין בכחם לבטל מחמת שכבר בא אל המדות. אבל חכם עדיף מנביא כי החכם עיניו בראשו שרואה הדבר כשהוא עדיין בראש למעלה מהמדות. והיינו מחמת שהחכם הוא בחי' אי"ן ולכך רואה הדבר גם כן בבחי' אי"ן. ולכך יכול להמתיק ולבטל. וסיים מה רואה כשרואה אי"ן רק שרואה שאינו רואה .

אח"כ אמר כשיש דינים חס ושלום על ישראל אזי אני חולה ועצב. וכשיש רחמים אני בריא ושמח. כי הצדיק יכול להרגיש בגופו כל ענייני השתנות שנעשה בעולם בכל פעם מרחמים לדין חס ושלום ומדין לרחמים....

ר' ישראל מריזין, ס' עירין קדישין, חלק א' דפ' 66-67.

[84] בן מלך שאביו השליטו בשליש מלכותו רק הכסא לאבי מלך, והוא עבר חקי אביו והפר את כל משפטיו לשנא אוהביו ולאהוב שונאיו, והמלך שלח אליו הרבה פעמים שרים רבים ונכבדים לצוותו ולהזכירו כי מאמר שהוא עושה משפט, ונלוו אליו בעלי העצה, אם לא יחזור מרה תהיה באחרונה, ולא אבה שמוע, ויצאה הגזרה מהמלך ומבעלי העצה לגרש לבן המלך ולשללו ולבוז את אשר לו ונשאר נע ונד, רק מכל טוב, נודד הוא ללחם איה, אמרו אתם אם בן המלך הזה ישארו לו תמיד יגון ואנחה, אל תבא רננה בו, והנמשל מובן איך נשמח ואיך נאכל בסעודת מרעות הא ודאי הוא חסרון דעת.

ר' חיים יוסף דוד אזולאי, ס' חדרי בטן, דף רפ"ד עמוד א'.

[85] ענין ט' באב... מדברי נביאים וכתובים ומדברי רבותינו ז"ל בתלמוד ובמדרשים ובזוהר נתבאר גודל החיוב המוטל להתאבל על חורבן בית המקדש ועל הגלות. וטעם הענין הוא, מפני כבוד השכינה, כי מפני חטאינו גלינו מארצינו וכביכול השכינה בגלות והשפחה תירש גבירתה, וגבר האויב מצד הקליפה סטרא אחרא, וכבוד בית ה' נשרף, ואין עולה ואין זבח, ופסקה הנבואה ורוח הקודש, ורוח הטומאה נתפשט, ועם ה' אומה הישראלית נתנו לדבר ולחרב ולרעב ולשבי ולבזה, ועד היום הם בין האומות ככבשה בין הזאבים ובחרפה ובבוז, וכל זה הוא חלול השם, אוי נא לנו כי חטאו אבותינו ואנחנו לא נטהרנו, על דא ודאי קא בכינו כי גרמנו כל אלה. ובשומינו על לבינו זה בצום ובבכי ובהספד ובהתעוררות לב לצעוק השיבנו ה' אליך ונשובה, אז כלה ענן וילד, דהיינו הקליפה מתמעטת ואנחנו מזדככים מכח הצער והחרטה.

ר' ישעיה הלוי הורוויץ, ס' שני לוחות הברית, מסכת תענית, כרך א' דף מ"ו עמוד א'.

[86] ציון נקראת עתה יתום ומלכות בית דוד נקרא' אתה בגלות אלמנה וכל המרחם על יתום ואלמנ' יזכ' לראות בנחמת ציון ומלכות ביד דוד על מכונה.

ר' לוי יצחק מברדישוב, ס' קדושת לוי, דף פ"ג עמוד ג'.

[87] א"א זצ"ל אמר שמן הג' שביעות [sic] יודע לו הימים טובים. ואני אומר שהג' שביעות הם כמו אבנים טובים שגדילים תחת הרי חושך אע"פ שהם בחי' חושך מ"מ יש בהם בחי' אור. וכשיבוא משיח צדקינו ויהיה אור הלבנה כאור

החמה אזי יהיו הג׳ שביעות ימים טובים כי הג׳ שביעות הם כנגד ג׳ רגלים. השי״ת יודע האמת כי בימי בחורתי שהיה לי כח הרגשתי בהג׳ שביעות בכל יום אור חדש. והאמת מה שאמרו חז״ל כל מה דעביד רחמנא לטב עביד הכוונה על הג׳ שביעות. אף על פי שהם בחי׳ ירידה לישראל מ״מ לטב עבוד.

ר׳ ישראל מריזין, ס׳ עירין קדישין,חלק א׳, דף 68.

[88] בכל מקום שהוא צר מאד, שם הוא בהעלם (הוא) התגלות אלקים, ולילה בכל מקום הוא סוד הדין ובפרט חצות הלילה, והיה שם הנס של מכת בכורות, ואצל בלעם הרשע היתה בו בהעלם גדול בחי׳ אחת [דנבואה] כמו אצל משה רבינו, וגם בתשעה באב שנחרב בו הבית היתה בו בהעלם גדול בחי׳ הגאולה, ולכך נולד בו משיח. וגם אצל אשה מעוברת, כ״ז שאין צירים אינה יכולה ללדת. וכדומה לי שאמר שלכך איתא בזוה״ק כד ייתי דוחקא בתר דוחקא ייתי פורקנא לישראל. וזה שאלת מה נשתנה.

ר׳ פנחס מקאריץ, ס׳ אמרי פנחס, סימן תרצ״ב, דף קל״ד.

[89] איכה ישבה בדד העיר וגו׳, [ברש״י ז״ל, ירמי׳ כתב ספר קינות הוא המגלה אשר שרף יהויקים על האח אשר על האש והיו בה שלש אל״ף ביתו״ת, איכה ישבה, איכה יעיב, איכה יועם, שוב הוסיף עליו אני הגבר שהוא שלש אל״ף ביתו״ת וכו׳, עכ״ל] הטעם שירמי׳ דקדק לסדר הקינות עפ״י סדר אל״ף בי״ת י״ל שהוא מחמת שכשירמי׳ ראה החורבן וגודל השפעה שניטל מאתנו הי׳ כמעט בדעתו שבלתי אפשרות לישראל ולעולם שום קיום ח״ו עד שכמעט כלתה נפשו מגודל המרירות לולא שראה שיור האל״ף בי״ת שיש לנו בצירופיהם כמ״ש בספר יצירה אז מצא לנו בדעתו שיור התורה וזה הי׳ לו ניחום וזהו באמת טעם קריאתינו החדש הזה בשם מנחם א״ב ומזה הטעם ג״כ הוידוי הוא באל״ף בי״ת.

ר׳ מנחם מענדל מקאצק, ס׳ אהל תורה, דף 70.

[90] טבעו בארץ שעריה פי׳ כי הנה בדבר שהוא במדריגות אי״ן לא שייך שבירה כי השבירה שייך בדבר שהוא מדה או כלי נמצא אם אדם מחזיק את עצמו לאי״ן מחמת דביקותו בבורא ית׳ כמו השר אפילו הוא גדול שבכל שרי מלוכה בעמדו לפני המלך הוא בעיניו כמו קטן ואינו רוצה שיעשה לו שום כבוד מחמת גדלו ושרבותו כמו שעושים לו כשהוא בביתו בפ״ע כי אז עושים לו כבוד ובושים ויראים ממנו אמנם כשהוא לפני המלך הוא וכל מדותיו נתבטלו מפני יראתו ובשתו לפני המלך וזהו טבעו בארץ שעריה ר״ל שמחזיק עצמו לארץ לאין בעיניו שעריה ר״ל המדות וכשאין לו שום מדה אזי אין שייך אצלו שום שבירה וזהו מכל חטאתיכם לפני יי׳ תטהרו.

ר׳ דוב בער ממזריטש, ס׳ מגיד דבריו ליעקב, סימן פ׳, דף ט״ו.

[91] אני הגבר ראה עני בשבט עברתו (איכה ג׳ א׳), יותר הווה ליה למימר ראה עני, אבל הכוונה כי כנודע במוצאי תשעה באב נולד משיח (ירושלמי ברכות

226

פרק ב' הלכה ד'), וזה שכתוב אני הגבר ראה עני, רוצה לומר שראה משיח
שנולד והוא נקרא עני ורוכב על החמור (זכריה ט' ט'), בשבט עברתו רצה לומר
ראו שאין כאלוקינו וכמו שכתוב (תהלים ל' ה') זמרו לה' חסידיו וכו' כי רגע
באפו, רצה לומר בעת שנחרב הבית דהיינו במוצאי תשעה באב שהיה חרון אף
גדול כמו שכתוב (איכה א' י"ב) אשר הוגה ה' ביום חרון אפו, חיים ברצונו
באותו פעם נולד משיח, שאמרו בחלק חיים שמו, וזה שכתוב ראה עני, היינו
לידת משיח, בשבט עברתו, בה בעת שהכה בשבט עברתו ודפח"ח.
ר' אורי מסטרעליסק, ס' אמרי קדוש, דף' פ"ג-פ"ד.

[92] פירש מורי מוהד"ב זצ"ל. כל רודפיה השיגוה בין המצרים (איכה א, ג),
שמי שרודף אחר הקדושה משיג אותה בין המצרים יותר ויותר.
ר' ישראל מקאזניץ, ס' עבודת ישראל, דף ש"מ.

[93] אומרים בשם הרב המגיד הגדול והקדוש ממעזיריטש נבג"מ זיע"א בפסוק
השיבנו ה' אליך ונשובה חדש ימינו כקדם שפי' כי נודע הוכוח שבין הקב"ה
לכנס"י שהקב"ה אומר להם שובו בנים שובבים שובה אלי ואשובה אליכם והיינו
שיהיה מקודם אתערותא דלתתא מכנס"י ואח"כ ישוב ירחמנו וכו'. וכנס"י
אומרים שובנו אלקי ישענו כו' פי' שיהיה אתערותא דלעילא מקודם להשיבם
אליו ית' ולפדותם מהגלות ולקבצם מכל העמים ואזי ישובו לה' בלב שלם ויתקנו
מעשיהם. ולזה בא ירמיה להשיב להש"י תשובה נוצחת באומרו השיבנו ה' אליך
מתחלה ואח"כ ונשובה. והנה שהאמת הוא שצריך להיות מתחלה אתעדל"ת.
עכ"ז חדש ימינו כקדם פי' כמו שהיה קודם בריאת העולם שלא נברא עוד שום
בריה בעולם רק שהיה אתערותא דלעילא ע"ש העתיד לבא שהיה צופה ומביט
עד סוף כל הדורות וראה הנח"ר שיגיע אליו מעבודת ישראל גוי קדוש כן עשה
גם עתה שיתגלה כבוד מלכותך עלינו מהרה ושם נעבדך ביראה כשנים קדמוניות
ודפח"ח וש"י [ושלומך ישגה?].
ר' ישראל מבאהאפאלי, ס' עטרת ישראל, דף 105.

## ראש השנה

[94] אמר, ראש השנה, האדם צריך לקחת הראש בחינת מוח, אל הלב. היינו
להתבונן להשגיח על עצמו על מעשיו, מראשית השנה עד אחרית השנה. וזהו
ראש השנה, שהאדם צריך להכין לו ולקחת לעצמו ראש, בחינת מוח, על כל
השנה.

ר' ישראל מסאדיגורא, ס' אור ישראל, דף רכ"ח (ליל ב, תרמ"ז).

[95] פ"א אמר באיזה אופן יוכל הבעל תפלה לגשת להתפלל בפני העמוד בימים
נוראים למשל למלך שקצף על המדינה וישב לשפוע את העם בדין נתכנסו כל
בני המדינה ואמרו מאן ייזיל לפייסא עלנא למלכא לבקש על נפשינו ולא נמצא
בכל המדינה מי שיבוא להתחנן לפני המלך כי כולם יראו פן יפשם פן בדברם לפני

המלך ישכלו בלשונם ויפגעו בכבוד המלך ויתחייבו ראשם למלך, והי׳ ביניהם איש אחד פושע ומורד למלכות וידע בנפשו כי כבר נתחייב ראשו למלכות, ואמר אנכי אלך ואבקש רחמים עליכם כי אנכי כבר נתחייבתי ראשי למלך וכשאמצא אני חן בעיני המלך בודאי כל המדינה ימצאו חן בעיני המלך, בזה האופן ובזו הכוונה יגש הבע״ת להעמוד בימים הנוראים לבקש ולהתפלל בעד הצבור.

ר׳ משה בן ישראל מקאברין, ס׳ אמרות טהורות, דפ׳ 32-31.

[96] כי תעביר ממשלת זדון מן הארץ, י״ל שמרמז על אותם אנשים שמתדמין במעשיהם לצדיקים ולבם לא נכון עמם והוא שאומרים כי תעביר ממשלת לשון משל ודמיון זדון היינו אדם בליעל שע״ז אנו מתפללים שלא יהא דומה הזדון להטוב רק שיהיה הבדל בין האור והחושך וידעו ויבינו זאת כל יושבי תבל יה״ר שיהיה בב״א.

ר׳ משה חיים אפרים מסודילקאב, ס׳ דגל מחנה אפרים, דף רס״ג.

[97] כי שמע אלקים וגו׳ באשר הוא שם (בראשית כא, יז). ואיתה במדרש (שם. פרשה נג), אמר רבי סימון קפצו מלאכי השרת לקטרגו, אמרו לפניו, רבון העולמים, אדם שהוא עתיד להמית את בניך בצמא אתה מעלה לו באר, אמר להם אני דן את האדם אלא בשעתו. וזהו באשר הוא שם. כלומר, שדנו ישמעאל לפי מעשיו בהווה. כך גם אנו מבקשים שהקב״ה יראה אותנו לפי המעשים שלנו בימי ראש השנה ויום הכפורים לא על שעבר ולא על העתיד, אלא לפי ההווה.

ר׳ יצחק מווארקא, ס׳ בית יצחק, דפ׳ קמ״ו-קמ״ז.

[98] אמר ר׳ אבהו למה תוקעין בשופר של איל. אמר הקב״ה תקעו לפני בשופר של איל כדי שאזכור לכם עקידת יצחק בן אברהם ומעלה אני עליכם כאילו עקדתם עצמיכם לפני עכ״ל.

...אין ראוי לאדם לבקש זאת שיבוא לידי מסירת נפש בפועל כמו שקרה לר׳ עקיבא שנהרג על קדושת שמו יתברך אמנם יכין עצמו לקדש ה׳ בכל עוז ומי שהוא נכון לזה באמת ובשמחה מעלה עליו השי״ת כאילו קיימו בפועל ממש וזהו הפי׳ שאזכור לכם עקדת יצחק ומעלה אני עליכם כאילו עקדתם עצמיכם לפני פי׳ אחרי שהמלכתם אליהכם עליכם ואתם נכונים לקדש שמו ולמסור נפשכם יזכור לכם עקידת יצחק שאפרו צבור אף שלא נשרף בפועל ומעלה אני עליכם כאילו גם אתם עקדתם עצמיכם לפני ונעשין עולות בפועל ולא תצטרכו לבא לידי מעשה ממש:

ר׳ קלונימוס קלמן הלוי אפשטיין, ס׳ מאור ושמש, רמזי ר״ה, דפ׳ ל״ד, עמוד ד׳, ל״ה עמוד א׳.

[99] בגין דא אברהם עקד ליצחק. בגין לאכללא ביה דינא... ולאשתכחא שמאלא כליל בימינא... ולאשלטא ימינא על שמאלא. ועל דא קודשא בריך הוא

228

פקיד ליה לאברהם. לקרבא בריה לדינא. ולאתקפא עלוי. ולא פקיד ליצחק. אלא לאברהם. ועל דא אשתכח. דא בדינא. ודא בחסד. וכלא חד. ואתכליל דא בדא.
ספר הזהר, חלק ב', דף רנ"ז עמוד א'.

[100] שמעתי, שאיש אחד שאל אותו: כיצד הוא הבחירה? השיב לו בפשיטות, שהבחירה היא ביד אדם בפשיטות, אם רוצה עושה, ואם אינו רוצה אינו עושה. ורשמתי זאת, כי הוא נצרך מאד, כי כמה בני אדם נבוכים בזה מאד, מחמת שהם מורגלים במעשיהם ובדרכיהם מנעוריהם מאד, על כן נדמה להם שאין בהם בחירה, חס ושלום, ואינם יכולים לשנות מעשיהם. אבל באמת אינו כן, כי בודאי יש לכל אדם בחירה תמיד על כל דבר, וכמו שרוצה עושה, והבן הדברים מאד.
ר' נתן מנמירוב, ס' ליקוטי מוהר"ן, ליקוטי תנינא, סימן ק"י, דף מ"ב עמוד ד'.

[101] שמעתי מאא"ז זלל"ה שמלת חטא האלף אינו ניכר בההברה והטעם לפי שהרשע שרוצה לעבור עבירה שוכח באלופו של עולם...
ר' משה חיים אפרים מסדילקאב, ס' דגל מחנה אפרים, דף רכ"ה.

[102] פ"א בעת התקיעות הי' הוא ז"ל רק המסדר הזהר והברכות כנהוג ואמר בקול גדול רבש"ע האב רחמנות אויף אידישע נשמות עפין זייא זייערע הערצער אז זייא זאלין קענין פאר דיר תשובה טאהן.
ר' משה בן ישראל מקאבריין, ס' אמרות טהורות, דף ל"א.

[103] תשובה נקראת אמא עילאה (זח"ג רעח ע"ב). ואמר על זה הגאון הקדוש ישראל ואורו אב"ד דק"ק נעשכיז, למה נקראת כן מפני שכמו שהתינוק הקטן יחבא תחת כנפי אמו להסתר מגערת המאיים עליו, כן השב בתשובה הוא מתכסה בה מהמקטרגין עליו במעלו אשר מעל וינצל מכל העונש.
ר' מרדכי מנעשכיז, ס' רשפי אש,סי' קסא, דף פ"ב.

[104] אך באמת הכל תלוי באמונה, כי ישראל מאמינים בהשי"ת שימחול להם כל חטאתם, והקב"ה מאמין בישראל שיעשו תשובה ויתקנו מעשיהם.
ר' ישראל מסאדיגורא, ס' אור ישראל, דף רכ"ז.

[105] בליל ראש השנה. אמר כי א"א לקבל יום הקדוש הזה רק ע"י ריעות. כאמור יום תרו"עה יהיה לכם. כי אי אפשר לקבלו רק ע"י אחדות וריעות וזהו דכתיב באחד לחודש השביעי לרמז כי הכל ע"י אחדות. וזהו דכתיב ביום ההוא יהיה ד' אחד ושמו אחד. כי בודאי באחדותו אין לספק ח"ו ואצ"ל רק לרמז כי הכל הוא ע"י אחדות. וד"ל. ואמר רק בשמחה ובישוב הדעת. כי ע"י שמחה המוח מזוכך ועיקר התשובה ע"י מוח זך.
ר' אהרן (השני) מקארלין, ס' בית אהרן, דף רס"ג.

[106] בראש השנה הראשון בטומשוב לפני תקיעות שופר אמר רבינו: "וציוונו" ס׳זאל אריין גיין אין אלע איברים דער ציווי, ואמר השומע שארבעים שנה לאחר מכן היה מזדעזע כשהיה נזכר בזה.

ר׳ מנחם מענדל מקאצק, ס׳ עמוד האמת, דפ׳ קע״ח-קע״ט.

[107] איתא בשם ר׳ סעדיה גאון, כי השופר להביא פחד, לכן התינוק מפחד מקול השופר ומכלי זמר אינו מפחד, ע״כ ראוי לפחוד ותיכף שמפחד נתעלה השכינה, וזה עלה אלקים וכו׳. פעם אחת אמר בבית-הכנסת קודם התקיעות והיה מעורר העולם לבכיה ביותר, וכשבא לביתו אמר לנו שהטעם בזה שאומרים קודם החקיעות כדי שישמעו העם, וכאשר השומע ישמע מאסף נשמתו אליו, ולוקח נשמתן ותוקע בהן לשופר מעלה נשמתו בזה. ואמר לנו כי לא יוכל להבין זאת לאחרים, כי הוא למעלה מהדיבור, כמו שאחד רוצה להראות על אדם ואינו אומר רק מראהו בראשו או בידו, כן הדבר הזה, וגם החולה כאשר כואב לו אינו יכול לומר איך הוא כואב לו והוא מתאנח בקול בלא דיבור אַ, כך השופר ג״כ קול בלא דיבור. ואמר אלמלא לא בא לעולם אלא [להשמיע] דבר זה די.

ר׳ פנחס מקאריץ, ס׳ אמרי פנחס, סימן תקע״א, דף קט״ו.

[108] פעם אחת ביום ראש השנה קודם תקיעת שופר ברח רבינו הרבי הק׳ ר׳ זוסיא מבית מדרשו ויצא לחוץ פתאום ושם באמצע הרחוב פגש עני אחד נער משולח ונעזב ערום ויחף ורעב ואמר לו הרב אל הנער הכי אין אתה מתקנא בנער כמוך מן אומות העולם ההולך לקראתך שהוא יש לו כל טוב ואוכל שותה ומלובש היטב והשיב הנער יהי לו אשר לו ואני בעזרת השם יהודי ומאמין בה׳ והלך תיכף לבית המדרש ובאלו הדברים הלך ללמוד זכות על בני ישראל קודם התקיעות וצעק ואמר רבונו של עולם מי כעמך ישראל הנה זה הנער עני ורעב וחוסר כך ואעפ״כ מקבל עליו הכל ואינו רוצה להחליף אמונתו וע״י לימוד זכות זה נפתחו שערי רחמים על כל ישראל זי״ע.

ר׳ זושא מאניפאלע, ס׳ בוצינא קדישא, דף ל״ה.

[109] אל״ב שמע והקשב עניניו של ר״ה ואחר תדבר דע שהקב״ה מנהיג את בריותיו ע״י מדותיו הן לדין הן לרחמים הוא שנאמר הרועה בשושנים והשושנים הם ו׳ עליון הרומזים בו׳ קצוות וכשהוא מרחם על הבריות מרחם בדרך אחד מדרכי הרחמים והוא החסד, ובשעה הכעס אחד מדרכי הדין הוא הפחד. וזהו תקיעת שופר אשר ממנו יוצא הדין והרחמים, תרועה ושברים דין, תקיעה רחמים, ואנו מעוררין מדותיו של הקב״ה להליץ בעדנו טובה...

ספר הקנה, דף קנ״ט.

[110] תקיעה שברים תרועה תקיעה. תקיעה היא לשון אהבה מלשון נתקע ביבמתו כי בתחלה באה האהבה מהקב״ה על ידי ישראל שישראל עובדים אותו באמת ובאהבה ובזה שישראל עובדים ה׳ באהבה משברים היצה״ר שרוצה

230

להרע לישראל וישראל משברים אותו וזהו שברים תרועה לשבר היצה"ר שרוצה
להרע אחר כך נוסיף האהבה מהקדוש ב"ה על ישראל וזהו תקיעה בסוף.

ר' לוי יצחק מברדיטשוב, ס' קדושת לוי, דף צ"ד עמוד ב'.

[111] משל לפני התקיעות מלך גדול מלך מפואר ששלח את בניו לצוד ציד ותעו
הבנים מהדרך, והיו צועקים אולי ישמע האב ולא נענו. ואמרו בלבם אולי שכחנו
את הלשון של אבינו, לפיכך אינו שומע צעקתנו, בכן נצעק בקול בלא דיבור,
ויעצו א"ם לשלוח את אחד לצעוק והזהירו אותו ראה והבן כי כולנו תלויים בך.
כך הנמשל: הקב"ה שלח אותנו להעלות ניצוצות הקדושה ותעינו מאבינו, ואולי
מפני ששכחנו הדיבור של אבינו אין אנו יכולים להתפלל בדיבור, נשלח אותך
בעל תוקע שתעורר רחמים עלינו בקול בלא דיבור, וראה והזהר כי כולנו תלויים
בך, ואעפ"כ יחזיק עצמו לאין, כי הוא רק כמגריפה שהיא עור ויש בה נקבים,
ודרך הנקבים מוציא הכלי זמר, וכי יתגאה העור במה שיוצא קול זמר ממנו. כך
האדם, המחשבה והדיבור וכל המדות שורים בו כבתוך כלי, ומה יתגאה, הלא
הוא בעצמו אינו כלום, ואין בו רק מדות רעות, והוא מחוייב להעלות אותם אל
הקב"ה והוא מביא ד' ח"ו בהם, ומלביש אותו בקליפה כביכול ח"ו, ר"ל. ואם בא
במחשבתו שהוא עובד ה', אזי הוא בודאי גרוע מקודם.

ר' דוב בער, המגיד ממעזריטש, ס' תורת המגיד, כרך ב' דף ח'.


## יום כיפור

[112] (מהבעש"ט) זלה"ה, אם אדם רוצה לשבח ישבח את הקב"ה, ואם רוצה
לגנות יגנח את עצמו. (שהמשבח מודה באחדות ומכובד, משא"כ המבזה ומגנה
שנפרד מהאחדות.)

ר' ישראל בן אליעזר, הבעל שם טוב, כתר שם טוב, חלק א', דף ח'
עמוד א', סימן נ"ד.

[113] לענין התחזקות לבל יפול האדם בדעתו מחמת רבוי הפגמים והקלקולים
שקלקל על ידי מעשיו, ענה ואמר: אם אתה מאמין שיכולין לקלקל, תאמין
שיכולין לתקן.

ר' נחמן מברסלב, ס' ליקוטי מוהר"ן, חלק ב' סימן קי"ב דף מ"ב עמ'
ד'.

[114] גלמי ראו עיניך וכו' ימים יצרו (תהלים קל"ט). כל יום הוא יצירה בפני
עצמו, ולו אחד בהם - זה יום הכפורים, כמו שפרש רש"י שם, שהוא תענית
שמחיה כל הימים, כי יום הכפורים הוא כללות כל הימים, ועליו נאמר: בעצם
היום הזה תענו את נפשתיכם; הינו הרצונות, כמו שכתוב בזהר הנ"ל: לאכללא
כלא גופא ונפשא ולאתכנעא בהאי יומא ויהא רעותא דילהון בקדשא בריך הוא

וכו'. כי נפש הוא בחינת רצון, והעקר - להכניע הרצון. וזה: בעצם היום הזה - על
ידי פנימיות העצמיות של היום, שהוא כלול מכל הימים, תענו וכו' ...

ר' נחמן מברסלב, ס' ליקוטי מוהר"ן, חלק א' סימן קע"ט דף ק"ט עמ'
א'.

[115] וסוד עיקר התעניות על כל זה הוא מזבח מוכן לכפר על חטאיו, כי
במיעוט אכילה ושתיה מתמעט מחלבו ומקריב אותו המיעוט בתפלתו לפני
אלהיו, והיה לפנות ערב בגבור עליו חולשת האברים אש שלהבת יסודתו תוקד
בו לא תכבה לאכול ולהמעיט חלבו ודמו.

ר' מאיר ן' גבאי, ס' תולעת יעקב, דף קכ"ד.

[116] ב' הרב פ"א בעי"כ היו העולם צועקים ורועשים מאד בתהלים קודם כל
נדרי, והפך הרב פניו כלפי העם ואמר מה יהיה שאתם צועקים והדיבורים אינם
עולים למעלה, כי אתם כל השנה מדברים שקר ואיך יכול [לעלות] דיבורים מפה
כזה וכו', ולמה אני אומר לכם דבר זה דוקא, כי אני עסקתי בדבר זה הרבה.
וביאר הוא נ"י כי דבר אחר אינו קשה לצאת ממנו כ"כ ואפשר יצאתם, ע"כ
קבלו על עצמכם שלא לדבר שקר ויהיה עליה לשכינה ויעלו התפלות שלכם.

ר' פנחס מקאריץ, ס' אמרי פנחס, סימן תרט"ז, דף קכ"ב.

[117] כי הנה כחומר ביד היוצר וכו', כן אנחנו בידך חסד נוצר (פיוט לליל יו"כ).
כי יש ביד ישראל לשנות הטבע בכח כמו שרוצים, אם עושים רצונו של מקום.
כי כן היה כוונת הבריאה, בשביל ישראל (ב"ר פג, ה), ובשביל אברהם אבינו
עליו השלום על דרך "בהבראם" (ב"ר יב, ט). וזהו 'כי הנה כחומר ביד היוצר כן
אנחנו' - בידינו לשנות הטבע, כי כן הוא 'חסד נוצר' מתחילת הבריאה. וזה אמר
ירמיה: "כחומר ביד היוצר כן אתם בידי בית ישראל" (ירמיה יח, א), שיש
לכם כח לשנות הטבע, רק אם יהיו עושים רצונו.

ר' חיים מקאסוב, ס' תורת חיים, דף ר"י.

[118] כי ביום הזה יכפר עליכם לטהר אתכם מכל חטאתיכם לפני ה' תטהרו.
קשה דהול"ל לכפר לכם וי"ל, דידוע שאם האדם חוטא ח"ו אינו פוגם רק בנפשו
אלא בכל העולמות העליונים. וזהו הפי' יכפר עליכם, דכיון שפתח בתשובה
בחודה של מחט מתקן כל מה שפגם אפילו בעולמות שמעליכם, והעולמות
העליונים יסייעו אותו לטהר אתכם מכל חטאתיכם, ואז לפני ה' תטהרו, כלומר
תחילה עליכם לשוב בתשובה שלימה על כל מה שפגמתם, ואח"כ יעזרו אתכם
מלמעלה להטהר לפני ה'.

ר' שלום רוקח מבעלזא - שר שלום, ס' מהר"ש בעלזא, [חלק ב'] דף
ע"ד.

[119] ...אומר אני, כי ביום הזה יכפר עליכם לטהר אתכם מכל חטאתיכם לפני
ה' תטהרו. ע"ד שאמר הרה"צ מבארדיטשוב זצ"ל על מה שאמרו ראשון לחשבון

232

עוונות (תנחומא אמור כב), כי כשישראל עושין תשובה מאהבה, והזדונות
נעשות להם כזכיות (יומא פו:), אז מחפשין את העוונות לעשות מהם זכיות.
וזהו כי ביום הזה יכפר עליכם לטהר אתכם, וכתיב באתנחתא, מכל
חטאתיכם לפני ה' תטהרו. היינו כי כשעושין תשובה מאהבה ומעוררין מדת
הרחמים, אזי, מכל חטאתיכם תטהרו, שהזדונות נעשים זכיות...

ר' ישראל מסאדיגורא, ס' אור ישראל, דף רמ"ו. (ליל יו"כ, תרס"ג)

[120] למה אנחנו אומרים ביום הכפורים כמה וכמה וידויים ועל חטא ואין אנו
נענים ולא מתבשרים שה' העביר חטאותינו, ודוד המלך ע"ה כיון שאמר אמנם
חטאתי, מיד נתבשר על ידי נתן הנביא ואמר לו (שמואל ב', יב) גם ה' העביר
חטאתך, מפני שדוד המלך ע"ה אמר חטאתי, היינו חטאתי ועשה עמי כרצונך
ומקבל את הדין על עצמו באהבה כי צדיק אתה ה', וזה הוא בחי' תשובה
אמיתית, ולכן נמחל מיד. מה שאין כן אנו, מיד כשאומרים אשמנו, מדמים
בבפשנו כי בזה ודאי הוא מוחל לנו, וכשאנו אומרים בגדנו, סוברים אנחנו כי על
ידי זה מוכרח להיות לנו כל טוב, ולכן אין זה התשובה בשלמות.

ר' שמחה בונם מפשיסחא, ס' מדרש שמחה, דף רל"ג.

[121] בענין על חטא ביאר הוא נ"י שיש הרבה שהם רק תנועה קלה .
באומץ הלב לפי פשוטו שייך רק לצדקה, אבל הוא בכל הדברים.....
בוידוי פה, פי' מה שאמרנו הודוי רק בפה ולבו בל עמו.
בנטית גרון, בסיקור עין, הוא רק תנועה נטיה או ראיה אחת, ואמר על
דעתו טוב לאדם שיבחר לו אחד מעל חטא עכ"פ ויחזק בו מאד, כי בכולם קשה
להזהר כראוי וכו'.

ר' פנחס מקאריץ, ס' אמרי פנחס, סימן תרכ"ב, דף קכ"ג.

[122] אשמנו בגדנו גזלנו וכו', מדוע חברו את תפלת הוידוי וגם תפלת על חטא
על סדר א"ב, בכדי שידעו מתי להפסיק, שאלמלא היה מסודר על סדר זה, לא
היו יודעים אימתי להפסיק להכות על הלב, כי החטא אין לו סוף, והתשובה גם
לה אין סוף, אבל לאל"ף בי"ת יש תחילה וסוף.

ר' יצחק מווארקא, ס' בית יצחק, דף קמ"ו.

[123] ובודאי מי שמתודה וחוזר לסורו, אז בשעה שהתודה לא נשבר לבו בקרבו
וענושו בכפל כפלים, כי אז הוא כאלו מתפאר ח"ו במה שעשה וכאלו אומר מי
אדון לי. וזהו פי' מ"ש בנוסח על חטא, על חטא ש"ל בוידוי פה, ר"ל שהוידוי לא
היה אלא בפה ולא בלב ...

ר' ישעיה הורוויץ, ס' שני לוחות הברית, מסכת יומא, הלכות תשובה,
כרך א', דף ס"ה, עמוד ב'.

[124] הרי אני ככלי מלא בושה וכלימה. יתכן לפרש לטיבותא, דכל העבירות
שעשינו אינן בגלל שכוח הרע מוטבע בעצמותנו ח"ו, אלא הוא רק כמו

233

שממלאים כלי ואפשר לרוקנו וישאר הכלי כבתחילה, כן אנחנו בידך להוציא
הדברים המאוסים מתוכנו ולנקותנו ולטהרנו ונעבדך בלב שלם כבשנים
קדמוניות.

ר' שלום רוקח מבעלזא - שר שלום, ס' מהר"ש בעלזא, [חלק ב'] דף
ע"ה.

[125] כתיב (דניאל ט' ט"ו) חטאנו רשענו כלל עצמו בכלל לפי שכל ישראל
ערבים זה בזה שנאמר בעכן (יהושע כ"ב ב') והוא איש אחד לא גוע בעונו לכך
צריך בלשון רבים לבקש סלח לנו אבינו כי חטאנו וכשאנו מתודים אנו אומרים
על חטאים שאנו חייבים עליהם סקילה שריפה הרג וחנק ואע"פ שידע אדם שלא
חטא בכך שיהא חיים אעפ"כ צריך שיתוודה כך לפי שכל ישראל ערבים זה בזה
ועוד כדי שיודה החייב יתבייש להודות.

ר' יהודה בן שמואל החסיד מרגנסבורג, ספר חסידים, סימן תר"א, דף
שצ"א.

[126] פקודא (מ"ד) דא למפלח כהנא רבא פולחנא דההוא יומא כמה דאצטריך
ולמשלח שעיר לעזאזל. רזא דא כמה דאת אמר בגין לאתתפרשא מעמא קדישא
ולא יתבע חוביהון קמי מלכא ולא יקטרג עלייהו דהא לית ליה תקיפו ושלטנו
(בה) בר כד אתקף רוגזא מלעילא. ובההוא דורונא אתהפך לבתר אפוטרופסא
עלייהו ועל דא אתדחייא מקמי מלכא...

ספר הזהר, רעיא מהימנא, כרך ג', דף ס"ג עמוד א'.

[127] והכהנים והעם העומדים בעזרה כשהיו שומעים את השם הנכבד והנורא
מפורש יוצא מפי כהן גדול בקדושה ובטהרה היו כורעים ומשתחוים ונופלים על
פניהם וכו'. ואף הוא היה מתכוין כנגד המברכים לגמור את השם וכו' ואומר
להם תטהרו. צריך לשים לב מפני מה דוקא ביום הכיפורים היו כורעים כשהיו
שומעים את השם מפי כה"ג הלא בבית המקדש היו שומעים בכל יום השם
הוי"ה ככתיבתו ומפני מה לא היה כריעה גם צריך לדעת שמלת מפורש לכאורה
הוא כמיותר שזאת ידוע שבבית המקדש לא היו מזכירין רק השם המפורש והיה
די באמרו השם הנכבד והנורא יוצא מפי כה"ג כו' . אך העניין הוא שבכל ימות
השנה הגם שהצדיקים עושין יחודים והעולמות מתעלין מ"מ אור הכתר אינו
מתגלה חוץ מיום הכיפורים שאז מתגלה אור הכתר עליון על ישראל ומופיע
עליהם כל היום הקדוש והוא המטהר את ישראל ביום זה כנאמר כי ביום הזה
יכפר עליכם לטהר אתכם וגו' לפני ה' תטהרו. ומלת תטהרו רומז על הכתר
שתיבת תטהרו עולה גימטריא תר"ך כמנין כתר וע"כ יש דעות בין המקובלים
לומר קדושת כתר גם בשחרית יו"כ כל ימות השנה לא היה כריעה בשעה
שהזכיר את השם המפורש מפני שלא היה היחוד גדול כ"כ אבל ביוה"כ שכה"ג
היה מכוין כשהזכיר את השם הנכבד והנורא להמשיך אור הכתר ע"כ היה צריך
כריעה מפני גודל קדושתו ועוצם בהירתו שאין בו השגה וזהו פי' כשהיו שומעים
את השם הנכבד והנורא מפורש יוצא מפי כהן גדול ור"ל שהיו שומעים את השם

מפי כה"ג בכוונה זו להמשיך הכתר עליון. ובמלת מפורש מרומז הכתר שכן
מפר"ש בגימטריא כתר ע"כ היו כורעם כי אז לא היה באפשרי בלא כריעה
שנפלו על פניהם מרוב קדושתו ועוצם בהירתו של כתר עליון שאין בו
השגה ואמר אח"כ ואף הוא היה מתכוין כנגד המברכים לגמור את השם ר"ל
לייחד את השם בכוונה זו להמשיך קדושת כתר וזהו ואומר תטהרו ר"ל באומרו
להם תטהרו היה מכוין להמשיך שיופיע עליהם אור קדושת כתר שמרומז בתיבת
תטהרו כנ"ל.

ר' קלונימוס קלמן הלוי אפשטיין, ס' מאור ושמש, רמזי יום הכיפורים
חלק ה', דף ל"ח עמוד ג',

## סוכות

[128] החג הזה נקרא בתורה (ויקרא כ"ג ל"ד) חג הסוכות, על שם המצוה
הנעשית בחג הזה, ומיהו יש להבין למה נקרא בלשון רבים סוכות ולא בלשון
יחיד חג הסוכה... ואמרו רז"ל (במדב"ר כ"א ס"ב) אפילו הצדיקים לא יהיו כל
אנפין שוין... על כן נקרא החג בלשון רבים חג הסוכות שאין סוכה אחת דומה
לחברתה...

ר' צבי אלימלך מדינוב, ס' בני יששכר, חלק ב' דף ל"ט ד'-מ' עמ' א'.

[129] ליל התקדש חג, צדיקים ישמחו יעלצו לפני אלהים וישישו בשמחה אשר
הרגל הזה זמן שמחה לכל היא כמ"ש בנוסח התפלה זמן שמחתנו וכו'. וראוי
לכל איש להעביר מעליו כל מיני דאגה ויגון ולאזור עצמו בשמחה ובטוב לבב,
ועל ידי כך תתעורר מקום השמחה למעלה...

ס' חמדת ימים, חג הסוכות, פרק ד', דף 375.

[130] א"ל ולמה סוכות אחר יוה"כ א"ל הכיפורים כיפר עונותיהם של ישראל.
וסוכה מה מורה אבע"א חכמה עלאה אבע"א חכמה תתאה בית הוא והבית
עושה צל הוא שאמר סוכות אחר כפורים. ור"ל אחר שנתכפרו ראוין הם
להתלונן בצילו של קב"ה שנאמר בצל שדי יתלונן.

ס' הפליאה, דף ק"ז עמוד א'.

[131] אשריהם ואשרינו מה טוב חלקנו, שה' יתברך בחר בנו והפליא עצה לנו
בכל כל דבר ודבר בעתו, כי אחר עבור ימים האלו מתחיל חג הסוכות, וכמו
שאמרו רבותינו ז"ל (ראה זהר פינחס ריד, ב) 'שמאלו תחת לראשי' (שיר
השירים ב, ז) - מראש השנה עד יום הכפורים, ומיום הכפורים עד הסוכות הוא
'וימינו תחבקני' ...

ו(ה)עניו הדבר, כי אחר שנמתקו הדינים למעלה מנפשותינו, והדינים
נקראים שמאל, אחר כך מתגלה לנו שמחת ה' יתברך, ששרש השמחה הוא
מתחלת בטהרת הנפש לפני ה' יתברך בתשובה, אבת אז בעת התשובה הדבר

235

בהעלם מחמת שבירת הלב, אבל אחר כך מתגלה התענוג והשמחה, וזהו חג הסוכות זמן שמחתנו.

ר' משולם פייבוש הלוי העליר מזבארידזא, ס' יושר דברי אמת, דפ' קס"ח-קס"ט.

[132] ג' ימים אחר יוה"כ נשאר הארה מיום הכיפורים ולכך מחמת הארת יוה"כ מוחל הקב"ה ג'וכ עוונותיהם של ישראל ובערב יו"ט עוסקים בסוכה ובלולב ולכך יו"ט הראשון הוא ראשון לחשבון עונות ואמר שנאמין לו שג' ימים אחר יוה"כ לא שמע מה שהי' מדבר אליו וכאילו אמר דברו לעץ כך לא שמע.
ר' רפאל מבערשד, בס' מדרש פנחס, דף 48.

[133] אמרו הראשונים ארבע ימים שבין יום הכפורים לחג הסוכות נזכרים ונעשים כימים מקודשים, כי הם מקדשים שקדשום שמים בכמה קדושות, הן מצד שהם ימים שבין שתי קדושות קדושת יוה"כ וקדושת החג והם כחול המועד. והן שבהם עוסקים עם הקדש כל איש ישראל במצות סוכה ולולב וד' מינים, ומעשים האלו מביאים את האדם לזכור את ה' אלהיו, לאהבה אותו ולדבקה בו ולשמוח בשמחה רוחניית לעבוד את ה' בשמחה ובטוב לבב...
ס' חמדת ימים, כרך ג' עמוד 334.

[134] מצות לולב. ענין המצוה הזאת וכונתה ליחד ש"ש בכל לבבו ובכל נפשו וכן ענין לולב לו לב שיהי' לבו שלם עם אביו שבשמי' וכמו שהלולב מקשר כל העלין שבו ונעשה הכל אגודה א' וקשר א' בלי פירוד ביחוד גמור כך צריך האדם שיקשר כל דעותיו ומחשבותיו ויפנה הכל אל מקום א' ואל יפנה במחשבתו אנה ואנה ז"ש תמים תהי' עם ה' אלהיך כלו' תהי' כל מחשבותיך כולם פונות אל מקום א' וכזה תהי' תמים ושלם בענין עבודתו ויראתו כמו ...
ר' משה ן' מכיר, ס' סדר היום, דף 91.

[135] וע"י בחינת תשובה עילאה זו שמעומקא דליבא מתגלה בסוכות בחינת ימינו תחבקני שימין עליון הוא בחינת אהבה רבה שלמעלה מן הטעם ודעת המתגלה ומאיר למטה בגלוי הלב שלא יהיה בבחי' נפרד ח"ו ממנו ית' וזהו תחבקני כמשל המחבק את חבירו שלא ילך ממנו, דהיינו ע"י הסוכה בחינת צל שהוא בחינת ה' צלך וגו' ... וע"י נענועי הלולב כי ד' מינים שבלולב הם רומזים בשם הוי"ה ומנענעים ומביאים ללב שכל הבאה הוא ללב כדי להיות מאיר ומתגלה בלבו של אדם וזהו שמנענעין לשית סיטרין מעלה ומטה ולארבע רוחות כי הוא ית' אחד בשמים ובארץ וד' רוחות ולפי שהוא מקומו של עולם כמ"ש הנה מקום אתי ... וצריך להמשיך ולהכניס בחינת אחד בלב שיהיה ה' אחד שורה ומתגלה בו ולמהוי אחד באחד...
ר' שניאור זלמן מליאדי, ס' לקוטי תורה, דרושים לשמע"צ, דף פ"ז עמ' א'-ב'.

236

[136] וזהו סוד סוכ"ה ולול"ב, סוכ"ה הוא בחינת אור מקיף (פרי עץ חיים, שער
חג הסוכות פרק א', פרק ג'), ולול"ב הוא בחינת אור פנימי (פע"ח ש' הלולב
פ"ב-פ"ג). סוכ"ה בחינת אור מקיף, כמאמר (מעריב דליל שבת) 'ופרוס עלינו
סוכת שלומך' (עיין פע"ח ש' השבת פי"ב), ועלינו היא בחינת אור מקיף. ולול"ב
הוא בחינת אור פנימי, ל"ו ל"ב (זהר חלק א' רס"ז עמ' ב', תיקוני הזהר תקון כ"א
דף נ"ו עמ' ב'). ולכך נהגו לנענע הד' מינים בסוכה (עיין פע"ח ש' הלולב פ"ג, וע'
משנת חסידים ימי מצוה וסוכה ס"ה), כדי שיתייחד בחינת אור פנימי עם אור
מקיף. וכן כשמנענע אפילו בבית הרי חלל הנשאר בין הלולב להכותל הוא בחינת
אור מקיף (פע"ח ש' הלולב פ"ג), ואח"כ (ואחר כך) כשמדבק אל לבו, יכוין
להכניס הארה מבחינת אור מקיף לאור פנימי, שיולך מזה יחוד אור מקיף עם
אור פנימי...

ר' מרדכי מטשערנאביל, ס' ליקוטי תורה, דף קע"ט עמ' ב'.


[137] ועיקר מצות ד' מינים ונענועים באים בחג הקדוש הזה כי כולו מלא
חסדים לכבוש דינים הקשים שנתגברו מראש השנה עד יום הכפורים, שהם
בסוד "שמאלו תחת לראשי" (שיר השירים ב' ו'). ומעתה על ידי הלולב ונענועיו
הוא בסוד "וימיני תחבקני" להמשיך חסדי המקום, חסד ה' מלאה הארץ (תהלים
ל"ג ה'), ומתייחדים המדות העליונות ייחוד גמור...

ס' חמדת ימים, כרך ג' עמוד 354.

[138] ...צריך כל אדם שיכוין בזה כשיושב בסוכתו ולהודיע לבני ביתו שאנו
יוצאים מבתינו לסוכה, שלא כדרך העולם שדרכם להכנס כל אחד מסוכתו
לביתו מפני שהצינה גוברת בחצי תשרי, ואנו עושים בחפך לקיים מצות הבורא
יתברך ....

ס' חמדת ימים, חג הסוכות, פרק ד', דף 391.


[139] ענין סוכה הוא דהשי"ת תקיף אותנו מכל צד בכל מקום ואפילו בחו"ל
בקדושת בית המקדש מארבע רוחות ולמעלה ולמטה, הן דפנות הסוכה
וקרקעיתה והסכך, וכן אויר הסוכה הוא אוירא דא"י.

ר' שלום רוקח מבעלזא - שר שלום, ס' מהר"ש בעלזא, [חלק ב'] דף
ע"ז.


[140] סכות תשבו שבעת ימים וגו' פקודא (מה) דא לישב בסכה והא אוקימנא
בגין לאחזאה דישראל יתבי ברזא דמהימנותא בלא דחילו כלל דהא מקטרגא
אתפרש מנייהו וכל מאן דאיהו ברזא דמהימנותא יתיב בסכה כמה דאוקימנא
דכתיב כל האזרח בישראל ישבו בסכות. מאן דאיהו ברזא דמהימנותא ומזרעא
ושרשא דישראל ישבו בסכות. ורזא דא אתמר בכמה דוכתי:

ספר הזהר, רעיא מהימנא, כרך ג', דף ק"ג, עמוד ב'.


[141] פ"א בליל חג הסוכות כאשר הלך הרה"ק ר' אברהם האדמו"ר מטריסק
זי"ע אל הסוכה בדרכו על מפתן הסוכה נשאר על עמדו זמן רב ולא נכנס אל

הסוכה וכל האנשים שעמדו אצלו ראו כן תמהו. פתח הרה"ק פיו ואמר בבואי קרוב אל הסוכה עלה במחשבתי הן זה לא כביר אמרתי בתפלת ימים נוראים משול כחרס הנשבר היינו שהאדם נדמה לכלי חרס א"כ איפה איך הותר לי לכנוס הלא ע"פ דין אסור להכניס כלי חרס אל הסוכה תוך הסוכה אך הרי אחז"ל שכלי חרס אין להם תקנה אלא שבירה. לכן נשבר לבבנו לפני אל איום ונורא ולב נשבר ונדכה לא יבזה ואז נכנס אל הסוכה.

אברהם איטינגא, ס' אמרי צדיקים, דף 33.

[142] סוכ"ה נוטריקון סומך ועוזר כל הנופלים וכל שמשפיל עצמו ומראה כאילו נופל הקב"ה מעמידו ומחזיקו ביד ימינו וזה למי שבעיניו חשוב כאין כדאיתא בגמר', וסוכה לשון שררה מלשון נסיכה ולכך אנו יושבים בסוכה בצלא דמהימנותא שאנו יושבים כנסיכים עלמא דחרות כמאן דנצח קרבא וכלי מלחמתו בידו הלולב והאתרוג ואינו ירא משום דבר.

ר' פנחס מקאריץ, ס' אמרי שפר סימן י"ח, דף 5.

[143] רבינו הקדוש היה אומר: "אין לך חביבה ממצות סוכה, שאדם נכנס לסוכה בכל אבריו, עם מלבושיו ומנעליו לתוך המצוה, מה שלא נמצא כן בשאר המצוות."

ר' שמחה בונם מפשיסחא, ס' מדרש שמחה, כרך ב', דף רל"ג.

[144] וקבלתי רמז בתיבת סכה, ובזה הרמז יתבארו דיני דפנות של סכה. מצוה מן המובחר ארבע דפנות, ויוצא לכתחילה אפילו בשלשה, והלכתא אפילו בשנים ושלישית משהו. בחינת ארבע דפנות רומזות לארבע חומות שזכרתי תשובה תפלה צדקה תורה, ונגד זה 'ס' ד ס כה הסובבת ומקפת כל צד. אמנם יש בישראל שאינם בני תורה ולא יש לב להבין, נמצא הם מחזיקים בשלוש דפנות, שהם שלוש חומות תשובה תפלה צדקה, נגד זה 'כ' דתיבת ס כ ה הסובבת שלוש רוחות. אמנם לפעמים יש שלא יוכלו להחזיק אף בשלוש, כי אינם בעלי תורה, וגם הם עניים שלא יוכלו ליתן צדקה, אזי יחזיקו בשני דפנות שהם שני חומות תשובה ותפלה, שזה יוכל לקיים כל איש ישראל, ועוד שלישית משהו דהיינו ליתן דבר מועט, וכמ"ש רז"ל (גיטין ז, ב) : אפילו העני הנוטל צדקה צריך ליתן מעט צדקה, נגד זה אות 'ה' מן סכ ה שהיא שתי דפנות שלימות ושלישית משהו, ולזה ההלכה שנים כהלכתן והשלישית והשלישית משהו.

ר' ישעיה הלוי הורוויץ, ס' שני לוחות הברית, בית הגדול, כרך א' דף כ"ז עמוד ג'.

[145] סוכות הוא מלשון סכך שמסכך על דבר ומסתירו כי הקב"ה ברא העולם בחסדו כדי לגלות אלהותו לנבראים והוא א"צ לשום דבר רק לגלות חסדו לנבראים וזהו אמרתי עולם מה שאמרתי שיהיה העולם כדי שיהיה בנין בני לחסד שיתגלה בעולם כי טרם בריאות העולם לא היה בנין לחסד כי היה למעלה מהבנין בלתי אפשר להשיג ואף שטבע הטוב להיטיב לא מפני זה

נאמר שהוכרח לברא העולמות כדי להיטיב אלא שברא בחסדו של אמת חסד
שעושין עם המתים היינו מדריגות הדלים דלית להו מגרמייהו כלום ...
ר׳ מנחם מענדל מטשארנאביל, ס׳ מאור עינים, דף 142.

[146] מצוה לשבות ביום הראשון של חג הסוכות, וביום השמיני בו, ולעשות
סוכה כדי לעשות רמז לחכמ׳ העליונ׳ שהיא כמין סוכה להקב״ה ית׳ שהיא בית
נתיבו׳ לכל הספירו׳ כי היא מקפת את הכל ...
ר׳ מנחם ריקאנאטי, ס׳ טעמי המצות, דף ע״ו, עמ׳ א׳-ב׳.

[147] סוכה נקראת דירת ארעי (סוכה ב.). אומר אני, דירת ארעי, כשהאדם
מהרהר ועוסק בתשובה הוא כבר בעל תשובה. (אז א מענטש טיהט און טראקט
אין תשובה איז ער שוין איין בעל תשובה).
השי״ת יעזור שיהיה דירת קבע, היינו שיהיה התשובה בקביעות על כל
השנה, השי״ת יעזור לכל אחד מישראל שיהיה להם אמונה ויעשו תשובה
בקביעות וישפע ישועות על כלל ישראל.
ר׳ ישראל מסאדיגורא, ס׳ אור ישראל, דף ר״נ.

[148] שלמה המלך ע״ה עשה בזקנותו ספר קהלת. ושמעתי דלכן קורין אותו
בסוכות, לא מפני שמבהיל שמחת עולם זה, רק שממנו נקח תוקף ועיקר
השמחה האמיתית ע״י ההבלת כל עניני עולם הזה, רק זה חלקי וכו׳:
ר׳ מרדכי יוסף ליינר מאיזביצא, ס׳ מי השלוח, חלק ב׳ דף רמ״ח:

[149] דברי קהלת בן דוד מלך ישראל ופירש״י שכל דבריו הי׳ בהקהל שכל
דיבור של דברי קדושה ותפלה כולל כל העולמות ומלאכים ונשמות וכו״כ [וכו׳]
וכך יראה כל אדם שבכל דיבור יכלול כנ״ל ושלמה המלך ע״ה היה כל דבריו כך,
שהיה כלול בו כל נשמות ישראל ומלאכים וכו״כ [וכו׳] כי שלמה אותיות למשה
כידוע והיה כל דבריו בהקהל ואם יתנהג אדם כך שבכל דיבור כנ״ל יתנשא על
כל הברואים וזה פירושו דברי קהלת וכו׳.
ר׳ פנחס מקאריץ, ס׳ מדרש פנחס, דף 48.

[150] ...יש תועלת ויתרון לאור מן החשך (קהלת ב׳) דהיינו מעלת יתרון האור
ניכר מצד החשך, וכן החכם מצד הטיפש, וניכר מעלת הצדיק מצד הרשע,
והתענוג מכח הנגע והיסורין, ומעלת הדעת נודע מכח השכחה, אם כן נעשה זה
כסא לזה ... אמנם לפי זה יש מקום לטעות לעבוד עבודה זרה מאחר שהכל
נעשה כסא לזה לזה, אם כן באמת הכל נכנס באחדות אחד וכו׳, אפס שזה אינו
כי יש הבדל וכו׳...
ר׳ יעקב יוסף מפולנאי, ס׳ צפנת פענח, דפ׳ שס״ו עמוד ב׳-שס״ז עמוד
א׳.

239

[151] כל מה שתמצא ידך לעשות בכחך עשה פי׳ להעלות אנשי עשי׳ אל המחשבה שנקרא יו״ד יד״ו.

ר׳ ישראל בן אליעזר, הבעל שם טוב, ס׳ כתר שם טוב, חלק א׳, דף 14, סימן מ״ט.

[152] (קהלת י,א)... זבובי מות יביא יביע שמן רוקח, הם המחשבות זרות ורעות המתרגשות לבא בעולם ...

ר׳ ישראל מקאזניץ, ס׳ עבודת ישראל, דף שנ״ג.

[153] ולזה סיים שלמה סוף קהלת סוף דבר הכל נשמע את האלהים ירא ואת מצותיו שמור כי זה כל האדם כי את כל מעשה האלהים יבא במשפט על כל נעלם אם טוב ואם רע ונתעוררו חז״ל כי זה כל האדם לא נברא אלא לצוות לזה וכבר בארתי הכוונה כל העולם מראש ועד סוף מפרטי הנבראים ודוממים וכל דבר הבא לכלל הוי״ה לא נבראו בעולם כי אם לצוות לזה משמעו לשון צווי שמצווים אותו בחי׳ עבודה כי בכל דבר בעולם יש התלבשות אלהות ...

ר׳ זאב וואלף מזיטומיר, ס׳ אור המאיר, חלק ה׳, דף מ״ג, עומד ד׳.

[154] נסוך המים בחג היה נעשה בעסק גדול (מסכת סוכה, פרק לולב וערבה). ולכאורה, מצוה גדולה זו למה לא נכתבה בתורה. אלא שרצה הקב״ה להשאיר מקום לישראל שיבינו זאת משכלם.

ר׳ מנחם מענדל מווארקה, ס׳ בית יצחק, דף קנ״ד.

## שמיני עצרת ושמחת תורה

[155] אמר על המנהג ישראל שבשמע״צ וש״ת מחברים יחדיו עם בנ״י עם לומדי תורה ופשוטי העם ושמחים יחד בשמחת התורה. דהנה איתא במדרש והובא גם ברש״י הקדושה משל למלך שעשה סעודה. וכו׳ ואמר קשה. עלי פרידתכם. עצרו עלי עוד יום אחד. ואמר דהפי׳ פרידתכם שיהי׳ ח״ו איזה פירוד ביניכם זאת קשה עלי. ע״כ ביום זה מתחברים יחדיו ושותים ואוכלים יחד באהב׳ וחיבה ובזה ניחא מה דאיתא בגמ׳ (שבת ל״א) בעכ״ם שבא לפני שמאי והלל. ואמר גיירני ע״מ שתלמדני כה״ת כולה על רגל אחד. הכוונה בזה דהנה כל החגים ומועדים שישראל עושים. יש טעם בתורה ע״ז. פסח זכר ליציאת מצרים. סוכות כי בסוכות הושבתי את בנ״י וכן כל המועדים טובים אבל על שמע״צ אין שום טעם בתורה. והנה אה״ע אין להם טעם על חגאיהם רק שעושין מה שישראל עושין - וזהו מה שאמר העכו״ם הנ״ל למדנו כל התורה כולה היינו שחפשתי בכה״ת ולא מצאתי טעם על הרגל האחת היינו חג שמע״צ שנקרא רגל כפ״ע ואני מתמה על הרגל הזאת. והשיב לו הלל מה דעלך סני לחברך לא תעביד שהרגל הנ״ל היא מחמת שקשה עלי פרירתכם כנ״ל שישראל יתחברו יחדיו ויקיימו ואהבת לרעך כמוך.

ר' ישראל מסדגורא, ס' בית ישראל, דפ' 28-29.

[156] שמחת תורה משום מה? מכיון שימי סוכות הם ימי שמחה, הרי בני ישראל משקיעים את שמחתם בתורה.
ר' מנחם מענדל מקאצק, ס' אמת מקאצק תצמח, סימן תצג, דף קנ"ז.

[157] אחר תפלת העמידה דערבית זו המנהג בכל תפוצות ישראל עם קדוש לעטר הס"ת בכתרים ולהקיף עמהם ז' הקפות והוא מנהג ותיקין ... וכבר הובא בספרים גודל מעלת האדם המרבה בכל מיני שמחות לפני הס"ת שבזה מעורר ג"כ למעלה בעולמות העליונים שמחה וחדוה עצומה וכל הזהיר בשמחה של תורה ביום הזה בטוח שלא יפסיק תורה מזרעו.
אלכסנדר זיסקינד, ס' יסוד ושורש העבודה, דף רנ"ח.

[158] ומהרח"ו זלה"ה קא מסהיד עליה דמר ניהו האר"י זלה"ה וז"ל ואני ראיתי למורי ז"ל שהיה הולך לפני הספרים והיה מרקד ומשורר שירים ותושבחות ומסבב עמהם הז' הקפות בשמחה גדולה בכל יכולתו. ואח"כ כשהיו הולכים לבית הכנסת אחר שהיו מתאחרים והיו עושים ז' הקפות עם הספרים ג"כ מורי זלה"ה היה סובב עמהם ומרקד ומרנן בשמחה גדולה. וכן אם מתאחרים בב"הכ אחר, היה עושה כן ומסיים שם. וכל זה הלילה, וביום לא ראיתיהו ע"כ .
ס' חמדת ימים, חג הסוכות, פרק ח', דף 458.

[159] ...ביום זה אין חשבון ומספר אל העולים לקריאת התורה (שו"ע או"ח סימן תרס"ט בהג"ה), כיון שהשארת היום מבחינת אור המקיף הכללי אל התורה, ממילא אין גבול וחשבון, וכן תבין מה שנוהגין תיכף אחר סיום התורה ביום זה מתחילין תיכף בבראשית לנעוץ סופה בתחלתה, כי אין סיום וגבול, הבן הדבר היטב.
בשמיני עצרת הוא יום שמחת תורה (זח"ג רנו:), הנה מסיימין התורה באות ל' ומתחילין באות ב', להיות יום ההוא יחודא שלים קוב"ה וכנסת ישראל...
ר' צבי אלימלך מדינאב, ס' בני יששכר, כרך ב' דף נ"ה עמ' ב'-ג'.

[160] ענין שמחת תורה הוא כי כלל ישראל שמחים בתורה, והתורה תשמח בזה שישראל קיימו את המצוות בראש השנה ויום הכיפורים וסוכות, וזהו עיקר השמחה.
וזאת הברכה אשר ברך משה את בני ישראל (דברים לב, א) - בראשית ברא אלקים את השמים ואת הארץ (בראשית א, א). זאת היא הברכה הגדולה, ועיקר הברכה, שידעו ויאמינו ישראל, כי בראשית ברא וגו', אשר בראשית הוא ראשית חכמה יראת ה' (תהלים קיא, י), ברא אלקים, שתדעו שיש אלקים בעולם, שהקב"ה ברא ומנהיג העולם וזהו העיקר .

241

וזאת הברכה - בראשית, כי זהו עיקר הברכה, שידע כל אחד ואחד כי עדיין לא עשה כלום בעבודתו ועדיין נמצא בתחילת עבודתו ובבראשית.

וזאת הברכה אשר ברך משה איש האלקים את בני ישראל. איתא (ילק"ש ברכה תתק"ן) שמשה רבנו ע"ה התחנן לפני הקב"ה יהי רצון שתשרה שכינה במעשה ידיהם. וזהו וזאת, רומז על השכינה (זוהר ח"ב רצ:), על דרך הכתוב (ויקרא טז, ג) בזאת יבא אהרן על הקודש. וזהו וזאת הברכה, היינו שברכם שתשרה שכינה על מעשה ידיהם, אשר ברך משה איש האלקים את בני ישראל, היינו שיהיה אלקים - על ישראל, היינו שתשרה השכינה עליכם כנ"ל. וזאת, וא"ו המוסיף, כי זהו עיקר הברכה.

ר' ישראל מסדיגורא, ס' אור ישראל, דפ' רס"ז-רס"ח.


[161] ...אמר רז"ל (תענית ד.) אמרה כנסת ישראל לפני הקב"ה (הושע ו ג) ויבא כגשם לנו, ואמר הקב"ה (שם יד ו) אהיה כטל לישראל, נראה לי החילוק בין גשם לטל, גשם אתערותא דלתתא (תענית כח:) אין לך כל טפה מלמעלה שאין טפיים עולים כנגדה מלמטה, לאפוקי טל הוא אתערותא דלעילא, על כן בחג הפסח שהאתערותא הוא שלא על ידי מעשינו רק בחפזון כידוע (פרע"ח שכ"א פ"א), אז מתפללין על הטל, מה שאין כן חג הסוכות התעוררות הוא על ידי מעשינו תשובה ומעשים טובים ומצות, מתפללין תפלת הגשם.

ר' צבי אלימלך מדינוב, ס' בני יששכר, כרך ב', דף נ"ה עמוד ב'.


## חנוכה

[162] עבד מלך המקבל חסדים פרטיים מהמלך יותר משאר עבדיו ודאי צריך לעבוד יותר מהשאר ולהוסיף מידי העבודה ובמה יתרצה עבד לאדוניו להראות שהכיר בחסדיו אם לא בהראותו עבודתו עבודה שלמה, וכשם שהמלך הוסיף בחסדיו עליו בפרטות מיתר עבדיו כן הוא מחוייב להראות עבודה פרטית למלך יותר מהשאר ...

ובפרט בימי חנוכה, דמעיקרא הצרה באה על ביטול עבודה, ראוי לנו להוסיף בעבודה ...

ר' חיים יוסף דוד אזולאי, ס' חדרי בטן, דפ' פ' עמוד א', פ"א עמוד א'.


[163] צדיקים הקדמונים אמרו כי בחנוכה יכול כל אדם לפעול בתפילתו מאת הבורא ברוך הוא להמשיך עליו שנה טובה, יותר מאשר בכל הימים הטובים.

אומר אני, כי בכל הימים טובים האתערותא היא מתתא לעילא, ובחנוכה היא מעילא לתתא. והוא משל למלך, שבשעה שיושב בבית מלכותו, הרי כשבא לפניו אדם עם איזה בקשה, המלך מתנהג עמו על פי הדין והמשפט ומדקדק עמו היטב אם הוא ראוי למלאות לו בקשתו, אבל כשהמלך בדרך, אז כאשר יבוא לפניו איזה בקשה לא ידקדק המלך על כשרון פעולת המבקש, ואע"פ שאינו ראוי, ימלא לו בקשתו מצד המצוה ורמחנות.


242

והנה חנוכה הוא נר מצוה (משלי ו, כג), שבת ויום טוב הוא תורה אור. חנוכה הוא נר מצוה, דהיינו שבחנוכה יוכל כל אדם להושע מאת הבורא ב"ה מצד המצוה והרחמנות אף על פי שאינו ראוי, אבל יום טוב ושבת שנקרא תורה אור, לכן מתנהג אז הבורא ב"ה עם האדם על פי התורה והמשפט ...

ר' ישראל מסאדיגורא, ס' אור ישראל, דף מ'.

[164] הנה חנוכה שבו היה חנוכת בית המקדש, והוא רומז לחנוך העולם. כי העולם נברא בשביל התורה וקיום המצות, והיונים רצו לבטל תורה ומצות מישראל. וכשהגברו החשמונאים אז נתגברו התורה והמצות, ממילא נתחנך העולם. וכמו שהעולם נברא בכ"ה לחודש, כי העולם נברא כ"ה לאלול, ומה שאמרו העולם נברא בתשרי זהו בריית האדם, אבל התחלת הבריאה בכ"ה לחודש, כן חנוכה כ"ה לחודש. וכמו שראשית הבריאה יהי אור, כן מצות חנוכה בנרות. וכמו שאור הראשון נגנז ואין משתמשין בו, כן הנרות הללו אסור להשתמש בהן:

ר' ישעיה הורוויץ, ס' שני לוחות הברית, תורה שבכתב, חלק ב', דף כ"ט, עמ' א-ב:

[165] בגמרא שבת (דף כ"א סוף ע"ב) תנו רבנן: בכ"ה בכסליו יומי דחנוכ' תמניא אינון וכו' נעשה בו נס והדליקו ממנו ח' ימים לשנה אחרת קבעום ועשאום ימים טובים בהלל והודאה, עכלה"ג, וקשה מה זה הנס הגדול בחנוכה הלא בכ"י אנו אומרים על נסיך שבכל יום עמנו ועל נפלאותיך וכו', ועוד למה לא קבעו על הנס שכבשו שלשים ואחד מלכים ... וגם על הנס של סנחרב ונראה ליישב דבאמת עיקר כונת היונים אז לא הי' על איבוד הגופות רק להשכיכם תורתיך ולהעבירם חוקי רצוניך וכדאי' בדחז"ל (ירושלמי חגיגה פרק ב', וב"ר פרשת ב', ותנחומא תזריע סי' יא) שהיו אומרים להם כתבו על קרן השור שאין לכם חלק באלהי ישראל והי' לישראל השפלה גדולה מזה שהיו סוברים שאין הקב"ה חפץ ח"ו במעשיהם, ונעשה להם נס שהקב"ה המציא להם פך שמן טהור שלא נגעו בו כדי שיהיו יכולים לקיים מצות הדלקת נרות אשר באמת עפ"י דין היו פטורים ממצוה זו דאונס רחמנא פטרי' שהראה להם השי"ת בזה שאף באמת פטורים ואינם בכלל מבטלי מצות עשה מ"מ מצד חפצו ית' במעשיהם עושה להם נסים שיוכלו לקיים מצותיו ית' אף שפטורים יען כי למעשה ידיהם יכסוף, ומשנתברר להם ע"ז שהקב"ה חפץ במעשיהם ודאי אין לשער גדול השמחה שנקבע בלבם אז מזה כי באמת כשהאדם מבין שהקב"ה רוצה במעשיו יכסוף לעשות רצונו ית' בשלימות יותר, והבן, וזה י"ל טעם על קריאת ימים האלה חנוכה שהוא כמו שמחנכין הקטן אעפ"י שאינו בר חיוב עדיין רק כדי שאחר שיתחייב ידע איך לעשות, כן ממש בנס זה חינכם השי"ת במצוה זו בעת שהיו פטורים ולא הי' היו בני חיובא כנ"ל כדי שמזה ידעו בכל מצוה שתגיע לידם בחיוב איך הקב"ה חפץ במעשיהם, ולכן כ' והדליקו נרות משום כי עיקר שמחתם הי' בהם שהמציא להם השי"ת המצוה כנ"ל, ונל"פ מ"ש הלשון קבעו'ם עפ"י מאה"כ (תהלים קיא פסוק ד) זכר עשה נפלאותיו וגר', שהקב"ה עשה זכר

שכשיביאו זמן הרגלים שיתעורר הכח שהי׳ מתחילה, וזהו קבעום, שקבעו בלב
זכר הנס לעולם.

ר׳ מנחם מענדל מקאצק, ס׳ אהל תורה מהרבי מקאצק, דף 18.

[166] נכו״ן לב״ו בטו״ח בד׳ ׳׳ וגו׳ ס״ת מנכון עד סמוך וסמוך בכלל, המה
אותיות ״חנוכה״ וב׳ תיבות היינו אות נ׳ מנ״כון ואות ס׳ מס״מוך הוא ״נס״ היינו
שנס מחנוכה הוא בא מזה שהי׳ בטוחים בד׳ והי׳ זוכין לראות בצריו.

ר׳ שמחה בונם מפשיסחא בס׳ שיח שרפי קודש, חלק ג׳, דף 52.

[167] וכמעט נר ישראל טרם יכבה, העיר ה׳ רוח כהני ה׳ משרתיו עושי רצונו,
להורותו נתן בלבם, ואמר חזקו ידים רפות, נקום נקמת ה׳, אחר תאסף (במדבר
ל״א ב׳). וחיזק ואימץ ידי חשמונאי ובניו להיות אמיץ לבו בגבורים הוא ובניו
אתו, ויעבירו קול במחנה לאמר מי לה׳ אלי, ויאסוף אליו כל זקני יהודה כל איש
חיל רב פעלים אשר נגע ב׳ בלבו לנקום נקמת ה׳, קנאת ה׳ צבאות תעשה זאת.
וילחמו בו ויגרשוהו, וילכו ויכו אותו ואת עמו עד בלתי השאיר לו שריד. ובשובם
נתנו שבח והודאה לאל, וחזקו את בדק הבית. והיה אור ישראל לאש והארץ
האירה מכבודו כימי עולם. ודבר זה היא לבדה תספיק לעשות זכרון לבני ישראל
לנס ההוא, ולקבוע ח׳ ימי חנוכה בהלל ובהודאה. ולא כמו שעלה על רוח רבים
לאמר אשר עיקר קביעותן היתה מפני נס הפך, כי אין לקבוע ימים טובים בהלל
ובהודאה מפני נס הנעשה באי זה ענין הפך הטבע, אלא כשיהיה ענין הצלה
מאיזו הצלה...

ס׳ חמדת ימים, כרך ד׳, דף 278.

[168] איתא במנהגים שיש להדליק בשבת קודש ל״ו נרות כנגד ל״ו שעות
ששימש אור הראשון דהיינו שאדם הראשון נברא בע״ש נמצא י״ב שעות של
ע״ש וכ״ד של שבת ואח״כ נגנזו. אמר מורי שהוא האור של ל״ו מסכתות
שבש״ס והוא ל״ו נרות דחנוכה (ופעם א׳ אמר שהאור נגנז בל״ו מסכתות) וע״כ
נעשה נס בחנוכה כי אז נתגלה אור הגנוז (ופ״א שמעתי ממנו שבכל חנוכה
בשעת הדלקת נרות נתגלה אור הגנוז והוא אור של משיח) והדברים הנ״ל
שמעתי מפיו בליל שבת בק״ק אוסטרהא ואח״כ כשבא בשחרית לביהכ״נ מנה
את הנרות שדלקו בביהכ״נ ומצא בצומצם ל״ו נרות לא פחות ולא יותר והנאהו
מאוד (גם היה מנהג בחנוכה בשעת הדלקת הנרות שלא לסגור את החלונות
ברחוב משום לפרסומי ניסא) ובשאר הלילות הקפיד מאד לסגור החלונות
בתחילת הלילה...

ר׳ פנחס מקאריץ, ס׳ מדרש פנחס, דף ב׳ עמוד א׳.

[169] מה שנתקן להדליק נרות להזכיר נס המנורה ולא נתקן לעשות זכר אחר
להזכיר הנסים אחרים שנעשו אז כי כתיב נר מצוה ותורה אור, והנה חכמת
היוונים היה גדולה בימים ההם והם אמרו שהחכמה הוא עד שישיג השכל ומה
שלמעלה מן השכל אפס יחשב לכן אנחנו מאמינים בני מאמינים לכן חושבים כי

244

אור התורה למעלה מן השכל הוא והנה נר מצוה הוא מן המצוה מן התורה אם
כן התורה למעלה מן השכל כי המצוה יקבל השפעה מן התורה והנה המנורה
ירמז לאור התורה ואם זה בעצמו מצוה שנצטווה להדליק נרות המנורה מוכרח
שכש עוד למעלה אור שהמנורה מקבל השפעה ממנו ובזה נצחו את היוונים
שהרגו להם כי יש עוד אור למעלה לכן הותקן דוקא להזכיר נס זה כי בזה נצחו
את היוונים.

ר' אברהם בן זאב בארנשטיין מסאקטשוב, בס' שיח שרפי קודש, חלק
ג' דף 124.


[170] ותדע כי סוד אלו הנרות הם דברים נוראים ורומזים לדברים עליוני'
רוחניים קדושים וטהורי' וכשם שמאירים למטה כך מאירים למעלה ומתעוררי'
שפע ואורה בעול' העליון כדי שיושפעו בעול' השכל וכל נר ונר הוא מצוה בפני
עצמה ולכן תקנו בכל נר ונר ברכה בפני עצמה והנר שהוא הכלי יש לה ג' דברים
גשמיים וא' רוחני הכלים הפתילו' והשמן הם גשיי' והלהב הוא רוחני והם רמז
לאדם התחתון שיש בו ג' דברים כבד לב מוח גשמיים...

ס' גלי רזיא, דף כ"ג עמוד ב'.


[171] הכלל הוא בר"ה ויום הכפורים הקב"ה פוקד את ישראל לטובה רק
בחנוכ' ישראל רואין הטובה בשכל והוא במחשבה כי עיני עדה ראי' ז"ל
חכמי העדה ולכך בחנוכה הנירות כי הוא לשון ראי' ואח"כ פורים הוא הדיבור כי
קורין את המגילה ובפסח הוא במעש' שאוכל מצה ולכך חנוכה שהוא על הראי'
והוא בחודש כסליו הצירוף הוא וירא יושב הארץ הכנעני שמור' על הראי'.

ר' לוי יצחק מבדיטשוב, ס' קדושת הלוי, דף כ"ג עמוד א' .


[172] הדלקה עושה מצוה. אין המקום מכבד את האדם אלא האדם מכבד
מקומו כי באיזה מקום ומדריגה שאדם עומד אם אין מדליק את נפשו בנר מצוה
ותורה אור אינו כלום ואם מדליק את נפשו בנר מצוה ותורה אור ועושה תשובה
הקב"ה ממשיך עליו חיות ממקום גבוה שבגבוה למקום שפלות שעומד וע"י
התקשרות האורות הוא ממשיך שפע לעולם וזה לא המקום מכבד האדם אלא
האדם מכבד את מקומו וזהו הדלקת עושה מצוה ולא הנחה.

ר' אברהם יעקב מסאדיגורא, ס' בית ישראל, דף 65.


[173] ...שכל עניני חנוכה הם להזכיר על ענין המצות, אסור להשתמש לאורה
כי המצוה צריך [שיכוין] לשם שמים [ולא ע"מ לקבל פרס]:

ר' חיים יוסף דוד אזולאי, ס' חדרי בטן, דף צ"ב, עמ' א"ב:


[174] למה לא נזכר שם הוי"ה בתפילת "על הנסים" יש לפרש כמו שלא נזכר
שם משה בפרשת ואתה תצוה, כי אחר כל הניסים והנפלאות נעשה משה כל כך
מקורב להשי"ת עד שלא היה צריך לקרוא לו בשמו אלא בלשון אתה, כמו אב
לבנו שאינו קורא אותו בשמו, וכזה נראה לי שאחר כל הנסים והנפלאות שעשה

245

השי"ת לישראל בימי יוון, נעשו ישראל כל כך כמו בן לאביו, עד שלא היו
צריכים לכתוב שם הוי"ה ב"על הנסים" של בימי מתתיהו, רק בלשון "ואתה",
ואתה ברחמיך הרבים עמדת להם.

ר' יצחק מווארקה, ס' בית יצחק, דף קנ"ו.

[175] ימי חנוכה הם ימי הודאה, כמו שכתבו: וקבעו שמונת ימי חנוכה אלו
להודות ולהלל וכו'. וימו הודאה זה בחינת שעשוע עולם הבא, כי זה עיקר
שעשוע עולם הבא - להודות ולהלל שמו הגדול יתברך ולהכיר אותו יתברך, שעל
ידי זה סמוכים וקרובים אליו יתברך. כי כל מה שיודעין ומכירין אותו יתברך
ביותר, סמוכין אליו ביותר. כי שאר כל הדברים יתבטלו לעתיד כולם. בבחינת:
כל קרבנות בטלין, חוץ מקרבן תודה (מ"ר צו פ"ט, אמור פ' כז ע"ש). שלא
ישאר לעתיד, רק בחינת תודה והודאה, להודות ולהלל ולדעת אותו יתברך, כמו
שכתוב (ישעיה יא): כי מלאה הארץ דעה את ה' כמים לים מכסים, שזה כל
שעשוע עולם הבא .

ר' נחמן מברסלב, ס' ליקוטי מוהר"ן, חלק ב', פרק ב', סימן א', דף ג',
עמוד א'.

[176] מה שנוהגים לרשום על הדריידיל נגה"ש, אמר הרב שהוא מרמז על כל
מצות חנוכה, היינו נ'רות הדלקה ואמירת הלל. וזה נ"ש נ'רות ש'מונה ה"ג ה'לל ג'מור,
ואמר הוא נ"י, כיון שמנהג ישראל תורה כשם שיש ע' פנים כך וכו' ונ"ל רמז לזה
שהד' אותיות בגימ' משיח.

ר' פנחס מקאריץ, ס' אמרי פנחס, דף קכ"ט, סימן תרס"ג.

[177] ...ובאמת דע כי כל העולם כולו הוא בחי' גלגל החוזר שקורין דריידיל.
והכל חוזר חלילה ונתהפך מאדם מלאך ומלאך אדם ומראש רגל ומרגל ראש וכן
שאר כל הדברים שבעולם כולם חוזרים חלילה ומתגלגלים ומתהפכים מזה לזה
ומזה לזה מעליון לתחתון ומתחתון לעליון. כי באמת בהשורש הכל אחד ...

ר' נחמן מברסלב, שיחות הר"ן, דף כ"ו, סימן מ'.

## פורים

[178] קודם תפילת שחרית בפורים נדחק אברך אחד ונכנס לפני ולפנים לרבינו
הקדוש עם פתקא על דברים גשמיים וכל דבר שהיה כתוב שם פירש רבבו על
דברים רוחניים וכך קרא קרא הפתקא עד גמירא, ואמר תורה על פתקא הזאת. אח"כ
אצל שלחן קדשו בסעודת פורים סיפר רבנו: קודם התפלה בא אלי אברך אחד
עם פתקא בדברים גשמיים והיה ממש בסכנת נפש כי היתכן היום זמן של קימו
וקבלו לדרוש דברים גשמיים, ולכן נתתי לי עצה שכל ענין הפתקא הוא על
דברים רוחניים.

ר' יצחק מווארקא, ס' בית יצחק, דף קנ"ח-קנ"ט.

246

[179] ואפשר, שזה טעם מצות זכירת מעשה עמלק, כי זכו"ר ר"ת זכרון כבוד
ואהבת רע ...
ר' חיים יוסף דוד אזולאי, ס' חדרי בטן, דף קנ"ב.

[180] זכור את אשר עשה לך עמלק וגו' (דברים כ"ה י"ז-י"ט) ... צריכין לזכור
תמיד את אשר עשה להם היצה"ר (היצר הרע) בחינת עמלק, ומפני כשיבא
בלבם מחשבה טובה תיכף יצרפו לזה דיבור ומעשה כדי שלא יבא היצר הרע
בחינת עמלק בחינת שכחה בלבם ויקלקל מחשבתם הטובה ח"ו...
ר' ישראל פרידמן מסאדיגורא, ס' אור ישראל, שבת זכור תרמ"ו, דף
ק"ה.

[181] ומ"ש רז"ל שצריך לשתות יין עד שישתכר עד דלא ידע הכוונה הוא
שלעולם בתוך הקליפה יש ניצוץ של קדושה המאיר בתוכה ומסיר אותה ובכצ"ל
ברוך המן להמשיך אור גם לניצוץ ההוא לכן צריך לאומרו שלא בכוונה אחר
שהוא שכור וכבר יצא מדעתו שאם היה כוונה ח"ו יאיר גם אל הקליפה ונראה
לפע"ד כשאנו ממשיכים אור מוח הבינה ברחל ע"י שתיית היין ברבוי גדול יש
הארה גדולה שיהא בה כח להאיר גם עד הניצוץ ההוא אשר בתוך הקליפה.
ר' יעקב בן חיים צמח, ס' נגיד ומצוה, דף קל"ט.

[182] ויש ניסים נסתרים כמו בימי מרדכי ואסתר שלא היה שנוי הטבעים רק
הנס היה בתוך הטבעים ואמר אדמו"ר הגאון בצ"ק מ"ו דוב בעריש זצ"ל שלכן
נקראת אסתר שהיה הנס בהסתר בתוך הטבעים.
ר' לוי יצחק מברדיטשוב, ס' קדושת לוי, דף קי"ד, עמ' ד'.

[183] והטעם מה שספר זה נקרא בשם מגלה, הוא שמום שמגלה הוא לשון
התגלות.
ר' מנחם מענדל מקאצק, ס' עמוד האמת, דף 68.

[184] שמעתי בשם הבעש"ט זלל"ה שאמר ע"פ באמרם המלך אחשורוש
אמר להביא את ושתי מלכה לפניו ולא באה ותוכן הדברים דברי קודש כי בחי'
הקליפות אין להם בחינת מציאות כ"א דרך הלבשה באיזה בחי' וכיון שאמר
המלך להביא את ושתי המורה על הקליפות נגד אסתר שבקדושה מצוה להביא
את הקליפות ערום בלא לבוש ולכן לא באה כי באה כי מאין לה לבוא שאין לה שום
מציאות בלתי אמצעיות הלבשה העניין עמוק ולאו כל מוחא סביל את דבריו
הקדושים ...
ר' זאב וואלף מזוטאמיר, ס' אור המאיר, חלק ב, דף 60.

[185] איש יהודי היה בשושן הבירה ושמו מרדכי בן יאיר בן שמעי בן קיש בן
ימיני, גלוי וידוע שם יהודי נקרא ע"ש יהודה ובאותיות יהודה יש שם הוי"ה ב"ה

247

שמורה היה הוה ויהיה והוא רמז איש יהודי היה והוא הוה בכל דור ויהיה תמיד
ולא יעבור מתוך היהודים בחינת יהודי ושמו מרדכי היינו הארת בחינתו היה רב
חסד גימט' מרדכי וזהו בכל דור ודור יש צדיקים שהם אנשי חסד ומעוררים
בפעולתם רב חסד היינו החסד הגדול המשפיע על כל העולמות מא"ס עד א"ת
בן יאיר היינו שנלקח ממקום המאיר באור זך ובהיר איש ימיני היינו כשמו כן
הוא שהוא בחינת רב חסד שהוא מצד הימין וזהו בכל דור ודור והבן.

ר' משה חיים אפרים מסודילקאב, ס' דגל מחנה אפרים, דף קל"ט<br>עמוד א'.

[186] איש יהודי היה בשושן הבירה וגו', במד"ר, למה נקרא שמו יהודי והלא
ימיני הוא לפי שייחד שמו של הקב"ה כנגד כל באי עולם, עכלה"מ, ואינו מובן
דהלא כתיב יהודי, ונראה שהמדרש מורה לנו בזה שמי שהוא יחידי שמיוחד
להיות דבוק ביחודו של עולם זהו יהודי ...

ר' מנחם מענדל מקאצק, ס' אהל תורה, דף 68.

[187] כי אין לה אב ואם ע"ד [תהלים מה] שמעי בת וראי והטי אזנך ושכחי
עמך ובית אביך ויתאו המלך יפיך היינו כשושוכה לגמרי בעמו ובית אביו ואינו
מדבק עצמו רק להשם ב"ה ואז ויתאו המלך יפיך, ובת צר היינו התורה היא לו
צר היינו רפואה כמו הצרי אין בגלעד [ירמי' ח, כב] עיי"ש וזהו ג"כ הרמז כי אין
לה אב ואם והשי"ת.

ר' משה חיים אפרים מסודילקאב, ס' דגל מחנה אפרים, דף ק"מ עמוד<br>א'.

[188] הנה מה שאומרים בפורים אשר הניא עצת גוים ויפר מחשבות ערומים
וגו' דהנה יש שני מיני צוררי יהודים יש שהמה צוררים בלא תחבולות וערמות רק
שרודפין כפשוטו בפה מלא ויש שעושין בדרך ערמה כמו המן הרשע שביקש
תחבולות ועשה גורלות והפיל פור הנה לאותם שרודפים בלי ערמות כנ"ל
השי"ת מודד להם מדה כנגד מדה ומבטל עצתם בלי סיבה כמו בפשטיות וזהו
אשר הניא הנאה היא כמו כי הניא אביו, אותה ויפר מחשבות ערומים היינו
לבעלי ערמות כמו המן הרשע ימ"ש שהי' עם ערמות והפיל פור הוא הגורל
השי"ת (?)שי"ת הפיר מחשבתו:

ר' אורי יהושע אשר אלחנן מפאריסוב, ס' אמרי יהושע, דף 47.

[189] עוד ירמוז כי ידוע מלכות הוא בחינת דין ע"ד דינא דמלכותא דינא
ומרדכי גימט' רב חסד וידוע כי העולם לא היה יכול להתקיים במדת החסד לבד
שלא היה עונש לרשעים ושיתוף מדת הדין עם מדה"ר והוא שמרמז ומרדכי היינו
רב חסד יצא מלפני המלך ממ"ה הקב"ה בלבוש מלכות היינו בשיתוף מדה"ד
בחינת מלכות עם מדת החסד והרחמים והבן.

ר' משה חיים אפרים מסודילקאב, ס' דגל מחנה אפרים, דף קמ"ב<br>עמוד א'.

[190] על כן קראו לימים האלת פורים וגו׳. עפ״י אשר ביארנו דעיקר העבדות
ליחד המדות עם המחשבה ובפרט בימי הפורים, דמבואר בספרים דיראת
הרוממות נתגלה למטה. וצריך האדם לחברה עם המדות. וממילא גורם שיומשך
רק רחמים וחסדים בעולם. שבמדות יש בחי׳ התחלקות בחי׳ טוב ורע יש מדות
רחמים וחסד ויש להיפוך. אבל בחי׳ מחשבה אין שם שום בחי׳ התחלקות. רק
בחי׳ רחמים וחסד. וכשאדם מיחד המדות והמה בטלים למחשבה. ממילא הוא
גורם למעלה להיות מושך רק רחמים וחסדים. וזהו ע״כ קראו לימים האלה קראו
הוא לשון מחשבה כמבואר בספרים. ולימים הוא המחשבה כנודע. והאלה הוא
המדות דששה פעמים ששה בגימ׳ אל״ה והיינו שימשיך המדות להמחשבה.
וע״כ פורים פור ים פור הוא גורל שהוא מורה על דבר והיפוכו שהוא מורה על
המדות שהוא בחי׳ התחלקות כנ״ל. וים הוא עולם הבינה עולם המחשבה והיינו
שע״י הוא מושך מעולם הבינה רחמים וחסדים להמדות. אמן כן יהי רצון:
ר׳ אלימלך בן חיים מאיר יחיאל מגראדזיסק, ס׳ אמרי אלימלך, דפ׳
ע״ז, עמ׳ א׳-ב׳.


[191] ...שהופיע אז כל יום פורים אור החכמה על כל העולמות ובכל שנה ושנה
בימי הפורים האלה מתנוצץ אור החכמה ומופיע על כל העולמות יותר מיום
השבת ובשבת אנו מחליפין לבושינו מפני ששבת אנו יוצאין מעה״ד ונדבקין בעץ
החיים שאור החכמה מופיע בשבת ע״כ פושטין לבשי חול שהן כתנות עור
ולובשין בגדי שבת שבשבת אנו דביקים בעץ החיים ונעשה מעור אור ובפורים
שאור החכמה מופיע כל היום יותר מבשבת ע״כ המנהג הוא להלביש בגדי
נכרים להראות שע״י לבושין אלו יוכל האדם להדבק בעץ החיים אם יתקן אותן
הלבושין לעשות מעור אור ...
ר׳ קלונימוס קלמן עפשיין, ס׳ מאור ושמש, על שמות כ״ב כ״ח.

# LIST OF ILLUSTRATIONS

Cover photo and design © Marc Michaels.
All illustrations were sourced from wikiart.com and are in the Public Domain, with one exception.
The Ten *Sefirot* as a Tree © Larry Tabick
Shabbat: The Education Center of the National Library of Israel - The National Library of Israel Collections.
Pesach: Doré's English Bible.
Shavuot: Doré's English Bible.
Tisha B'Av: Doré's English Bible.
Rosh Hashanah: Doré's English Bible.
Yom Kippur: Library of Congress.
Sukkot: The Jewish National and University Library.
Shmini Atzeret & Simchat Torah: Jewish Museum London
Chanukah: Doré's English Bible.
Purim: Doré's English Bible.

# INDEX OF TEACHERS AND SOURCES

**Abulafia, Avraham ben Shmuel** (1240–after 1291), was a self-proclaimed prophet and founder of the school of prophetic kabbalah, based on Maimonides' *Guide to the Perplexed* and the mysterious *Sefer Yetzirah* ("Book of Formation"). He was born in Saragossa, Spain, grew up in Toledo, and spent many years traveling and teaching around the Mediterranean. A prolific writer, he composed many books of prophecy (only one is extant), numerous books expounding his method, and five books of commentary on the Torah, of which four are in print, one having disappeared. [79]

**Aharon (II) ben Asher of Karlin/Stolin** (1802-1872) was the fourth leader of the Karliner Hasidim in Lithuania after his grandfather, Aharon the Great, and led them for almost 50 years. He was a great proponent of the importance of joyfulness in worship and in life, but incurred the wrath of the *Mitnagdim* ("Opponents" of Hasidism), who forced his departure to Stolin before 1864. Yet in his day, the Karliner Hasidism reached its greatest numbers. He is said to have had a confident and imposing appearance. [56] [105]

**Alexander ben Moshe Süsskind** (d.1793) was a kabbalist who lived in Grodno, Lithuania. He was a recluse, but many stories are told of him which demonstrate his staunchness in the face of adversity, especially imprisonment. His teachings emphasize ethics and concentration in prayer, but above all joy in the service of God. [157]

**Ari** – see Luria, Yitzchak.

**Attar, Hayyim ben Moshe (ibn)** (1696-1743) was a kabbalist and author of a popular Torah commentary called *Or HaHayyim* ("The Light of Life"). He was born in Morocco, but decided to move to the Land of Israel. On the way, he stopped in Leghorn, Italy, where he soon gained renown in the community for his erudition and saintly qualities. He traveled extensively throughout Italy, encouraging emigration to Israel, and eventually settled in the holy land, establishing a *yeshivah* in Jerusalem. [40] [42]

**Avraham of Trisk** (Turzysk), Volhynia in modern Ukraine, was also known as the *Trisker Maggid* (Preacher) (1806–1889). He was the fifth of seven sons of Rabbi Mordechai Twersky of Chernobyl (see below), and like most of his brothers, set up a Hasidic court of his own, where many thousands of followers would visit. [141]

**Avraham ben Ze'ev Nachum Bornstein of Sochtchov** (Sochaczew) was married to the daughter of Menachem Mendel of Kotzk, and studied with him for ten years. He was a considerable legal scholar and head of a rabbinic court, and only became a Hasidic *rebbe* on the death of Hanoch Henich of Alexander. [169]

**Avraham Ya'akov ben Yisra'el of Sadagora** was the second son of Yisra'el of Ruzhin, descendant of the Maggid of Mezritch and founder of this important Hasidic dynasty. He succeeded his elder brother Shalom Yosef as leader of the community when the latter died just months after their father, while their four younger brothers established courts of their own. Avraham was a considerable leader and organizer and maintained relationships with important people outside the Hasidic community, including the Anglo-Jewish philanthropist and campaigner Sir Moses Montefiore. In 1856 he was imprisoned for alleged involvement with a counterfeiting ring, but was released after fifteen months. As is the case here, his sermons are found embedded in books presenting those of his father. (*Bet Yisra'el* is devoted to the father's teachings, but the subsection headed *Emet LeYa'akov* [Truth to Jacob, Micah 7:20] contains those of the son.) [40] [87] [172]

**Avraham Yehoshua Heschel of Apt/Apta** (Opatow) (1755-1825), was a disciple of Elimelech of Lyzhansk, and known as the *Ohev Yisra'el* ("Lover of Yisra'el") after his reputation for concern for all Jews and the title of his collection of sermons. He was a key figure in the spread of Hasidism in Poland and Rumania. One of his descendants was his namesake, the great American-Jewish thinker, Abraham Joshua Heschel (1907-1972). [26]

**Azriel of Gerona** was a central figure, perhaps the leader, of an influential group of Kabbalists in Gerona, Catalonia, in the early thirteenth century. Nothing is known of his life, but he was the author of a commentary on aggadic material in the Talmud, giving them a kabbalistic twist. He was a particularly profound thinker, bringing Neo-Platonic thought to bear on the Kabbalah, and was a major influence on the Zohar. [78]

**Azulai, Hayyim Yosef David** (1724-1806), was a renowned mystic and kabbalist, bibliographer and writer, and outstanding rabbi of the Ottoman Empire and Italy. He studied with Hayyim ibn Attar, among others. He traveled widely, collecting funds for his *yeshivah* and the Jewish community in Jerusalem, and making extensive notes of the Hebrew books and

252

manuscripts he found. He was born in Jerusalem and died in Leghorn, Italy. Also known as the *CHIDA*, an acronym of his name. [73] [84] [162] [173] [179]

**Ba'al Shem Tov** – see Yisra'el ben Eliezer, the Ba'al Shem Tov.

**Chemdat Yamim** is an anonymous work, usually running to four volumes, of extensive ethical and kabbalistic essays on Shabbat and the festivals. It was first printed in the early 1730's and was probably written not long before that. As we have it, it is probably incomplete, the sections of ordinary weekdays having apparently disappeared. Its author, though unknown, made extensively use of contemporary sources and was almost certainly a follower of the failed messiah Shabbetai Zevi. The book is still studied among Hasidic communities, who seem to be unaware of its heretical origins. [6] [7] [9] [38] [129] [133] [137] [138] [158] [167]

**Cordovero, Moshe** (1522-1570) was one of the great kabbalists of Safed, author of *Pardes Rimmonim* ("Orchard of Pomegranates" [Song of Songs 4:13]), and other influential kabbalistic works. He was a student of Yosef Karo, compiler of the *Shulchan Aruch*, and of Shlomo Alkabetz, his father-in-law, and the author of the Friday night hymn *Lecha Dodi*, as well as a teacher of Yitzchak Luria, the Ari. [59]

**Dov Baer, the Maggid ("Preacher") of Mezritch** (Mezhirech) (d. 1772), might be considered the second "founder" of the Hasidic movement. He was a learned scholar of Talmud, keen student of Lurianic Kabbalah, and renowned for his ascetic way of life. He was the teacher and mentor of a whole generation of Hasidic masters, and all his teachings were recorded by others. [90] [92] [93] [111]

**Elazar ben Yehudah of Worms** (c.1160-1237) was a leader of the *Hasidei Ashkenaz* (German Pietists), author of *Sefer HaRokeach* ("The Book of the Pharmacist"), a law code, and a Torah-commentary that places great emphasis on *gematria* (numerology) and other techniques of manipulating the text, plus other works of an esoteric nature. His wife and two of their children were murdered, and he himself injured, in anti-Jewish riots during the Crusades. [30] [35] [61]

**Elimelech ben Hayyim Meir Yechiel of Grodzisk** (Grodzisk Mazowiecki) (1824-1892), grandson of two Hasidic masters: Yisra'el, the Maggid of Koznitz, and Elimelech of Lyzhansk. He founded a Hasidic dynasty centered in his town in Poland. His thousands of followers are said to have included many great Torah scholars. [45] [190]

**Epstein, Kalonymus Kalman HaLevi of Cracow** (d.1823), disciple of Elimelech of Lyzhansk and Ya'akov Yitzchak, the Seer of Lublin, author of the Hasidic Torah commentary *Ma'or VaShemesh* ("Luminary and Sun"). [98] [127] [191]

**Ettinga (or, Ettinger), Avraham of Dukla** (1874–1924) came from a long line of rabbinic figures and became a genealogical expert researching Eastern European families. He wrote and published a number of such studies, plus several volumes of Hasidic tales. [141]

*Gallei Razayya* (Heaps of Secrets) was written in the sixteenth century by an unknown author in Safed during the period when it was the center of kabbalistic speculation. Its primary focus is on the doctrine of the transmigration of souls through the generations, and in particular, attempts to explain the more questionable deeds of biblical heroes by invoking that doctrine. [170]

**Hanoch Henich HaKohen of** Alexander (Aleksandrow) (1798-1870) was a disciple of Simchah Bunam of Pshische and Menachem Mendel of Kotzk. Later he took up the leadership of the Gur Hasidim, before settling in Alexander in central Poland. He believed that the *tzaddik* was merely a guide and that anyone could become a *Hasid* by their own efforts. [2] [12] [19]

**Hayyim ben Menachem Mendel Hager of Kosov** (Kosów) (1795-1844), was a Hasidic teacher who studied with his father Menachem Mendel of Kosov and his father-in-law Ya'akov Meir of Shepetovka, and visited the Seer of Lublin. He succeeded his father as leader of the Hasidim of Kosov. [38] [117]

**Hayyim Haike (or Haikl) ben Shmuel of Amdur** (d. 1787) was a disciple of Dov Baer, the Maggid of Mezritch, and after setting up as a *rebbe* in his own right, became a controversial figure because he encouraged extreme ecstatic behavior in his community, including turning somersaults during services. This aroused the ire of other Hasidic leaders, but he was also zealous in the propagation of Hasidism, which provoked considerable anger among the *Mitnagdim*. He preached complete self-abnegation before God. [4]

**Ibn Gabbai, Meir ben Yechezkel** (1480–after 1540). Few details of his life are known. He may have been a Spanish exile, and seems to have lived in Turkey and died in the Land of Israel. His works were the most influential kabbalistic books of his generation, between the Expulsion and the rise of mystical center in Safed. [47] [115]

**Ibn Machir, Moshe** (16th century) was a kabbalist and Talmudist who seems to have headed a *yeshiva* in Ein Zeitun, a village near Safed in the Galilee. Few other facts of his life can be ascertained. His book *Seder HaYom* ("The Order of the Day") detailing kabbalistic practices developed in Safed was instrumental in bringing them to a wider Jewish audience. [134]

**Ittamari, Eliyahu ben Shlomo Avraham of Izmir Eliyahu HaKohen of Izmir** (Smyrna) in what is now Turkey, was a renowned preacher in his day, a member of a prominent Sefardi rabbinic family and author of numerous works. He served the Jewish community of Izmir for his entire career, despite the fact that he was undoubtedly a secret follower of failed messiah Shabbetai Zevi. Eliyahu HaKohen is sometimes called *HaIttamari* after the title of one of the books he authored: *Midrash HaIttamari*, consisting of ethical sermons. Another book of sermons, *Shevet Musar* (A Rod of Discipline) was so popular that it was translated into Yiddish for a non-scholarly Ashkenazi readership. He also compiled an anthology, known as *Midrash Talpiot*, of kabbalistic quotations (sometimes with his own comments) arranged alphabetically by topics, though only the first half of the alphabet has appeared in print. [55]

**Levi Yitzchak ben Meir of Berditchev** (Berdichev) (1740-1810) was disciple of Dov Ber, the Maggid of Mezritch and one of the best loved Hasidic *rebbes*, author of *Kedushat Levi* ("The Holiness of Levi"). His outspoken Hasidic views led to the loss of two rabbinic positions. He placed great emphasis on joy in all aspects of life, attachment to God, and on fervent prayer. He is reputed to have shown great love and concern for the common people. [21] [86] [110] [171] [182]

**Luria, Yitzchak ben Shlomo, the Ari** ("Lion") (1534-1572), the greatest kabbalist of Safed, his ideas and interpretations are transmitted in the works of his disciples, notably Hayyim Vital. His ideas changed the language and imagery of Kabbalah forever, adding a greater emphasis on the historical drama of the conflict between the forces of good and evil. He came to be known as the Ari from the initial letters of the Hebrew words of *Ha-elohi Rabbi Yitzchak*, "the divine Rabbi Yitzchak." He is said to have spent seven years in seclusion on an island in the Nile in Egypt studying Kabbalah, before coming to Safed, where he lived only a few years before his death. [158]

**Menachem Mendel Morgenstern of Kotzk** (Kock) (1787-1859), a disciple of Ya'akov Yitzchak, the "Holy Jew" of Pshische (1765-1814) and Simchah Bunam of Pshische, he was known for his stern, challenging approach. This provoked much criticism, but also drew many followers to him. A troubled soul, he locked himself away from his Hasidim for twenty years, seeing only a select few. He also burned the books he had written, and opposed the collecting of his teachings for publication. Fortunately for us, this was done after his death. [44] [46] [50] [65] [71] [89] [106] [156] [165] [183] [186]

**Menachem Mendel of Rymanov** (Rymanow) (d.1815) was one of the closest disciples of Elimelech of Lyzhansk, and a key figure in the next generation of Polish Hasidism. He was known in his own day for his asceticism. [53]

**Menachem Mendel of Vorki** (Warka) (d.1868) was the second son of Yitzchak of Vorki, and was known as the "Silent *Tzaddik*" because he rarely spoke. He believed that one should speak only when one could no longer contain it, and that the real work of prayer takes place in silence. Out of humility, he succeeded his father only reluctantly. [154]

**Menachem Nachum Twersky of Chernobyl** (1730-1797), usually referred to simply as Nachum, was a disciple of the Maggid of Mezritch, after having visited the Ba'al Shem Tov. He became an itinerant preacher, spreading the Hasidic message, and incurring the wrath of the movement's opponents. He was a great believer in the value of moral purification. [75] [145]

**Meshullam ben Kalonymus** (10th-11th century) was a Talmudic scholar and poet. Not much is known of his life. He seems to have been based in Rome for a time, but ultimately moved to Mainz in Germany, where he is buried. His grandfather is said to have learned esoteric matters from Aharon of Bagdad, said to be the source of much of the ideas and interpretations of the Hasidei Ashkenaz, the German pietists of the period. [8]

**Meshullam Feibush ben Aharon Moshe HaLevi Heller of Zbarazh** (d. 1785) was a disciple of Yechiel Michal of Zlotchov, having also studied with the Maggid of Mezritch. He placed great emphasis on attachment to God, and the infallibility of the *tzaddik*. [10] [54] [76] [131]

**Mordechai ben Noach of Lachowicze** (Lyakhovichi; 1742-1810) was a disciple of Shlomo of Karlin and (briefly) of Baruch of Medzhibodz, a grandson of the Besht. His involvement in the Hasidic movement in Lithuania meant that he had to go into exile, and was once imprisoned, as a result of persecution by *mitnagdim*, opponents of Hasidism. For a time, his group was important in the north of Lithuania. [20]

**Mordechai of Neschiz** (Neskhiz, Nesukhoyshe) (d. 1800) was the founder of his dynasty, having been a disciple of Yechiel Michal, the Maggid of Zlotchov. He was famous in his own day as a miracle-worker, and also served as a communal rabbi in several towns. [31] [33] [74] [103]

**Mordechai ben Menachem Nachum Twersky of Chernobyl** (d. 1837) succeeded his father as *maggid* (preacher) of Chernobyl, and is considered the real founder of the Twersky dynasty of *rebbes*. Unlike his father, who was poor throughout his life, Mordechai of Chernobyl had a sumptuous court, sustained by his large following. [22] [58] [60] [136]

**Mordechai Yosef Leiner of Izbica** (1814-1878) was originally a disciple of Simchah Bunam of Pshische, but switched his allegiance to Menachem Mendel of Kotzk when the former died. Gradually, he came to oppose Menachem Mendel's teachings and leadership style, and broke away amid a great deal of strife. An original and controversial thinker, his book, *Mei HaShiloach* ("The Waters of the Shiloach"), was burned upon publication by followers of other *rebbes* for its "heretical" views, often contradicting talmudic and other traditional Jewish teachings. [148]

**Moshe Hayyim Efraim of Sudylkov** (Sudylkow) (d.1800) was a grandson of the Ba'al Shem Tov, and famous as the author of the Hasidic classic *Degel Machaneh Efraim* ("Flag of the Camp of Ephraim"), which is a rich source of his grandfather's teachings. He served as a preacher in Sudylkov, but remained in poverty throughout his life. His book played an important role in popularizing Hasidism. [96] [101] [185] [187] [189]

**Moshe ben Nachman** (Nachmanides, Ramban; 1195-1270) is one of the most famous commentators on the Torah, and the first to incorporate kabbalistic teachings, though often in the form of hints, rather than explicit statements. He was also a considerable legal scholar and attempted to bring about reconciliation between supporters and opponents of the study of medieval philosophy, particularly that of Maimonides. He took part in a disputation with Christian scholars about the validity of Christ's messiahship, and as a result had to leave his native Catalonia for the Holy Land. [77]

**Moshe ben Yisra'el Polier of Kobrin** (1784-1858) was the founder of the Kobrin Hasidic dynasty, having been a disciple of Mordecai of Lachowicze and his son Noach. He was known for his short pithy sayings, and concern for his followers. In his teachings, he stressed humility, truth, and patience in suffering. [95] [102]

**Moshe Eliakim Beri'ah**, son and successor of the R. Yisra'el, the Maggid of Koznitz. Although he succeeded him as *tzaddik*, it is said that he took some time to grow into his father's shoes. [51]

**Nachman of Bratzlav** (Bratslav, Breslov) (1772-1811) was the great-grandson of the Ba'al Shem Tov, and one of the most original thinkers in the Hasidic movement. Today he is perhaps most famous for his inventive tales. He was also a controversial figure, not least because he claimed to be the "righteous one of the generation." He famously tried to go to the Land of Israel, but was forced to return because of war. Surprisingly, after his death, his followers did not appoint a successor. [100] [113] [114] [175] [177]

**Nachmanides** – see Moshe ben Nachman

**Naftali Hertz ben Ya'akov Elchanan Bacharach** (1st half of 17th century) was born in Frankfurt, but the date of his birth and death are unknown. He also spent some years in Poland. His book, *Emek HaMelech* ("The Valley of the Sovereign"), presents the Lurianic Kabbalah, but in ways that emphasize its magical, demonic and messianic aspects. It had a strong influence on later Kabbalah, including some Hasidic schools, and on Eliyahu ben Shlomo, the Vilna Gaon. [69]

**Naftali Zevi Horowitz of Ropshitz** (Ropczyce) (1760-1827) is considered a student of Elimelech of Lyzhansk, Yisra'el the Maggid of Koznitz, and Menachem Mendel of Rymanov. He ultimately became one of the main Hasidic leaders in Galicia, Poland, after the death of Ya'akov Yitzchak, the Seer of Lublin. Details of his life are found only in legends. [25] [48] [57]

**Natan Steinhartz of Breslov/Nemirov** (1780-1844) was Nachman of Bratzlav's primary disciple, amanuensis, and an outstanding Hasidic teacher in his own right. He maintained the unity of the R. Nachman's followers after the death of the latter without appointing a successor. This ultimately earned the group the nickname of *die tote hasidim*, "the dead Hasidim," because their *rebbe* was dead. [100]

**Pinchas ben Avraham Abba Shapiro of Koretz** (Korzec) (1726-1791) was an early Hasidic teacher. It has been said that R. Pinchas of Koretz was a master of the aphorism. Certainly, the teachings we have in his name tend to be short, but that may have more to do with the process of their transmission than with his talents. These sayings were first published some sixty years after his death. He was a younger contemporary of the Ba'al Shem Tov, but was probably independent of him rather than a disciple, as frequently stated in histories produced by the Hasidim themselves and by early academic students of the movement. After the death of the Ba'al Shem Tov, R. Pinchas became embroiled in the controversy surrounding the choice of a successor. He preferred Ya'akov Yosef of Polonnoye, the Besht's closest disciple and author of the first Hasidic books, over Dov Baer, the Maggid of Mezritch, the ultimate victor. It is said that opposition from supporters of the Maggid drove him from Koretz to Ostrog in about 1770. His teachings emphasize modesty and inner devotion. [14] [28] [81] [88] [107] [116] [121] [142] [149] [168] [176]

**Rafael of Bershad**, in the Ukraine, (died between 1816 and 1826) was the principle disciple and successor of Pinchas of Koretz, such that their collected sayings are so intertwined that it is sometimes difficult to tell who is speaking. Very little is known of his life. [132] [176]

**Ra'ya Mehemna** ("The Faithful Shepherd") is one of the units that make up the Zohar. It consists of kabbalistic comments on the *mitzvot* of the Torah. It was written perhaps a decade or two later than the main body of the Zohar, probably by the same anonymous author who wrote *Tikkunei HaZohar*. [140]

**Recanati, Menachem ben Binyamin** (late 13th-early 14th centuries) was an Italian kabbalist, author of three kabbalistic books, one of which is referred to here: his *Perush al HaTorah* ("Commentary on the Torah"). Little is known of his life, although there is a family tradition that his knowledge and wisdom came to him in a miraculous fashion. [146]

**Reuven Hoeschke ben Hoeschke Katz** (died 1673) was a rabbi and kabbalist who lived in Prague. He was the grandson of Efraim of Luntschits, a well-known Torah commentator (author of *Keli Yaqar*, "A Precious Vessel") and preacher, but there are few biographical details of Reuven's life. [17]

***Sefer HaPeli'ah*** (The Book of Wonder) is an anonymous work of Kabbalah attributed to a grandson of the mysterious Talmudic figure Nechunyah ben HaQanah (the supposed author of *Sefer HaBahir*). In fact, it was written 1350 and 1390 and includes much from earlier works alongside additional material. Its main focus is the creation story. *Sefer HaQanah* is by the same author. Both are presented in the form of a dialogue between teacher and student. [130]

*Sefer HaQanah* (The Book of [Nechunyah ben] HaQanah] offers kabbalistic interpretations of the commandments of the Torah. By the same person who wrote *Sefer HaPeli'ah*. [13] [109]

**Shalom Rokeach of Belz** (d. 1855) was a disciple of Yisra'el ben Shabbetai Hapstein, the Maggid of Koznitz and Ya'akov Yitzchak HaLevi, "the Seer" of Lublin, and was also known as *Sar Shalom* ("Prince of Peace," Isaiah 9:6). He was a descendant of Elazar of Worms; hence his name *Rokeach* ("the pharmacist"). He founded the Belz Hasidic dynasty, one of the most important in Galicia. He was known as a miracle worker, but also as an outstanding talmudist. [118] [124] [139]

**Shneur Zalman of Liady** (1746-1813) was the youngest of the disciples of Dov Baer, the Maggid of Mezritch who set him the task of compiling a new code of Jewish law to replace the *Shulchan Aruch*. He was the founder of the movement that became known as *HaBaD*, and acronym of *Hochmah, Binah, Da'at* (Wisdom, Understanding, Knowledge) or Lubavitch, after the town where his son and successor came to live. Among Lubavitcher Hasidim, he is known as *Der Alter Rebbe* (the old rabbi). He was perhaps the greatest systematic thinker that Hasidism ever produced, as exemplified in his magnum opus, known as the *Tanya* ("It has been taught"). There are also several volumes of his sermons in print. [135]

**Simchah Bunam of Pshische** (Przysucha) (1765-1827) was a disciple of Ya'akov Yitzchak, the "Holy Jew" of Pshische, and succeeded him upon his death. Simchah Bunam is an extraordinary figure in the Hasidic movement: he was trained and worked as a pharmacist, wore modern western European clothing, spoke German, French and Latin, and was friendly with "enlightened" (non-religious, westernized) Jews. [49] [50] [120] [143] [166]

*Ta'amei HaMinhagim uMkorei HaDinim* (The Book of the Reasons for Customs and the Sources for Laws) is an anonymous work offering an anthology of interpretations, many of them Hasidic, of Jewish customs and laws. It was published in 1944 in Brooklyn, NY. [51]

*Tikkunei HaZohar* ("Repairs to the Zohar") is an anonymous work that appeared in Spain perhaps a decade or two after the publication of the Zohar in the late thirteenth century. It offers more than seventy commentaries on the opening verse of Genesis. It is by the same author as the *Ra'ya Mehemna*. [67]

260

**Tzemach, Ya'akov ben Hayyim** (died after 1665) was born into a family of Portuguese Jews who had converted to Christianity in order to avoid expulsion from the country. He trained and worked as a doctor, but went to the Land of Israel, specifically to Safed in the Galilee, between 1610 and 1620, where he studied Talmud and Kabbalah. Later, he continued his kabbalistic studies with Hayyim Vital's son, Shmuel, in Damascus. He is last recorded as signing a document excommunicating the failed messiah Shabbetai Zevi in 1665. He wrote numerous books, and his *Nagid Umetzaveh* (Telling and Commanding) was an important conduit for the kabbalistic practices of Yitchak Luria, the Ari, to enter into popular usage. [64] [181]

**Uri ben Pinchas of Strelisk** (d. 1826), was known as the *Seraph* because of his "fiery," enthusiastic prayer style. He had been a disciple of Shlomo of Karlin, the second *rebbe* of that dynasty. He de-emphasized miracles in Hasidism and instead, tried to focus his followers on ethical behavior. [91]

**Uri Yehoshua Asher Elchanan of Purisov** (Parysów) (1865-1941) was a descendant of the Holy Jew of Pshische. At the age of twenty-four, he succeeded his father Ya'akov Zevi as head of the community. In 1915 he moved to Warsaw where he survived the First World War. He was famous for his perseverance in Torah study, his lengthy and emotional prayers and his outstanding generosity to the poor. He died of a heart attack in the Warsaw Ghetto on 5 September 1941. [188]

**Vital, Hayyim ben Yosef** (1542-1620) was the primary disciple of Yitzchak Luria ("the Ari"), having previously studied with Moshe Alsheich and Moshe Cordovero, in Safed, in the Galilee. Later he moved to Damascus. He was a prolific writer, not only producing extensive versions of the Ari's teachings, but also a number of independent works, including a mystical diary. He proved to be one of the most influential kabbalists in history. [43] [158]

**Ya'akov Yitzchak HaLevi Horowitz, "the Seer" of Lublin** (1745-1815) was a descendant of Yeshaya Horowitz, the author of the *Shnei Luchot HaBrit* (The Two Tablets of the Covenant). He was a disciple of Elimelech of Lyzhansk, but caused a rift with his teacher when he set up his own "court" without the latter's permission. He was a key figure in the spread of Hasidism in Poland and Galicia, and taught many of the next generation of Hasidic masters. Known as a wonder-worker, mystic and prophet, he was given the epithet of "Seer" after his death. [15] [34]

**Ya'akov Yosef of Ostrog** (d. 1790) is known from the acronym of his name as *Rav Yeivi*, which was also the title of the book of his sermons. He is said to have admired the Ba'al Shem Tov, his older contemporary, but was perhaps not strictly speaking a disciple. He worked as a *maggid* (preacher) but was always poor. His teachings emphasize social justice. [70]

**Ya'akov Yosef of Polonnoye** (died c.1782) was the chief disciple of the Ba'al Shem Tov, author the first Hasidic books, notably *Toldot Ya'akov Yosef* ("The Generations of Jacob Joseph"), *Ben Porat Yosef* ("A Fruitful Bough is Joseph"), and *Tzafnat Paneach* (the Biblical Joseph's Egyptian name, cf. Genesis 41:45). His books reveal him to have been a penetrating scholar and keen critic of the social order. His propagation of Hasidism led him into communal difficulties, particularly in the first community he served where he was expelled from his post. [16] [18] [150]

**Yehudah ben Shmuel HeHasid of Regensburg** (d.1217) was the first leader of the Hasidei Ashkenaz movement, and reputed author of *Sefer Hasidim* ("The Book of the Pious"). He came from a long line of scholars and mystics stretching back to the ninth century. Little is known of his life, apart from legends which describe his great humility, and the miracles he performed on behalf of others. The *Sefer Hasidim* is one of the most important works of medieval Jewish ethics and folklore. [8] [125]

**Yeshaya HaLevi Horowitz** (c.1570-1626), rabbi, kabbalist and preacher, is the author of *Shnei Luchot HaBrit* ("The Two Tablets of the Covenant"), one of the most popular and comprehensive books of its day, and the kabbalistic prayer book commentary *Sha'ar HaShamayim* ("The Gate of Heaven"). He served as communal rabbi in Frankfurt, Prague, and for the Ashkenazim in Jerusalem. He was independently wealthy and refused payment for his rabbinic work. [37] [85] [123] [144] [164]

**Yisra'el ben Avraham of Bopoli** (?) (d. 1847) was a grandson of (Menachem) Nachum of Chernobyl on his mother's side, but beyond that there seem to be few facts about his life. The book of his teachings, *Ateret Yisrael* ("Israel's Diadem") appeared after his death and is an important source of the teachings of his grandfather and his brother-in-law, Shalom Shachna, the father of Yisra'el of Ruzhyn. [93]

**Yisra'el ben Eliezer, the Ba'al Shem Tov** ("Good Master of the Name [of God]" or the Besht) (1700-1760), founder of the Hasidic movement, his recorded sayings and the events of his life come down to us through his disciples and folk-stories; he offered a new approach to mysticism, making aspects of it accessible to non-scholars. Legend says that he traveled the region extensively, but modern research has revealed that he had a salaried position in the community of Medzhibodzh in Ukraine. [3] [5] [11] [39] [112] [151] [184]

**Yisra'el ben Shabbetai Hapstein, the Maggid of Koznitz** (Kozienice) (1733-1814) was a halachic scholar, a popular preacher and one of the first Hasidic *rebbes* in Poland. His sermons and his style of prayer were said to have had a great impact of his followers. His teachers included Dov Ber, the Maggid of Mezritch, Levi Yitzchak of Berditchev and Elimelech of Lyzhansk. [92] [152]

**Yisra'el ben Shalom Shachna Friedman of Ruzhyn** (Ruzhin) (1797-1850) was the great-grandson of Dov Ber, the Maggid of Mezritch. He was a great organizer and "held court" in opulent surroundings. In 1838, he was accused of ordering the execution of two Jewish informers, and spent time in a Czarist jail. In order to avoid surveillance, he fled to Austrian Empire, settling eventually in the town of Sadagora where he re-established his court. He is said to have been able to go to the heart of any issue with his penetrating intellect. [68] [72] [82] [83] [87] [155]

**Yisra'el Friedman of Sadagora** (1853-1907) was a descendant of Yisra'el Friedman of Ruzhyn, and succeeded his father, Avraham Ya'akov as *rebbe* in Sadagora, while his older brother Yitzchak held court in Boyan. [39] [94] [104] [119] [147] [160] [163] [180]

**Yitzchak Kalish of Vorki** (Warka) (1779–1848) was a disciple of Simchah Bunam of Pshische, and friend of Menachem Mendel of Kotzk and Mordechai of Izbica. He was well known for his love and support of the Jewish people against persecution, notably against the Czarist policy of forcibly conscripting Jewish young men into the Russian army. This attitude earned him the nickname *Ohev Yisra'el*, Lover of Israel. [66] [97] [122] [174] [178]

**Yitzchak Meir Rothenberg Alter of Gur/Ger** (Gora Kalwaria) (1789-1866) was a student of the Maggid of Koznitz and a disciple of Simchah Bunam of Pshische and Menachem Mendel of Kotzk. He established the Gerer dynasty, and was acknowledged as leader by the majority of the Kotzker's followers after the latter's death. He was active in campaigning against the imposition of western styles of dress on the Jews of the Russian empire. [23]

**Yo'etz Qayyam (or, Qim) Qadish Rokotz**. The introduction to his anthology entitled *Siach Sarfei Qodesh* (The Conversation of the Holy Serafim) says that he was from the town of Pristik (Przytyk), apparently in Ukraine. He was said to be a scholar, and was known to many of the rabbis of Poland in his day. There are few other details. [23] [65] [71] [166] [169]

**Ze'ev Wolf of Zhitomir** (d.1800). Little is known of the life of Ze'ev Wolf of Zhitomir in Ukraine. He was a disciple of both Dov Baer, the Maggid of Mezritch, successor to the Ba'al Shem Tov, and Yechiel Michal, the Maggid of Zlotchov, as well as an important teacher in his own right. His book, *Or HaMe'ir* (The Illuminating Light), is an important source of his teachers' sayings, but in it he offers his own views as well. An independent thinker, he was often critical of other Hasidic leaders, particularly with regard to shouting and excessive movement in prayer. *Or HaMe'ir* is composed of sermons for each weekly Torah reading, plus the Five *Megillot*. [63] [153] [184]

**Zevi Elimelech of Dinov** (Dynow) (1785-1841) was a disciple of, among others, Ya'akov Yitzchak, the Seer of Lublin, and Yisra'el, the Maggid of Koznitz. He served as communal rabbi in four towns, and opposed rationalism. He is most famous for his book *Benei Yissachar* ("The Children of Issachar"), a compendium of Hasidic and kabbalistic essays on the fasts and festivals of the year, so-called because of his belief that he was descended from Issachar, son of the patriarch Jacob. [1] [26] [52] [128] [159] [161]

**Zohar** ("Book of Splendor") is the classic text of the Kabbalah. It was published in Spain in the late thirteenth century, but is traditionally ascribed to the second century teacher R. Shimon bar Yochai and his school. It is made up of twenty-two largely independent units, and recent scholarship suggests that it may have been the work of a group of kabbalists building on, and re-shaping, earlier material. For some three hundred years, it stood, and still stands in some quarters, on a par with the Bible and the Talmud in sanctity. [27] [33] [62] [80] [99] [126] [140]

**Zusya of Hanipol** (Hanipoli or Anipoli) (died 1800), properly Meshullam Zusya ben Eliezer Lippa. He was the brother of Elimelech of Lyzhansk, and the two of them attached themselves to Dov Baer, the Maggid of Mezritch, as disciples. There are a great many legendary tales about Zusya, often describing his wanderings in voluntary "exile" with his brother, and most depict him as an example of a "holy fool," a type well known in Russian and Ukrainian folklore. [108]

# ABOUT THE AUTHOR

Rabbi Larry Tabick is emeritus rabbi of Mekor Hayim (formerly Shir Hayim) Reform Jewish Community, London, UK, after nearly 30 years of service there, and was lecturer in Kabbalah and Hasidism at the Leo Baeck College for the training of rabbis and teachers in London. He is the author of *Growing into Your Soul* (Hylas Books, 2005) and *The Aura of Torah: A Kabbalistic-Hasidic Commentary to the Weekly Readings* (Jewish Publication Society, 2014).

# OTHER TITLES FROM KULMUS PUBLISHING

Kulmus Publishing specialises in producing books of Jewish interest, *sofrut* (scribal arts), art and stories with a Jewish or ethical theme. For other titles from Kulmus Publishing visit **www.kulmus.co.uk**. Print, pdf and epub versions all available through www.lulu.com and some through other on-line booksellers.

A HIGHER LIGHT
SEFER BINSOA (THE BOOK OF BINSOA)
TAM (SIMPLE)
TEN (GIVE!)
THE TORAH IN THE WARDROBE
THE EMPTY TORAH
MEGILLAT B'NEY CHASHMONAY
(THE SCROLL OF THE HASOMONEAN SONS)
MEGILLAT HA'YESHUAH
(THE SALVATIONS SCROLL OF THE YEMENITE JEWS)
RESTORING THE TYBURN MEGILLAH
GHOSTLIGHT AND OTHER STORIES
CARE OF YOUR TORAH - A GUIDE
TIKKUN MEGILLAT HASHOAH
THROROUGHLY MODERN MOSES
THE EAST LONDON SYNAGOGUE -
OUTPOST OF ANOTHER WORLD
WOMEN RABBIS IN THE PULPIT
WELCOME TO THE CAVALCADE
SHIRAT HA-OLAM (SONG OF THE WORLD)
THE DOT ON THE OT

www.ingramcontent.com/pod-product-compliance
Lightning Source LLC
Chambersburg PA
CBHW031945090426
42739CB00006B/92